The Challenge of Public–Private Partnerships

The Challenge of Public–Private Partnerships

Learning from International Experience

Edited by

Graeme Hodge

Director, Centre for Regulatory Studies, Faculty of Law, Monash University, Australia

and

Carsten Greve

Department of Political Science, University of Copenhagen, Denmark

Edward Elgar

Cheltenham, UK • Northampton, MA, USA

Published by
Edward Elgar Publishing Limited
Glensanda House
Montpellier Parade
Cheltenham
Glos GL50 1UA
UK

Edward Elgar Publishing, Inc.
136 West Street
Suite 202
Northampton
Massachusetts 01060
USA

A catalogue record for this book
is available from the British Library

ISBN 1 84376 509 8

Printed and bound in Great Britain by MPG Books Ltd, Bodmin, Cornwall

Contents

Contributors

Roland Almqvist
Institute of Local Government Economics, Stockholm University.
Anthony E. Boardman
Strategy and Business Economics Division, Saunder School of Business, University of British Columbia.
Diana Bowman
Centre for Regulatory Studies, Faculty of Law, Monash University.
Ken Coghill
Department of Management, Faculty of Business and Economics, Monash University.
David Corner
United Kingdom National Audit Office.
Niels Ejersbo
Department of Political Science and Public Management, University of Southern Denmark.
Linda M. English
Faculty of Economics and Business, University of Sydney.
Joanne Evans
Blake Dawson Waldron.
Carsten Greve
Department of Political Science, University of Copenhagen.
Graeme Hodge
Centre for Regulatory Studies, Faculty of Law, Monash University.
Olle Högberg
Institute of Local Government Economics, Stockholm University.
Jocelyn M. Johnston
Department of Public Administration, University of Kansas.
Erik-Hans Klijn
Department of Public Administration, Erasmus University Rotterdam.
Lawrence L. Martin
Center for Community Partnerships, University of Central Florida.
Maria Oppen
Research Unit Innovation and Organization, Social Science Research Center Berlin (WZB).

Michael Pollitt
Judge Business School, University of Cambridge.
Finn Poschmann
C.D. Howe Institute, Toronto.
Barbara S. Romzek
College of Liberal Arts and Sciences and Department of Public Administration, University of Kansas.
Detlef Sack
Social Science Center Berlin and the Faculty of Social Science, University of Kassel.
Jean Shaoul
Manchester Business School, University of Manchester.
Geert R. Teisman
Department of Public Administration, Erasmus University Rotterdam.
Aidan R. Vining
Faculty of Business Administration, Simon Fraser University.
Alexander Wegener
interpublic berlin.
Roger Wettenhall
Centre for Research in Public Sector Management, University of Canberra.
Dennis Woodward
School of Political and Social Inquiry, Monash University.

Acknowledgements

The editors would like to thank the authors for their contributions, support and encouragement; Diana Bowman at the Centre for Regulatory Studies, Monash University for her project management skills, her patience and her diplomacy; staff at Edward Elgar; and finally both our families for their ever present support and love.

1. Introduction

Carsten Greve and Graeme Hodge

Public infrastructure and services both play a huge part in any modern society. We use the roads each day, our children attend schools or universities, and we rely on hospitals and medical developments funded from the public purse. We even depend on communications through the world wide web, the result of publicly funded research. But public infrastructure and services are a paradox, too. On the one hand they are both necessary for day to day living and fundamental to the longer term development of our communities. But on the other, issues concerning funding and daily operation do not excite the public and it is rare to see any real interest in such matters. That is, until it is suggested that private funds be used for future public infrastructure, education and hospital care as part of the growing world wide political support for privatization of government services and the subsequent movement towards 'public–private partnerships' (PPPs).

Public–private partnerships (PPPs) – loosely defined as cooperative institutional arrangements between public and private sector actors – have now gained wide interest around the world. But few people agree on what a PPP actually is. Some see it as a new governance tool that will replace the traditional method of contracting out for public services through competitive tendering. Others see PPPs as a new language in public management, designed to cover older established procedures involving private organizations in the delivery of public services (Linder, 1999). Yet others view PPPs as a new way to handle infrastructure projects such as building tunnels and renewing harbours (Savas, 2000). Then there are also a number of people who seem to use 'contracting' and 'PPPs' almost interchangeably.[1]

Governments have certainly contracted with the private sector for centuries. Since the beginnings of civilization there has been a distinction between what is public and what is private,[2] and there has often been tension between the two. As the state gradually increased its role in underpinning citizen welfare, higher living standards were accompanied by the growth of major public enterprises, often in place of failed embryonic private markets.

1

Even up until the mid 1970s, nationalizations were still being witnessed in the United Kingdom in order for the government to take the 'commanding heights' of the economy. The mixed economy was deemed to be necessary to ensure that the public good was not left to the vagaries of the market, which experience through periods of depression had shown was a rather unstable and flawed system. Increasing financing pressures and a reducing political support base saw the more recent period of economic rationalism evolve. These notions, along with policies tied to individual rationality and a maximum role for market mechanisms, also implied a minimum role for government. The slogan 'steering not rowing' was even taken by some as the recipe for a new ideology to shape government.

The benefits or otherwise of private service provision versus government service provision and intervention in the economy has driven an important continuing debate. There is a certain amount of 'neologism' attached to the use and discussion of PPPs, though. PPPs are hailed as the main alternative to contracting-out and privatization and thereby seen as a qualitative jump ahead in the effort to combine the strong sides of both the public sector and the private sector. Many articles and books (including this one) are devoted to the study of PPPs because the concept promises a new way of managing and governing organizations that delivers service to citizens. Yet the history of private provision in the public sphere indicates that in many aspects, there has always been some degree of public sector and private sector cooperation. The stories of private contracting in the public sphere are numerous; Mathew the private tax collector from the Bible, the private cleaning of public street lamps in 18th century England, private railways of the 19th century or the fact that 82 per cent of the 197 vessels in Drake's fleet that successfully conquered the Spanish Armada in 1588 were private contractors to the Admiralty.[3] And the first ship that sailed to America was a joint effort between public and private actors. Moreover, we might also view many of these contracting arrangements as early forms of cooperative partnerships. Arguments over efficiency, service quality and accountability in the two sectors have been well rehearsed over the centuries.[4] Today, the desire to adopt private capacities for government purposes continues, with public–private partnerships (PPPs) having now become a central tenet of 'third way' governments.

There is some merit in not only looking at today's PPP organizational arrangements, but starting to examine yesterday's organizational arrangements from a PPP perspective. Looking at partnerships from an historical perspective allows us examine how PPPs have developed, how different challenges have been faced, and how solutions to problems have been constructed. In Denmark, for instance, the commercial company, Falck (now part of the global company Group 4 Falck) has had a partnership with the Danish public sector for nearly a hundred years. Falck started its business by providing an ambulance service in the capital city Copenhagen, and has since expanded its services to include fire fighting and other rescue operations. Falck is now the preferred partner for most of Denmark's local governments in providing ambulance services and fire fighting. Although the contract is awarded through a 'contracting-out' procedure, the fact that Falck has been a market player for so many decades makes it more a partner than just 'another business firm'. The classic work of Selznick (1957; 1984) who describes the way an organization transforms into an institution through 'infusion with value' might be one place to begin the analytical inquiry into the development of PPPs from basic contracting-out arrangements.

So, why a book on PPPs if nobody seems to know what they are, yet everyone is talking about them? The reasons are threefold. First, there is a need to re-examine the different meanings and definitions given to PPPs in order to find out if the concept is worth keeping and using for empirical studies. How do PPPs challenge the public sector, and the policymakers, public managers and citizens who participate in the debates? Second, there is now a critical need to review the experience with PPPs as they have evolved throughout the world. Even though the precise boundary surrounding PPPs is still evolving, there are now sufficient experiments and developments taking place around the world in the name of PPPs to bring these to account and learn lessons from experience. By gathering such evidence from different countries, we might be better able to grasp what PPPs are, and how they should be understood. Third, governments nowadays are beginning to enter into long term business relationships with private partners under more sophisticated and far-reaching contracts than ever before. The huge financial commitments being made by governments in the names of citizens now make such inquiries even more important. In the case of the Blair government, the NAO (2001) reports that some £100 billion has been committed by the UK government for 400 PFI contracts currently in force. In Australia, over AUD$20 billion of private finance may be channelled into public assets over the coming five years according to Gray (2002).

If privatization is a story about private organizations delivering government services over the past few centuries, PPPs appear to be the latest chapter in the book. Given that the public versus private debate has always attracted its share of policy spin and advertizing from both sides, a book devoting careful attention to the advantages and disadvantages of PPPs and learning from empirical experience to date seems to meet a critical need.

DEFINING THE PUBLIC–PRIVATE PARTNERSHIP (PPP) CONCEPT

Scholars have been divided so far in determining how we might think about PPPs. The greatest divide seems to be between those researchers who think of PPP as a tool of governance and those who think it is a 'language game' (Teisman and Klijn, 2002). For many people, PPPs are connected with infrastructure projects and PPPs are institutional arrangements for cooperation expressed through the establishment of new organizational units. Also in the world of infrastructure projects, PPPs are seen as financial models that enable the public sector to make use of private finance capital in a way that enhances the possibilities of both the regional government and the private company involved. Let us examine the theme of the institutional arrangement or governance tool first, and then return to the discussion of PPPs as a discursive term.

PPPs as Organizational and Financial Arrangements

Most definitions of PPPs emphasise that PPPs are established because they can benefit both the public sector and the private sector. The line of reasoning seems to be that both the public sector and the private sector have specific qualities, and if those qualities are combined, then the end result will be better for all (Vaillancourt Rosenau, 1999:1). There is an agreement in the literature that risk sharing is one of the big incentives for both the public sector and the private sector. Furthermore, there is the aspect of uncertainty of the future to take into account, and the knowledge that not everything can be written into a detailed contract (Williamson, 1985). There is also the prospect that the cooperation can result in some new product or service that no one would have thought of if the public organizations and private organizations had kept to themselves. Finally, it has been noted that a partnership involves a longer term commitment which means that contracts will be written that can continue for a number of years.

One definition to start off comes from the Dutch public management scholars van Ham and Koppenjan (2001:598) who define a PPP as 'co-operation of some sort of durability between public and private actors in which they jointly develop products and services and share risks, costs and resources which are connected with these products'. This definition has several advantages: first, it underlines cooperation of some durability. The collaboration cannot only take place in short-term contracts. Second, it emphasizes risk sharing as a vital component and other factors to be shared as well. Both parties in a partnership come together on equal terms in the sense that both have to bear parts of the risks involved. There can indeed be many types of such risks. One immediately thinks of financial risks, but van Ham and Koppenjan add democratic risks and political risks as well as substantive risks connected to the subject matter at hand. Third, they jointly produce something (a product or a service), and, perhaps implicitly, both stand to gain from mutual effort. Similar definitions can be found in other texts. Collin and Hansson (2000:*x*), for instance, define PPPs, perhaps more narrowly, as 'an arrangement between a municipality and one or more private firms, where all parties share risks, profit, utilities and investments through a joint ownership of an organization'.

Other writers have underlined how cooperation can take place in mutually built organizations like a joint venture company or a purpose built organization. But public organizations and private organizations may not need go so far as establishing a mutual organization. In the infrastructure literature on public–private cooperation, a number of mutual financial arrangements are mentioned (see Savas, 2000, for an overview). These financial arrangements include BOT (build–own–transfer), BOOT (build–own–operate–transfer), as well as so-called 'sale-and-lease-back' arrangements where local governments sell their buildings and then rent them back on a 20- or 30-year contract from a financial organization. It is no surprise that under such infrastructure arrangements, a narrower definition of PPPs exists. For instance, Campbell (2001) suggested simply that 'a PPP project generally involves the design, construction, financing and maintenance (and in some cases operation) of public infrastructure or a public facility by the private sector under a long term contract'.

A wider interpretation, and one that keeps the organizational aspect but sees it in inter-organizational terms, is to conceive policy networks as special arrangements for public–private cooperation. The literature of policy networks and governance is huge (see Börzel, 1998; Klijn and Koppenjan, 2000; Kickert et al., 1997; and Milward and Provan, 2000). In this literature the intermingling and cooperation of public and private actors in inter-organizational settings is emphasised. A policy network in agriculture involving government departments, farmers, farmers' organizations and other interest groups could in some senses be viewed as a PPP because it entails cooperation of some durability between public and private actors.

Overall then, the organizational aspect of PPPs seems to have at least two dimensions. The first dimension is finance: How are public and private actors engaged financially in PPPs? The other dimension is organizational. How tightly organized is the relationship between public and private actors? Do inter-organizational policy networks exist or have joint venture companies or other types of organizational units been established where both contribute to the governance and management of the organization?

A typology of PPPs based on the nature of financial and organizational relationships is shown in Table 1.1.

Table 1.1   A PPP typology based on financial and organizational relationships

Finance/Organization	Tight organizational relationship	Loose organizational relationship
Tight financial relationship	Joint venture companies	BOOT, BOT,
	Joint stock companies	Sale-and-lease-back
	Joint development projects	
Loose financial relationship	Policy communities	Issue networks

The notion of viewing PPPs in terms of organizational and financial arrangements also covers many other uses of the PPP concept. A few years ago, Osborne (2000a) noted that as well as being a cornerstone of 'New Labour's' stakeholder society in the UK, they have also become a tool for providing public services and developing a civil society in post-communist regimes such as Hungary, and a mechanism for combating social exclusion and enhancing community development under European Union policy. In the USA, PPPs have traditionally been associated with urban renewal and downtown economic development. As Osborne (2000a) put it, PPPs have 'been central to national and state-government initiatives to regenerate local urban communities, as well as often arising out of community-led attempts to deal with the crisis of government in American communities'. Evidently, a huge range of definitions for PPPs exists, with each having different organizational and financial characteristics.

Such partnership arrangements can cover quite different territory to the traditional contracting-out of services, however, with longer term implications, a larger potential role in infrastructure decision making possible, bigger financial flows and greater capacity for risks to be shifted to either side of the partnership.[5] Teisman and Klijn (2002) go further, seeing PPPs as involving joint decision making rather than having a principal–agent relationship, with both parties being involved early on in developing effective joint outputs and arrangements rather than government alone defining both the problem and the solution, and then choosing the most cost-efficient private company for production. Each of these differences with traditional contract arrangements will no doubt require an appropriate mechanism to ensure the protection of the public interest for the long term and ensure that accountability to citizens is maintained at the highest level.[6]

PPPs as a Language Game

There are indeed, as Linder puts it, 'multiple grammars' to the meaning of the PPP. The language of PPPs, in this view, is a game designed to 'cloud' other strategies and purposes. One such purpose is privatization, and encouraging private providers to supply public services at the expense of public organizations themselves. The privatization proponent, Savas (2000), openly admits in his book that 'contracting out' and 'privatization' are expressions that generate opposition quickly, and that expressions such as 'alternative delivery systems', and now 'public–private partnerships' invite more people and organizations to join the debate and the cause of letting private organizations get a market share of public service provision. Thus, Teisman and Klijn (2002), Linder (1999) and Savas (2000), writing from different perspectives, all agree that the use of the term PPP must be seen in relation to previous more pejorative terms such as contracting-out and privatization.

It seems fair to say that a number of governments have tried to avoid using the term 'privatization' or 'contracting-out' in favour of speaking of 'PPPs'.[7] This may stem from a government's desire for a genuinely new and different policy direction not to be judged harshly and inappropriately on the basis of policy failures from the past. But it is just as likely that the avoidance of these terms is part of a general trend within public management of having to renew the buzz words from time to time, or the trend towards advancing a consistent private market-based policy thrust under a different and more catchy title.

Viewed from this perspective, researchers should be careful how they approach empirical analysis of PPPs. Should researchers look for similarity between policies conducted in the name of PPPs and contracting-out in order to reveal the continuation of policy instead of a break with policy? Or should researchers concentrate on analysing the 'language game' itself and the way governments deliberately change discourse in the pursuit of getting policy votes from citizens? A number of researchers have dealt with the 'language' of public management reform, and ways in which new practices are introduced through the construction of meaning (Stewart and Newman, 1997; Miller and Simmons, 1998).[8] There is no doubt that PPPs have become a favourite expression when describing new institutional arrangements for governments. The Blair government in Britain has earned global fame for putting political emphasis on public–private cooperation and on PPPs especially. Interestingly, the UK Treasury has, below the political radar, explicitly acknowledged the sale of state-owned enterprises as one type of public–private partnership, rather than anything separate (HM Treasury, 2003). In Britain, the centre-left think tank, The Institute for Public Policy Research (2000, 2001), published influential reports recommending a continuing use of PPPs, but also encouraging the use of PPPs in a balanced way. Trade unions in Britain, on the other hand, have been sceptical about the Blair government's real intentions in stressing the advantages of PPPs.

So, are PPPs the next chapter in the privatization story, another promise in our attempts to better define and measure public sector service performance,[9] a renewed support scheme for boosting business in difficult times, a language game camouflaging the next frontier from the conquering transaction merchants, legal advisors and merchant bankers seeking fat commissions? Or through the PPP quest, are we simply seeking more refined processes for providing infrastructure and services, and giving communities better value for money? Perhaps the PPP phenomenon is all of these, and we simply need a more detailed understanding of it.

PPP PROMISES AND PERFORMANCE

Like the broader privatization reform family, the PPP concept has been the subject of much policy rhetoric. At this level, the extremes see a remarkably similar colourful salesmanship and praise on the one hand, and stinging criticism on the other. Bowman (2001), for instance, reports PPPs being seen by some in the UK as 'yet again screwing the taxpayer' with private project sponsors being caricatured as 'evil bandits running away with all the loot', and with London Underground issues being labelled as 'son of fat cat'. Similar attitudes in Canada have seen PPPs there being coined in terms of the memorable phrase 'Problem, Problem, Problem'.[10] On the other side of the rhetoric, PPPs have been dubbed as a 'marriage made in heaven' by other commentators and the notion of better defined and controlled services through tight contracts seems alluring. We are certainly now drowning in promises by governments around the world that PPPs will provide public sector services more cheaply and quickly with reduced pressure on government budgets. Additionally, strengthened monitoring and accountability are also claimed, with stronger business and investor confidence implicit in this reform.

Serious evidence on the veracity of these claims and counter claims is less voluminous – indeed it is one of the surprises of the existing PPP literature to find that for the size of the financial commitments to PPPs being entered by governments around the globe, the evidence on cost and quality gains for techniques such as the PFI seems to be limited.[11] Given that PPPs are an inherent part of the ongoing privatization debate, this may not be so surprising. But stewardship in the public interest demands that this deficit be addressed.

What is important to recognize here is that there is a portfolio of international empirical evidence on PPPs and that its findings are mixed.[12] Existing international evidence varies along a continuum between two extremes. At the positive end are the findings of UK commentators such as Pollitt (2002) who reviewed a sample of ten major PFI case evaluations undertaken by the National Audit Office and concluded that the best deal was probably obtained in every case, and that good value for money was probably achieved in eight of the ten cases. At the other end are the stinging attacks of several commentators. These include for instance, Monbiot (2000) who accuses the UK Treasury of failing to represent the public interest in its haste to sign up to these deals, and Australian analysts such as Walker and Walker (2000) who see PPPs as 'misleading accounting trickery of the worst entrepreneurial kind', along with Davidson (2004:15) who argues that PPP policies have 'nothing to do with economics and everything to do with powerful vested interests that are happy to hide behind the complexity of this issue to enrich themselves'.

It seems overall that the economic and financial benefits of PPPs are still subject to debate, and hence, considerable uncertainty. One of the aims of this book is to add to the level of reliable empirical information available to assess PPPs.

Other dimensions of the PPP phenomenon also deserve careful deliberation. In particular, there is always potential for enthusiastic governments to make trade-offs implicitly in the midst of fervent reforms. For instance, with contracts of up to several decades, to what extent are governments now entering these arrangements reducing the capacity and flexibility of the Crown to make future decisions in the public interest? There appears to have been little discussion of this at political and administrative levels throughout the PPP era, though independent analysis of such issues exists in the research literature.[13] PPPs also seem to have provided only limited opportunity for meaningful levels of transparency or public participation. With limited transparency and complex adjustment formulae in PPPs, the clarity of partnership financial arrangements can be difficult to fathom. This does not give citizens confidence in the arrangements when, despite the rhetoric of risk sharing with private financing, a significant financial role for government often nevertheless seems to be the reality.

These issues could broadly be interpreted as concerns over fundamental accountability at the levels of policy, project governance and financial transparency. As has occurred in other areas of the privatization arena, negative judgements can be formed by community leaders about the efficacy of partnering and private financing, and these policy doubts grow if reformist governments create an atmosphere of secrecy. Less information, in this instance, can amount to guilt in citizens' eyes, whether the case is proven or not. When such doubts are married together with the observation that PPPs can offer short term political attractions to governments by providing early project infrastructure and moving capital expenditures off-budget, the implication is that far greater attention to accountability mechanisms is warranted.

CONCEPTUAL FRAMEWORKS FOR PPPS

What conceptual frameworks are available to assist us in better understanding and managing PPPs? There are many.

There seem to be few restrictions on the types of policy arena for which PPPs may be applied, judging from the literature. Infrastructure projects include the construction of buildings, tunnels (Hodge, 2002), port development (Klijn and Teisman, 2002) and sports stadiums (Greve, 2003) as well as wastewater management schemes (Johnson and Walzer, 2000). PPPs seem to be one of the preferred policy models for delivery nowadays, with public sector organizations getting access to private capital and construction expertise and private sector organizations getting new orders and securing new customers.

PPPs have also been used in social policy areas including human services and welfare service provision in the USA especially (Rom, 1999; Romzek and Johnston, 2002). Also, PPPs exist within the governance structures of several other areas of the public sector including the construction and operation of prisons (Schneider, 1999; and Sands, 2004), education (Levin, 1999), in the transport sector (Teisman and Klijn, 2002) and administrative and managerial services.

Adopting the primary variables earlier discussed of organizational and financial relationships, one first possible way to conduct research on PPPs would be to explore the relationship between the types of organization and the policy areas. In certain areas, construction of buildings and tunnels, for example, the most common organizational form could be the financial partnership through 'BOT' or 'BOOT' models, where governments get projects financed.

This framework might assist researchers in studying the possible organizational and financial factors influencing different types of services. Table 1.2 shows these ideas.

Table 1.2   A PPP typology based on service types and partnership dimensions

Type of services/dimensions in PPPs	Financial dimension	Organizational dimension
Social and welfare policy Buildings and tunnels (infrastructure) Prisons Transport Other services		

A second useful framework could be based on the early account and organizational description of a PPP sketched by the American scholar Ruth DeHoog (DeHoog, 1990), as a result of her work with contractual governance. After presenting an empirical study of contracting out of human service production in the USA, DeHoog outlined three different models for service contracting: the competitive model, the negotiation model, and the cooperation model. While the first two models are fairly well-known in the literature on contracting, and correspond with Williamson's split between (neo-) classical and relational contracting, the third 'cooperation model' appears to have many of the features connected with PPPs in today's literature. Table 1. 3 shows this taxonomy.

Table 1.3   A PPP typology based on service types and contractual dimensions

Type of services/contract dimensions in PPPs	Competition	Cooperation	Negotiation
Social and welfare policy Buildings and tunnels (infra-structure) Prisons Transport Other services			

The use of this taxonomy, which potentially articulates both the benefits and drawbacks of each of these contracting models, may assist researchers in framing the analysis of different partnership cases.

A third way of conceptualizing PPP evaluation is in terms of the type of empirical evidence used in an assessment of performance. This has not been a major concern of the literature thus far, but is of importance to the editors of this book. In evaluating PPPs, evaluation discourse may be based primarily on policy rhetoric, the legal contract, or on the historical outcomes of experience. These three sources of evidence form a continuum varying from weakest proof of success at the policy rhetoric end, to the strongest proof of success at the historical outcomes end. Thus, for the narrower view of PPPs as PFI, we might recall that PPPs, for say infrastructure, now typically cover a continuum of operations that can include the financing, design and development, operation and ownership for a long period of time as well as the traditional concern for simply the provision of a constructed facility: European Commission (2003), Asian Development Bank (2000) and AusCID (2003).[14] Some remind us that PPPs may be based on either public financing or private financing (Jones, 2002), whilst others assume that private finance is an integral part to the partnership arrangement. Yet others such as the Department of Treasury and Finance (2001a, 2001b) in Victoria, Australia, focus more on the risks involved in contractual relationships, and on which sector ought bear these risks in the contract.

Putting these three conceptual dimensions of risk type, the primary sector bearing risk and evaluation evidence together, the PPP 'evaluation cube' would be formed as indicated in Figure 1.1, below.[15]

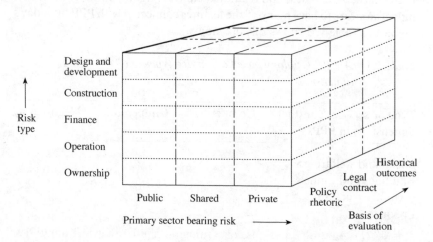

Figure 1.1   Evaluation cube for public–private partnerships

Investigating any public and private advantages of PPPs through this framework ought to assist in our search for patterns in terms of both the types of risk under discussion and review, and the strength of the evidence being used as the basis for any judgements made for success or failure. Of course assessments may also compare actual PPP performance against either perfection, which is unobtainable in the real world, or against the next best 'counter-factual' real world alternative. Both have their uses, but the latter is probably more realistic.

THE RESEARCH AGENDA

A number of theoretical and empirical works have already been published, and our aim is to build on those insights in our search for the meaning and impact of PPPs. Early studies included Stephen Osborne's edited book in 2000 dealing with both theoretical insights and empirical evidence from around the globe and Pauline Vallaincourt-Rosenau's special issue of *The American Behavioral Scientist* in 1999, which provided another contribution looking into a variety of policy areas.[16] Two further edited editions also became available through Perrot and Chatelus (2000) and Berg et al. (2002), both of which looked at the use of PPPs as the mechanism to provide public sector infrastructure. As well, PPPs have been the subject of special editions of academic journals such as *Accountability Quarterly* (May 2002) and *Accounting, Auditing and Accountability Journal* (vol. 16, no. 3) in 2003 and *Australian Accounting Review* (vol. 14, no. 2) in 2004. The number of studies on PPPs has been growing fast, and understanding PPPs has become an essential matter central to the challenges now facing public policymaking, management and governance.

An early formal agenda was originally published by Broadbent and Laughlin (1999) and re-stated in their more recent work (Broadbent and Laughlin, 2003) for the case of PFIs as partnerships. They defined three central research questions: 'what is the nature of PFI (PPP) and who is regulating its application?', 'how are definitions of PFI (PPP) in terms of value for money and risk transfer derived and operationalised?', and 'what is the merit and worth of PFI (PPP)?' Moreover, we might wish to consider other concerns including those from Berg et al. (2002), who question both performance shortcomings or successes and what lessons we have learned from the PPP experience thus far, along with several more technical accounting questions concerning difficulties in evaluating PPPs (PFIs), estimating the 'public sector comparator', articulating the sector on whose balance sheet any assets should be shown and describing how risks are treated in such decisions (Broadbent and Laughlin, 2003).

The questions that this current book raise revolve around historical perspectives on PPPs, financial issues and risk transfer, the legal aspects of getting the partnership contract right, political issues that frame the appearance of PPPs on policy agendas around the world, managerial and governance issues of how to run PPPs and accountability issues. These perspectives will be applied across a range of different partnership definitions.

The specific questions to be explored are many. For example, from an historical perspective, which aspects of PPPs are new today; how have PPPs 'evolved' over time; and how should a better understanding of PPP history inform our actions now? From the perspective of finance and risk transfer, how are PPP financial deals constructed; to what degree are modern PPPs a 'financial deal' driven exercise, and what are the financial 'drivers'; how 'successful' (in financial terms) have PPPs been for citizens and other parties; on what criteria ought PPP success be evaluated, and which criteria are currently adopted; to what degree do PPPs adhere to 'traditional' stewardship requirements in accounting; and to what degree do risk transfer promises match risk transfer experience? In terms of legal issues and getting the contract right, do different 'models' of PPPs exist; to what degree are PPPs really 'legal partnerships'; and what have we learned to date, from a legal perspective, about PPP contracts?

In the field of politics, what are the important political interests at stake in typical PPPs; and what are the implications for making future governance decisions in the public interest? When managing and governing PPPs, how is management and governance practised when decision-making is shared between public actors and private actors in PPPs; and what are the resulting management and governance challenges that arise? Lastly, in terms of accountability issues, how is accountability practised in PPPs; are there typical models applied to PPPs; what are the most useful models and constructs that might help us better understand PPP accountability; and what are the resulting accountability challenges for future PPPs?

This book sets out to extend these agenda items further, and puts a particular emphasis on learning from the empirical evidence of international experience in order to better meet tomorrow's PPP challenges. One of the key aims of the book is to inform readers interested in public policy matters such as PPPs in an accessible manner. A primary concern of this book is therefore to outline some of the more important aspects in what is fast becoming, despite its central place in today's public policy debates, yet another policy sector dominated by technical terminology and jargon.

BOOK STRUCTURE

This book on public–private partnerships addresses these agenda items in three parts. First, a range of frameworks and theoretical constructs is presented to improve our understanding of PPP events and outcomes. We take a thoughtful perspective and look carefully at conceptual issues through the lenses of history, finance and risk, legal aspects, political issues, management and accountability. In each of these areas the aim will be to present useful new theoretical or conceptual insights and ideas. Chapters 2 to 7 will thus form the initial 'theory' section of the book.

The second section of the book, comprising Chapters 8 to 16, will look more at empirical experience internationally and cover the United States, the United Kingdom, Scandinavia, Germany, and Australasia. The aim here will be to provide new information on international case study experiences and enhance our appreciation of PPPs through independent evaluation.

Last, we seek to probe recent public policy learnings on PPPs based on shared international understandings of this phenomenon and contribute, through comparative analyses, suggestions and strategies to improve our ability to meet the challenges of PPPs in the future. Chapter 17 thus synthesizes common issues, and sorts the rhetoric from the reality with the aim of providing strategies for better meeting the various common international challenges.

This book therefore aims to build on previous contributions in several ways. We certainly wish to take the next step forwards in our thinking on PPPs and build on current understandings, particularly in the areas of risk transfer, financial implications, contractual matters and accountability. We also aim to take the next step forward in terms of better documenting and understanding international empirical evidence from case study experience. In particular, the aim will be to separate out learnings in areas where human services are provided, from those more traditional areas of providing physical infrastructure. But as well, this book aims to have a strong thread of 'accountability' through all chapters, and thereby attempt to redress one of the most persistent concerns of citizens in governing PPPs.

CONCLUSIONS

PPPs present governance and public management scholars with several challenges. First, there is the challenge of finding an adequate definition of what constitutes a PPP. Is the conception of PPP as an institutional arrangement one that is best subject to an empirical examination, and superior to viewing PPPs as simply a language game that reconstructs the way public service production and delivery is presented to the public? Second, is the challenge of finding out which, if any, are the policy areas best suited to PPPs. Some preliminary evidence seems to suggest that PPPs have gained a stronghold in big infrastructure construction projects like tunnels and bridge building. Other types of evidence suggest that PPPs can be applied successfully to education policy and prison management. Again, we do not know how different types of PPPs (different institutional arrangements) 'fit' to which policy areas (that is, if they are meant to 'fit' at all). Third, there is the challenge of seeing PPPs in an historical perspective. PPPs may not be all that new, and the way that PPPs have developed (and matured?) in earlier times, could inform the way they are managed and governed now and in the future.

PPPs are therefore now an increasingly relevant and popular public policy option throughout the world. They may even symbolize the new relationship between the citizen and the state. This book aims to investigate both how PPP reforms are working compared with the more traditional methods of providing public sector service and infrastructure, and identify the biggest winners and losers in these reforms. The essays in this book reflect on our experience, and evaluate our international learnings to date within the context of the concerns and demands relevant to the 21st century. As such they present an exciting series of perspectives.

NOTES

1. In his well-known book on contracting in the public sector, Donald F. Kettl (1993) sometimes describes contracting as 'public–private partnerships' and points out how the United States has had a long tradition of using PPPs.
2. See Parsons (1995:3).
3. See Wettenhall (2003).
4. See McIntosh et al. (1997).
5. It is perhaps also not surprising that the public does not care for the fine distinctions made by some professional groups of what is and what is not a PPP or whether one type of relationship is the same as another. As a consequence, the demise of the British Railtrack, although itself not strictly a PFI/PPP, carries with it judgements of all PPPs and takes the sheen off of a wide range of partnership possibilities with different characteristics: Hodge (2002).
6. We ought remind ourselves that traditional methods of infrastructure and service delivery do not necessarily have any high moral ground here. In the past, governments would quite happily fund, through public debt, a 100-year water storage dam project, or construct a public highway, which would be expected to last many decades. Such decisions, however, would usually be accompanied by careful scrutiny through parliamentary debate and policy transparency.
7. The PPP policies of the Western Australian and Northern Territory governments in Australia, for instance, are explicit at the political level that their partnerships policy is not privatization (Government of WA, 2002; Government of NT, 2004). They also attempt to carve out their own unique linguistic niche in saying that this local policy is not 'public–private partnerships broadly understood', like the Private Finance Initiative of the UK, and whilst 'it is [about] private sector investment' there is 'no ideological preference for private provision' Maguire (2002). The attempt here at a local language monopoly for political gain is a creative example of PPP as rhetorical spin.
8. Stewart and Newman (1997) see 'managerialism' and the focus on 'customer orientation' as a way to shift minds in the public sector.

9. The recent history of the public sector internationally has been replete with schemes that have promised a nirvana in our desire to better define public sector services and measure performance. Examples of such schemes have included but are not limited to: performance indicators and targets, management by objectives, total quality management, benchmarking, contracting and outsourcing, systems analysis, zero based budgeting, performance budgeting, output-based budgeting, results budgeting, programme budgeting, programme planning and budgeting systems, competitive tendering and best value in local government. Many of these have been sold with enthusiasm and the allure has attracted huge investments by governments. Whilst there have undoubtedly been significant benefits delivered through many of these initiatives, most have also fallen well short of fully meeting the initial glowing promises made.

10. See Bowman (2000).

11. Interestingly, the evidence on the effectiveness of PPPs appears to come from two distinct research domains; public policy and public finance on one hand, and construction engineering and economics on the other. There appears to have been little cross-fertilization occurring between these two areas. This book draws mainly from the public policy and public finance domain while others, such as Grimsey and Lewis (2004), appear to draw more from the engineering and economics domain.

12. Shepherd (2000) for instance suggests cost savings of between 10 per cent and 30 per cent, whilst earlier estimates include 17 per cent cost savings from Arthur Andersen and LSE Enterprise in their analysis of 29 business cases, and 10–20 per cent based on seven empirical cases from the National Audit Office (2000). Historical empirical experience also reminds us that the London Underground (under public ownership) 'has had a history of completing investment projects over budget and late', with, for instance, line upgrades for the Jubilee Line being six years late and 30 per cent over budget, and an analysis of some 250 projects by LU between 1997 to 2000 revealing cost over-runs averaging 20 per cent Department of Transport (2002) US commentators such as Bloomfield et al. (1998) were less buoyant, with Massachusetts correctional facility experience suggesting lease purchase financing arrangements were 7.4 per cent more expensive than conventional financing and that 'inflated sales pitches' camouflaged the real costs and risks to the public. Likewise, Monbiot (2000) has mounted a stinging attack on PPPs accusing the UK Treasury of failing to represent the public interest in the midst of a corporate takeover of Britains' public governance. Australian analyses of PPPs such as Walker and Walker (2000) were also not complimentary either, likening off-balance sheet PPP infrastructure financing deals to the misleading accounting trickery of the worst entrepreneurial kind, and judging that PPPs eroded accountability to Parliament and to the public. In support, they cite Australian projects providing real rates of return of up to 21–25 per cent compared to the return to the public via government of 2 per cent. They nevertheless concede that 'there can be situations where BOOT schemes are good deals for both government and private sector'. Likewise, Davidson (2004:15) sees PPPs as a policy that 'has nothing to do with economics and everything to do with powerful vested interests that are happy to hide behind the complexity of this issue to enrich themselves'.

What might we make of all this? Hall (1998), in his early careful analysis of UK experience, noted that value for money in PFI schemes depends on any gains in efficiency through private sector involvement more than compensating for higher finance costs and that it is difficult to obtain clear evidence on this in the absence of an accurate and uncontroversial public sector comparator. He presented initial evidence on PFI deals in the UK as achieving significant savings overall for roads projects, two prison contracts (generating around 10 per cent savings compared with publicly financed prisons), and the National Insurance Recording System (NIRS2) contract (claiming a 60 per cent cost saving). These estimates however, were provided within the general context of the initial UK contracts being subject to considerable uncertainty, and being qualified to the extent that managers may have aimed to deliver cost-saving successes for political reasons and knowing that outcomes for long term contracts are always uncertain. Overall, Hall saw the evidence on performance as nevertheless providing 'some grounds for optimism'. The later analysis of Pollitt (2002) also resulted in a careful 'pass mark' being given again to PPPs. He observed that in the late 1990s even the UK Treasury did not appear to know what its PFI commitments were, that unions were critical of the PFI initiative and cited IPPR (2001) which judged PFIs as being 'successful for prisons and roads but of limited value to date in hospitals and school projects'. Importantly, he summarized the findings of NAO (1999) showing that in a sample of ten major PFI case evaluations undertaken by the National Audit Office, the best deal was probably obtained in every case, and good value for money was probably achieved in eight of the ten cases. More recently independent support has come from Mott-Macdonald (2002) and National Audit Office (2003) with both reporting PPPs as being delivered on time far more often than traditional infrastructure provision arrangements. They note that whereas traditional 'public' infrastructure provision arrangements are on time and on budget 30 per cent and 27 per cent of the time, PFI-type partnerships are on time and on budget 76 per cent and 78 per cent of the time respectively. Assessments of the empirical effectiveness of PPPs, therefore, remain mixed and controversial.

13. For instance, Daniels and Trebilcock (1996) observe that public policy decision making cannot be avoided through the PPP mechanism, despite instances of problems occurring and these being passed off as simply contractual concerns between the two parties rather than being public policy concerns. Likewise, Hodge (2002) outlines some of the governance issues present when delivering privately funded public infrastructure.

14. AusCID (2003) for instance lists the most common PPPs as Design and Construct (D&C), Operate and Maintain (O&M), Design–Build–Operate (DBO), Build–Own–Operate–Transfer (BOOT), Build–Own–Operate (BOO), Lease–Own–Operate (LOO) and Alliance.

15. Of course many dimensions are possible in constructing such an evaluation cube, and these three represent only one of many possibilities for a conceptual framework to assist readers.

16. These essays were later published as a book in 2000; see Vallaincourt-Rosenau (2000).

REFERENCES

Arthur Andersen and LSE Enterprise (2000), *Value for Money Drivers in the Private Finance Initiative*, report commissioned by the UK Treasury Task Force on Public–Private Partnerships.

Asian Development Bank (2000), *Developing Best Practices for Promoting Private Sector Investment in Infrastructure*, Expressways, Tasman Asia Pacific.

AusCID (2003), 'Public Private Partnerships – A Brief Summary', www.auscid. org.au, July.

Berg, S., M. Pollitt and M. Tsuji (2002), 'Introduction', in Sanford V. Berg, Michael G. Pollitt and Masatsugu Tsuji (eds), *Private Initiatives in Infrastructure: Priorities, Incentives and Performance*, Cheltenham, UK and Northampton, MA, USA: Edward Elgar, pp. 1–9.

Börzel, T.A. (1998), 'Organising Babylon – on the different conceptions of policy networks', *Public Administration*, **76**, 253–73.

Bowman, L. (2000), 'P3–Problem, Problem, Problem', *Project Finance*, *206*, 25.

Bowman, L. (2001), 'Pfist Fight', *Project Finance*, **221**, 26–28.

Broadbent, J. and R. Laughlin (1999), 'The Private Finance Initiative: clarification of a future research agenda', *Financial Accountability and Management*, **15** (2), 95–114.

Broadbent, J. and R. Laughlin (2003), 'Public Private Partnerships: an introduction', *Accounting, Auditing and Accountability Journal*, **16** (3), 332–41.

Campbell, G. (2001), *Public Private Partnerships – A Developing Market?*, Melbourne, unpublished.

Collin, S. and L. Hansson (2000), 'The propensity, persistence and performance of public–private partnerships in Sweden', in Stephen P. Osborne (ed.), *Public–Private Partnerships: Theory and Practice in International Perspective*, London: Routledge, pp. 201–18.

Daniels, R.J. and M.J. Trebilcock (1996), 'Private provision of public infrastructure: an organisational analysis of the next privatization frontier', *University of Toronto Law Journal*, **46**, 375–426.

Davidson, K. (2004), 'How union leaders are selling out the workers', *The Age*, **11** (June), 15.

DeHoog, R.H. (1990), 'Competition, negotiation, or cooperation. three models for service contracting', *Administration and Society*, **22** (3), 317–40.

Department of Transport (2002), *London Undergroud PPPs: Value for Money Review*, London: Department of Transport.

Department of Treasury and Finance (2001a), *Partnerships Victoria: Practitioners' Guide*, March, Melbourne.

Department of Treasury and Finance (2001b), *Partnerships Victoria: Risk Allocation and Contractual Issues*, June, Melbourne.

European Commission (2003), *Guidelines for Successful Public–Private Partnerships*, Directorate General – Regional Policy, March, Paris.

Ghere, R.K. (2001), 'Probing the strategic intricacies of public–private partnerships: the patent as a comparative reference', *Public Administration Review*, **61** (4), 441–51.

Government of Western Australia (2002), *Partnerships for Growth: Policies and Guidelines for Public–Private Partnerships in Western Australia*, Department of Treasury and Finance, December, Perth.

Government of Northern Territory (2004), *Territory Partnerships: Policy Framework*, Department of Treasury and Finance, April, Darwin.

Gray, J. (2002), 'Going private: a twenty bn shake up', *Australian Financial Review*, 1 and 52–3.

Greve, C. (2003), 'When public–private partnerships fail. The extreme case of the NPM-inspired local government of Farum in Denmark', paper for the EGPA Conference, 3–6 September, Oerias, Portugal.

Hall, J. (1998), 'Private opportunity, public benefit?', *Fiscal Studies*, **19** (2), 121–40.

HM Treasury (2003), *PFI: Meeting the Investment Challenge*, London: Stationery Office.

Hodge, G. (2002), 'Who steers when the government signs public–private partnerships?', paper for the ASPA Conference, March, Phoenix, AZ.

Institute for Public Policy Research (2000), *Building Better Partnerships*: The Final Report from the Commission on Public Private Partnerships, London: IPPR.

Institute for Public Policy Research (2001), *Significant Reforms of PPPs Necessary for Labour to Deliver on Public Services, Current Topics*, www.ippr.org.uk, 25 June.

Johnson, R.A. and N. Waltzer (eds) (2000), *Local Government Innovation. Issues and Trends in Privatization and Managed Competition*, Westport, CT: Quorum Books.

Jones, D. (2002), 'Policy development in Australia for public–private partnerships – what more is there to do?', presentation to the seminar, 'Providing value for money through public–private partnerships: the lessons learnt so far from economic and social infrastructure projects', 2 June, The Avillon Hotel, Sydney.

Kettl, D F. (1993), *Sharing Power. Public Governance and Private Markets*, Washington, DC: The Brookings Institute.

Kickert, W., E.-H. Klijn and J. Koppenjan (eds) (1997), *Managing Complex Networks*, London: Sage.

Klijn, E.H. and J. Koppenjan (2000), 'Public management and policy networks. Foundations of a network approach to governance', *Public Management Review*, **2** (1), 35–58.

Klijn, E.H. and G.R. Teisman (2000), 'Governing public–private partnerships: analyzing and managing the process and institutional characteristics of public–private partnerships', in Stephen P. Osborne (ed.), *Public–Private Partnerships: Theory and Practice in International Perspective*, London: Routledge, pp. 84–102.

Levin, H. (1999), 'The public–private nexus in education', *American Behavioral Scientist*, **43** (1), 124–37.

Linder, S.H. (1999), 'Coming to terms with the public–private partnership: a grammar of multiple meanings', *The American Behavioral Scientist*, **43** (1), 35–51.

Maguire, G. (2002), *Partnerships Victoria*, Presentation to University of Melbourne law students, 10 October.

McIntosh, K., J. Shauness and R. Wettenhall (1997), *Contracting Out in Australia: An Indicative History*, University of Canberra: Centre for Research in Public Sector Management.

Miller, H. and J. Simmons (1998), 'The Irony of Privatization', *Administration and Society*, **35** (5), 513–35.

Milward, H.B. and K.G. Provan (2000), 'Governing the hollow state', *Journal of Public Administration Research and Theory*, **10** (2), 359–79.

Monbiot, G. (2000), *Captive State: The Corporate Takeover of Britain*, London: Pan Books.

National Audit Office (1999), *Examining Value for Money of Deals Under the Private Finance Initiative*, London: Stationery Office.

National Audit Office (2000), *Examining the Value for Money of Deals under the Private Finance Initiative*, London: Stationery Office.

National Audit Office (2001), *Managing the Relations to Secure a Successful Partnership in PFI Projects*, a report by the Comptroller and Auditor General, HC 375, London: Stationery Office.

Osborne, S.P. (2000a), 'Introduction: understanding public–private partnerships in international perspective: globally convergent or nationally divergent phenomena?', in Stephen P. Osborne (ed.), *Public–Private Partnerships: Theory and Practice in International Perspective*, London: Routledge, pp. 1–5.

Osborne, S.P. (ed.) (2000b), *Public–Private Partnerships: Theory and Practice in International Perspective*, London: Routledge.

Parsons, W. (1995), *Public Policy: An Introduction to the Theory and Practice of Policy Analysis*, Aldershot, UK and Brookfield, USA: Edward Elgar.

Perrot, J.Y. and G. Chatelus, (eds) (2000), *Financing of major infrastructure and public service projects: public–private partnerships*, Paris: French Ministry for Public Works, Transport and Housing.

Pollitt, M.G. (2002), 'The declining role of the state in infrastructure investment in the UK', in Sanford V. Berg, Michael G. Pollitt and Masatsuga Tsuji (eds), *Private Initiatives in Infrastructure: Priorities, Incentives and Performance*, Cheltenham, UK and Northampton, MA, USA: Edward Elgar.

Rom, M.C. (1999), 'From welfare state to opportunity inc.: public–private partnerships in welfare reform', *The American Behavioral Scientist*, **43** (1), 155–76.

Romzek, B and J. Johnston (2002), 'Effective contract implementation and management. A preliminary model', *Journal of Public Administration Research and Theory*, **12** (3), 423–53.

Sands, V.J. (2004), 'Victoria's partly-privatised prison system', *The Asia Pacific Journal of Public Administration*, **26** (2), 137–56.

Savas, E.S. (2000), *Privatisation and Public–Private Partnerships*, New York: Chatham House Publishers, Seven Bridges Press.

Savas, E.S. (2002), 'Competition and choice in New York City social services', *Public Administration Review*, **61** (1), 82–91.

Schneider, A.L. (1999), 'Public–Private Policy Partnerships in the U.S. Prison System', *The American Behavioral Scientist*, **43** (1), 192–208.

Selznick, P. (1984) [1957], *Leadership in Administration*, California: University of California Press.

Shepherd, T. (2000), 'A Practitioner's Perspective', presentation to the Productivity Commission Workshop on Private Sector Involvement in Provision of Public Infrastructure, 12–13 October, Melbourne.

Stewart, J. and J. Newman (1997), *The Managerial State*, London: Sage.

Teisman, G.R. and E.H. Klijn (2002), Partnership Arrangements. Governmental Rhetoric or Governance Scheme?', *Public Administration Review*, **62** (2), 197–205.

Vaillancourt Rosenau, P. (1999), 'Introduction: the strengths and weaknesses of public–private policy partnerships', *The American Behavioral Scientist*, **43** (1)

Vaillancourt Rosenau, P. (ed.) (2000), *Public–Private Policy Partnerships*, Cambridge: The MIT Press.

van Ham, H. and J. Koppenjan (2001), 'Building public–private partnerships: assessing and managing risks in port development', *Public Management Review*, **3** (4), 593–616.

Walker, B. and B.C. Walker (2000), *Privatisation: Sell Off or Sell Out? The Australian Experience*, Sydney: ABC Books.

Wettenhall, R.A. (2003), 'The rhetoric and reality of public–private partnerships', *Public Organisation Review: A Global Journal*, **3**, 77–107.

Williamson, O.E. (1985), *The Economic Institutions of Capitalism*, New York: The Free Press.

2. The public–private interface: surveying the history

Roger Wettenhall

INTRODUCTION

As the conception of this book will indicate, 'partnership', particularly in the form of 'public–private partnership' (or 'PPP'), has become one of the dominating organizational ideas circulating at the beginning of the 21st century. It has all the popular appeal of a new messianic slogan, and it can plausibly be argued that it has taken over that role from 'privatization' (and its variant, the softer 'corporatization') which had that role through the later 1980s and the 1990s. Privatization was itself, of course, the antidote to the earlier 'nationalization', a dominant idea around the mid-20th century. PPP, indeed, has the virtue of claiming a sort of middle ground between the hard-line positions occupied by nationalization at the left pole and privatization at the right pole of the public–private spectrum. Its appeal, the very term implies, should be all the greater because it offers something to the adherents of both those earlier positions. Seemingly it moves us towards endeavours organized on a collaborative basis, whereas both those older bases were adversary by their very nature and so socially divisive in their effects.

However, many who want to be associated with the new fashion use the term without attempting to define their purpose – or its relevance to that purpose – with any precision. For some, it seems that almost any modern organizational innovation where public and private elements are found can be described as a PPP; for others, it seems that there is only one acceptable application – the private funding of public infrastructure – so that others with some claim to that descriptor are ignored. The latter approach is, of course, far too limiting. But it is also likely that many of the arrangements that are now popularly regarded as 'partnerships' will contain elements of mix, but that they are far from being genuine partnerships in the sense of an equitable distribution of contribution, benefit and authority among the involved parties.[1]

The other conceptual problem is that, whatever the new enthusiasts may think, there is nothing new about the mixing of public–private endeavours, and the main purpose of this chapter is to review the long history of such relationships. Delving back into the history of the 'public–private interface'[2] may help to introduce a note of caution here, and it has a further advantage. If we simply assume that PPP is a new social movement without antecedents, we deprive ourselves of the possibility of benefiting from an understanding of strengths and weaknesses in older mixing/partnering arrangements that might emerge from historical inquiry. The more we know of the relevant past, the less we are likely to fall short in today's designs. A short survey such as this will not, of course, reveal the extent of the valuable insights to come from knowing past strengths and weaknesses; it may, however, point the way to other researchers who want to delve further.

PUBLIC AND PRIVATE THROUGH THE AGES

Much has been written in the recent period about the blurring of the public and private realms in the commerce of society and the economy. Mostly, however, such analysis is not much concerned to work back through the ages to see whether this is an entirely new development, or rather just the latest manifestation of an ongoing pendulum swing backwards and forwards across that public–private spectrum.[3]

It is relevant here to consider the evolution of state systems and the place of the public and private realms within those systems. It may well be that the very clear distinction between public and private that advanced western polities brought into the 20th century was a mark of the maturing of their state-governance systems, and that such clarity has rarely been present at other times and in other circumstances. This would be entirely consistent with the proposition that 'differentiation of the instruments of government from other sorts of organization and monopolization of the means of coercion' were vital ingredients in the formation of modern nation states in Western Europe (Tilly, 1975:40). And, if that is so, it is at least arguable that the blurrings with which those polities have approached the 21st century indicate a retreat from that state-governance maturity.

Developments in late 20th century thinking about governance are also relevant. Governance is increasingly seen as a process shared by the state, the market and civil society, with 'networking' between the three sectors much studied. It is even speculated that there can be governance without government (Rosenau and Czempiel, 1992; Rhodes, 1996; 1997), and studies in the history of policing suggest a connection with the so-called fiscal crisis of the state arising from the growing tension of the 1950s and 1960s between the popular demand for more services and that for lower taxes (O'Connor, 1973), and exacerbated by the oil shortages of the 1970s. This crisis, of course, induced the economic retrenchment policies of the late century and, arguably, gave rise to the New Public Management (NPM) movement.

The connection between public interest and private interest, it is suggested, can be usefully analysed in terms of three forms of interaction: coercion, commercial exchange, and gift. And asking the question 'who pays and who benefits?' quickly shows that various kinds of malversation are possible, such as organizational corruption, extortion and the displacement of the public service goal by that of cost recovery or outright profiteering. The 'rise of the state' through the 19th century, it is further suggested, saw the eclipse of gift in this relationship by coercion. But the fiscal crisis beginning in the 1970s produced a reversal, with the increasingly under-resourced state looking for mechanisms of coproduction involving commercial exchange (sale, outsourcing, user pays) and gift. The market becomes stronger and state activity varies inversely with that development. The notion of the 'public good', as in policing, fades accordingly: either the state retreats altogether (full privatization) or there is increased emphasis on forms of mixing (Grabosky, 2004; drawing particularly on Damaska, 1984:91; and Davis, 2000:9).[4]

Nine 'theatres' of economic and social activity in which there has been, over at least two millennia, evidence of such mixing are identified. There may well be others, and these nine are far from watertight categories – there are obvious overlaps between some of them. For the most part they also defy ordering in a chronological sense, for their time-limits are indistinct and in several the time-line is indeed a long one. The ordering here is thus fairly capricious.

NINE THEATRES OF PUBLIC–PRIVATE MIXING IN HISTORY

1. Privateer Shipping

The mixing of public and private initiatives was vital to England's rise as a major sea power, and the so-called Spanish War of 1585–1603 was of major importance in setting the stage for this development.[5] The nation wanted both to share the riches that came to Spain from its possessions in the New World and to curb Spanish influence in the Netherlands, and Elizabeth I and many of her wealthier subjects combined effectively in seeking to achieve these objectives. The navy was still in its infancy, and vessels captained by now-famous navigators such as Sir Francis Drake and Sir Walter Raleigh and financed by powerful merchants and aristocratic landowners, some of them related to the queen, were to play a major part. In the practice that came to be known as privateering, 'public and private interests were inextricably mixed', and the privateers 'far outnumbered the queen's ships during this war' (Andrews, 1964:21, 237).

Thus, in Drake's 'West Indian raid of 1585', Elizabeth supplied just two of the 25 ships involved, though she also made a cash subscription sufficient to give her 'an investment officially assessed as £20 000 in a total stock of £60 400'. Also, however, Drake 'was acting as the queen's admiral and had his official instructions'. In the better-known example – the English fleet under Drake which defeated the Spanish Armada in 1588 – 163 out of the 197 vessels in that fleet were privately owned. Sometimes it was difficult to distinguish between the privateers and pure pirates, and some former pirates who escaped the gallows became fairly well respected as privateer captains. The 'licensing' mostly took the form of the issue of 'letters of reprisal' (later described as 'letters of marque'), which authorized the holders 'to set forth armed vessels for the capture of Spanish goods at sea'. In this early form of contracting, they were required in return to 'enter into a bond to observe certain rules in the conduct of the enterprise and the disposal of the prizes', one-tenth of the value of which (the proportion was later reduced) had to be surrendered to the Crown.[6]

The chief regulator was an official known as the Lord High Admiral, exercising his powers variously through the High Court of Admiralty and its judge (at this time the quaintly named Dr Julius Caesar) and through vice-admirals in the major ports. The system did much to protect the nation from foreign threats, to develop trade and commerce generally, and in particular – through 'the school of privateering' – to build up the 'race of skippers', shipbuilders and seafarers who made it possible to develop a real navy and establish an overseas empire. But it was also a 'feeble and corrupt' system, weakened by political interference and by the prevailing pattern of remunerating officials not by fixed salary but by the fees and perquisites they could attract from their work – the leading officials were themselves promoters of privateering ventures, and the queen 'joined in the scramble by lending her ships and money for expeditions in which the motive of plunder was scarcely secondary' (Andrews, 1964:3, 5, 22–31, 222–38).

So here the mixing of public and private had both good and bad effects. Whether the bad could have been overcome by a sounder system of regulation is an interesting question. But the mingling of the public and private interest was a primary cause of the corruption in the system. The changes ahead – the development of a clearly separate, public and professional navy, and the administrative reforms that would substitute remuneration by fixed salary based on the type of work performed and the degree of responsibility involved in it – would not only be marks of maturing state institutions but also a move away from public–private mixing.

There is paradox here: in contributing to the development of a powerful body of merchants, privateering became a social force which helped shape expansionist state policies and underlined the mutuality of many state and private interests, but which at the same time demanded, for the efficient operation of the state, clearer lines of distinction between state and private spheres.

Though the national navies developed, it took several centuries for privateering to disappear. Naval lay-offs in formal non-war periods actually contributed to its survival, naval ships being lent to private trading companies through the 1600s and 1700s. In the French case, what has been described as a 'system of royal partnership' emerged, both to take up otherwise redundant ship and dockyard labour and facilities and as part of 'a positive strategic plan' to assist in bringing competing world trading powers to their knees (Bromley, 1987:187, 216).[7] It is estimated that some 11 000 vessels were commissioned as privateers through 18th century Britain; nonetheless the navy was now itself a significant force, and privateering was no longer the 'characteristic form of maritime warfare' that it had been in earlier centuries (Starkey, 1990: especially 253).[8]

2.   Mercenary Armies

Some similar issues are presented by military mercenaries, whom a leading military historian tells us 'have been in existence for as long as there have been states of any size' (Corvisier, 1994:501). Before the 18th century they were generally not viewed with disfavour, but that came with increasing acceptance that the mature modern state will have a standing army, provided and provisioned by the state itself. However not all of today's states are mature in that sense, and it was estimated that around 90 private military groups were operating in Africa in the mid-1990s. They were particularly likely to appear in states torn apart by civil war, such as Angola and Sierra Leone.

The biggest at that time was called Executive Outcomes (EO), made up mostly of former members of the regular South African Defence Force who had become redundant at the end of the apartheid regime, and closely associated with a mining company specializing in diamonds and registered in the tax-haven Isle of Man. It needed to win contracts from and be financed by governments, but its primary task in Sierra Leone, under changing governments, was to defend diamond and rutile mines in danger of being looted by rebels; the mines were mostly owned by foreign private interests, though it is likely that government had some investment in them; the government in turn was heavily dependent on those companies as a source of state revenue and moreover, with a small and highly unreliable official army and weak legitimation among its citizens, it soon came to see the advantage of using EO to protect its own installations.

Not surprisingly, the use of such mercenaries in Africa has been condemned alike by the United Nations, the Commonwealth and the Organization of African Unity (Correy, 1996). EO was a volatile mix whose relationships were incapable of clear definition and so very likely to spawn corruption: certainly a public–private mix, but could we call it a partnership?

As suggested by the interest taken in the public–private interface by scholars of policing (noted in the introduction), mixing has also occurred over the years in the civil policing function. The late 20th century movement towards the 'multilateralization' of policing (Bayley and Shearing, 2001) – marked by developments such as the growth of private security services, user-pays policing, provision of complimentary office space for police by some businesses, increasing reliance on 'neighbourhood watches' for community policing, and recognition of the need for sponsorship guidelines by some police services – is in a sense a return to the past, and it demonstrates the decline of state monopolization and the return of commercial exchange and gift in this important area of social activity (Grabosky, 2004).

3. Trade, Commerce and Colonial Expansion

Privateering was closely connected with the expansion of trade, commerce and empire. As one chronicler of British privateering enterprise points out, the capital accumulation that came to its leaders through that enterprise 'played no small part in the launching of the East India Company and the financing of the Virginia plantation' (Andrews, 1964:230–32). The first settlements of English subjects overseas in the 1600s were 'the work of private enterprise', with the crown's initial function simply that of conferring on the grantees authority to govern lands acquired in its name, usually by charter. So-called proprietary governments were thus established in North America and the Caribbean; gradually revenue, customs, survey and other officials with salaries borne by the home government were placed in these colonies. Eventually the charters expired or were forfeited, and the colonies came to be directly administered by the Crown (Keir, 1953:345–9).

The East India Company (there were French and Dutch counterparts) is probably the best known of these companies. Initially a private commercial organization – though chartered by the Crown and with strong government interest in the trades it developed – it too soon acquired territorial and governmental responsibilities throughout India and the East. However its officers, underpaid and inadequately controlled, cheated on the company; it got into financial difficulties and could not meet its financial obligations to the Crown. The British state intervened several times by legislation or charter revision, increasingly directing its affairs and curtailing its power. Eventually, in 1858, its dominions were brought under the sole control of the Crown (Keir, 1953:157, 169–70).[9]

Even more so than the British empire, the Spanish empire was built on such public–private mixes: 'Down to 1700, the (Spanish) government relied principally on private contractors to supply both soldiers and ships'. In the 1550s, most of the galleys employed by the Crown in the Mediterranean and around the Spanish coast 'were contracted from private owners, mostly Italians'. And, through most of the 16th century, the fleets connecting Spain with its rich American possessions 'consisted exclusively of private vessels sailing under charter' (Kamen, 2003:157, 169–70). In such ways were colonial empires established through a major mix of private initiatives and public policies. Again, however, whether partnerships resulted is a moot point.

4.   Treasury Organization

It is often forgotten just how recent in the history of western states is the emergence of the Treasury, the system of annual parliamentary appropriations and the associated consolidated revenue fund and auditing service, which bring a large measure of coordination and control to public financing. Naomi Caiden (1989:53–5) has presented a model of the system of 'pre-budgetary financial administration' that applied in western states before the major administrative reforms of the 19th century. Essentially, 'the backbone of the system' was a body of businessmen on own account functioning as private accountants, contracted to rulers of states. They:

> made a very fine living as receivers and payers of taxes. They had the right to collect taxes and make profits if they were able to collect more than the amount contracted for the state. But much of their profit came simply from using state monies for their own banking activities, from discounting unpaid claims against the state, and from advancing funds to the king when – as was often inevitable – the king's account with them was overdrawn. One particularly famous group in France, the tax-farmers, who bid at auction for particular sources of revenue, even banded together in a syndicate, thereby improving their efficiency and acting as the major source of royal credit.

The system was dynamic, flexible, incoherent and, above all, it 'depended on corruption to sustain it'. For efficiency and probity in government it had to be replaced, and accordingly the 19th century reformers moved these states forward into what Caiden described as 'the budgetary era'. The answer was the nationalization of public finances, another indication of the maturing of the involved state-governance systems.

The mixing becomes even more apparent if we consider the involvement of the church in the international military/commercial enterprise that emerged in and after the Wars of the Crusades in the form of the medieval orders of the Knights Templars and Knights Hospitallers. Formalized by orders of the then Christian states of the Levant and of the Catholic Church and sponsored by various European kings, these knightly orders performed military duty in support of the crusader enterprise, established themselves in agriculture and finance in Europe, and developed expertise in accounting and banking. They came to provide numerous services for European monarchs such as collecting debts and taxes, providing loans, paying royal pensions, transferring funds and providing repositories for governments; one of them, the Hospitallers (otherwise the Order of St John), underwent the ultimate transformation to publicness by governing Malta as a sovereign state from 1530 to 1798; and they left legacies that would surface much later in a variety of fields such as legal education in London and provision of the St John Ambulance Service, now regarded as a charitable community organization.[10]

5. Public (Government-Owned) Enterprise

Outside the 20th century world of the centrally planned economies, public enterprise has usually been a field which has brought together elements of the state (public) and the market (mostly private in the conventional view). As the Indian scholar Ramanadham reminded us almost a generation ago (1984), public enterprises have two faces, one governmental (in that they are owned by the state and need to serve public goals) and the other enterprise-oriented (in that they are expected to be business-like in their operations). While they are properly seen as part of the public sector, few would dispute that, however they are organized,[11] their operations have linked public and private in important ways.

When the modern privatizing 'bug' gained hold in the 1980s, reformers began to ask why there was such a thing as public enterprise (Wettenhall, 1988). Economists then produced explanations based on the concept of 'market failure' (i.e. private enterprise failures forcing state intervention), followed by the alleged 'government failure' seen as justifying the removal of public enterprise and much else from the public realm. But, leaving aside the fact that the economists rarely seemed to allow for the sheer absence of private enterprise capacity that marked so many developing country contexts[12] (which was not really 'failure'), these were essentially 20th century constructs. It is instructive to look back to a time before such interpretations became fashionable, and to see just how much earlier public enterprise mixed state and market spheres as we currently understand them.

A few historical examples will show the extent of such mixing. In Pharaonic Egypt, the state granary department bought (from temple and peasant producers), stored and distributed the staple food on which the early civilization depended (Erman, 1969:81, 107). In Imperial China around the time of the birth of Christ, state and private enterprises were both involved in salt and iron mining, with movement between them (Gernet, 1982:140). In the old Persian empire, 'contracting, partnership building and marketization' – all involving connections between large government and small business – developed as the state engaged in the provision of roads, bridges, canals, irrigation systems and textile and silk production, and used private financial firms to collect taxes for it (Farazmand, 2001:176; also Farazmand, 1998). In Europe in 1628, the Geneva state provided a publicly owned 'chamber' to purchase, store and distribute corn, and this prospered for nearly two centuries through complex relations with individual suppliers, investors and merchants (Blanc, 1940).

Such connections are apparent also in the activities of many public enterprises of the modern era; indeed, the mixing has sometimes gone further, towards the establishment of actual shared ownership arrangements. These arrangements are not so uncommon, and several generations of students of public enterprise through the middle decades of the 20th century had a class-name for them: 'mixed enterprise' (e.g. Daintith, 1970; Musolf, 1972; and see Eckel and Vining, 1982, who preferred 'joint enterprise').

6. Mixed Enterprise

Governments became involved in order to promote or protect enterprises considered to have strategic value for the state, especially where private capital resources were inadequate as in many developing country situations, or were failing as in various industrialized country situations.[13] The developing country case is well illustrated in a recent report from the Caribbean which sees the private sector as 'the engine of economic growth', but also sees that it cannot 'effectively engage in the process of change' without significant public support. Perhaps too glibly, it describes the equity mixes that are likely to result as PPPs, though it wants them to be 'smart partnerships' marked by features such as shared vision, a code of ethics, trust, longevity, networks and transparency (Springer, 2003). The industrialized country case was very clearly exemplified by depression Italy, where state rescue imperatives led to the creation of the vast *Instituto per la Ricostruzione Industriale* and *Ente Nazionale Idrocarburi* (IRI and ENI) networks with their controlling state holding corporations and state investments in a mass of financial, transport, communications, electricity and production companies (Posner and Woolf, 1967; Holland, 1972).

As one British observer has remarked, in a mixed economy 'Government assistance to private business and industry is a familiar feature' (Samuels, 1968:296); cynical Australians and Americans have suggested that such 'business welfare' or 'corporate welfare' should be seen as a counterpart to 'social welfare' (Mitchell, 1995; Barlett and Steele, 1998). Not infrequently, governments take up equity in the enterprises receiving assistance: this entitles them to appoint directors to governing boards, and sometimes other controls are instituted.[14]

The mixed enterprise that has probably been most discussed in relevant circles is British Petroleum (BP) with its predecessors. Under the advocacy of Winston Churchill as First Lord of the Admiralty, the British government in 1914 signed a 'convention' (Davies, 1938:423) with the infant private Anglo–Persian Oil Company in order to secure a regular supply of oil for the Royal Navy: the government subscribed capital and acquired shares giving it around 50 per cent ownership, it gained the right to appoint two directors, those directors had power to veto any board resolution subject to appeal to the government, and of course the deal secured a vast ongoing contribution to Treasury revenue by way of dividends. Much later, in the era of Margaret Thatcher, the government bailed out, only to see the Kuwaiti government take up some of the shares being divested – still a public–private mix, but now a different 'public'![15]

Mixed enterprises of this sort have often enough been thought of as partnerships. But, again, this requires a significant degree of equality among the 'partners', and so much will depend on what is established in the contract that sets up the mix. In the Anglo–Persian/Anglo–Iranian/BP case the shareholding was virtually even, but the motivations were not.[16] In the more recent case of Australia's Telstra, the major telecommunications corporation, the Commonwealth government with just over half the shares faces over two million other 'owners', some large investment houses but mostly a mass of ordinary citizens who were persuaded to take up small shareholdings in the 'public float' pandemic of the 1990s – it is hard to see that there is any element of partnership there.

It is arguable that the syndicalist doctrine associated mostly with the developing socialist parties of Western Europe in the 19th and early 20th centuries had partnership objectives as its primary goal. Given perhaps its best practical application when major industries were brought into public ownership in early post-Second World War France, it was seen as a sort of 'nationalization beyond the state': the governing boards of the affected industries were made up of representatives of the state, workers and consumers in close to equal numbers, who were in theory expected to operate collaboratively and autonomously from direct state institutions.

Unfortunately for the theory, the inter-party collaboration did not emerge, and the state was soon exerting itself over the other parties in an attempt to achieve efficient operation (Einaudi et al., 1955:93–104).

There is another theatre which is highly productive of mixing arrangements even though governments and private interests do not share actual ownership. It is more inchoate and less amenable to clear labeling, and it manifests itself particularly in the fields of agriculture, health and education.

7.   Intersectoral Collaboration on Agriculture, Health and Education

Throughout history these fields have demonstrated much mixing; in respect of the first, it has been observed that the 'use of public food enterprises (has) been a key element in public management in even the most autocratic governments' (Somasundram, 1987:154). But this has rarely amounted to the totality of growing, storing and distributing food products; the world only came close to that when the notion of nationalizing the entire means of production, distribution and exchange was largely implemented in the Marxist–Leninist planned economies of the 20th century. The mixing character of the industry has already been noted in the cases of Pharaonic Egypt and 17th and 18th century Geneva. It has so often involved a mass of usually small-scale private operators in farming, trading and selling, along with state enterprises operating in a variety of facilitating roles such as lending to farmers, storage, marketing, quality control, and research and development (R&D).[17]

Brief reflection will show that, again outside the centrally planned economies, such mixing has also been a characteristic feature of the education and health sectors over a long period. Private schools have existed alongside public ones, many of them church-operated. Similarly private hospitals – again, some church-operated – have existed alongside public ones. In contexts as different as Australia and Hong Kong (on which see Scott, 2003), church-provided schools mostly preceded the state-provided ones, but as those state or quasi-state systems matured much of the educational effort became public sector-based. As public health systems developed, it often fell to the public sector to provide the large general hospitals, but private boutique hospitals continued to operate. Supporting health facilities could be either public or private, with the non-profit sector often very active in this area. The Red Cross blood transfusion service, active in many countries, is a significant example of this sort of contribution. In pharmaceutical production the private sector has mostly dominated, but in Australia in its developmental period it was a public enterprise – the Commonwealth Serum Laboratories or CSL – which did so much to provide for community protection from life-threatening diseases and pestilences affecting livestock.

The privatizing mood of the late 20th century has brought changes in all these industries. They have not eliminated the mixing, but may have changed its character. In agriculture in Australia, for example, there has been a subtle change in many rural industries shifting 'ownership' of marketing, testing and other functions to producer groups without having much effect on the funding or other generally collaborative arrangements. In education, governments have been increasing their financial support to private schools at the expense of public schools, leading in the Australian case to the formation of a new political party, the Defence of Government Schools (DOGS) Party, in an unsuccessful effort at reversal. Today, in the context of the symbolic enshrinement of the idea of partnership, the highly controversial split between public and private in education has itself been described as a partnership by Bill Daniels, the executive director of the Australian National Council of Independent Schools Associations (Daniels, 2002; and for discussion Aulich, 2003).

So this survey comes to another important theatre for public–private mixes, seemingly thought by many 'moderns' to be the only theatre of PPP. But manifestly it is not the only one, and whether it actually produces partnerships is open to doubt.

8. Private Provision of Public Infrastructure

There is little dispute that it is the responsibility of governments to provide public infrastructure facilities deemed essential to community living. But it is also obvious that private firms and private contractors have long been involved in such provision (Neutze, 1995, 1997:ch.9). The Australian case illustrates.

While convict labour provided the infrastructure in the first European settlements in Australia, the colonial governments were soon feeling the need to call for private tenders for the construction of roads, bridges, drainage systems and public buildings. The inefficiencies of the contractors led to a significant swing back to government as constructor at the end of the 19th century; thereafter political preferences produced swings backwards and forwards between public and contracted private constructors. When the great Sydney Harbour Bridge was built in the early 1930s, common sense ensured that the central span was built under contract by one of the world's leading private bridge construction firms; the massive approaches were, however, constructed by the New South Wales Public Works Department. In the post-Second World War period, Australian governments had no hesitation in employing private firms to undertake much of the construction and even design and project management work in big projects such as the development of Canberra as the national capital and the building of the vast Snowy Mountains hydro-electric scheme (McIntosh et al., 1997). What distinguished all these cases from the modern BOOT-type schemes was that public authorities raised the capital within prescribed borrowing limits, paid the contractors for their services, owned and operated the resulting assets, and retained the revenues they produced.

From the 1980s, however, 'financial engineering' was employed to get around the borrowing limits and establish 'off balance sheet financing arrangements' (Walker and Walker, 2000:189). It was discovered that existing properties could be refinanced, or new projects financed, through leases or sale-and-buy-back arrangements (effectively purchases on credit from private firms). Increasingly Australian state governments chose to send government-underwritten streams of cash flows to private sector financiers to provide new public infrastructure assets like hospitals, schools, prisons, highway and railway extensions and tunnels. Several varieties of BOOT (build, own, operate, transfer) schemes resulted, and there has been much argument about whether the initiating governments are unduly favouring the private firms involved and so preventing their publics from getting a fair deal; the relevant contracts follow much jockeying to achieve favourable deals, much manipulation of accounting conventions, and often much long-term uncertainty.[18]

The Private Finance Initiative introduced by the Conservative government in Britain in 1992 and continued by New Labour when it won office (but given the 'friendlier-sounding 'Public–Private Partnerships'' label (EIU, 2002)) came out of this family of arrangements. Other chapters in this book will deal more extensively with it. What is surprising is that many came to see this as a ground-breaking development; as indicated, even Australians had been doing it for a decade or more and in Britain there were important, though now often-neglected antecedents, such as the Channel Tunnel (Marcou, 1992).

And it had a counterpart in the so-called French concession model, which has figured importantly in the provision of water supply systems in many countries and, to a more limited extent, in highway construction and maintenance and the provision of public transport services. The origins of this model can be tracked back to the mid-1800s, when the water company Générale des Eaux (which became the modern Vivendi Environment) won contracts to supply water to cities such as Lyons, Paris and Venice. The essential feature is that public authorities retain ownership of a facility or service but grant concessions or leases under which private contractors carry the cost of operation and maintenance, collect the resulting revenues, and retain the surpluses as profit (Hall, 2000; Adam Smith Institute, 2002).

9.   A Note on Hallmark Events

There is massive public–private mixing also in the planning and management of events such as international exhibitions and trade fairs and the Olympic Games.[19] Though my examples are of fairly recent vintage, the world has a century or more of relevant experience.

When a state or a city wants to be a host, it has to enter into binding contracts with a variety of domestic and international interests, some public and some private. In the case of World Expo 88 held in Brisbane in Australia's Bicentenary Year (1988), there was a Queensland statutory authority with a major coordinating mission relating to other state and commonwealth (federal) agencies, a variety of international organizations, and important sections of the business community (Carroll, 1989). In the case of the XXVII Olympiad held in Sydney in 2000, the main 'players' were the New South Wales (NSW) government on the public side and the International and National Olympic Committees on the private side, operating under 'host city' and 'endorsement' contracts awkwardly justiciable under Swiss law (because the IOC is based in Switzerland). Though the outcome was generally well regarded, there were major relationship difficulties which brought seriously into question whether any element of 'partnership' could be discerned; it is fairly widely agreed that success came only when the NSW government asserted its authority and sidelined the other parties in organizing the facilities for the games. Thus then IOC President Samaranch conceded that 'the State Government's involvement in the organization of the games had underpinned its success and created a model [likely to be] adopted in future host countries' (reported in Silmalis, 2000; see also Horin, 2000a, 2000b; Mantziaris and Wettenhall, 2000; Wettenhall 2003:96).

CONCLUSION: RETROSPECT AND PROSPECT

As demonstrated by this survey, clear elements of public–private mixing have existed in all these theatres of state and international development. The mixing has taken place over many centuries, has often been deeply embedded in society, and has produced many positive outcomes. No serious observer or analyst should be allowed to suggest that it is simply a product of the recent reform period – though, of course, it is entirely proper to explore the various forms of mixing in this reform period to see what useful refinements and adaptations have emerged.

This survey has also suggested a positive connection between the displacing of some of the earlier mixes and the maturing of government systems: in several of the contexts noted, the mixing has been a contributing cause of inefficiency and corruption, so that earlier reforming impulses have pushed towards clearer recognition of the special character and needs of public sector management. In moving away from such recognition, in championing public–private blurring and mixing, the recent reform movement is re-introducing some of those earlier problems. And, if that is indeed so, further governance reform some distance ahead may well produce another bout of public sector purification and turn us away from our current enthusiasms.

Often enough, in both past and present discourse, this mixing is described as partnering. But the question must be asked again: at what point is it semantically legitimate to describe such a mix as a partnership? A simple but persuasive response comes from adapting another insight from the literature on policing history noted above. This proposes that there are three parties to the kinds of mixes we are discussing: not only the involved public organization and the associated private actor or institution, but also the general public being served. If *all* benefit from a given configuration, then we have a 'win–win–win or "trifecta"' situation (Grabosky, 2004:72). And if a public–private mix achieves that, then it is likely to be a genuine partnership.

But a fuller response requires that some attention be given to the nexus between public–private mixing and the contracting process. This process is ubiquitous: it is present, in one form or another, in virtually all the cases of mixing noted in this chapter. Of course it also has much wider applications, and it has attracted by now an extensive descriptive and analytical literature. What is important here is that it is increasingly accepted that most forms of contracting involve competition, which is antithetical to collaboration (see Milward and Provan, 2003). Kay's division of the field into three classes (spot, classical and relational contracts) is helpful (Kay 1983:ch.4). Since collaboration is a *sine qua non* of partnership, only the relational contracts, which are usually long-term, mostly implicit, involve a large measure of trust between the parties, and have elsewhere been described as 'social contracts' (Macneil, 1980), have any chance of qualifying. It is argued more generally that 'collaborative advantage' (from Huxham, 1996), perceived in such ways, 'presents an attractive alternative to the market, quasi-market and contractualized relationships that have dominated the public management reform movement internationally in the past decade' (Lowndes and Skelcher, 1998:313). Elsewhere the editors of this book have expressed somewhat similar views (Hodge, 1999: 117–18; Greve and Ejersbo, 2002:46). Lowndes and Skelcher (1998:314) propose that, in an effective partnership, 'concrete expression' needs to be given to the collaborative relationship 'through creation of an organizational structure (such as) a partnership board or forum'; and Robinson (1999:1) similarly sees a PPP as 'a new form of organisation created from the bodies that come together'. As a final example of this sort of thinking, in his most recent exploration Kooiman (2003:ch.7) relates the very notion of PPP to collaboration, cooperation, 'communicative governance' and 'co-management'.

It seems axiomatic that, unless the public–private relationship is of this kind, there is no partnership. Many mixes, yes; but fewer partnerships. It is important that our current discourse accommodates itself to this finding, and that future research focuses on exploring the conditions necessary to achieve such partnerships. The intention here is not to suggest that there is some mathematical formula that will allow us to measure the point at which a mix becomes a partnership. It is rather to warn against erection of the term 'public–private partnership' into a slogan which confuses where we need clarification. The cause of public sector reform over the past few decades has suffered greatly because of the reformist liking for such slogans: corporatization, privatization, marketization, agencification and 'new public management' ('NPM') itself are other examples. They all carry the unsupportable implication that steps taken in their name will necessarily lead to improvement. It is not that change is not needed, and some of the reforms of the recent period have certainly had beneficial effects. Without clear thinking about the many possible variations within them, without close attention to the needs of particular situations, and without reflection about past practices which contain many similarities and offer important lessons, however, continued shouting from the rooftops that seeks to eulogize these slogan-processes is scarcely helpful.

NOTES

1. The fashionable appeal of the idea of PPP (as distinct from the reality) is perhaps nowhere better demonstrated than in the progression of book titles used by that great pro-privatization polemicist E.S. Savas. His first position-defining book, advocating the mass abandonment of direct state provision of services, was titled *Privatization: The Key to Better Government* (1987). By 2000 he saw the need to cash in on the new fashion and so produced a rehash of the first, with a new title, a limited amount of updating in the original chapters, and a new final chapter dedicated to partnership: *Privatization and Public–Private Partnerships*.

2. Some of these issues were addressed in a preliminary way in an earlier paper: Wettenhall, 2003. The term 'public–private interface' is taken from an essay on policing which addresses a number of issues of relevance to the current inquiry: Grabosky (2004:76).

3. Indeed, it may be that the meanings of the words 'public' and 'private' have been changing over the centuries, and that cross-century comparisons will be misleading unless this possibility is factored into the exercise. There is, of course, an extensive literature ranging over many aspects of public–private differentiation. For some examples which do not bear much on the issues of primary concern here, see Benn and Gaus, 1983; Boyd, 1997; Kaminski, 1991; Weintraub and Kumar, 1997. And views will differ across cultures: see Silver's explanation that, while in the USA 'community' (i.e. civil society) is seen as part

of the private sphere, in France it is seen as an expression of the nation and so is deemed public (quoted in Brinkerhoff and Brinkerhoff, 2002:14).

4. Thanks again to Peter Grabosky, Professsor in the Regulatory Institutions Network in the Australian National University, Canberra, for a very useful summary of relevant sections of the recent policing literature. The term 'malversation' is taken from and extends a part of Hood's more general exploration of late 20th century trends in public management: Hood (1989:352). And, of course (like public–private mixing), sale, outsourcing and user-pays were not new practices, though they were refined and used more frequently in the recent reform period.

5. However Starkey's work, which focuses mostly on the 18th century, showed that the Norman kings of the 13th century would, in emergencies, mobilize privately owned vessels in the Channel ports and order them 'to commit every possible injury on the enemy at sea' (Starkey, 1990:21).

6. Such consideration of the role of the Crown requires a caveat: throughout history, it has often been difficult to distinguish between the private investments of a monarch and those of his/her functions that are firmly located within the public realm.

7. Followers of Patrick O'Brian's fictional Royal Navy hero Jack Aubrey will recall how, in the early 1800s, both when dismissed on spurious charges of financial impropriety and during a lay-off period between campaigns of the Napoleonic Wars when he was on the half-pay inactive list, he and other half-pay officers took a former naval frigate somewhat ambiguously into privateering colours (O'Brian, 1988, 1993).

8. An American naval historian concludes that the end of privateering came with the Crimean War, when Britain and France found themselves fighting on the same side and agreed to bring their rules of maritime conflict into conformity (Petrie, 1999:140–1). Thanks to Daniel Guttman of the Center for the Study of American Government in Johns Hopkins University, Washington, for this reference and for the reference to Kamen's work on the Spanish empire noted below.

9. Much has been written about the East India Company, often described contemporaneously as 'The Honourable Company' or 'John Company', and described near the 400th anniversary of its creation as 'the largest multinational business that the world has ever seen' (Wild, 1999: dust jacket). A good general source is Furber, 1948, while an amusing picture of what it was like to be one of its servants is to be found in a tracking of the career of Sir Stamford Raffles, founder of Singapore: Barley (1991).

10. For a general review, see Wettenhall, 2001. On the Hospitallers' role in governing Malta, see Pirotta, 1996:24–39.

11. Public enterprise is sometimes seen incorrectly as an organizational category in its own right. The reality is that a public enterprise can be organized as a department or part of a department, as a statutory corporation, as a state-owned company, or as a local government activity.

12. Which included Britain's overseas dominions in the 19th century – see, for example, Wettenhall, 1990, 1996.

13. Some have been short-term outcomes of the privatizing measures of the late 20th century, as governments have divested enterprises in stages. The concern here is with more enduring mixed enterprises. It should be noted, however, that some cases of mixed ownership emerging in the recent NPM period also seem destined for longer life: notably utility service providers in continental Europe which now have multiple governments as well as private interests as owners (Lane 2002), several major world airports (Graham, 2001: ch.2), and the outcomes of India's 'disinvestment' policy (Ghuman and Wettenhall, 2001:150–2).

14. The position of the 'mixed economy' itself deserves attention. Thus an economic historians' review of the Australian developmental situation in the late 19th and earlier 20th centuries speaks of 'a strongly supportive relationship, almost a partnership, of government towards major business interests and a private acceptance (and use of) this supportive relationship' (Butlin et al., 1982:10).

15. Anglo–Persian had a highly significant precursor: the Suez Canal Company, in which the then British government bought the shareholding of the Khedive of Egypt in 1875 in

order to obtain a strong voice in maintaining communications with the empire; in 1938 that was the British government's largest shareholding in a mixed enterprise, amounting to 39 per cent of the company and contributing revenue to the Treasury of £2 812 500 in 1937–8 (at 1937–8 values!); the British government appointed three directors, and the arrangement survived until Nasser 'expropriated' (or nationalized) the canal in 1956 (Davies, 1938:422–3; Samuels, 1968: 299). On the propensity of one country's public sector to be active in the public sector of another, see Wettenhall, 1993.

16. Mostly the private side wanted to make money, whereas the public side was moved by strategic considerations and so retained some special power – even though, when put to the test, it proved to be a chimera (see Wettenhall, 2003:94, drawing on Bailey, 1979; and Yergin, 1991:622–4).

17. The notion of state intervention in agriculture as facilitation emerges very clearly in many of the mixing examples, drawn mostly from developing countries, discussed by Curtis (1991). This is, of course, rather more than the notion offered by Osborne and Gaebler (1993) that the state should merely steer while non-state agents do the rowing.

18. There have been some highly critical reports by Australian Auditors-General: see eg AG/NSW, 1996:15–19, which reports on the cases of the Port Macquarie Base Hospital and a water filtration plant in the Sydney catchment area – in both, 'the complex financial arrangements ... provide the plausible appearance but not the reality of reducing risk for the State'. On Port Macquarie Base Hospital, see also Collyer et al., 2001:ch.10; on the Sydney Harbour Tunnel, see Harris, 1991:533–6; on Melbourne's CityLink road project, see Quiggin, 1999 (and see also Quiggin, 1996:ch.12). A litany of problems associated with such private funding arrangements in Australia is exposed in Walker and Walker, 2000:ch.7.

19. On the notion of 'hallmark events', see Hall, 1992.

REFERENCES

Adam Smith Institute (2002), 'Contract management of water systems', in 'Around the world in 80 ideas', accessed at www.adamsmith.org/80ideas/idea/51htm.

AG/NSW (Auditor-General of New South Wales) (1996), *Annual Report to Parliament*, Sydney: NSW Government Printer.

Andrews, Kenneth R. (1964), *Elizabethan Privateering: English Privateering During the Spanish War, 1585–1603*, Cambridge: Cambridge University Press.

Aulich, Chris (2003), 'Governance through community partnerships', *The Innovation Journal*, **8** (2) (online at: http//www.innovation.cc/peer_reviewed/AulichPartnerships.pdf).

Bailey, Martin (1979), *Oilgate: The Sanctions Scandal*, London: Coronet.

Barlett, Donald L. and James B. Steele (1998), 'Corporate welfare', Time, 9 November.

Barley, Nigel (1991), *The Duke of Puddle Dock: In the Footsteps of Stamford Raffles*, London: Viking.

Bayley, David and Clifford Shearing (2001), *The New Structure of Policing: Description, Conceptualization and Research Agenda*, Washington: National Institute of Justice.

Benn, S. and G.R. Gaus (eds) (1983), *Public and Private in Social Life*, London: Croom Helm.

Blanc, Hermann (1940), 'A great state enterprise of olden times: The Geneva Corn Chamber, 1628–1798', *Annals of Collective Economy* (now *Annals of Public and Cooperative Economics*), **16** (1), 136–91.

Boyd, Susan B. (ed.) (1997), *Challenging the Public/Private Divide: Feminism, Law and Public Policy*, Toronto: University of Toronto Press.

Brinkerhoff, Jennifer M. and Derick W. Brinkerhoff (2002), 'Government–nonprofit relations in comparative perspective: evolution, themes and new directions', *Public Administration and Development*, **22** (1), 3–18.

Bromley, J.S. (1987), *Corsairs and Navies, 1660–1760*, London: Hambledon Press.

Butlin, N.J., A. Barnard and J.J. Pincus (1982), *Government and Capitalism: Public and Private Choice in Twentieth Century Australia*, Sydney: Allen and Unwin.

Caiden, Naomi (1989), 'A new perspective on budgetary reform', *Australian Journal of Public Administration*, **48** (1), 53–60.

Carroll, Peter (1989), 'The origins of EXPO 1988', *Australian Journal of Public Administration*, **48** (1), 41–52.

Collyer, Fran, Jim McMaster and Roger Wettenhall (2001), *Public Enterprise Divestment: Australian Case Studies*, Suva: Pacific Institute of Management and Development, University of the South Pacific.

Correy, Stan (1996), 'The Diamond Mercenaries of Africa', *Background Briefing*, Radio National, Australian Broadcasting Corporation, 4 August.

Corvisier, André (1994), 'Mercenaries', in André Corvisier (ed.), *A Dictionary of Military History and the Art of War* (trans. Chris Turner; revised and expanded by John Childs), Oxford: Blackwell, 501–4.

Curtis, Donald (1991), *Beyond Government: Organisations for Common Benefit*, London: Macmillan.

Daintith, T.C. (1970), 'The mixed enterprise in the United Kingdom', in W. Friedmann and J.F. Garner (eds), *Government Enterprise: A Comparative Study*, London: Stevens, 53–78.

Damaska, Mirjan (1984), *The Faces of Justice and State Authority*, New Haven: Yale University Press.

Daniels, Bill (2002), 'Funding debate needs collaborative approach', *Canberra Times*, 11 June.

Davies, Ernest (1938), 'Government directors of public companies', *Political Quarterly*, **9** (3), 421–30.

Davis, Natalie Zemon (2000), *The Gift in Sixteenth-Century France*, Madison: University of Wisconsin Press.

Eckel, Catherine and Adrian Vining (1982), 'Toward a positive theory of joint enterprise', in W.T. Stanbury and Fred Thompson (eds), *Managing Public Enterprise*, New York: Praeger, 209–22.

Einaudi, Mario, Maurice Byé and Ernesto Rossi, (1955), *Nationalization in France and Italy*, Ithaca: Cornell University Press.

EIU (Economist Intelligence Unit) (2002), *Public v Private*, London: The Economist Newspaper Group.

Erman, Adolf (1969), *Life in Ancient Egypt* (trans. H.M. Tirad), New York: Benjamin Blom (first published 1894).

Farazmand, Ali (1998), 'Administration of the Persian Achaemenid world-state empire: implications for modern public administration', *International Journal of Public Administration*, **21** (1), 25–86.

Farazmand, Ali (2001), 'Privatization and public enterprise reform in post-revolutionary Iran', in Ali Farazmand (ed.), *Privatization or Public Enterprise Reform? International Case Studies with Implications for Public Management*, Westport, Connecticut: Greenwood Press, 175–200.

Furber, H. (1948), *John Company at Work: A Study of European Expansion in India in the Late Eighteenth Century*, Cambridge, Massachusetts: Harvard University Press.

Gernet, Jacques (1982), *A History of Chinese Civilization* (trans. J.R. Foster), Cambridge: Cambridge University Press.

Ghuman, B.S. and Roger Wettenhall (2001), 'From public enterprise and privatisation towards sectoral mixes: guest editors' introduction', *Asian Journal of Public Administration*, **23** (2), 143–66.

Grabosky, Peter (2004), 'Toward a theory of public/private interaction in policing', draft of chapter for inclusion in Joan McCord (ed.), *Beyond Empiricism: Institutions and Intentions in the Study of Crime*, (vol. 13 of *Advances in Criminology Theory*), Picataway, New Jersey: Transaction Books.

Graham, Anne (2001), *Managing Airports: An International Perspective*, Oxford: Butterworth Heinemann.

Greve, Carsten and Niels Ejersbo (2002), 'Serial organizational monogamy: building trust into contractual relationships', *International Review of Public Administration* (Seoul, South Korea), **7** (1), 39–51.

Hall, C.M. (1992), *Hallmark Tourist Events: Impacts, Management and Planning*, London: Bellhaven Press.

Hall, David (2000), 'Water in public hands', in 'Problems with water privatisations and concessions', accessed at www.france.attac.org/a2952.

Harris, G.T. (1991), 'Cost benefit analysis: its limitations and use in fully privatised infrastructure projects', *Australian Journal of Public Administration*, **50** (4), 526–38.

Hodge, Graeme (1999), 'Contracting-out and competition: learning to get the best value balance', *Journal of Economic and Social Policy* (Southern Cross University and [Canberra] Centre for Policy and Research), **4** (2), 105–25.

Holland, Stuart (ed.) (1972), *The State as Entrepreneur*, London: Weidenfeld and Nicolson.

Hood, Christopher (1989), 'Public administration and public policy: intellectual challenges for the 1990s', *Australian Journal of Public Administration*, **48** (4), 346–58.

Horin, A. (2000a), 'Just relax! The games have given us Sydney at its best', *Sydney Morning Herald*, 23 September, p. 1.

Horin, A. (2000b), "Rare praise, indeed, for public servants', *Australian Journal of Public Administration*, **59** (4), 128.

Huxham, C. (ed.) (1996), *Creating Collaborative Advantage*, London: Sage.

Kamen, Henry (2003), *Empire: How Spain Became a World Power 1492–1763*, New York: HarperCollins.

Kaminski, Antoni Z. (ed.) (1991), 'The public and the private', symposium in *International Political Science Review*, **12** (4), 263–351.

Kay, John (1993), *Foundations of Corporate Success: How Business Strategies Add Value*, Oxford: Oxford University Press.

Keir, Sir David Lindsay (1953), *The Constitutional History of Modern Britain 1485–1951*, London: Adam and Charles Black.

Kooiman, Jan (2003), *Governing as Governance*, Sage: London.

Lane, Jan-Erik (2002), 'The transformation and future of public enterprises in Continental Western Europe', *Public Finance and Management*, **2** (1), 47–66.

Lowndes, Vivien and Chris Skelcher (1998), 'The dynamics of multi-organizational partnerships: an analysis of changing modes of governance', *Public Administration*, **76** (2), 313–33.

McIntosh, Kylie, Jason Shauness and Roger Wettenhall (1997), *Contracting Out in Australia: An Indicative History*, Canberra: Centre for Research in Public Sector Management, University of Canberra.

Macneil, Ian R. (1980), *The New Social Contract: An Inquiry into Modern Contractual Relations*, New Haven, Connecticut: Yale University Press.

Mantziaris, Christos and Roger Wettenhall (2000), 'The Olympic Games, corporatisation and (ir)responsible government: three papers', *Public Law Review* (Sydney), **11** (1), 19–66.

Marcou, Gerard (1992), 'Public-private partnership for public infrastructure delivery: the Channel Tunnel case in international perspective', in Zhang Zhijian, Raul de Guzman and Mila Reforma (eds), *Administrative Reform Towards Promoting Productivity in Bureaucratic Performance*, vol. 1, Manila: EROPA Secretariat-General, pp. 316–37.

Milward, H. Brinton and Keith G. Provan (2003), 'Managing the hollow state: collaboration and contracting', *Public Management Review*, **5** (1), 1–18.

Mitchell, William (1995), 'Business welfare: a legitimate role for government?', *Current Affairs Bulletin* (Sydney), **71** (6), 4–13.

Musolf, Lloyd D. (1972), *Mixed Enterprise: A Developmental Perspective*, Lexington, Massachusetts: Heath.

Neutze, Max (1995), *Private Sector Involvement in Public Infrastructure*, background paper no. 4, Canberra: The Australia Institute.

Neutze, Max (1997), *Funding Urban Services*, Sydney: Allen and Unwin.

O'Brian, Patrick (1988), *The Letter of Marque*, London: Collins.

O'Brian, Patrick (1993), *The Wine-Dark Sea*, London: HarperCollins.

O'Connor, James R. (1973), *The Fiscal Crisis of the State*, New York: St Martins Press.

Osborne, David and Ted Gaebler (1993), *Reinventing Government: How the Entrepreneurial Spirit is Transforming the Public Sector*, New York: Plume.

Petrie, Donald A. 1999. *The Prize Game: Lawful Looting on the High Seas in the Days of Fighting Sail*, Annapolis, Maryland: US Naval Institute.

Pirotta, Godfrey (1996), *The Maltese Public Service 1800–1940: The Administrative Politics of a Micro-State*, Msida, Malta: Mireva Publications.

Posner, M.V. and S.J. Woolf (1967), *Italian Public Enterprise*, London: Gerald Duckworth.

Quiggin, John (1996), *Great Expectations: Microeconomic Reform and Australia*, Sydney: Allen and Unwin.

Quiggin, John (1999), 'Privatisation: who gains?', *Australian Financial Review*, 19 August.

Ramanadham, V.V. (1984), *The Nature of Public Enterprise*, London: Croom Helm.

Rhodes, R.A.W. (1996), 'The new governance: governing without government', *Political Studies*, **44** (4), 652–67.

Rhodes, R.A.W. (1997), *Understanding Governance: Policy Networks, Governance, Reflexivity and Accountability*, Buckingham: Open University Press.

Robinson, David (ed.) (1999), *Partnership: From Practice to Theory*, Wellington: Institute of Policy Studies, Victoria University of Wellington.

Rosenau, James N and Ernst-Otto Czempiel (1992), *Governance Without Government: Order and Change in World Politics*, Cambridge: Cambridge University Press.

Samuels, Alec (1968), 'Government participation in private industry', *Journal of Business Law*, October, 296–302.

Savas, E.S. (1987), *Privatization: The Key to Better Government*, Chatham, New Jersey: Chatham House.

Savas, E.S. (2000), *Privatization and Public–Private Partnerships*, New York: Chatham House.

Scott, Ian (2003), 'Organizations in the public sector in Hong Kong: core government, quasi-government and private bodies with public functions', *Public Organization Review*, **3** (3), 247–67.

Silmalis, L. (2000), 'Praise keeps coming as games chief departs', *Canberra Times*, 3 October.

Somasundram, M. (1987), 'Successes are the pillars of failure? A case study of the Cereal Marketing Public Enterprise', in Colm O Nuallain and Roger Wettenhall (eds), *Public Enterprise: The Management Challenge*, Brussels: International Institute of Administrative Sciences, 153–66.

Springer, Basil G.F. (2003), 'Creating effective public private partnerships', paper presented at CAPAM Regional Conference on Caribbean Public Service Leadership and the Challenge of Globalization, Barbados, 7–9 May.

Starkey, David J. (1990), *British Privateering Enterprise in the Eighteenth Century*, Exeter: University of Exeter Press.

Tilly, Charles (1975), 'Reflections on the history of European state-making', in Charles Tilly (ed.), *The Formation of National States in Western Europe*, Princeton, New Jersey: Princeton University Press, 24–82 .

Walker, Bob and Betty Con Walker (2000), *Privatisation – Sell off or Sell Out? The Australian Experience*, Sydney: ABC Books.

Weintraub, Jeff and Krishnan Kumar (eds) (1997), *Public and Private in Thought and Practice: Perspectives on a Grand Dichotomy*, Chicago: University of Chicago Press.

Wettenhall, Roger (1988), 'Why public enterprise? A public interest perspective', *Canberra Bulletin of Public Administration*, (57), 44–50.

Wettenhall, Roger (1990), 'Australia's daring experiment with public enterprise', in Alexander Kouzmin and Nicholas Scott (eds), *Dynamics in Australian Public Management: Selected Essays*, Melbourne: Macmillan, 2–16.

Wettenhall, Roger (1993), 'The globalization of public enterprises', *International Review of Administrative Sciences*, **59** (3), 387–408.

Wettenhall, Roger (1996), 'Australia: a pioneer among developing countries', in Ali Farazmand (ed.), *Public Enterprise Management: International Case Studies*, Westport, Connecticut: Greenwood Press, 237–61.

Wettenhall, Roger (2001), 'The Templars and Australia: crusading orders and a statutory authority', *Australian Studies*, **16** (2), 131–50.

Wettenhall, Roger (2003), 'The rhetoric and reality of public–private partnerships', *Public Organization Review*, **3** (1), 77–107.

Wild, Antony (1999), *The East India Company: Trade and Conquest from 1600*, London: HarperCollins.

Yergin, Daniel (1991), *The Prize: The Epic Quest for Oil, Money and Power*, New York: Simon and Schuster.

3. The United Kingdom Private Finance Initiative: the challenge of allocating risk

David Corner

INTRODUCTION

The United Kingdom (UK) has been at the forefront of the development of innovative approaches to engaging the private sector in the delivery of public services. In 1992 the UK embarked upon a new type of public–private partnership, known as the Private Finance Initiative (PFI). Under the Private Finance Initiative, private sector firms take on the responsibility for providing a public service including maintaining, enhancing or constructing the necessary infrastructure required. A total of 563 Private Finance Initiative contracts had been let by April 2003, with a total capital value of £35.5 billion (HM Treasury, 2002–3), and accounting for more than ten per cent of total investment in the UK public sector in 2003–4.

This chapter explores the value for money of the Private Finance Initiative. It argues that there are powerful performance incentives in Private Finance Initiative contracts which at least potentially offer significant improved performance compared to past practices. It suggests that Private Finance Initiative contracts enable risks to be better estimated than in the past, but that the real success of Private Finance Initiative projects also depends on the degree to which risk is genuinely transferred from the public to the private sector and optimally shared. It also considers some of the difficulties this presents for accounting for Private Finance Initiative projects. It draws on the work of the United Kingdom National Audit Office and the House of Commons Committee of Public Accounts which have both examined and reported to the United Kingdom parliament in detail on a number of individual Private Finance Initiative projects as well as other general issues arising from the initiative.[1]

RISK UNDER CONVENTIONAL PROCUREMENT IN THE PUBLIC SECTOR

Public service delivery is a risky business. The operation of any organization, public or private, involves risk. But public service agencies operate across a diverse range of activities, markets and locations. Many of the projects they have responsibility for delivering are large or unique. They may not have precedents on which to draw to help guide implementation. And they are usually more exposed to political and reputational risk. Despite this it is only in the last ten years, that public sector policy makers and implementers have turned their attention in earnest to risk management techniques.

Effective risk management involves anticipating, preparing for, and mitigating adverse outcomes, without eradicating, or unnecessarily hindering, beneficial risk taking. Well managed risk taking also presents opportunities to innovate, experiment and develop new ideas where more traditional ways of working are not able to deliver real change; for example, in providing an environment where radically new or different approaches can be developed in the confidence that the associated risks will be well managed. Indeed the greatest risk of all may be not taking any risks, where services and the way they are delivered do not anticipate change or evolve to meet new demands from citizens.

Constructing and operating a public building entails a number of risks. These include the risk of construction overruns, higher than expected costs of maintenance, increases or decreases in demand for the services provided in the facility, and changes in legislation or the regulatory regime affecting how the building or the services it houses are delivered. In a traditional construction contract the public sector has accommodated a number of types of risk: design and construction risk – delivering to cost and time; commissioning and operating risks – including maintenance; demand (or volume/usage) risks; residual value risk; technology and obsolescence risks; regulation and similar risks (including taxation, planning permission); and project financing risk.

For each project, some risks are more relevant than others. In a road project, the key risks will be demand and design/asset construction and maintenance, whereas in a prison project, the key risks relate to availability, performance and operating costs alongside design/asset construction and maintenance.

The record of conventional public sector procurement in assessing these risks is not good. The full costs of projects have often not been calculated accurately beforehand, risk management procedures have often been weak and there have been insufficient incentives to ensure that projects are driven forward successfully. Recent examples in the UK include the following:

- The initial cost estimates of Guy's and St Thomas's Hospital rose by £124 million to £160 million and the completion date slipped by over three years (NAO, 1997–98b);
- The cost of the Trident submarine shiplift and berth at Faslane rose from an estimate of £100 million to a final cost of £314 million and was delivered two and a half years late (NAO, 1993–4);
- The London Underground Jubilee Line extension was delivered two years late and cost £1.4 billion more than original estimates; and
- The top 25 equipment projects in the Ministry of Defence experienced cost overruns amounting to £2.8 billion with average delays of three and a half years (NAO, 2003–4).

A recent National Audit Office study found that only 30 per cent of conventional procurement construction projects were delivered on time and only 27 per cent were within budget (NAO, 2001–2a). An independent report commissioned by the Treasury found that outturn costs of conventional procurement construction projects were between 2 and 24 per cent higher than the estimate in the business case (HM Treasury, 2002).

WHAT IS THE PRIVATE FINANCE INITIATIVE?

Under conventional procurement, the government typically enters into one contract with a builder to develop a government-designed asset and then either operates this itself or enters into a second contract for operation. A common problem is that the operator or service provider, having no role in the design and construction stages, finds that the asset has been designed or built in a way that limits flexibility when it comes to delivering services more efficiently. This often results in substantial operating cost implications over the typical 25–30 year life of the asset.

The Private Finance Initiative is a form of public–private partnership that combines procurement, where the public sector purchases capital items from the private sector, with an extension of contracting-out, where public services are contracted from the private sector. It differs from privatization in that the public sector retains a substantial role as the main purchaser of services or as the enabler of the project. It also differs from contracting out since the private sector provides the capital asset as well as the services. A Private Finance initiative contract is intended to provide a continuing commercial incentive for synergy, flexibility and efficiency right through from initial design, build and operation.

Under the most common form of Private Finance Initiative, the private sector designs, builds, finances and operates facilities based on specifications of outputs determined by public sector bodies. The requirements of the public service body would normally be framed not as precise input specifications and designs, but as an output specification defining the service required; for example supporting hospital beds for a certain number of patients, or prison accommodation for a specific category of inmates. Under a Private Finance Initiative contract the public body usually pays a stream of committed revenue payments for the use of the facilities over the contract period. Once the contract has expired, ownership of the asset may remain with the private sector contractor or pass to the public sector, depending on the terms of the contract.

For example, in 1999 the Ministry of Defence identified that improvements were necessary to the accommodation and working environment available in its principal office building and decided to redevelop it. This was a large and complex project. It involved moving over 3000 staff into other central London accommodation, carrying out an extensive redevelopment, disposing of surplus properties and then moving staff back into the redeveloped building. In May 2000, the Ministry of Defence let a Private Finance Initiative contract with a net present value of £746 million (at 2000 price levels) to a private sector consortium called Modus. The 30-year contract covered the redevelopment and limited refurbishment and provision of support to other buildings needed to accommodate staff while redevelopment was undertaken, followed by the provision of maintenance and facilities management services (NAO, 2002–3).

Private Finance Initiative deals have ranged from very small projects, such as a £100 000 scheme to improve Information Technology facilities at a local school, to Europe's largest construction project – the Channel Tunnel Rail Link, worth £4 billion (NAO, 2000–1b). Private Finance Initiative contracts have been signed in over twenty different sectors and by over one hundred different public sector organisations within central and local government and the National Health Service. The largest users of Private Finance Initiative have been the Department for Transport which accounts for about 20 per cent of all Private Finance Initiative projects by capital value and the Department of Health which has signed about 120 separate Private Finance Initiative contracts (HM Treasury, 2002–3).

The UK's Treasury has stated that one of the main objectives of Private Finance Initiative is to transform public sector bodies from being owners and operators of assets into purchasers of services from the private sector. Private firms become long term providers of services rather than simply upfront asset builders, combining the responsibilities of designing, building, financing and operating the assets in order to deliver the services demanded by the public sector (ibid.).

THE POTENTIAL ADVANTAGES AND DISADVANTAGES OF PRIVATE FINANCE INITIATIVE DEALS

Private Finance Initiative contracts are generally long term arrangements involving public expenditure over extended periods, often for 30 years or more. The public sector does not have to find the money up-front to meet the initial capital costs. But the cash payments thereafter will generally be higher than in an equivalent conventionally-financed project (Figure 3.1).

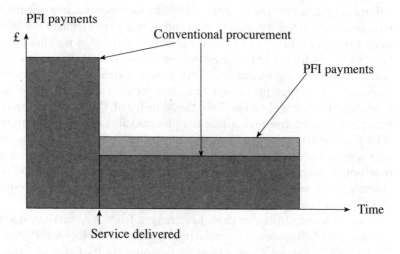

Source: Public Accounts Committee (2003)

Figure 3.1   Timing of payments under the Private Finance Initiative and conventional procurement

The Private Finance Initiative approach can enable the public sector to undertake projects which they would be unable to finance conventionally since they do not need to find all the money for the capital asset during its construction. Private Finance Initiative deals can therefore be attractive in the short term. But there is a risk that this attractiveness may distort priorities in favour of those projects which are capable of being run as Private Finance Initiative projects. For the Private Finance Initiative route to be worthwhile, the higher financing costs of raising funds in private markets and any other potential disadvantages need to be more than outweighed by the benefits achieved. Some of the potential advantages and disadvantages of Private Finance Initiative deals are set out in Table 3.1.

Table 3.1 *Potential advantages and disadvantages of Private Finance Initiative deals*

Advantages	Disadvantages
There can be greater price certainty. The public sector body and contractor agree the annual unitary payment for the services to be provided. This should usually only change as a result of agreed circumstances.	The public sector body is tied into a long-term contract (often around 30 years). Business needs change over time so there is the risk that the contract may become unsuitable for these changing needs during the contract life.
Responsibility for assets is transferred to the contractor. The public sector body is not involved in providing services which may not be part of its core business.	Variations may be needed as the public sector body's business needs change. Management of these may require renegotiation of contract terms and prices.
Private Finance Initiative brings the scope for innovation in service delivery. The contractor has incentives to introduce innovative ways to meet the public sector body's needs.	There could be disadvantages, for example, if innovative methods of service delivery lead to a decrease in the level or quality of service.
Often, the unitary payment will not start until, for example, the building is operational, so the contractor has incentives to encourage timely delivery of quality service.	The unitary payment will include charges for the contractor's acceptance of risks, such as construction and service delivery risks, which may not materialize.
The contract provides greater incentives to manage risks over the life of the contract than under traditional procurement. A reduced level or quality of service would lead to compensation paid to the public sector body.	There is the possibility that the contractor may not manage transferred risks well. Or public sector bodies may believe they have transferred core business risks, which ultimately remain with them.
A long-term Private Finance Initiative contract encourages the contractor and the public sector body to consider costs over the whole life of the contract, rather than considering the construction and operational periods separately. This can lead to efficiencies through synergies between design and construction and its later operation and maintenance. The contractor takes the risk of getting the design and construction wrong.	The whole life costs will be paid through the unitary payment, which will be based on the contractor arranging financing at commercial rates which tend to be higher than government borrowing rates.

Source: Public Accounts Committee (2003)

THE PUBLIC SECTOR VERSUS PRIVATE SECTOR DECISION

Up until recently the main tool public bodies have relied on in evaluating up-front whether a Private Finance Initiative option provides better value for money over conventional procurement is a public sector comparator. A public sector comparator is a costing of a conventionally financed project delivering the same outputs as those of the Private Finance Initiative deal under examination.

The use of public sector comparators has been the subject of considerable debate. The accuracy of public sector comparators is limited because they are prone to error owing to the complexity of the financial modelling that is often used. They are also dependent on uncertain forecasts. And a great deal depends on assumptions about the time cost of money – i.e. the discount rate.

There is a risk that the users of the public sector comparator will believe that it is more accurate than it could ever be. Decisions can be made on the basis of small and spurious differences between the public sector comparator and the Private Finance Initiative option. In the case of the Private Finance Initiative contract for a new accommodation programme at the Government Communication Headquarters, the management made a highly uncertain assumption that a conventionally procured building would have overrun its budget by 24 per cent. That alone accounted for the comparative cost saving that the Government Communications Headquarters estimated the Private Finance Initiative deal would offer, but was simply an average over past projects and hid the wide range of possible outcomes (Public Accounts Committee, 2004–5).

The UK House of Commons Committee of Public Accounts believes there have been many cases where the public sector comparator has been incorrectly used as a pass or fail test. In these cases the desire to show that the Private Finance Initiative deal is 'cheaper' than the public sector comparator has led to manipulation of the underlying calculations and erroneous interpretation of the results (Table 3.2). There are likely to be qualitative and non-financial differences between the options that cannot simply be subsumed in a difference in forecast cost. The UK Treasury has recently recognised this and instituted reform of the public sector comparator as only a single element within an approach which is intended to provide a more sophisticated long-term and analytically robust approach to appraisal and investment evaluation (HM Treasury, 2002–3).

This chapter goes on to suggest that a key element of the evaluation of the value for money of individual Private Finance Initiatives is the success with which risk is genuinely transferred from the public to the private sector and optimally shared between the two sectors.

Table 3.2   Weaknesses in the use of public sector comparators

Private Finance Initiative deal	House of Commons Committee of Public Account's findings
Dartford and Gravesham Hospital	The NHS Trust did not detect significant errors in the public sector comparator. The Trust also did not quantify the full effects of changes in contract terms and of the sensitivity of the deal to changes in key assumptions, as the deal went forward. Had the Trust known that the savings were marginal when negotiating the deal, it might have made different decisions and achieved better value for money (Public Accounts Committee, 1999–2000b).
Airwave	A public sector comparator was not prepared until late in the procurement, and after a decision to use the Private Finance Initiative had already been made. It is therefore doubtful that the use of a comparator added to the decision-making process (Public Accounts Committee, 2001–2b).
Ministry of Defence Main Building	The public sector comparator gave a central estimate for the cost of a conventionally financed alternative to the Private Finance Initiative deal as £746.2 million, compared to an expected deal cost of £746.1 million. Such accuracy in long term project costings is spurious, and the small margin in favour of the Private Finance Initiative deal provided no assurance that the deal would deliver value for money (Public Accounts Committee, 2002–3a).
West Middlesex Hospital	The NHS Trust's advisers strove to make slight adjustments to the calculations, well within the range of error inherent in costing a 35-year project, so that the Private Finance Initiative cost appeared marginally cheaper than the public sector comparator (Public Accounts Committee, 2002–3b).

THE ALLOCATION OF RISK

The main benefit of transferring risk from the public sector is that it should generate the incentives for the private sector to supply cost effective and higher quality services on time. Risk and reward go hand in hand. Private Finance Initiative suppliers usually only start to receive their service payments when a flow of services actually starts, and continued payment depends on meeting performance criteria.

Private sector management skills are better harnessed and incentivized by having private finance at risk. The transfer of project financing risk generates incentives for the private sector to supply services on time and of a higher quality as they only start to receive payments when a flow of public services actually starts, and continued payment depends on meeting specified performance criteria.

The lenders to a Private Finance Initiative have a powerful incentive to identify, allocate and ensure the effective management of all the risks the private sector assumes in a project. One of the valuable features of private sector financing of Private Finance initiative projects is the extensive due diligence work that private sector risk-takers carry out on projects. But the returns to financiers need to be commensurate with the risks that they are actually taking and this in turn depends on the market being well informed and truly competitive. In some Private Finance Initiative projects the Committee of Public Accounts has found this not to be the case (Table 3.3).

The assessment of risk, and who is best able to manage it, needs to be carefully considered in the design of Private Finance Initiative projects. Value for money will be achieved where there is optimum transfer of risk such that individual risks are allocated to those best placed to manage them. If the public sector seek to transfer risks which the private sector cannot manage, value for money will reduce as the private sector seeks to charge a premium for accepting such risks.

The principle governing risk transfer is that the risk should be allocated to whoever from the public or private sector is able to manage it at least cost. An optimal sharing of risk between the private and public sector should recognize that there are certain risks that are best managed by the government and to seek to transfer these risks would either not be available or not offer value for money for the public sector. The government pays for inappropriately transferred risks through higher service charges. The optimum allocation of risk, rather than maximizing risk transfer, should be the objective, and it is vital to ensure that value for money is not diminished.

This is illustrated by the case of the Private Finance Initiative contract to develop a benefits payments card system. In May 1996, the Department

Table 3.3   Examples of Inadequate Competition

PFI deal	Committee of Public Account's findings
Immigration and Nationality Directorate (Public Accounts Committee, 1999–2000a)	Key figures, on which future increases in productivity would be measured and payments to the contractor calculated, had not been finally agreed until more than a year after the contract was signed. Such important issues need to be finalized before a contractor is selected and the benefits of competition fall away (Public Accounts Committee, 2003).
Dartford and Gravesham Hospital (Public Accounts Committee, 1999–2000b)	The NHS Trust selected two firms to submit final bids but one of the firms did not submit a bid. The Trust therefore ended up with only one final bidder on this major pathfinder project for the use of the PFI in the NHS. The bidder's final bid was 33 per cent higher in real terms than its indicative bid. The Trust did not undertake a detailed analysis of the reasons for the increase in the final bid, especially given the absence of other bids. Such action might have helped the Trust to secure a greater price reduction in the subsequent negotiations (Public Accounts Committee, 2003).
Newcastle Estate (Public Accounts Committee, 1999–2000c)	In this deal the Department of Social Security appointed a preferred bidder whilst important issues remained unresolved. Exclusive negotiations with the preferred bidder continued for 18 months (Public Accounts Committee, 2003).

of Social Security and Post Office Counters Ltd jointly awarded a contract to Pathway, a subsidiary of the ICL computer services group, for delivery of the benefits payment card. The project was intended to replace by 1999 the existing paper-based methods of paying social security benefits with a magnetic strip payment card, and to automate the national network of post offices through which most benefits are paid across Great Britain and Northern Ireland. The project was vast in its scale and complexity, and estimated to cost some £1 billion in payments to Pathway. It was also one of the first information technology contracts awarded under the Private Finance Initiative. After delays and problems the government decided to cancel the benefits payment card with upwards of £1 billion in abortive costs, the write-down of assets and delayed reductions in benefit fraud.

The contractor chosen was selected because they were willing to take on a level of risk for preventing benefit fraud which the other two bidders for the contract would not accept, even though the contractor came third on eight out of eleven technical and management criteria. At the time, there was a mistaken view that Private Finance Initiative bidders should compete on the level of risk they were prepared to take on, rather than achieving an optimum allocation of risk (Public Accounts Committee, 2001–2a).

Private Finance Initiative schemes need to transfer to the private sector risks where the supplier can influence the outcome. The supplier is able to influence the likely performance of the building and its services by the quality of the design, construction and refurbishment work undertaken. The quality and frequency of maintenance also has an important bearing on on-going performance. Therefore, risks transferred should usually include design, build, financing and operating risks.

The ability to secure risk transfer on worthwhile terms means ensuring that the scope of a contract is sufficiently widely drawn. If the private sector has clear ownership, responsibility and control, it will take all the risks it can manage. If the public sector seeks to reserve to itself many of the responsibilities and controls that go hand in hand with ownership, and yet still seek to transfer the risk, the private sector will simply increase its price (and thus potentially damage value for money).

The National Audit Office recently surveyed a number of PFI contractors and the public sector bodies that had contracted them (NAO, 2001–2b). It showed that in some projects there is disagreement on whether risks have been allocated to the party best able to manage them. Only two-thirds of contractors shared the public sector bodies' view that risks had been allocated appropriately. Seventy-nine per cent of authorities thought the risk allocation was totally satisfactory but only 53 per cent of contractors had this view. Contractors recognized that risk allocation was an important area where there were often problems. All the contractors who were dissatisfied with the risk allocation thought that risks had been inappropriately transferred to them rather than inappropriately retained by authorities.

For example, in the case of the first Private Finance Initiative contracts awarded to design, build, finance and operate roads, payments to operators were based primarily on traffic volumes which are, however, notoriously difficult to forecast. This was done to test the ability of the private sector to bear one of the risks involved in running tolled roads, but it created a new financial risk which bore both on the public sector and on the private sector and which neither party was able to manage effectively (NAO, 1997–8a). Bidders included a premium in their pricing for taking this risk which is likely to have reduced the value for money offered by these contracts. Private Finance Initiative contracts can deliver better value than traditional methods of procurement if risks are transferred to the parties best able to handle them. In this case risk transfer was confused with risk creation, which is simply likely to increase costs to the public sector.

Some contractors may be too willing to accept inappropriate risk. Some authorities may have been tempted to transfer as much risk as possible to the private sector. But if contractors accept inappropriate risk to win the competition, the subsequent realization of those risks within a very competitively priced contract may lead to problems for the contractor and, therefore, for the authority. The due diligence carried out by contractors' banks may sometimes stop contractors taking on too much or inappropriate risk but this work is done on behalf of the bankers themselves and may not give full reassurance about project risks to other parties.

Some public sector authorities may transfer risk back to themselves. The essence of Private Finance Initiatives is that authorities provide contractors with an output specification of the services they require. Contractors then have the responsibility and risk for deciding how they will provide those services. If public sector bodies tell contractors how the services are to be provided, they are transferring the risk back to themselves. Contractors sometimes attempt to define the technical solution, or have expectations on how a service should be provided, which limits contractors' freedom to propose alternatives.

In the case of the road contracts mentioned above, following their signing, the operators put forward more than 3000 variations and innovative ways of varying standards, which the Agency accepted. This suggests the core requirements in the original tender documents were too tightly drawn to encourage novel ideas. However, the exploitation of private sector innovation is critical to the success of the Private Finance Initiative in delivering improved value for money.

Under Private Finance Initiative contracts not all risks can be or are suitable for transfer to the contractor. It is clearly important that authorities continually monitor risks to which they may be exposed and take steps to manage them. For example, under the terms of the Ministry of Defence's Fixed Telecommunications Service contract, it had become exposed to the possibility of having to pay the contractor (British Telecom) compensation of up to £12 million because the anticipated numbers of users paying for secure speech services was not sufficient to enable British Telecom to recover its initial investment in developing this service. Proactive management by the Ministry, working in conjunction with British Telecom, enabled a satisfactory resolution of this situation which involved changes to required volumes of users and the mechanisms for funding British Telecom's investment in the service. On this basis, British Telecom agreed not to press for the compensation to which it was entitled under the contract (Public Accounts Committee, 2003).

Where a Private Finance Initiative project concerns the delivery of an essential public service the public sector body may have no option, if the project fails, but to take back responsibility for delivering the service. In these circumstances it would be misleading for the contract to be drawn up on the basis that the risk of failing to deliver the service had been wholly transferred to the private sector supplier.

If contractors successfully manage the risks that have been allocated to them and deliver the services required they can expect to earn rewards commensurate with the level of risk that they have borne. But commercial discipline is undermined if contractors get the impression that risks will be taken back by the public sector if they materialize in any serious way. There are a number of examples where central government has done just this.

For example, in one case the Private Finance Initiative contractor was required to build and operate a new museum in Leeds for the Royal Armouries. However the government effectively bailed the company out to the tune of over £10 million when it ran into financial difficulties and faced imminent insolvency. There were no contingency plans in place, as it was considered that the risk of the project's failure lay with the contractor. However the business risks ultimately lay with the public sector as the government were unwilling to countenance the closure of the museum and therefore stepped in to rescue the project (NAO, 2000–1a).

The need to ensure that services to the public are maintained means that the risk of ultimate failure is one that sometimes cannot be transferred to the private sector. In the case of an operational facility, such as a hospital, it would be normal in current contracts to have provisions enabling the public sector partner to take over the assets and their operation in the event of failure and/or to seek a new private sector partner. The contract might provide for the private sector partner to receive compensation for the transfer of assets to the public sector, thus addressing the problem of security for the project's financing.

Private Finance Initiative deals need to be structured so that, if the contractor gets into difficulties, there is a strong incentive for the financier to step in and either get the contractor back on track or, if that is not possible, replace the contractor with an alternative. Only where both these options fail should the public sector body normally step in. Even here this should not mean that the contractor is rescued or should not still pay a substantial financial price in the event of a rescue.

Good risk management requires a thorough appraisal of all the possible risks attached to a deal and the development of contingencies should the risks crystallize. This emphasizes the importance of developing a successful partnership-based relationship between the public sector body and a contractor. Such a relationship is assisted by the right contractual framework, which includes allocating risks appropriately, establishing clearly defined quality of service and value for money mechanisms, and building in arrangements to deal with change. It is also essential that both parties to the deal understand their respective objectives, assess the prospects for a partnership, and make efforts to understand each other's business. As a deal progresses, the risks inherent in it will change and risk management arrangements therefore need to be reviewed regularly as deal risks change over time.

ACCOUNTING FOR THE ALLOCATION OF RISK

Generally accepted accounting practice draws a distinction between property and services, the former accounted as an asset and the latter as current expenditure. When a property has been built through conventional procurement methods, the public sector is almost always considered to bear the risks of ownership and the capital invested in that property is booked as an asset in the Government's account and counts against the public sector borrowing requirement.

Generally accepted accounting practice also requires both private and public sector bodies to account for the economic substance of a transaction, rather than simply its legal form. This means that a party in a contractual relationship that reaps the benefits and bears the balance of risks of ownership of a property has an asset of the property and must report this on the balance sheet. But this raises difficulties for Private Finance Initiative projects where, as we have seen, value for money depends on sophisticated allocation of risk between the private and public sectors.

The UK Accounting Standards Board has recognised these difficulties. It has issued guidance to help public sector bodies and their auditors determine ownership for balance-sheet purposes (UK Accounting Standards Board, 1994). It is based on an assessment of which party bears the majority of potential variations in returns relating to the Private Finance Initiative property. The UK Treasury has issued a Technical Note to supplement the Accounting Standards Board guidance (HM Treasury, 1997). The methodology recommended by this guidance for assessing which party has the majority of these risks identifies three sets of indicators that should be considered: qualitative, quantitative and other indicators.

The qualitative indicators are based on the concept that if the contractor defaults and, despite this, the debt financiers still get a full pay-out, if the equity input is minimal, or if the purchaser effectively determines the nature of the property, then these all indicate that the asset should be on the purchaser's (i.e. the public sector's) balance sheet.

The quantitative indicators are those risks – demand risk, design risk, residual value risk, etc., that are capable of some sort of allocation and evaluation. And there will be some risks (the 'other indicators') that are so uncertain that it would be foolhardy to attempt a meaningful quantification, for example the risks of financial impacts arising from future changes in technology or public policy.

It is possible that a qualitative analysis of such indicators and risks for a particular project will give a clear idea of which party should include the asset on its balance sheet. The Treasury guidance states that 'where demand risk is significant, it will normally give the clearest evidence of who should record an asset of the property', and that 'where it is significant, residual value risk will normally give clear evidence of who should record an asset of the property' (HM Treasury, 1997).

However it may not always be clear who should record an asset of the property without further detailed quantitative analysis of the risks to the property costs and revenues. The audited body and its advisers will typically start this process with some brainstorming by risk assessment workshops to consider all the potential risks and their likely quantum and who bears them. This process might not be carried out just for accounting purposes – it might be part of a wider process in assessing the likely benefits or otherwise of a Private Finance Initiative proposal generally.

The outcome of this exercise could be a risk register with a preliminary broad brush evaluation of the quantum of each identified risk for each of the parties. This should consider the probability of each of the identified risks materialising, the average financial impact and range and distribution of possible outcomes. This may then be refined by statistical methods to combine the range and impact of the risks through modelling techniques. The net present value of the quantified risks for each party would be compared and, subject to the qualitative and other indicators not providing a strongly contrary indication, the asset would be attributed to the party bearing the majority of the quantified risk.

There are a number of difficulties and judgements surrounding a quantitative risk analysis, and different interpretations of demand risk have arisen with public sector bodies and their advisers seeking to exploit these to ensure off-balance-sheet accounting. Small changes in 'guestimates' and assumptions used in quantitative analyses can tip the results so as to provide an off-balance-sheet assessment when a more rounded and intuitive view based on all the relevant risk considerations would provide a different answer. This has led to a situation in the health and local authority sectors where Private Finance Initiative hospital and schools are commonly not recorded on either the public sector's or the private sector's balance sheets. These difficulties tend to stem from a mechanical application of quantitative techniques combined with inaccurate assumptions and contentious argumentation to downplay the role of demand risk rather than a commonsense application of 'Generally Acceptable Accounting Practice'.

An obvious effect of the Private Finance Initiative is to reduce the current public sector balance-sheet and replace it with a stream of future liabilities. A private contractor picks up the bill for the construction of a new prison while the taxpayer guarantees it an income spread out over the lifetime of the asset so that today's capital investment becomes tomorrow's current spending. The signing of Private Finance Initiative contracts usually involves a commitment on the part of government to a future stream of payments for the services provided.

Future liabilities are recorded and published by the UK Government but until recently it was difficult to disaggregate those that were commitments as a result of the Private Finance Initiative. In response to a recommendation from the Treasury Committee in 1996 (HM Treasury, 1996–7), the Treasury now publishes forecasts of the committed expenditure for public services flowing from private sector investments under the Private Finance Initiative. Payments under Private Finance Initiative contract were estimated in April 2004 to rise to between £6.1 and £6.3 billion each year between 2006–7 and 2016–17 before declining to between around £2.5 billion each year between 2027–8 and 2029–30. In total over the 25-year period some £123 billion is committed (NAO, 2001–02b). These figures represent best estimates. Actual expenditure will in future years depend upon the payment mechanism details for each contract.

CONCLUSIONS

This chapter has argued that the success of the Private Finance Initiative cannot be judged solely of itself, but in relation to the record of conventional public sector procurement projects, which is not good. One of the benefits of its introduction has been to focus greater attention on the need to identify and manage better risks in the delivery of public sector procurement projects, not just those involving private finance. But the real success of Private Finance Initiative projects depends on the degree to which risk is genuinely transferred from the public to the private sector and optimally shared.

NOTE

1. These reports can be read at www.nao.org.uk.

REFERENCES

HM Treasury (1996–7), *The Private Finance Initiative*, Treasury Select Committee, HC 315, London: Stationery Office.

HM Treasury (1997), Treasury Task Force Technical Note No 1, London: Stationery Office.

HM Treasury (2002), *Review of Large Public Procurement in the UK*, Mott MacDonald, London: Stationery Office.

HM Treasury (2002–3), *PFI: Meeting the Investment Challenge*, Report of Comptroller and Auditor General, Session 2002–3, London: Stationery Office.

National Audit Office (1993–4), *Ministry of Defence: Management of the Trident Works Programme*, HC 621, Session 1993–4, London: Stationery Office.

National Audit Office (1997–8a), *The Private Finance Initiative: The First Four Design, Build, Finance and Operate Roads* Contracts, Report of Comptroller and Auditor General, HC 476, Session 1997–8, London: Stationery Office.

National Audit Office (1997–98b), *Guy's Hospital Phase III Development*, Report of Comptroller and Auditor General, HC 761, Session 1997–98, London: Stationery Office.

National Audit Office, (2000–1a), *The Re-negotiation of the PFI-type deal for the Royal Armouries Museum in Leeds*, Report of Comptroller and Auditor General, HC 103, Session 2000–1, London: Stationery Office.

National Audit Office (2000–1b), *The Channel Tunnel Rail Link*, Report of Comptroller and Auditor General, HC 302, Session 2000–1, London: Stationery Office.

National Audit Office (2000–2a), *Modernising Construction*, report of Comptroller and Auditor General, HC 87, Session 2000–2001, London: Stationery Office.

National Audit Office (2001–2b), *Managing the relationship to secure a successful partnership in PFI deals*, Report of Comptroller and Auditor General, HC 375, Session 2001–2, London: Stationery Office.

National Audit Office (2002–3), *Redevelopment of MOD Main Building*, Report of Comptroller and Auditor General, HC 748, Session 2002–3, London: Stationery Office.

Public Accounts Committee (1999–2000a), *Home Office: The Immigration and Nationality Directorate's Casework Programme*, 7th Report, House of Commons, London: Stationery Office.

Public Accounts Committee (1999–2000b), *The PFI Contract for the New Dartford and Gravesham Hospital*, 12th Report, House of Commons, London: Stationery Office.

Public Accounts Committee (1999–2000c), *The Newcastle Estate Development Project*, HC 104, 19th Report, House of Commons, London: Stationery Office.

Public Accounts Committee (2001–2a), *The Cancellation of the Benefits Payment Card Project*, HC 358, 3rd Report, House of Commons, London: Stationery Shop.

Public Accounts Committee (2001–2b), *Airwave*, HC 783, 64th Report, House of Commons, London: Stationery Shop.

Public Accounts Committee (2002–3a), *Private Finance Initiative: The Redevelopment of MOD Main Building*, 4th Report, House of Commons, London: Stationery Office.

Public Accounts Committee (2002–3b), *The PFI Contract for the Redevelopment of the West Middlesex Hospital*, 19th Report, House of Commons, London: Stationery Shop.

Public Accounts Committee (2003), *Delivering better value for money from the Private Finance Initiative*, HC 764, 28th Report, House of Commons, London: Stationery Shop.

Public Accounts Committee (2004–5), *Government Communications Headquarters (GCHQ): New Accommodation Programme*, HC 65, 23rd Report, House of Commons, London: Stationery Shop.

UK Accounting Standards Board (1994), 'Application note F "Private Finance Initiative and similar contracts"', in *FRS 5 'Reporting the Substance of Transactions'*, London: Accounting Standards Board.

4. Getting the contract right

Joanne Evans and Diana Bowman

INTRODUCTION

Public–private partnerships (PPPs) are notoriously hard to define. Stern and Harding (2002:127) characterize PPPs as 'a loose term applied to any venture that embraces both public and private sectors'. In the wider sense, pretty much any form of public procurement of private goods and services would constitute a public private partnership. This is consistent with the approach of Broadbent and Laughlin (2003:332) who assert that 'PPPs involve organisations whose affiliations lie in the public and private sectors working together in partnership to provide a service.'

In contrast, PPPs may be more narrowly defined as partnerships between the public and private sectors for the financing, design, construction, operation and maintenance, and/or provision of assets or infrastructure and associated services, which have traditionally been provided by the public sector (Webb and Pulle, 2002). Liddle (1996:12) argues that PFIs, a narrower form of PPP, are 'basically a hire–purchase scheme that enables the government to buy big-ticket items without paying cash on the nail'.

In the context in which the term is increasingly used, a public–private partnership is constituted by combining different aspects of public infrastructure and associated services to be provided by the private sector (Evans, 2003). This chapter will focus on PPPs in this context in its discussion of contracts.

Despite the obvious difficulties in reaching a universal definition of PPPs, a number of key features of today's PPP arrangements can been identified. Amongst the most important of these key features are the contractual nature of the relationship between the public and private sectors, long term commitments by the parties, a significant capital funding requirement with contractual models invariably based on the application of risk allocation theory.

As illustrated below, the project delivery options offered by PPPs are often defined by the contractual models under which they can be delivered. Contractual considerations will set the parameters of each PPP arrangement, as well as influencing the performance and achievements of each contracting partner. With contractual documentation therefore providing the primary mechanism for determining PPP success, the significance of 'getting the contract right' should not be under-estimated.

PPP MODELS

The flexible nature of PPPs as a procurement form encourages the development and adaptation of existing structures in response to the individual needs and specifications of each project and project partner (English and Guthrie, 2003).

The models used to facilitate PPPs will accordingly be a function of a range of factors. These include the sector in which the project takes place, the risks associated with that project, whether the infrastructure is capable of generating revenue itself or will always be provided at a net cost to government, whether there are opportunities for non-government use of the infrastructure, whether there are aspects of the project owned or controlled by government (for example, land), and whether there is competition as to the infrastructure and the need to regulate access and pricing.

Apart from the project's structural considerations, the legal framework within which a PPP project operates will also be a determinant of the optimal PPP model. PPPs will be subjected to legal issues that may encompass many facets of law including (amongst others) commercial, taxation, insurance, environmental, property, industrial relations and constitutional law. The complex interaction of these areas must be reinforced by efficient institutional structures to ensure 'sufficient clarity, continuity and security' (European Commission, 2003:36) to all 'partners'.

PPPs, even for this narrow area of public infrastructure provision, therefore encompass a broad continuum of project delivery models, which have been fashioned by the parameters of the project, as well as the legal and regulatory environment in which the project will operate.

It is useful, before examining the risk allocation impetus behind PPPs and the key aspects of the principal documents involved, to have a broad understanding of the definition and characteristics of the various models, which are illustrated in Table 4.1.

Conventional public sector procurement methods are today viewed as appropriate for relatively small capital projects or straightforward service provision. This form of project delivery may be beneficial in transferring design and construction risk where the public sector wishes to retain operating and ownership responsibility (VDTF, 2001; European Commission, 2003). This option, however, does not enable an optimal level

Table 4.1   Public–private partnership models

Project delivery options	Characteristics
Traditional public sector procurement	Traditional procurement is characterized by infrastructure ownership remaining within the public sector. • Under this model, governments may specify asset or service requirements to the private sector, who are individually contracted to build or provide the asset or service. • This form of procurement may be subdivided into distinct forms, including design and construction contracts, service contracts, operation and management contracts and leasing. • Assets or services are usually paid for by the government upon delivery or completion.
Build–Own–Operate–Transfer (BOOT)	The BOOT structure is the most dominant form of PPP. • Under this form of procurement, the private entity is responsible for the design, construction, finance and operation of the asset. • Under the concession contract, the government agrees to allow the private entity to provide a public asset for a specified time, which may extend for a period of 25–30 years. • The private sector bears all commercial risks and maintenance costs associated with the asset for the duration of the concession period. • The asset generates revenues solely or predominantly on a user-pays basis. • At the conclusion of the contract, ownership of the asset reverts to the public sector, usually at no cost or at a negligible cost.
Design–Build–Finance–Operate (DBFO)	DBFOs represent the most successful form of PPP, the most common being projects under the United Kingdom's Private Finance Initiative. • Under a DBFO/PFI, the private sector finances, designs, constructs and operates a revenue-generating asset for a pre-determined period of time (the concession period). • The government agrees to purchase the services provided by the private entity under a concession contract, commonly for a duration of 25–30 years. • Ownership of the infrastructure is retained by the private sector for the duration of the contract life but may revert to the public sector at the conclusion of the concession period.
Design–Build–Operate (DBO)	DBO projects incorporate many elements of the traditional public sector procurement model, and may often be viewed as a unification of a Design & Construction approach with an Operation & Maintenance contract. • This approach can be advantageous, as it commonly integrates the design, construction and maintenance within one contact. • The public sector purchases the infrastructure at the time of commission and retains ownership thereafter. The private entity is responsible for the asset's operation for a period after commissioning.

Notes: Adapted from European Commission (2003); AusCID (2003); Victorian Department of Treasury and Finance (2001); and Department of the Environment and Local Government (2000).

of risk allocation for the public sector or encourage private initiative to be incorporated into the contracting process (Queensland Government State Development, 2002; International Financial Services London, 2003; European Commission, 2003).

The BOOT (Build–Own–Operate–Transfer) finance method has formed the backbone of Australia's PPP experience since the 1980s (Jones, 2002:7) as well as in other jurisdictions. This form of PPP enables innovation and initiation from the private sector and is often associated with accelerated infrastructure construction and improved value for money. The 'whole-of-life' contracting approach adopted by BOOT projects enables optimal risk allocation for the public and private sectors, and cost distribution for the concession period (Jones, 2002). The capital investment required by the private sector and the trans-generational concession period requires superior contract and performance management arrangements to ensure quality and availability of service for the whole life of the contractual period, allowing the private sector to service its financial commitments and realize appropriate returns.

The variations of the BOOT model (such as the BOO, Build–Own–Operate) depend on where ownership of the infrastructure (and capital risks) resides during and after the period of private sector operation or whether that period is indefinite. There are also variations of this structure in which existing infrastructure may be provided to the private sector to be refurbished or upgraded, and operated and maintained by the private sector for a term or permanently. Unfortunately, BOOT projects have traditionally been characterized by their high tendering and transaction costs, in conjunction with complex contractual arrangements, although these factors are often necessary to generate the superior contracting outcomes sought by both private and public parties.

DBFOs (Design–Build–Finance–Operate projects) are often considered a subset of the BOOT model, with the only significant difference being that the term BOOT is usually used with reference to economic infrastructure projects, in which the service is provided direct to the public (particularly in transport projects), whereas DBFOs are characterized by the provision of services to government, predominantly in the social infrastructure context (that is, in relation to infrastructure that is always provided at a net cost to government, such as schools and hospitals). Projects under the private finance initiative ('PFI'), a series of policies first implemented in the United Kingdom in 1992 in order to facilitate the involvement of the private sector in the provision of public infrastructure and services, are the best known and most successful form of DBFOs (Allen, 2001).

DBO (Design–Build–Operate) projects contain the elements of BOOT or DBFO projects without the financing component, so that the private sector is not required to make a large up-front capital investment in the infrastructure. The developer is paid for the design and construct components at completion and paid separately for operation and maintenance of the infrastructure during the term. Therefore, there is some separation of the functions which are integrated by virtue of the financing structure of the BOOT projects, although there is still some opportunity to capitalize on the synergies produced by attaching a long term service contract to a design and construction contract (Evans, 2003).

RISK ALLOCATION

The primary contributor to achieving value for money in public private partnerships is generally thought to be transfer of appropriate risk to the private sector (Arthur Andersen and Enterprise LSE, 2000). The theory of optimal risk allocation involves the transfer of risk to the party best able to manage it (Allen, 2001).

Accordingly, PPPs involve a new approach to risk identification and management for projects through defining contractual obligations as outcomes, and thus transferring risks associated with the design, construction, implementation, ownership and operation of the infrastructure asset to the private sector (Victorian Department of Treasury and Finance, 2001). This transfer of risks has been termed a 'new paradigm for government contracting'.

Management of a risk may involve mitigation through due diligence, certain technical performance requirements, and satisfaction of prerequisites before accepting the risk, as well as risk transfer to a third party by way of subcontract or insurance. The private sector will price risks based on the probability of the risk crystallizing and its likely effect on costs and/or revenues. A central concept here is that if the private sector is better placed than the public sector to manage a risk through one of the techniques described above, or in some other way, the private sector will price that risk at a lower level than the public sector, giving rise to improved value for money. As a corollary to this premise, each time a risk is transferred to the private sector that it is either unable to manage or is no better able than the public sector to manage, the value for money of the project will tend to decrease (Arthur Andersen and Enterprise LSE, 2000).

The marketplace commonly defines risks by reference to certain well-settled categories, in order to identify the contractual treatment of particular risks which are similar in their character.

Some key risk categories which arise for consideration in the context of PPP projects are outlined in Table 4.2. It is ultimately the project contracts through which the theory of risk allocation is implemented and, if the

Table 4.2   Risk categories

Risk Category	Description
Site risk	• Risks associated with tenure, access, site suitability (including ground conditions, environmental, native title, heritage and planning considerations). • Allocation will generally depend on site ownership and selection process and availability of information to the relevant parties.
Design, construction and commissioning risk	• Risks that designs and construction do not meet the requirements for the infrastructure, that there are delays (for reasons such as competency, weather, industrial disputes and the like) or that the cost of design and construction is more than budgeted. • Most of these risks are allocated to the private sector through mechanisms such as an output specification and performance payment regimes.
Operating and maintenance risks	• These include risks that operation and maintenance of the infrastructure costs more or is more difficult that anticipated (for example due to issues with inputs, construction, competency or usage). • Again, most of these risks are allocated to the private sector through mechanisms such as an output specification and performance payment regimes.
Financial risks	• Risks of increases in interest rates, inflation and taxes. • Risks to do with financing and taxes are generally borne by the private sector, with some sharing of inflation risk suggested for long term projects.
Uptake/patronage risks	• These include risks to do with the market, competition and usage of the infrastructure. • Who bears these risks will depend on the PPP delivery option (e.g. private sector in BOOTs and public sector in DBFOs).
Force majeure risks	• Risks of significant adverse weather or other specified events which cause material loss or damage to the asset or otherwise prevent performance. • These risks are generally shared as they are beyond the control of either party.
Legislative risks	• This category includes risks that a change in law causes an increase in costs of constructing or operating the PPP project or prevents performance of the project. • These risks are often shared, depending on the application and effect of the change in law. Compliance with law is generally a private sector risk.

parties get the contract right, the benefits of optimal risk allocation are achieved.

PARTICIPANTS IN A PPP

Public Sector Parties

One of the threshold issues in any PPP will be determining the correct public sector entity to enter into the contracts and ascertaining the powers it has to enter into contracts or arrangements for the provision of infrastructure and services by the private sector.

A government entity or a minister contracting on behalf of the government may have express power under legislation to enter into a transaction. However, as the private provision of public infrastructure is a relatively new phenomena, it is often the case that legislation relating to the provision of public assets, infrastructure and services or establishing government entities does not specifically deal with such powers.

Generally, ministers of governments have prerogative power (the authority, power and privileges of the Crown) which can be exercised in the ordinary course of administering their portfolio. This is a relatively wide power, which facilitates entry into contracts for the provision of public assets, infrastructure and services, provided such power has not been limited or excluded by legislation. Prerogative power can, of course, be subject to legislative regulation, limitation and exclusions.

Once the government has entered into a contract for the provision of public assets or infrastructure the private sector will be concerned about the principle of sovereign immunity, which can apply to exclude or limit the jurisdiction of courts over the acts of sovereign States. These immunities have been slowly eroded within the Australian context following the passing of colonial legislation.[1] In recognising the increasing reliance of governments upon contractual relationships, the provisions of the Crown Proceedings Act 1958 (Vic) similarly reinforce the commercial and economic imperative of being able to bind the state. With formality and frequency, the enforceability of PPP contractual agreements will rarely be in doubt (Hodge and Bowman, 2004).

In extreme cases, and to avoid doubt, it may be necessary for project or concession deeds to be ratified by an Act of Parliament, so as to provide greater security for the private sector and protect against shortcomings in the powers of the contracting government entity, or to extend powers and protections to the private sector, which the government would otherwise have if it were providing the infrastructure itself.

Private Sector Parties

The private sector parties to a PPP project will usually include a special purpose project vehicle established especially to carry out the project, which is funded through private equity investors and private sector debt financing.

Traditionally, equity for PPPs has been provided by parties involved in some aspect of the project, such as the construction or facilities management contractors. Indeed, governments often derive comfort from the long-term equity commitment of such project participants. However, increasingly, institutional investors and specialist infrastructure funds have been established and are investing in PPPs.

PPPs are generally financed through project financing – also often called limited recourse financing (see Millhouse, 2002). Worldwide, project finance is the most common means by which private sector money is channelled into PPPs. Project finance is important for infrastructure development because it is the technique by which large amounts of money can be raised from financial institutions and markets for a specific purpose, whilst limiting the financial exposure of the project sponsors. Project lenders finance the project on the basis that they will look only (or at least substantially) to the cashflows and earnings of the project as the source of funds from which they will be repaid and to the assets of the project as collateral for the loan. There is limited or no financial recourse to project sponsors. This allows sponsors to insulate their balance sheets from riskier projects and also allows them to take on projects which might otherwise be too big for them to finance alone.

It is commonly said that project financing of PPPs, which is only serviced and repaid over a significant proportion of the term of the contract with the government, enhances performance under PPPs by ensuring that the private sector provider (and its financiers) are highly incentivized to ensure services are supplied on time and to a higher standard. This is the case as revenues only commence once the infrastructure is complete and operational, and continued payment generally depends on meeting specified performance criteria (UK Treasury Taskforce, 1997).

The benefit to the government of dealing with a single project financed entity which is fully accountable for all aspects of the project is that this is the most effective structure for extracting the life cycle or whole of life approaches to risk (Victorian Department of Treasury and Finance, 2001). That is, there is a strong incentive to ensure that the design and construction convert into an efficient operation phase.

However, a special purpose vehicle does not have the technical expertise to carry out all aspects of the project, and the private sector parties will therefore also include subcontractors, such as design and construction contractors and operation and maintenance contractors, who provide various aspects of technical input to the project.

CONTRACTUAL STRUCTURE

A PPP arrangement is essentially contractual in nature (Stern and Harding, 2002), with project potential predominantly determined by contractual provisions as opposed to market forces (Gerrard, 2001). The complex and far reaching character of PPP projects has resulted in the evolution of labyrinthine legal documents, as public sector and private sector parties attempt to address complex project specifications and all potential contingencies. With intergenerational concession periods for PPPs, clear procurement and service requirements and performance evaluation are imperative to the success of any project (Parker and Hartley, 2003). However, preserving flexibility and provisions to deal efficiently with unforeseen risks are essential if infrastructure is to meet its social objectives. While lessons learnt over time have transformed much of the PPP contractual landscape, the main elements of the framework have endured. A brief description of each of the primary contractual documents within the PPP context is set out below.

Project Deed

Although the type of contracts in a privately financed project will vary to some extent depending on the PPP model used, the core contract for a PPP project is the project or concession deed. This agreement sets out the terms under which:

- the private sector must finance, design and construct the relevant asset or infrastructure;
- the private sector must operate, clean, maintain and repair the infrastructure;
- the private sector partner must give up possession of the infrastructure to the state at the end of the term of the project (this obligation may be an option or may be subject to a payment of some kind, depending on the structure of the transaction);
- some kind of site tenure such as a lease or a licence is provided to the private sector partner over the site on which the infrastructure is to be constructed;

- the revenue arrangements for the privately financed project are established, whether these comprise performance based fees or provisions permitting the charging of fees or levying of tolls direct to the users of the infrastructure; and
- establishes the risk allocation framework for the project in relation to other aspects such as environmental requirements, latent conditions, planning approvals, changes to requirements and law, loss, damage and insurance, taxes and intellectual property amongst others.

Financing

The obligation to finance the infrastructure is usually satisfied through various shareholders' subscription arrangements, subordinated debt arrangements, and senior project financing arrangements.

The project financing arrangements are generally documented via funding documents (loan agreements, subscription agreements and the like), security arrangements (mortgages, charges, security assignments and the like), guarantees and other sponsor support documents (limited guarantees are often given, even in project financing structures, particularly during the construction phases of projects), and subordination and intercreditor documents (where there is more than one source of funding).

The most important aspects of these documents are the commitment and timing of funding, the ability to cancel commitments or withdraw funding, the security requirements of the funding parties and the flexibility to accommodate the risk allocation in the underlying contract with the government, including with respect to changes to the project and application of insurance.

Subcontracting

The private sector partner satisfies its obligations under the project deed to design and construct and commission the PPP facilities through one or more subcontracts with design and construction contractors. These arrangements are generally further secured through traditional construction securities, such as bonding and guaranteeing arrangements.

The private sector partner satisfies its obligations to operate, clean, maintain and repair the infrastructure through one or more operations and maintenance agreements with sub-contractors. Again, these may be secured by various bonding or guaranteeing arrangements.

The nature of the passing of obligations from the special purpose project vehicle to the subcontractors often involves the requirement for a coordination document between the subcontractors, in order to facilitate interface between the subcontractors without recourse being had to the special purpose project vehicle.

Security, Tripartite Deeds and Consent Deeds

The private sector special purpose vehicle may be required to give security to various parties, including to the lenders, to secure its obligations under the debt arrangements and to the state to secure its obligations under the project deed, particularly where the private sector party pays concession fees to the government, as is often the case in economic infrastructure projects.

A tripartite or direct deed between the State entity, the private sector special purpose vehicle and the financiers is entered into for a number of purposes. It:

- records the consent of the State to the security granted in favour of the financiers, particularly over the rights under the project deed;
- sets out priorities as between the security granted in favour of the state, and that granted to financiers;
- regulates enforcement of financier's security via step in and assignment; and
- contains other agreements relating to exchange of information, application of insurance proceeds and the like.

There are generally other tripartite or consent deeds between the state and the subcontractors and between the financiers and the subcontractors. These also facilitate the enforcement of security and, importantly, allow continuation of the design and construction or operation functions upon a default by the head contractor or private sector special purpose vehicle.

Others

There may be other important project agreements, depending on the structure of the transaction and the parties involved. For example, PPP projects may require interface deeds, development deeds, government guarantee arrangements (where the contracting party is a statutory body not otherwise financially supported by the government) and, of course, insurance policies.

The typical contractual structure therefore, looks something like Figure 4.1.

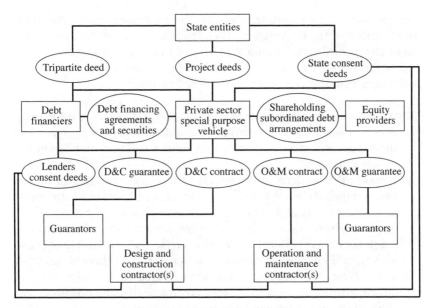

Source: Evans, J. (2003)

Figure 4.1 Typical PPP contractual structure

KEY ASPECTS OF GETTING THE CONTRACTS RIGHT

Getting the PPP project documents right is largely a function of how the more unusual aspects of PPP contracting are dealt with. PPP projects are, by their nature, long term, involve significant investment of time and capital, are generally of social significance and have public policy considerations applied to them that would not be applied to most purely commercial contracting arrangements within the private sector.

Accommodating Change and Flexibility

The transgenerational nature of PPP contracts and their social significance affects all contracting parties and their subsequent participation within a project. With projects involving public assets and a risk-sharing relationship over periods of as many as 25–30 years, flexibility is mandatory for success (Robinson, 2000). The requirement to accommodate change in order for the infrastructure to meet its social objectives, must be balanced against the certainty and commitment required by a private sector participants at the outset of the PPP project. Therefore, the degree of flexibility needs to be clearly articulated within the terms of the project contracts and not left to the unfettered discretion of each party. There is a range of possible solutions, including provisions such as the following:

1. A regime which allows either party to propose a change, and the relevant effects of such change on performance and costing on the project, and the parties will meet to discuss and agree a solution by reference to certain criteria.
2. It may be that, under a government funded project, the financing impact of any required change can be agreed in advance by reference to certain base case input rates and maximum rates of return.
3. There may be provisions whereby the government undertakes to provide assistance or take performance and/or revenue and costs risks associated with specific changes, in respect of which it would otherwise take risk in any event. For example, in relation to increased demands on social infrastructure, the government may pay the capital and operating cost effect of the need to expand a hospital or school.
4. It may be that a modular approach to certain infrastructure can be adopted, whereby a pricing mechanism can be built into the project at the outset for additional components to be added on as and when they become necessary.
5. In addition to or as an alternative to the modular solution, a change mechanism within a project of concession deed may specify a range of solutions to accommodate particular changes, which may involve, for example extension of the term of the concession or project deed, government funded capital additions or refinancing solutions.

Gain Sharing

In concept at least, the provision of financial incentives to all partnership members should encourage active cooperation, successful risk allocation and management success, and thereby benefit all parties, especially in projects where revenue generation is central to project success. Mandatory gain-sharing provisions between the private and public sectors are now commonly incorporated within PPP contractual arrangements to enable both sectors to benefit from any excess financial gain. These provisions include benchmarking, market testing, upside, and refinancing gain sharing clauses.

However, balance is needed, and care must be taken not to usurp incentives to improve efficiency and performance in the private sector, by expecting returns to the public sector of 'super profits' where the downside would not have been similarly shared. Likewise, distribution of gains on refinancing should focus on market maturity and government funding factors, where the cooperation and contribution of both the public and private sectors play a role, and sharing is therefore appropriate.

Performance Payment Regimes

The performance payment mechanism in a PPP contract puts into effect the risk allocation for the project (UK Office of Government Commerce, 2002). For example, in the traditional BOOT projects, the private sector proponent will usually take market or patronage risk, that is, the risk that anticipated usage, volumes or prices are not achievable, and therefore revenues, are less than those forecast. Risks associated with delays in construction due to contractor non-performance are generally also allocated to the private sector by virtue of revenue not being available until the relevant asset is available and/or performing according to certain specifications. In each of these cases the revenue effects of the event determine where the risk of that event lies.

Where the payment for services by the public sector is determined by contracted performance specifications, including the quality, quantity and accessibility of the service (VDTF, 2001), economic viability of the project will be a product of the private sector parties' ability to ensure stated delivery objectives are fulfilled. Failure to meet performance requirements will result in deductions or abatements to service payments, dependent on the nature and severity of the failure.

Excusable Non-performance

Excusable non-performance covers a range of issues which must be considered when structuring a PPP. Whilst the government will generally have an overriding duty and obligation to provide infrastructure to the public, there are certain circumstances where the private sector's provision of infrastructure under a PPP may be interfered with or prevented by circumstances in which they should be properly relieved of their obligations. These types of events generally fall into four broad categories:

1. Government prescribed items: These events relate to a part of the infrastructure or the project which the government is intended to provide or has made undertakings in relation to provision. For example, this may involve the site of the infrastructure, certain permits, licences or approvals in relation to the infrastructure, certain interconnecting infrastructure or network, certain non-competitive undertakings, certain government

furnished equipment or items in relation to the infrastructure. In accordance with general risk allocation theory, it is appropriate for the government to take revenue and performance risks associated with such events or circumstances. This may involve payment of compensation, continued payment of performance related payments, notwithstanding prevention of performance, as well as relief of the obligation to perform and suspension of any right the government might otherwise have to step in or terminate the concession or project deed.

2. Government interface: The second category of excusable non-performance relates to other potential areas of government interference, such as discriminatory changes in law. For public policy reasons the government cannot be influenced in making laws for the good government of its jurisdiction by commercial arrangements it has entered into with the private sector. For this reason, changes in law which cannot be anticipated at the time of entering into the project or concession deed, and which are of general application, must be implemented by the private sector infrastructure provider without recourse to the government. However, if a new law or regulation requires significant alteration or addition to the infrastructure, there may be an argument for government to take this risk, particularly if such additional work cannot be funded by market revenues. If a government changes law or regulation which is directly, specifically and exclusively aimed at the infrastructure, the private sector provider of the infrastructure should, on risk allocation theory principles, be excused from performance to the extent that new law prevents its proper performance of the PPP project.

3. Force majeure events, such as fire, explosion, lighting, storm, flooding, civil commotions, blockades or embargoes and certain industrial action and even inability to obtain certain consents and approvals in some circumstances, may cause loss or damage to infrastructure, service discontinuity or inability to provide the infrastructure at all. In these circumstances, it may be appropriate to excuse the private sector party from its obligations to provide the infrastructure for a certain period, whilst it reinstates or replaces the infrastructure. However, as many of these events are insurable events, and are therefore covered by material loss and damage as well as consequential loss or business interruption insurance, governments are usually unwilling to take revenue and cost associated effects related to such events, and, accordingly, it is usually thought appropriate for deductions or abatements to be made under relevant performance payment regimes.

4. Emergencies: Emergency situations may require the government to step in and physically take possession of the infrastructure or assets: for example, in times of war, civil unrest or where a major natural disaster

gives rise to security, strategic or exceptional requirements. In these circumstances, the private sector provider of the infrastructure should be relieved of performance and should also be compensated for, or take no revenue risk in connection with, such emergency action.

Defaults, Cure Rights and Step In

Whilst PPP contracts will almost invariably contain rights for a government to step in and take over infrastructure in certain emergency situations, the project documents may also contain step-in rights which will enable the government to take over the operation of the infrastructure if a problem arises which cannot be cured or rectified by the private sector. Such rights must be reserved to the government, as it has an overriding obligation to ensure safe, accessible infrastructure services to the public. This, of course, must be weighed up against the private sector's large investment in the project and its obvious desire to control the infrastructure and any problems which may arise.

Step-in rights are therefore generally limited in their scope, duration and impact on the private sector parties, under a step-in protocol to be observed as between the government and the private sector infrastructure provider. Such a protocol will usually allow the private sector infrastructure provider some opportunity to cure default or provide services (other than in exceptional emergency situations) before the government steps in. Where the infrastructure has not been provided in accordance with the private sector providers' obligations under the project or concession deed, there will usually be provision for the government to give notice of that default and for the private sector provider of the infrastructure to remedy the default or come up with a cure plan detailing steps to remedy or mitigate the effect of the default. Where the default cannot be remedied, a prevention plan containing full details of the programme to be implemented to ensure prevention of the recurrence of the default may be required. The government will often also want its own cure rights (and right to recover from the private sector party) where a default warrants something less than a full step in.

In getting the contract right, the interests of the government in ensuring the ongoing provision of the infrastructure (particularly social infrastructure) and its desire to take control of the infrastructure if it is not satisfied of its operation or availability must be balanced against the financial interest of the private sector infrastructure provider.

Obviously, the ultimate right of the government upon default of the private sector provider of infrastructure is to terminate the PPP and retake possession of the relevant infrastructure. Termination is a drastic and irreversible process and should only be resorted to once the reasonable tolerances of the government's step-in rights and the private sector parties' cure rights have been exceeded. Those tolerances will be dictated by many factors including the strategic importance of the infrastructure to the government and the ability of the government to replace the private sector provider and its subcontractors in the provision of the infrastructure.

CONCLUSION

With PPPs 'a central government policy priority' (Newburry and Pallot, 2003:483) private investment within the public sector appears destined to become 'the most important means of infrastructure procurement' (Brown, 1999:25). Increasing capital expenditure within this context will necessitate facilitative legislative and regulatory provisions. However, with risk allocation theory and the contractual relationship forming the basis of the public–private partnership, 'getting the contract right' will be fundamental to the success of a PPP project.

PPP procurement so far has seen the development of extensive and intricate legal documents, underpinned by the public and private sectors' twin goals of achieving value for money and optimal risk allocation. This chapter has argued that a number of key contractual documents, including but not limited to, the project deed, financing, subcontracting, security and tripartite deeds, will form the foundation of any PPP procurement venture in the arena of privately financed infrastructure. However, recognition of inherent risks within transgenerational project delivery led to contractual considerations focusing on the need for clear procurement and service requirements, in conjunction with transparent performance evaluation criteria, in preference to a series of template documentation. It is argued that the application of this elastic approach to the contractual arrangement has underpinned the success of the broad continuum of project delivery models within Australia and internationally.

In concluding this discussion on contractual considerations within the PPP sphere, it is also important to recognize the practical limitations posed by the procurement form. Whilst academic discussion regarding the preferential contract character and content is possible, significant supposition may only be made when the first wave of transgenerational contracts expires. With average contract life ranging between 25 to 30 years, it appears that questions regarding 'best contractual practice' may well remain unanswered for a further 20 years. With the 'jury still out' on PPPs, cautious implementation and evaluation must guide private sector procurement of public assets and infrastructure.

NOTES

1. See for example *Judiciary Act 1903 (Cth)* s.64 and the *Commonwealth of Australia Constitution Act 1901* (UK), s.75(iii).

REFERENCES

Allen, G. (2001), *The Private Finance Initiative (PFI)*, London: UK Parliament.

Arthur Andersen and Enterprise LSE (2000), *Value for Money Drivers in the Private Finance Initiative*, London: Commissioned by the UK Treasury Taskforce.

Broadbent, J. and R. Laughlin (2003), 'Public Private Partnerships: An Introduction', *AAAJ*, **16** (3), 332–41.

Brown, C. (1999), 'United Kingdom: Public private partnerships', *International Financial Law Review*, **25**.

Department of the Environment and Local Government (Ireland) (2000), *Introduction to Public Private Partnerships: Public Private Partnerships Guidance Note 1*.

Department of Treasury and Finance (2001), *Partnership Victoria Guidance Material: Risk*, Melbourne: State Government of Victoria.

English, L.M. and J. Guthrie (2003), 'Driving privately financed projects in Australia: what makes them tick?', *AAAJ*, **16** (3), 493–510.

European Commission (2003), *Guidelines for Successful Public–Private Partnerships*, Paris, France: European Commission, Directorate-General Regional Policy.

Evans, J (2003), 'Public Private Partnerships: A New Direction in Australia', paper presented at the Twenty-Seventh Annual AMPLA Conference, Adelaide, South Australia.

Gerrard, M.B (2001), 'Public–Private partnerships', *Finance & Development*, **38** (3), 48.

Hodge, G.A. and D.M. Bowman (2004), 'PPP contractual issues – big promises and unfinished business', in Abby Ghobadian, Nicholas O'Regan, David Gallear and Howard Viney (eds), *Public–Private Partnerships: Policy and Experience*, London: Palgrave Macmillan.

International Financial Services London (2003), *Public Private Partnerships: UK Expertise for International Markets*, London: IFSL, www.ifsl.org.uk/uploads/PPP%20report%202002.pdf, 8 July 2004.

Jones, D (2002), 'Policy Development in Australia for Public Private Partnerships – what more is there to do?', paper presented at the 'Providing value for money through PPPs: the lessons learnt so far from economic and social infrastructure projects' conference, Sydney, Australia: 26 June.

Liddle, R. (1996), 'Alistair Darling: Private Finance Initiative', *New Statesman*, **9** (418), 12.

Millhouse, A (2002), *Public Private Partnerships – the Dawn of a New Era for Project Financing?*, Brisbane: Allens Arthur Robinson.

Newberry, S. and J. Pallot (2003), 'Fiscal (ir)responsibility: privileging PPPs in New Zealand', *AAAJ*, **16** (3), 467–92.

Parker, D. and K. Hartley (2003), 'Transaction costs, relational contracting and public private partnerships: a case study of UK defence', *European Journal of Purchasing and Supply Management*, **9**, 97–108.

Queensland Government State Development (2002), *Public–Private Partnerships Guidance Material: Value for Money Framework*, Brisbane: Queensland Government.

Robinson, P. (2000), 'The Private Finance Initiative', *New Economy*, 7 (3), 148–9.

Stern, S. and D. Harding (2002), 'Profits and perils of public private partnerships', *Euromoney*, 394, 126.

UK Office of Government Commerce (2002), *PFI Contract Guidance – Standardisation of PFI Contracts*, London: HM Treasury.

UK Treasury Taskforce (1997), *Partnerships for Prosperity*, London: HM Treasury.

Victorian Department of Treasury and Finance (2001), *Partnership Victoria Guidance Material: Risk Allocation and Contractual Issues – a Guide*, Melbourne: State Government of Victoria.

Webb, R. and B. Pulle (2002), *Public Private Partnerships: An Introduction*, Canberra: Parliament of Australia.

5. Political issues of public–private partnerships

Ken Coghill and Dennis Woodward

INTRODUCTION

Public–private partnerships (PPPs) appear to be an emerging feature of public policy in many parts of the world. While it is arguable whether this is a new creation or is qualitatively different from 'contracting out', the use of PPPs to *finance* infrastructure development and the *tighter organizational linkages* between public and private sector actors does seem to mark a departure from previous practice. PPPs, in this respect therefore, might mark the emergence of a new phenomenon rather than simply being a new term for something long in existence. They are, however, a manifestation that has emerged out of the privatization movement and that has been justified by the ideology that has informed the drive for privatization. The use of the new expression, therefore, can be seen in part as a means to avoid the opprobrium that has come to be associated with both 'contracting out' and 'privatization' in some quarters (Savas, 2000). To this extent, PPPs can be seen as 'rebadged' privatization.

Unlike privatization, however, PPPs have thus far failed to become a major political issue. Governments have generally been able to pursue them without opposition and indeed, almost without having to justify their use. This, in itself, requires some explanation. This chapter, therefore, seeks to examine this and other political issues associated with PPPs. In particular, it endeavours to explore why governments have embraced PPPs; who benefits from their use; what problems or criticisms might arise from them; who stands to lose from their adoption; and, lastly, why they have managed to stay off the agenda of electoral politics.

THE LURE OF PPPs

Seeking to explain why governments have come to embrace PPPs, both for major infrastructure projects and other activities, cuts to the heart of government decision making in general. Public choice theory would have us believe that governments are largely (if not solely) motivated by their desire to remain in office (Pincus, 1993). From this perspective, therefore, it can be assumed that there are electoral benefits to be gained for governments by pursuing the PPP option. What, then, are these benefits?

PPPs can be used to deliver goods and services desired by the electorate. Governments generally gain kudos from announcing (and eventually opening) new projects that can be seen as providing employment in their construction (and possibly in their operations) and as enhancing the lives of voters. While governments could conceivably gain this benefit from providing such projects without the assistance of private sector 'partners', using PPPs brings with it certain advantages. This is not to suggest, however, that all these advantages are beyond contestation. Indeed, it will be argued that some benefits are more claimed than real and that many of the claims are based on acceptance of the neo-liberal economic paradigm which itself might be open to challenge. Rather, it is contended that so long as there is a preponderant acceptance of these key assumptions amongst the economic policy community, they provide a powerful rationale for governments acting according to their prescripts. What then, are the perceived advantages of PPPs for governments?

Possibly the biggest advantage of PPPs can be seen in their use for constructing substantial infrastructure projects such as major highways, tunnels, and buildings. Where such projects involve the private sector partner providing the finance for the project through a BOOT scheme, the government concerned is able to enjoy the provision of infrastructure at seemingly no cost. There are clear gains to be derived from such a situation. First, the government can avoid the need to either divert revenue with concomitant levels of revenue raising or alternatively borrow the funds to build the project and thus prevent any contribution to public debt. Second, it is spared the necessity of servicing that debt – freeing it either to keep revenue extraction low or to use taxes in some other way. It would appear that there are electoral gains on both counts, although there is some evidence to suggest that, given the choice, the electorate would support higher taxes to improve services (Willacy, 2001; Jacobs, 2003).

Within Australia, it has almost become conventional wisdom that public sector debt is necessarily a bad thing, leading to extraordinarily low levels of public debt by international standards (OECD, 2004). It is seen as 'crowding out' private sector investment and pushing up interest rates, and hence the public sector borrowing requirement (PSBR) needs to be kept as low as possible (Argy, 1998:70–79). Governments that can minimize public debt, or better still, reduce it, are seen as 'good economic managers' by the majority of financial journalists and presumably by the general (voting) public. Minimizing public debt, like delivering balanced or surplus budgets, gains the applause of international financial markets, and governments appear to be acutely conscious of the need to maintain their support. In particular, winning the approval of the major credit rating agencies, Moody's and Standard and Poor's, and being able to boast of an AAA credit rating, enables governments to impress electors with their financial credentials.

There is a certain irony in this situation, as the ostensible advantage of a better credit rating comes in the form of being able to borrow funds at a lower interest rate (reflecting the reduced risk involved for 'creditworthy' customers) and yet the governments concerned are not seeking to borrow but rather to avoid public debt. Moreover, the nature of credit ratings that are the product of a tiny club of (private) international rating agencies are open to challenge (Sinclair, 2003). The ratings are essentially subjective assessments but in reality governments of highly developed countries virtually never default on their borrowings, such that all but a few deserve the lowest possible risk assessment. They should be rated equally highly and well ahead of private sector borrowers, none of whom can underwrite their capacity to service debt through the authority to raise taxes.

In addition, using private sector finance for infrastructure development might lead to reduced taxes, but the actual real cost to the community might in fact be greater than had governments taken charge of raising the finances. This is because governments are able to borrow funds at rates below those of private sector borrowers since they are (correctly) seen as better credit risks (Millar, 2001). Private sector partners, moreover, not only have to pay more for their borrowing, but their need to operate profitably means that they will need to recoup from their public customers more than just the extra cost of borrowing. This means that private sector financing and operation of projects will cost the community more than public provision unless the private sector can deliver greater efficiencies than the public sector. That the private sector can operate more efficiently than the public sector and achieve quicker and cheaper outcomes, is a central tenet of the neo-liberal economic paradigm that underpins privatization and PPPs. It should not, however, be accepted uncritically (as will be discussed further below). However, to the extent that government can override lengthy public consultations and debate by signing contracts, infrastructure projects may be delivered more quickly and hence PPPs became attractive for government.

Clearly, another reason for governments treading the PPP path is to develop and maintain the approval of the business community. Those businesses that are direct beneficiaries of government contracts are unlikely to oppose that government directly and might even support it through donations and/or public statements. Other businesses, mindful of possible future partnerships, would also have an incentive to seek harmonious relations with government, and the business community in general is liable to be well disposed towards a government that strives to be 'friendly towards business'.

Another explanation for government acceptance of PPPs lies in the advice that they receive. Whether that advice is derived from public servants or from private consultants, it is most likely to reflect the dominant neo-liberal economic view that has been described as the 'Washington consensus' (Balaam and Veseth, 2005:64). At least in the Anglo-Saxon world (and increasingly elsewhere as well) there has been a transformation of the public service in line with the New Public Management that has seen government bureaucracies adopt private sector practices (Hughes, 1998; Lane, 2000). This has entailed moves towards 'smaller government', contracting out, and notions of 'steering not rowing' (Osborne and Gaebler, 1993). The civil service that is being constructed by these means, unsurprisingly recommends PPPs.

Yet, as Heald (2003) has shown, there are dangers of seemingly technical analysis of funding options disguising essentially ideological assumptions which disregard fundamental political principles. Writing in the British context in which Private Finance Initiative (PFI) is the policy instrument with which PPPs are associated, Heald points out that value for money (VFM) has incentives embedded within it which bias it in favour of private sector financing. These incentives range from informal encouragement by government ministers operating in a culture which appears to be committed to a strong role for the private sector to methodological features that distort the distribution of costs and benefits in favour of PPPs. These issues are compounded by the perspectives of private sector advisors whose future income streams rely on a continuing flow of private provision projects and who rarely share the commitment to serving the public interest that has motivated most public servants. As Heald (ibid.:343) states, '(t)he concern in the PFI context is that the sources of professional advice available to purchasers are not neutral on the choice between PFI and alternatives'. This process, once again, has been informed by the neo-liberal paradigm. Dissenting views held by opponents or sceptics tend to be denied credibility while emulation of overseas examples reinforces the dominant trend.

Lastly, the political leaders themselves have increasingly embraced the hegemonic neo-liberal paradigm. Such an outcome is hardly unexpected given the lack of credible alternatives since the apparent discrediting of Keynesian views in the 1970s and the collapse of communism in the late 1980s and early 1990s. Even the democratic socialist project has retreated into the discourse of a 'third way' (Giddens, 2000, 2001). Surrounded by opinions from the major institutions propagating the 'Washington consensus' – the World Bank, the International Monetary Fund (IMF) and the Organization for Economic Cooperation and Development (OECD), reinforced by the reports of right wing think tanks, the articles of economic journalists, and the advice of their public servants and consultants, there is little wonder that political leaders (whether in government or opposition) have absorbed the neo-liberal agenda and its latest manifestation, PPPs.

PPP BENEFICIARIES

Clearly, the private sector benefits from PPPs whereas it is excluded, except often from construction, under traditional provision. The neo-liberal push for 'smaller government' might have seen the number of government employees shrink, but it has generally not seen the percentage of revenue collected (proportional to the size of the economy) fall, nor levels of government expenditure reduced (OECD, 1995, 2003). Vast sums of money are at stake with PPPs, depending whether the private firm is a partner in a major long-term project, a major contractor or simply a short-term consultant. Government contracts can be quite lucrative with private businesses benefiting in terms of providing employment for their workforce, generating profits and attaining tax advantages or other incentives. Some companies derive most (if not all) of their business from governments. This is particularly true of some US companies such as General Dynamics, McDonnell Douglas and, controversially, Halliburton[1] that produce equipment and services for the US military, but it is not confined to military contractors (Weidenbaum, 1999).

Governments also benefit from PPPs as outlined earlier in our discussion of the reasons governments have come to adopt them. To briefly reiterate, they gain business support or acquiescence. They gain a favourable press for their 'good management' as well as high ratings from credit rating agencies for minimizing debt. They gain accolades or at least avoid retribution from financial markets for their 'fiscal responsibility'. Lastly, to the extent that the public accepts (or acquiesces in) the strictures of the neo-liberal paradigm, governments gain electoral support by pursuing PPPs. Such support is founded on governments being rewarded by voters for providing needed infrastructure and services (without raising taxes) and for acting as 'sound economic managers'. After all, governments can hardly be accused of inefficiency and waste if their activities are conducted by the seemingly always efficient and customer oriented private sector! The government gains the electoral benefit of removal of the real costs to the community from the public sector capital budget and their conversion into less visible annual expenditures or direct costs to consumers of services. In Hodges' words, the costs go on a 'mega credit card' (Hodge, 2004).

Whether the public also benefit from PPPs is a debatable question. Clearly, if they get needed infrastructure that otherwise would not have been built (because the government feared major debt, or faced insurmountable political problems in acting alone), then they have benefited. In addition, provided that the neo-liberal assumptions of the superiority of private sector over public sector provision holds true such that services and projects are delivered more quickly and efficiently, then a solid case can be mounted to suggest the public benefited. If, however, the private sector is not able to perform more efficiently than the public sector, then the public stand to lose when governments opt for PPPs since the private sector borrowing costs and need for profit returns (discussed above) mean that the overall cost to the community will be greater than purely government provision. (The empirical evidence showing that the private sector is not always more efficient than the public sector will be discussed further below.)

Even in those cases where it can be clearly demonstrated that PPPs do produce better results in terms of speed of construction or provision, service and efficiency, there is still a case to be made that other factors might outweigh these advantages and undermine any public benefit. Again, this will be discussed further below but it revolves around the argument that values other than those of a purely economic nature might be more important. For example, the public might have great concerns with issues of principle, such as participation in decisions, democratic control and accountable governance, rather than with the economies of earlier provision of facilities or services or lower costs.

CRITICISMS OF PPPs

Despite the widespread acceptance of PPPs and the limited criticisms of their use, they are not above challenge. Most fundamentally, some of the underlying principles and assumptions of the neo-liberal economic paradigm that justifies PPPs are problematic (Stilwell, 1993; Richardson, 1997). In addition, there is evidence to suggest that some of the values underlying PPPs do not and probably have never had majority support (Argy, 2003). It is not, however, the purpose of this chapter to question neo-liberal economics in its entirety, but rather to focus on those of its aspects that particularly bear on the issue of PPPs.

One of these is the view that public debt is necessarily bad (whereas private debt poses no problems) (Pitchford, 1990). Public debt can be deleterious. There are numerous examples of countries falling into 'debt traps' – being forced to devote more and more of their output to repaying loans until they reach a stage where they are unable to service their debt and need to be 'bailed out' by structural adjustment loans from the IMF and World Bank. Typically these come with a regimen of policy directives of the neo-liberal type that involve cutting back on government spending (particularly on welfare), privatizing state owned enterprises (which are often subsidized by government), and removing any impediments to unrestricted foreign investment (Cohn, 2003:195).

Notwithstanding this, public debt need not be an unmitigated evil (Oatley, 2004:329). First, it depends on the purposes to which the borrowed funds are devoted. If government debt is applied to increase consumption levels, is squandered on grandiose (non-productive) public monuments (such as presidential palaces), or worse, siphoned off by corrupt leaders into Swiss bank accounts, then clearly such debt is bad. If, however, the government debt is used for productive purposes, the returns that it generates to the national economy will exceed the costs of borrowing. In this respect, there is considerable evidence to suggest that those countries that have invested in infrastructure, education and research and development have fared best in the economic development stakes (Gilpin, 2001:129–47).

Second, provided that government debt is not excessive and the interest on the loans can be serviced, government debt should not pose any problems. Over time the productive investments of government undertaken with the loans will see the economy expand sufficiently such that the increased revenue will enable not only the servicing of loans but their repayment. In this context, it is noteworthy that the United States (George W. Bush Administration) and Japan have used huge levels of government debt as vehicles to stimulate economic growth.

Another major assumption (as noted above) is that the private sector is inherently more efficient than the public sector (Langmore, 1988:13). In part, this is an ideologically held view based on certain beliefs about the competitive nature of markets. In reality, however, perfectly competitive markets appear to be increasingly the exception rather than the norm as they are replaced by monopoly and oligopoly and governments are often compelled to regulate in order to achieve competitive outcomes (Gow and Maher, 1994). Additionally, the apparent inefficiency of some public sector enterprises can be readily explained by their need to conform to government charters demanding pursuit of multiple objectives which are inconsistent with maximizing profits as a measure of efficiency (Hodge, 1996). For example, there may be cross subsidies for certain sections of the public or some services might need to be provided irrespective of costs.

The empirical evidence sheds some interesting light on this issue of private versus public sector efficiency. There are now quite a few studies that have compared the relative performance of public sector enterprises and activities with those of privatized enterprises and 'contracted out' operations (Hodge,

2000; Langmore, 1988). The results are somewhat mixed. Some types of activities appear to be often more efficiently performed by the private sector, most notably physical services such as garbage collection, cleaning, and road construction (Hodge, 1996). Other activities, however, have been more efficiently carried out 'in house' by the public sector (Hodge, 2000). Moreover, where public enterprises have been corporatised, their results have tended to equal those in the private sector (Wiltshire, 1994). The point to note from this is that the private sector is not always more efficient than the public sector. PPPs, therefore, need to be justified on a case-by-case basis. However, this needs to take account of any limitations in the capacity of the public sector to fulfil the task, whether due to downsizing or other factors.

Much of the justification for PPPs has been based on the purported efficiencies to be gained by their use. For example, Fitzgerald (2004:4) suggested that there were seven motivations for PPPs:

1. an improved focus on service delivery, by reducing the time and effort that an agency will spend on property-related matters;
2. a requirement to pay only for contract infrastructure or facility related services and pay only when those services are delivered;
3. a very high level of confidence that infrastructure will be available on time and without cost blow-out;
4. an ability to hold a provider financially accountable for the performance of particular infrastructure throughout its lifetime;
5. access to the best technical and management skills, from whatever source;
6. improved outcomes, by using competitive forms to stimulate creativity, pricing and delivery;
7. access to infrastructure financing without additional government borrowing.

Clearly, the merit of PPPs is in terms of their ability to deliver services quickly and cheaply through their superior efficiency. While (as argued above) it cannot be simply assumed that PPPs will inevitably produce the most efficient outcomes, there is a larger issue at stake here concerning social goals.

Put simply, technical efficiency should not displace other social values. Indeed, it is meaningless to talk of efficiency without reference to goals. Should considerations of equity be ignored in the drive for greater efficiency? Should democracy be sacrificed if it stands in the way of greater efficiency? Yet, there are dangers that PPPs threaten to bring about these results. Nonetheless, governments may sometimes find reason to adopt PPPs as a means of service or infrastructure provision. For example, governments sometimes act in advance of public opinion and sometimes their actions lag behind.

This is because PPPs change the relationship from government provision of services to *citizens,* to one of private provision to *consumers/customers* (Smyth and Wearing, 2002:240–1). The democratic rights and entitlements of citizens are reduced to the dictates of the market place where their rights as consumers are greatly curtailed. The very ability to partake as a consumer is limited by one's wealth. That is, universal entitlements to all become available only to those able (or willing) to purchase the service. Clearly, there are issues of equity at stake here.

Similarly, the avenues for redress of grievances by citizens are far greater than those available through market mechanisms. Recourse to administrative law and bodies like the Administrative Appeals Tribunal or oversight of government actions by an Ombudsman, are far more transparent and provide greater access for citizens than consumer complaints and legal action. Ultimately, in a democracy, the government is held accountable by voters for its activities, but this accountability can be weakened by the use of PPPs.

In part, this is because the public are excluded from the decisions to take the PPP path. What are in fact *political* decisions, tend to be presented to the public as though they were *technical* decisions. Negotiations between government and private sector partners are typically conducted in private under the mantra of 'commercial in confidence' such that the public has little or no input into such negotiations but are presented with the outcome as a *fait accompli* (Davidson, 2002). This poses less of a problem if the result is the awarding of a short-term contract, but if the PPP involves a major long-term relationship stretching over decades, then there is a major point of contention.

Current governments (with limited public input) are committing future governments and future voters to particular courses of action. By doing so, they are limiting the future choices of citizens. Yet, a democratic polity must be able to change policy direction and priorities. A polity may express its desire through signals to an incumbent government or by voting for a change in government. PPPs which lock in certain policy assumptions, however, can severely limit a society's capacity to manage its response to new policy factors. For example, the desirable mix of public rail transport and toll roads may prove dramatically different at some future time depending on future energy prices but long-term partnerships for a particular mix might restrict needed changes. PPPs, therefore, can cut across democratic precepts.

A final criticism of PPPs is that they add to the potential for corruption of the political process. The very fact that huge sums of money flow from discretionary decisions immediately introduces the potential for biased decisions to be sought by tenderers, or offered by decision-makers. These have been the source of corruption in many jurisdictions (Procurement Watch Inc., 2002). Large corporate donations to political parties clearly have the potential to influence (however subtly, indirectly or subconsciously) the actions of government in determining policies and awarding PPPs. The relationship between the Bush administration and Enron provides a case in point (Press, 2002). Perhaps the Canadian example of banning corporate and union donations and severely limiting individual donations to candidates and political parties (Munroe, 2003) would overcome the problem.

THE NON-POLITICAL NATURE OF PPPs

Given the above possible criticisms of PPPs and the prospect that the voting public might lose as a result of their use, it would appear somewhat surprising that they have (so far) largely failed to become the subject of political debate or feature as a major issue in elections. A number of tentative explanations, however, might be posited.

First, the very terminology might lessen contention. As a relatively new expression, what it actually encompasses might not be well known by the public. Additionally, as a new term, it comes without any unfavourable connotations. Public opposition to privatization, for example, does not seem to be carried over to PPPs. The public is well aware when a public asset is sold to the private sector (and forever lost to the public sector) but a PPP (such as a BOOT scheme) means that ultimately the infrastructure in question will revert to public ownership. Similarly, the public might view more favourably something being constructed from new being (initially) in private hands as opposed to *losing* ownership of something previously in public hands. Moreover, the term 'partnership' brings with it favourable associations. There are implications of agreement, mutual benefits and equality between the partners – there is no hint that the benefits might flow more to one partner than the other or that one partner might be subordinate in some way to the other.

Second, the lack of public disquiet about PPPs may be a function of the public's lack of capacity to understand and interpret the nature, effects and implications of what they entail. The complexity of the arrangements of some PPPs and their technical nature militates against the public being in a position to judge whether PPPs are in their best interests or not. Such calculations, moreover, are made more difficult if the PPP involves a long-term commitment with future costs pushed beyond the time scales of normal cost–benefit calculations. Furthermore, to the extent that details of PPPs are kept confidential, or are too complex to be readily understood, the public's ability to make reasoned assessments is reduced.

Third, the lack of opposition to PPPs from within the public policy community has kept them off the political agenda. The attraction of PPPs to incumbent governments has already been discussed above, but why opposition parties have generally uncritically accepted their use needs some explanation. Once again, the answer may lie in the overwhelming dominance of the neo-liberal economic paradigm. For a party to take a contrary position would expose it to virtual ridicule as being economically incompetent – it certainly could not be seen as a 'good economic manager' capable of being trusted with the public finances. To question the merits of PPPs (whether as a government or opposition party) would be to confront the conventional wisdom espoused by almost the entire range of the public service, consultants, the business community, economic and political commentators in the media, financial markets and ratings agencies. The lack of any acceptable alternative ideology in the public or political domain leaves opponents of PPPs with little room for manoeuvre, limits the credibility of critical analysis and assessment of PPPs and, as a consequence, reduces public awareness of potential failings of PPPs.

There was a second factor in the UK, Australia and some other polities. In these countries, privatization had been vilified by left-of-centre opposition political parties which were later elected to government at national or subnational levels. These new governments were then faced with finding ways of providing goods and services. In doing so, they had to preserve the credibility of their political opposition to privatization whilst accommodating the neo-liberal paradigm. PPPs emerged as something seemingly different and new. Their adoption was all the easier for governments faced with right-of-centre opposition parties which had an ideological predisposition to close relationships between business and government and therefore to PPPs. PPPs were therefore attractive politically, seeming to be an innovative departure from privatization and yet a difficult target for the opposition.

A third factor which may have had some influence is the industrial relations implications. For left-of-centre governments, especially the Labour/Labor parties of the UK, Australia and NZ with organizational links with trade unions, labour relations can be extremely difficult to handle. PPPs remove the government from involvement in labour relations involved in either the construction or provision of public facilities and services.

In addition, if more recent American critics of the pluralist model of power are correct and power is not relatively, evenly dispersed between competing interest groups but rather heavily biased in favour of the corporate sector (Held, 1987:202), then parties seeking office cannot afford to alienate business. Since PPPs generally favor business interests, for a major political party to oppose their use would be tantamount to political suicide.

CONCLUSION

The popularity of PPPs and their apparent failure to arouse political debate can be traced to the dominance of the neo-liberal economic paradigm and certain of its assumptions on which they are largely based and justified. So pervasive has this view become within the public policy community, that there are effectively no alternative views that a political actor or the general public could credibly espouse to challenge the use of PPPs. In addition, it is a politically attractive strategy in certain circumstances.

This chapter has argued that governments benefit from the use of PPPs as do the various consultants, contractors and members of the business community directly involved. Whether the general public, however, are net beneficiaries is less clear cut. They may well benefit if the use of PPPs enables desirable projects to be executed that otherwise would not have been undertaken by government alone. They also stand to benefit in those instances where PPPs are able to deliver quicker, cheaper and more efficient outcomes because private sector performance is superior to that of the public sector. It is argued, however, that this is not always the case and the public could end up paying more for provision of services than they needed to because of the higher interest rates paid for private company borrowings and the higher prices paid to ensure private profitability. Policy, therefore, must be evidence based, resting on proper piloting and trials of creative ideas and their innovative use. Claims of efficiency must be checked against the criteria applied.

It is also argued that PPPs need to be judged on more than just economic criteria. The potential for corruption of the body politic is a serious risk to good, democratic governance. These risks dictate that PPP processes must be supported by strong anti-corruption infrastructure of lore, law and enforcement. PPPs should not undermine democracy. Nor should their impact on equity issues be ignored. Distributional effects need to be exposed and cost effects should be calculated over the whole economy rather than merely the budget sector.

In sum, this chapter argues that PPPs need to be subjected to greater scrutiny, used where clearly beneficial to the public (both economically and socially), but avoided where they damage the public interest. Perhaps the time has come for PPPs to take a more prominent place on the political agenda.

NOTE

1. Halliburton has a ten-year master contract for the provision of goods and services to support the US Army, which could be seen as amongst the world's largest PPPs.

REFERENCES

Argy, F. (2003), 'Balancing efficiency with equity – the big challenge for public policy' paper presented at Towards Public Value conference, 24–25 November Monash University, Australia.

Argy, F. (1998), *Australia at the Crossroads: Radical Free Market or a Progressive Liberalism?*, Sydney: Allen and Unwin.

Balaam, D. and M. Veseth (2005), *Introduction to International Political Economy*, 3rd edn, Upper Saddle River, NJ: Pearson.

Cohn, T. (2003), *Global Political Economy: Theory and Practice*, 2nd edn, New York: Longman.

Davidson, K. (2002), 'Privatisation policy doesn't hold water', *The Age*, 31 October.

Giddens, A. (2000), *The Third Way & Its Critics*, Cambridge: Polity Press.

Giddens, A. (ed.) (2001), *The Global Third Way Debate*, Cambridge: Polity Press.

Gilpin, R. (2001), *Global Political Economy: Understanding the International Economic Order*, Princeton, NJ: Princeton University Press.

Gow, D. and A. Maher (1994), 'Regulation in Theory and Practice' in R. Stewart (ed.) *Government and Business Relations in Australia*, Sydney: Allen and Unwin.

Heald, D. (2003), *Accounting, Auditing and Accountability Journal*, **16**, 342–71.

Held, D. (1987), *Models of Democracy*, Stanford: Stanford University Press.

Hodge, G. (2000), *Privatisation: An International Review*, Boulder CO: Westview Press.

Hodge, G. (2004), 'Are public private partnerships really good value for taxpayers?', Australian Broadcasting Corporation, 16 May, available at http://www.abc.net. au/insidebusiness/content/2004/s1109185.htm, accessed 17 September 2004.

Hughes, O. (1998), *Public Management and Administration: An Introduction*, 2nd edn, Basingstoke: Macmillan.

Jacobs, M. (2003), in *ABC Radio National In the National Interest*, T. Lane (ed.), Melbourne.

Langmore, J. (1988), 'Privatisation: abandoning public responsibility', *Current Affairs Bulletin*, March.

Lane, J.-E. (2000), *New Public Management*, London: Routledge.

Millar, R. (2001), 'Preserving the myth of public inefficiency', *The Age*, 6 August.

Munroe, S. (2003), 'Canadian political financing reform', Canada Online, available at http://canadaonline.about.com/cs/govtethics/a/polfinancebill.htm, accessed 28 September 2003.

Oatley, T. (2004), *International Political Economy: Interests and Institutions in the Global Economy*, New York: Pearson.

OECD (1995), *The OECD Jobs Study: Taxation, Employment and Unemployment*, Paris: OECD.

OECD (2003), 'General government outlays. Annex 26', in *OECD Economic Outlook*, June, Paris: OECD, available at http://www.findarticles.com/cf_dls/ m4456/73/105851465/print.jhtml, accessed 14 July 2004.

OECD (2004), 'Fiscal balances and public indebtedness – EO75 Annex Tables: Annex Table 33. General government net financial liabilities', 14 July, Paris: OECD, available at http://www.oecd.org/topicstatsportal/0,2647,en_2825_ 495684_1_1_1_1_1,00.html, accessed 14 July 2004.

Osborne, D. and T. Gaebler (1993), *Reinventing Government: How the Entrepreneurial Spirit is Transforming the Public Sector,* New York: Plume.

Pincus, J. (1993), 'Market failure and government failure' in S. King and P. Lloyd, (eds), *Economic Rationalism: Dead End or Way Forward*, Sydney: Allen and Unwin.

Pitchford, J. (1990), *Australia's Foreign Debt: Myths and Realities,* Sydney: Allen and Unwin.

Press, B. (2002), 'Enron case shouts for campaign finance reform', Tribune Media Services, 13 February, available at http://www.cnn.com/2002/ALLPOLITICS/02/13/ column.billpress, accessed 25 June, 2004.

Procurement Watch Inc. (2002), '(Philippines) Senate passes anti-corruption measure on 2nd and 3rd reading', Procurement Watch Inc., available at http://www. procurementwatch.org.ph/dec0902.htm, accessed 28 September 2003.

Richardson, J. (1997), 'Economics: hegemonic discourse', *Quadrant*, March, 52–60.

Savas, E. (2000), *Privatisation and Public–Private Partnerships*, New York: Chatham House Publishers.

Sinclair, T. (2003), *New Political Economy*, **8**, 147–61.

Smyth, P. and M. Wearing (2002), 'After the welfare state? Welfare governance and the communitarian revival', in S. Bell (ed.), *Economic Governance and Institutional Dynamics*, Oxford: Oxford University Press.

Stilwell, F. (1993), 'Economic rationalism: sound foundations for policy?', in S. Rees, G. Rodley and F. Stilwell (eds), *Beyond the Market: Alternatives to Economic Rationalism*, Leichhardt, NSW: Pluto Press.

Weidenbaum, M. (1999), *Business and Government in the Global Marketplace*, 6th edn, Upper Saddle River, NJ: Prentice Hall.

Willacy, M. (2001), 'Opinion polls on tax cuts', 2003 Australian Broadcasting Commission radio AM programme, available at http://www.abc.net.au/am/ s345825.htm, accessed 9 November 2003.

Wiltshire, K. (1994), 'Privatisation and Corporatisation' in R. Stewart (ed.), *Government and Business Relations in Australia*, Sydney: Allen and Unwin.

6. Public–private partnerships as the management of co-production: strategic and institutional obstacles in a difficult marriage

Erik-Hans Klijn and Geert R. Teisman

INTRODUCTION: THE FOCUS ON PUBLIC–PRIVATE PARTNERSHIP

Public–private partnerships have enjoyed popularity in western Europe recently (see Osborne, 2000). Public–private partnerships are also an important component – at least in the rhetoric – of Tony Blair's New Labour policies (Falconer and McLaughlin, 2000; Sullivan and Skelcher, 2002). This has led to an enormous growth in both strategic partnerships (principally the LSP, the local strategic partnerships) as well as those of a more implementational nature (for example for regeneration projects) (Sullivan and Skelcher, 2002). Even in the European Union, traditionally the bastion in which the division of public and private enterprise and market operation forms part of the standard repertoire – there is an increasing focus on PPPs (Teisman and Klijn, 2000).

The expertise centre (Kenniscentrum) within the Ministry of Finance in the Netherlands set up at the end of the 1990s to support PPP initiatives in the Netherlands states that: 'International experiences show that a faster and more efficient implementation of infrastructure projects is possible by means of public–private partnership (PPP). In the Netherlands both public and private actors show great interest in and willingness to adopt PPPs' (Kenniscentrum, 1998). In short, public–private partnership has everything going for it and it is considered as one of the most important new horizontal forms of governance in the modern network society.

What are Public–Private Partnerships?

Public–private partnership may be considered as a form of co-production, of cooperation, in which the parties realize products, services or policy outcomes jointly. Above all, PPP assumes that through a more intensive cooperation between pubic and private parties, better and more efficient policy outcomes and policy products can be realized. With this in mind, the idea is that private parties would need to be involved earlier and more intensively in decision making on joint projects.

Public–private partnerships may be described as 'more or less sustainable cooperation between public and private actors in which joint products and/ or services are developed and in which risks, costs and profits are shared' (Klijn and Teisman, 2000). Although PPP projects are to be found in many areas, partnerships appear to be formed primarily for the purpose of tackling urban problems (regeneration processes, accessibility, economic vitality, improving the living environment and so on) and infrastructural projects. However, partnerships in the health care sector are cropping up increasingly (Teisman and Klijn, 2000).

Structure of this Chapter

In this chapter we examine public–private partnerships as a form of co-production and look at how they are organized and managed. We focus first on the reason for cooperation: the possibility of generating surplus value. We also discuss different forms of surplus value. Then we examine the two prevailing ways of organising public–private cooperation: contracts and partnership. The two forms are contrasted and examples of both forms are discussed.

CO-PRODUCTION IN PPP: THE SEARCH FOR SURPLUS VALUE

Cooperation between public and private actors should lead to additional returns. In most publications this is called surplus value (or collaborative advantages: see Huxham, 2000) and refers to extra revenues which would not come about without this cooperation.[1] The expertise centre for PPP states that:

> ... Involving private parties in the delivering of public services must provide added value. This may be added value in financial terms. For example, motorways or railway infrastructure which can be developed and are maintained during their life cycle at lower costs ... Just as important is the substantive added value. For example, a higher degree of availability of motorways and railway infrastructure due to optimisation of its maintenance, but also the possibility that teaching staff are able to concentrate fully on teaching while other people ensure that the school

is kept running effectively ... Finally, PPP could contribute to public goals being delivered more quickly. (Kenniscentrum PPP, 2001:10–11)

In short, the motivation behind the setting up of PPPs in various countries is that they should be capable of generating extra profits.

Forms of Surplus Value

Surplus value can take different forms (Teisman and in 't Veld, 1992; Osborne, 2000; Huxham, 2000). A distinction is often made in simple cost savings, for example because permits are provided more quickly, and the achieving of real synergy. In the first case, public and private parties continue to do only what they can do themselves and generate profit though joint coordination of operations. In this form of co-production no substantive surplus value is realized.

If substantive surplus value is achieved, this is termed synergy. For instance, the real estate value of housing financed by investors is increased by a well-formulated master plan drawn up jointly by public and private actors whereby the area acquires a more prestigious character. An even greater substantive surplus value is achieved when really innovative products are realized, for example in the sphere of service provision, where at high-speed railway stations, forms of public transport are better geared to one another via an easily accessible information channel. In the latter case an innovative product (an information system) is realized whereas in the master plan example only quality improvement is achieved by combining existing products and services.

There is thus a rising scale of surplus value: cost savings, substantive improvement and innovative products.

Surplus Value and Organizational Form

It is important to recognize that having higher ambitions for achieving surplus value, in other words realizing substantive surplus value as well, or realizing innovative products and services, also requires a more complicated and sophisticated organizational form. In order to achieve synergy, a great deal of contact, coordination and exchange of information among the actors is necessary, plus the will to look beyond one's own organization's boundaries. In this sense public–private cooperation does not differ from strategic alliances in the private domain (Faulkner, 1995; Nooteboom, 1998). There, too, and particularly for the joint development of new products (principally in research and development alliances) information exchange on a large scale is necessary in order to develop a really innovative product.

It is an interesting feature of that world that we find companies frequently cooperating on the development of a new product and/or standards for new products, only to subsequently compete with each other when they market their own version of that product.

METHODS OF CO-PRODUCTION: ORGANIZING THE RESPONSIBILITY

It is not only in practice that we find many different forms of co-production in PPP projects. From a theoretical perspective, too, there are different ways of looking at the forms of co-production.

Two Forms: Contracts and Partnerships

In most publication we find a distinction between PPP concessions or contracts and PPP as an organizational cooperation project or partnership (Teisman, 1998; Osborne, 2000; Kenniscentrum, 2002).

- In a PPP concession various components of the value chain of an investment project are integrated and then put out to tender via a *contract*. In this way the design, construction, financing and, if appropriate, commercial operation of an infrastructural project (such as a road), for instance, are integrated in a contract. The surplus value in this case derives from the fact that greater efficiency can be attained in this way. This is achieved among other things by the lower costs of coordination between the various components. But the idea is that substantive surplus value can also be achieved in this way which should convert into financial advantages. There is a tendering system used in England, for example, whereby road building is contracted out to private consortia for a period of 30 years. By using more sustainable building materials the consortium can save on future maintenance (Haynes and Roden, 1999). But the devising of new products is also stimulated, according to this view, because any innovations have a long period over which to get a return on investment.
- In a PPP as an organizational cooperative project, the key feature is that different projects are integrated with each other in order to achieve surplus value. In this case, PPP is a *partnership*. This sort of cooperation is usually found in urban reconstruction and regeneration projects. Here, for example, measures which endeavour to strengthen transport are combined with measures which are aimed at improving the living environment and/or housing and at strengthening the economy. In this

method of cooperation the surplus value is generated by combining substantive measures and projects which then reinforce each other. This also makes it possible to effect a financial trade-off between profitable and less profitable but socially worthwhile components.

The method of co-production in the two forms of PPP is regulated in a very different way. In the first form there is only limited co-production. This primarily consists of interaction between public and private actors at the start of a PPP project regarding the basic principles of the project to be contracted out. This mode of operation is in fact a variation on the classic method of contract allocation in which attempts are made to increase the surplus value via a whole range of new forms of contract. Ideas about new contract forms crop up in a large number of countries but are perhaps worked out in most detail in the UK Private Finance Initiative. The ideas of the Netherlands expertise centre for PPP, for example, have been largely adopted from the UK PFI model.

Box 6.1   Private Finance Initiative as contract form: road contracting

---

AN EXAMPLE: PRIVATE FINANCE INITIATIVE IN ROAD SERVICE IN THE UK

The Private Finance Initiative is a perfect form of 'new contracting'. Ideas for using the Private Finance Initiatives (PFI) for road services in the UK date back to the early 1990s. In 1992, the Private Finance Initiative was started to encourage the private sector to become involved in government projects. At the end of 1992, the Department of Transport in the UK announced that private parties should be able to provide the possibility of designing, building, financing and operating (DBFO) roads over a long period of time.

The idea of contracting
Most of the ideas in these DBFO contracts were specified in a policy document entitled 'Paying for Better Motorways' which was published in May 1993. This outlined the two main benefits of contracting the obligations for building and operating the road service to private partners. The first was that private partners could absorb the risks at each stage of the project. Because the contract would run for a long period, private actors could experiment with new ways to build and operate roads. A second aim of the Private

Finance Initiative was to promote a private sector road maintenance industry which scarcely existed at that time, according to the Department of Transport.

The nature of the contract
In general, the contract between the Highway Agency and the contractor is specified according to the desires of the agency and to some fundamental requirements for design, construction, operation and maintenance of the projected road. To ensure that the DBFO company (the contractor) operates within and fulfils the obligations of the contract, the Highway Agency monitors the activities of the DBFO company. It does this by appointing representatives who monitor the construction, operation and maintenance activities. The contract contains a penalty point mechanism. This allocates penalty points for failures in the performance of the contract. If the number of points exceeds specified values, the monitoring activities are increased. If the number of penalty points reaches a certain maximum, the Agency has the right to terminate the contract.

Source:　Koppenjan and Klijn, 2004.

The precondition for success for this type of approach to co-production is that the public party should be able to specify the problem clearly and that clear rules for the tendering process should exist.

The second method of co-production in PPP, organizational cooperation constructions or partnerships, involves a far more intensive interaction because the various project components which are often the domain of diverse private and public actors have to be coordinated with each other and it is rather more difficult to clearly delineate in advance the content and ambitions of the cooperation.

Box 6.2　An example of partnership

THE AMSTERDAM SOUTH AXIS

The South Axis project concerns the (re)development of the area surrounding the Amsterdam South/WTC Railway Station and the southern part of the motorway around Amsterdam. During the eighties, there had been a rapid expansion in the construction of new office space in this area. One example is the new headquarters of the large ABN-AMRO Bank. The City of Amsterdam had to make decisions on this expansion case by case, and in 1994 it wanted to develop more systematic planning for this area.

A partnership arrangement
For this purpose the City managers set up the so-called 'South Axis Coalition' in December 1994, in which all the prominent private actors took part. It was a kind of informal strategic group without any fixed membership. To support the coalition, a working group was set up consisting of civil servants from the main departments of the Amsterdam civil service in order to direct research towards possible solutions and start working on a master plan. A first draft of the plan was presented in October 1996. Sections of the master plan were discussed with interest groups in late 1996. As a result, additional housing (1500) and other functions were added to the existing proposals. In 1997, the Dutch Railways (NS) real estate department joined this strategic group, and the partners started working together on further development of the plan. They paid special attention to the idea of constructing an underground infrastructure (the motorway and heavy and light rail) in order to create the necessary space aboveground for the construction of new offices and housing.

This master plan was approved by the City Council in January 1998. The area would be developed into a high-potential area of office space and private housing combined with transport facilities. On the basis of this document, certain areas were already undergoing further development (such as investments in the large, already existing RAI Conference Centre which were made in February 1998, and plans for an office site called Mahler IV in May 1998).

Source: Adapted from Klijn and Teisman, 2003.

The preconditions for partnership success lie predominantly in the way in which the partners' ambitions and goals can be linked and in effective rules for interactions being laid down.

Contracts and Partnerships: A Comparison

The difference in responsibility and risk division between the two forms is crucial. In a contract relationship a clear delineation of responsibility and risk is effected. The commissioning party (the public party) is responsible for the problem/project specifications. After a degree of co-production in the early phase, responsibilities are then very strictly divided between public and private parties. Once the tendering process has been concluded the relationship is no longer one of co-production but of regulation. The principle (the public actor) monitors the behaviour and actions of the agent (the private actor or actors).

In a partnership the co-production is usually more close-knit and intensive since parties are also jointly responsible for the implementation (or at least coordination is necessary because the parts of the various measures have to be tailored to one another) and more joint product or policy development takes place. A comparison between a contract – in whatever form – and a partnership is illustrated in Table 6.1.

Table 6.1   Co-production in PPPs via contracts and partnership

Characteristics	Contract arrangements	Partnership arrangements
Type of relationship	Client (public party) and contractor (private party)	Joint decision making (searching for linkages)
Nature of problem and specification of solutions	Public party specifies problem and solution/ product	Public and private parties involved in joint process of problem and solution specification
Scope of project	Tendency to search for clear divisions; any expansion of scope must fall within the delineated responsibilities	Tendency to search for expansion of scope and linking of elements
Preconditions for success	Clear contract and tendering rules and clearly formulated problems/project requirements	Linking ambitions and goals, effective rules for interaction to create commitment and profitable cooperation
Management principles	Strongly based on principles of project management (specifying goals, organizing time planning, organizing manpower)	Based more on principles of process management (searching for goals, linking and connecting actors' activities, and linking of decisions)
Sort of co-production	Limited and occurring primarily prior to the tendering process; after that only monitoring; no co-production	Extensive during the whole process; at first primarily regarding nature of ambitions and searching for linkages, later on more co-production in jointly realizing ambitions

Sources: Teisman, 1998; Klijn and Teisman, 2000.

Conclusion: New or Old?

It should be mentioned that it is highly debatable whether the contract form of public–private partnership, as found, for example, in the UK Private Finance Initiative, should be considered as a PPP. In fact this form is no different from classic forms of contracting out and tendering. The only difference is in the division of responsibility. Real joint risk taking and product development hardly take place at all. In short, the contract form of PPP, which is considered by many authors to be a PPP, is not actually a PPP at all but a revamped form of tendering in which there is still a sharp risk division.

DEVELOPMENT OF CO-PRODUCTION IN PPP: BETWEEN AMBITIONS AND RISK AVOIDANCE

Generally speaking, interactions in PPP projects are complex. Often, different parties are involved, each with its own perceptions and strategies, and the decision making can only progress if these are coordinated to some extent. But in addition, for co-production in PPP projects, many different decisions are often necessary which must frequently be made in very different arenas.

In PPPs therefore, the ambitions are considerable – creating value, innovation, greater efficiency and faster decision making – but so are the necessary organizational efforts. The general picture that emerges when examining the research into co-production decision making in PPP projects is that interactions are frequently a time-consuming and laborious process and it is often difficult to actually realize the intended surplus value (see particularly van Ham and Koppenjan, 2002; but also Canoy et al., 2001; Klijn and Teisman, 2003; Klijn et al., 2003). On the basis of extensive research into PPP projects in the Netherlands (van Ham and Koppenjan, 2002; Klijn et al., 2002) we discuss three of the most striking phenomena: the need for attractive plans and selection of appropriate ambitions, the problem of risk avoidance behaviour, and the need for effective process management.

Substantive Ambitions: the Need for an Attractive Plan and the Proper Scope

The substantive ambitions are strongly linked to the scope which parties decide on for the PPP cooperation. This refers to the extent of the project and the number of subjects and subprojects which have to be linked with each other. On the one hand, linking subjects and subprojects enables exchange and the trade-off of profitable components for less profitable but nevertheless socially desired components. On the other hand, the linking of subjects and subprojects makes the cooperation more complex, which means that greater demands are made on the management of the cooperation.

The scope of a public–private partnership project depends not only on the nature of the problem and its cohesion but also on what opportunities there are to interest actors in cooperation. The nature of the problem concerns the question of whether the problem should be tackled together with other problems or not. For example, an attempt can be made in an urban regeneration project to create jobs for people, but if they are then unable to find accommodation to match their higher income and ambition and subsequently leave the area, the measure will have failed in at least a part of its intention, namely to improve parts of the city. In selecting the scope of a project, the manager has to always be aware that an objective formulation of the problem does not exist (Derry 1984; Schon and Rein, 1994) and that different actors have different views of the problem (and therefore also of the desired scope of a project) (Koppenjan and Klijn, 2004).

This means that the scope of a PPP project is the choice of the actors involved and is not fixed beforehand. The fact that a choice is involved, however, is not always realized by the parties. Too often in PPP projects the scope is regarded as a given so that opportunities for possible expansions (or sometimes contractions) which could help the process move forwards are missed. This emerged from a study conducted into a large number of PPP projects in the Netherlands (van Ham and Koppenjan, 2003). The scope of PPP projects must be consciously dealt with if for no other reason than that the actors who are involved in the process need to have something to gain. If that is not the case then the actors' cooperation will leave much to be desired.

This means that the content of proposals must not only be attractive but also has to be interesting enough to induce a large number of actors to engage in action and cooperation. In short, making a conscious choice about the scope of the project is not only necessary in view of the nature of the problem and the desired exchange of profitable and non-profitable components of the partnership project, but also with a view to obtaining the desired cooperation from the actors involved.

Although ways for expansion in the scope of a project are sometimes seen, it remains difficult to reach joint action because the behaviour of parties is characterized by risk avoidance or because the management of the project is not well operated.

Box 6.3   Failures in the South Axis case

SOUTH AXIS FAILURES

Despite the promising start of the South Axis project and the joint decision making efforts of public and private actors, no concrete results were obtained for the financing of the underground transport infrastructure. The enthusiastic cooperation between city managers and private actors began to stagnate. They began to resume their traditional roles. Public actors felt that they needed to invest a great deal of time and effort in keeping the process going while failing to obtain any clear commitments on the financial involvement of private actors. Private actors criticised their insufficient influence on the decision making and the lack of impact of their efforts.

Joint fact-finding instead of joint decision making
According to previous negotiations, agreements should have been signed by early 1999. But in reality no agreement was reached on how to proceed further. The public–private cooperation structure began to unravel, and the focus shifted to the realization of real estate projects that were not dependent on the new underground car and public transport infrastructure. The public managers once again took on a central role in the planning process. They negotiated on a bilateral basis with several private and public actors for commitments, money (from public actors) or partial investment projects (with private actors). Although the interaction between public and private actors remained intensive, their joint organization began to come apart, and responsibilities split up along traditional lines. *In other words, the interaction that existed was used mainly for joint fact-finding, not for joint responsibility and joint decision making.*

As an illustration of this, the City of Amsterdam and its central departments initiated a number of fact-finding studies to explore the technical and financial possibilities of locating infrastructure below the ground. In early 2000, the City Council once again declared that infrastructure should be located underground. This solution was expected to lead to great environmental and economic improvements. Three important private actors, the ING Bank, the ABN-AMRO Bank, and NS Real Estate, started to organise their strategies in a consortium. After some negotiations with the City of Amsterdam, they guaranteed an investment of 2 billion Dutch guilders (about 630 million Euros) in real estate above the tunnel (if it was constructed and financed by the government).

From joint organisation to bilateral agreements

In November 2000, the urban and national public authorities produced a preliminary document containing various options for improvements in the infrastructure. The 'dock model' (rail and roads underground) optimized the possibilities and created the best conditions for achieving the targets set. It was, however, also the most expensive one. Two other models are still being worked on: a 'dike model' and an 'art model'. The first option aims to achieve expansion more or less within the given physical situation. In the second model, light rail infrastructure and motorways are to be moved underground, while the long-distance rail infrastructure is maintained in its current position.

The period after the initial document was presented was used to consult with the societal actors. In June 2001 the City managers and national authorities presented an initial document outlining procedures for further decision-making. In accordance with public law, they initiated a formal legal procedure (MER) which was intended to result in a definite public decision within two years. One of the basic principles of this procedure was that the motorway should be located underground. Discussions on how to deal with the railway and light rail infrastructure continued. In February 2002, the City Council reaffirmed its preference for the dock model.

In the meantime, various forms of interaction surrounding parts of the project continued. In November 2001 a consortium consisting of the ING Bank, ABN-AMRO Bank and NS signed an agreement with the City Council for the development of a 'Business Park' (the Drenthe Park) in the area. Bilateral agreements were concluded with the University in this area and with the RAI Conference Committee. In terms of partnership, we may conclude that the South Axis is a good example of the type of cooperation that starts with high ambitions in terms of strategic alliances and joint decision making, but in reality develops towards a network structure in which traditional roles are played and cooperation is based on bilateral agreements.

Risk Avoidance

Risk avoidance is a frequently occurring pattern in co-production in PPP projects (van Ham and Koppenjan, 2002; Klijn and Teisman 2003). The box above, which discusses the Amsterdam South Axis, demonstrates this phenomenon very clearly.

Comparable patterns emerge in many PPP projects in spite of high expectations being expressed regarding surplus value and transboundary interactions (see Klijn and Teisman, 2003; van Ham and Koppenjan, 2003). After an enthusiastic start but noncommittal consultations, the parties start to make motions of withdrawal as soon as commitment is called for. This is accompanied by risk avoidance behaviour which leads to one-sided project definition (by public parties), limitation of the scope, disaggregration and splitting up of the project into subprojects, and minimizing interactions between public and private parties. This behaviour clearly does not help the creation of surplus value. On the other hand, it is a tried and tested strategy for dealing with the ever-increasing complexity of cooperation (and thus the interweaving of actors and subjects).

Management of Co-production

The Achilles' heel of co-production in PPP projects is the management of interactions according to the study into PPP projects in the Netherlands mentioned earlier (van Ham and Koppenjan, 2002). On the one hand parties have great difficulty in giving shape to an organization. For want of anything better, tried and tested forms of contract making are drawn up accompanied by public plan preparation and division of responsibilities wholly in line with the organizational recommendations from a contract view of PPP as discussed in Section 3. The gain from such a rigid contractual plan, however, is disappointing. It allows little room for substantive enrichment and opportunities for scope expansion are missed. Moreover, it shifts the laborious negotiations between public and private parties to the tendering phase. In practice, it appears that contract negotiations are often laborious processes and companies further impose additional requirements (van Ham and Koppenjan, 2002:465).

But in cooperative projects where initially a broad approach, strongly aimed at co-production, is chosen, management also forms a stumbling block. In this case, parties often find it too much trouble to support and supervise such a complicated process. Much variation in terms of solution is created but due to the absence of good selection mechanisms, projects become an accumulation of a huge number of ambitions which makes them either prohibitively expensive or unachievable. In sum, it seems to be difficult to manage the selection effectively.

Interactions in Public–Private Partnership: Conclusion

In short, on analysing the interaction progress of co-production in PPPs it appears that the connection between the level of ambition, the chosen organizational form and the form of management is not always clearly recognized. A high ambition level with intensive co-production requires much effort in the sphere of process management whereas rushing into the choice for a limited ambition level and strong emphasis on contracts and division of responsibility usually leads to limited surplus value or substantive enrichment (van Ham and Koppenjan, 2002; Klijn 2002). Before linking any conclusions to this statement about the management of PPP as co-production it is necessary to shed light on the institutional background to these strategy patterns in PPP.

THE BACKGROUND TO CO-PRODUCTION IN PPP: INSTITUTIONAL FACTORS

The institutional complexity within which PPP projects come about has already been pointed out. Relevant decisions for PPP projects are often taken in a whole range of different places in diverse networks.

The Institutional Complexity of PPP

In PPPs, projects mostly involve diverse actors with a variety of backgrounds. But in addition, decisions are usually taken in diverse arenas which frequently are not and cannot be connected. If the actors also come from diverse networks and thus use differing rules, the decision making can become extremely difficult (Klijn and Teisman, 2003).

Box 6.4   Example of institutional complexity

THE DELFT CASE

In the municipality of Delft the busy Rotterdam–Amsterdam railway line runs right through the centre of the city. Moreover, this is just about the only section that is still two-track whereas the rest of the line is four-track. There have thus been plans for some considerable time to double the line and at the same time to reroute it underground. Although the municipality of Delft is the initiator, a lot of central public actors (such as the Ministry of Transport, Public Works and Water Management as biggest financial backer and the Ministry of Public Housing, Spatial Planning and the Environment (VROM) involved in the aboveground restructuring) as well as private actors (such as the Dutch Railways as transporter and Ballast Nedam as major project developer) are involved in the decision making.

The Delft Railway Zone project, the plan for the line that at present runs through the centre of Delft to be placed under the ground so that space is created above the ground for a valuable addition to the city centre, is thus anything but a local project. It is linked with a large number of decision arenas in other networks. It was for this purpose that the municipality of Delft at the end of the 1990s applied for a subsidy under the multi-utilisation of space scheme. Using that money a master plan was developed by the Spanish urban developer, Busquets, which in turn functioned as a basis for further developing the space that will become available. In addition, this serves to link the Delft Railway Zone project with decision making on multiple use of space by the Ministry of Public Housing, Spatial Planning and the Environment (VROM) from which it also receives a contribution. The decision making about Delft is of course also strongly linked with the decision making within the Ministry of Transport, Public Works and Water Management regarding funds for infrastructure (the MIT). Furthermore, the decision making is also linked with decision making on safety. As a pilot project, a safety impact assessment for Delft has been drawn up together with all those involved in the plans for the projected tunnel. The outcomes of this assessment have been continually brought into the decision making on the subject of the tunnel which took place chiefly between the municipality of Delft and Pro-rail. In this way, a PPP project of this kind, which is realized at a local level, is continually linked with supra-local arenas which are located across a whole range of different networks.

These institutional characteristics make PPP projects complex and help account for the complicated and often laborious interaction patterns (see also Koppenjan and Klijn, 2004). Many different actors have to be linked together, sectoral and network divisions have to be overcome, and any variations in rules and deep-seated convictions held by actors from different networks have to be dealt with.

Differing Backgrounds of Public and Private Actors

On top of this complexity, moreover, there are the differing backgrounds and identities of public and private actors. The value patterns and identities of public and private parties tend to differ (see for example Jacobs, 1992). In short, the values of private actors (who are highly competitive, with a respect for commercial contracts) lead to strategies in which the certainty of a market share and returns are the key issues, but where there is also a strong emphasis on seizing market opportunities. Although private parties are willing to take on market risks they are chary of political risks. Here lies an important difference from the public sector. National and local government can safely allow itself loss-making behaviour as long as this is tolerated by its political and public supporters. So long as the budget is not exceeded, usually no political problems arise. This usually means that the project remains within the specified budget. The chief problem for public actors is expectations which cannot be lived up to and which lead to political problems. This leads to public actors wanting to control the (content of the) process as much as possible. Table 6.2 summarizes the value orientations of public and private parties and the strategy dynamic that this produces which is often to be found in PPP projects.

Table 6.2   Relationship between core business, values and strategies of public and private actors

	Public actors	Private actors	Tension
Core business	Objectives: (sectoral) public objectives Continuity: political preconditions	Objectives: realizing profit (margins) Continuity: financial preconditions	Different risk perceptions: political risks in expectations versus market risks in annual figures
Values	Loyalty Dedication to self-defined public business Auditability of process and approach (political/social) Emphasis on risk avoidance and preventing expectations	Competitive Dedication to consumer preferences Auditable by shareholders on results Emphasis on market opportunities and risk and on innovations	Government reticent in process versus private party reticent in knowledge Government reticent in result versus private party reticent with own commitment

Table 6.2   continued

	Public actors	Private actors	Tension
Strategies	Seeking ways to guarantee substantive influence (public primacy) Minimizing expectations and implementation uncertainties in terms of costs	Seeking for certainties for production, and/or opportunity for attaining commissions Minimizing political risks and organizational costs as consequence of sluggish public procedures	Conflict leads to mutual demarcation of agreements and thus to tried and tested forms of cooperation (contracts)
Consequences for PPP	Emphasis on risk limitation and laying down of decisions leads to laying down of procedures and public dominance	Emphasis on certainty of market share and returns leads to waiting behaviour and limited investment until the date the commission is attained	Creation of surplus value through trans-boundary interaction fails to occur

Source: Klijn and Teisman, 2002.

A strategy pattern thus develops in which private actors, as long as no commission has been attained, adopt a reticent attitude, while public actors attempt to limit the risk and endeavour to pin down the content of the project. The result is that the creation of substantive surplus value often fails to occur, as can be seen in Table 6.2. This shows that the interaction problems in PPP cooperation discussed in Section 4 are not just accidental patterns but are strongly linked to the complexity of the decision-making and the institutional backgrounds of the actors involved.

MANAGEMENT STRATEGIES FOR PUBLIC–PRIVATE PARTNERSHIP

If a manager or initiator wants to achieve real synergy in public–private partnership projects, this requires major efforts and exceedingly good process management. Three aspects are central to this (Klijn et al., 2002; also Klijn and Teisman, 2000; Huxham and Vangen, 2000) and these will be further elaborated in the rest of this section:

- content: working towards integration and variety;
- process: intensifying the interactions;
- management: supporting the cooperation process.

Content: Attractive Ideas and the Creation of Variety

An attractive content is an important booster for public–private partnership. After all, both public and private actors need to be given an incentive to devote their best efforts to the cooperative project. This means that a unilateral substantive arranging of the project by public actors has a demotivating effect because it leaves no room for private input.

However, a fixed content at the start also fails to do justice to the complexity of the substantive task. This usually concerns difficult problems (Koppenjan and Klijn, 2004) about which the various actors involved have different perceptions and for which they sometimes also advocate different solutions. This means that during the process, new ideas have to be developed and solutions have to be tried out. Thus, although certain substantive frameworks and benchmarks are necessary, flexibility and creativity are indispensable during the process in order to bring the cooperation to a favourable conclusion.

During the cooperation, and particularly during the phase in which plans and/or products are developed, the substantive variety can be increased by making more use of creative competition (Teisman, 1997). Allowing different ideas to develop at the same time prevents solutions being pinned down at an early stage, which later turn out to be inadequate. An important difference compared to classical methods of problem solving is that ideas are worked out in minute detail so that the alternatives being considered really are comparable and optimal creativity is stimulated by the competition and discussion among the various consortia who are developing the plans. These consortia, incidentally, may contain differing combinations of public, private or third party stakeholders.

Process: Promoting Interactions and Arranging

For cooperation to be achieved, it is important that joint images about the content and form of cooperation should evolve among the parties. Intensive interactions are not an adequate precondition for this but are certainly a necessary one. These interactions must also lead to the creation of a certain trust among actors. This seems to conflict with the recommendations from the contract form of public–private partnerships which emphasize a division of responsibilities, formalizing the interactions between actors and agreeing clear sanctions.

In order to achieve this cooperation, private actors have to play a prominent role in the process: for example, by choosing a robust cooperation construction, by contracting out the role of process manager or by offering remuneration to participants (for which explicit efforts are expected to be made). Making clear agreements with representative political bodies (local councils, parliament, etc.) also prevents interactions suddenly stagnating at a later stage. In order to get the process to run smoothly, clear organizational arrangements are also needed which support these interactions.

The Need for Process Management

The complexity – both institutional and in process terms – makes it impossible to anticipate everything in advance or even to lay everything down in advance in process agreements. Room is needed in which to tackle unforeseen developments and unexpected turns in the process and this is why good and active process management is necessary (see Klijn and Teisman, 2000). Management of trust, and the gradual development of a basis for trust, are also part of this. Effective process architecture (Bruijn et al., 1998), i.e. a set of agreements on the mode of interactions and associated matters such as agreements on solving conflicts, is the first step in the necessary process management. But sustaining interactions, making headway in substantive agreements and maintaining the organizational arrangements on the part of the process manager during the course of the interaction is just as important.

For components of the cooperation project that have crystallized and can be implemented, a switchover must be made to principles of project management in which the classic control instruments (fixing content, monitoring time and money, planning methodologies) can be used. In this way project management thus complements such strategies of process management as linking contents, facilitating interactions, making arrangements, and so on (see Kickert et al., 1997; Koppenjan and Klijn, 2004).

IN CONCLUSION: LESSONS FOR CO-PRODUCTION IN PPP

In this chapter we have drawn attention to the different uses of the phrase 'public–private partnerships'. There are forms, like the UK Private Finance

Initiative, that are strongly contract based and there are forms that have a more partnership orientation. In the first form, the level of co-production is low and the risks are mostly clearly shared among partners in a strongly contractual manner. In the second form there is more co-production and sharing of risks and costs. It is doubtful if the contractual form of public–private partnership really can be described as a PPP because it does not differ much from classic contractual tendering procedures. It is however a well-known form of collaboration with relatively few risks. The opportunities however to achieve worthwhile added value are more limited because of the limited co-production involved.

Partnership constructs are more difficult to manage. Opportunities certainly exist for achieving excellent results through co-production in PPP projects. Nevertheless, it seems that if co-production is to deliver successful results, huge efforts are required and the process management has to be exceptionally well-organized. A few pointers are crucial to this (see Klijn, Koppenjan and van Ham, 2002; Kenniscentrum, 2001; Huxham, 2000):

- *Attractive content*: an attractive content is the motor of progress in decision making. To that end, a great deal of investment is needed in searching for interesting solutions, linking existing solutions with the ideas and wishes of other stakeholders. On the other hand, there should be a willingness to adapt ideas that have already been developed to changing circumstances. In this sense they are learning processes rather than progress towards fixed frameworks.
- *Intensive interactions and involving third parties*: there is often a tendency to interpret the co-production in too limited a way with the result that PPP projects arouse resistance at a later stage. Co-production between public and private parties must be accompanied at the outset by co-production with other involved parties (not necessarily all around the same table!).
- *Gearing ambitions and management to each other*: it has been shown that there is a relationship between the chosen ambitions and the chosen organizational form and mode of management. If division of responsibility and clear contract forms are chosen, little can be expected of the substantive surplus value. In that case, the co-production addresses itself to the early phase of the PPP and primarily to achieving greater efficiency.
- *Provide good process management*: good process management is the key to engineering co-production that results in rich, substantive solutions with surplus value. In particular, if greater ambition and broad co-production have been chosen, the supervision of interactions, a good process design and the arranging of interactions is essential. Without

this type of process management, there is a serious risk that a broadly designed process will turn out to be a disappointment due to the unrestricted piling up of wishes.

The conclusion can thus be that real partnership between public and private actors requires a lot of work and often has to conquer many institutional obstacles but given the changing nature of society where knowledge resources are divided and required (policy) products are complex in nature we probably have no other choice than to go on and struggle to find workable relations.

NOTE

1. The term has an affinity with another frequently used term: win–win situations (see for example Bruijn et al., 1998).

REFERENCES

Bruijn, J.A., E.F. Ten Heuvelhof and R.J. in 't Veld (1998), 'Procesmanagement; over procesontwerpen en besluitvorming' ['Process management; about designing processes and decision-making'], Amsterdam: Academic Service.

Canoy, M., M. Janssen and B. Vollaard (2001), *PPS: een uidagend huwelijk, publiek–private Samenwerking bij Combinatieprojecten*, The Hague: CPB.

Derry, D. (1984), *Problem definition in policy analysis*, Lawrence, KS: University Press of Kansas.

Falconer, P.K. and K. McLaughlin (2000), 'Public–private partnerships and the "New Labour" government in Britain', in S.P. Osborne (ed.) *Public–Private Partnerships; Theory and Practice in International Perspective*, London: Routledge.

Faulkner, D. (1995), *International Strategic Alliances*, McGraw-Hill.

Ham, J.C. van and J.F.M. Koppenjan (2002), *Publiek–private samenwerking bij transportinfrastructuur, wenkend of wijkend perspectief* [*Public–Private Partnerships in Transport Infrastructure*] Utrecht: Lemma.

Haynes, L. and N. Roden (1999), 'Commercialising the management and maintenance of trunk roads in the United Kingdom', *Transportation*, **26** (1), 31–54.

Hodge, G. (1996), *Contracting Out Government Services: A Review of International Evidence*, Melbourne: Montech Pty Ltd.

Huxham, C. (2000), 'The challenges of collaborative government', *Public Management Review*, **2**, 337–57.

Huxham, C. and S. Vangen (2000), 'What makes partnerships work?', in S.P. Osborne (ed.) *Public–Private Partnerships; Theory and Practice in International Perspective*, London: Routledge, pp. 293–310.

Jacobs, J. (1992), *Systems of Survival: A Dialogue on the Moral Foundations of Commerce and Politics*, Mississauga, OT: Random House.

Kenniscentrum PPS [Knowledge Centre] (1998), 'Eindrapport Meer Waarde door Samen Werken' ['Final report on added value through cooperation'], The Hague: Ministry of Finance, Projectbureau PPS.

Kenniscentrum PPS [Knowledge Centre] (2001), *Voortgangsrapportage 2001 [Progress Report 2001]* The Hague: Ministry of Finance.

Kenniscentrum PPS (2002), *Voortgangsrapportage 2002 [Progress Report* 2002], The Hague: Ministry of Finance.

Kickert, W.J.M, Klijn and J.F.M. Koppenjam (1997), *Managing Complex Networks, Strategies for the Public Sector*, London: Sage.

Klijn, E.H., J.F.M. Koppenjan and J.C. van Ham (2002), 'Slotbeschouwing: partnerships passing through the night?' ['Conclusion: partnerships passing through the night'] in van Ham and Koppenjan (2002), 457–82.

Klijn, E.H. and G.R. Teisman, (2000), 'Governing public–private partnerships; analysing and managing the processes and institutional characteristics of public–private partnerships', in S.P. Osborne (ed.) *Public–Private Partnerships; Theory and Practice in International Perspective*, London: Routledge.

Klijn, E.H. and G.R. Teisman (2003), 'Institutional and strategic barriers to public–private partnership: an analysis of Dutch cases', *Public Money and Management*, **23** (3), 137–46

Koppenjan, J.F.M. and E.H. Klijn, (2004), *Managing Uncertainties in Networks; A Network Perspective on Problem Solving and Decision Making*, London: Routledge.

Kouwenhoven, V.P. (1991), *Publiek–private samenwerking: mode of model? [Public–Private Cooperation: Mode or Model?]*, Delft: Eburon.

Nooteboom, B. (1998), *Management van Partnerships [Managing Partnerships]*, Schoonhoven: Academic Service.

Osborne, S.P. (ed.) (2000), *Public–Private Partnerships; Theory and Practice in International Perspective*, London: Routledge.

Schon, D.A. and M. Rein (1994), *Frame Reflection: Toward the Resolution of Intractable Policy Controversies*, New York: Basic Books

Sullivan, H. and C. Skelcher (2002), *Working Across Boundaries; Collaboration in Public Services*, Houndsmills Basingstoke: Palgrave.

Teisman, G.R. (1997), *Sturen via creatieve concurrentie [Governance through creative competition]*, Nijmegen: Catholic University of Nijmegen.

Teisman, G.R. (1998), 'Procesmanagement: de basis voor partnerschap?' ['Process management: the basis for partnership?'] *ESB*, **83** (4170), 21–26.

Teisman, G.R. and E.H. Klijn (2000), 'Public–Private partnerships in the European Union: officially suspect, embraced in daily practice', in S.P. Osborne (ed.), *Public–Private Partnerships; Theory and Practice in International Perspective*, London: Routledge, p. 165–86.

Teisman, G.R. and R.J. in 't Veld (1992), *Innovatief investeren in infrastructuur* (studie voor GWWO), The Hague: GWWO.

7. Traditional contracts as partnerships: effective accountability in social services contracts in the American states

Jocelyn M. Johnston and Barbara S. Romzek

The current international trend toward globalization and devolution has given rise to multiple new forms of government service delivery and governance, including public–private partnerships (PPPs).[1] These range from the urban PPPs observed in Europe, perceived by some analysts as 'corporatist forms of governance' (DiGaetano and Strom, 2003), to the heavy reliance of the United States Department of Defense on contractors to deliver post-war reconstruction services in Iraq (Center for Public Integrity, 2003). While the precise definition of a PPP is not yet firmly established (Greve and Hodge, 2004), PPPs are generally understood to entail service delivery partnerships between public and nongovernmental sector agents – partnerships that incorporate the sharing of responsibility, authority, risk, and accountability (Linder and Rosenau, 2000). A substantial portion of the international privatization movement that supports PPPs takes the form of contracting (Reidenbach, 1997). The extensiveness of privatization, PPPs and government contracting has stimulated a keen interest on the part of scholars interested in how these strategies are managed by public officials and their partners (Pollitt and Talbot, 2004; Hodge, 2000).

In the USA and Westminster, models of governance, parallel trends of devolution and government reform have prompted an explosion of government contracting across various levels of state activity (Romzek, 2000). This is especially true in the USA, with shifts in the locus of control for programme delivery and a blurring of the traditional boundaries among governments, private companies and nonprofit organizations across federal, state and local levels of government. In this setting, governments at all levels have expanded the range of services they deliver through contracts – from the traditional 'make–buy' decisions for defence weaponry, highway construction, and refuse collection – to contracting for ongoing provision of specialized services such as programme management for the National Aeronautics and Space Administration (NASA) and state social welfare services (Johnston et al., 2003; US GAO, 2002; Savas, 2000; Sclar, 2000; Salamon, 1999).

Our interest here is in a traditional contracting context, but one that is undergoing substantial change in the USA. The American states are the front line deliverers of most social welfare services, and they have increasingly turned to contracting to reform their delivery systems. Contracting is hardly a new phenomenon for the states, but new programme areas and unprecedented levels of contract complexity raise important questions about how governments and contractors are adapting, and whether governments are able to hold contractors accountable for their performance. As contracts become more complicated and deal with more difficult social welfare programme areas, both sides of the contracting relationships – government and nongovernmental organizations – have begun to refer to each other as 'partners' in service delivery. Thus, although the traditional contracting regime implies a relationship with some hierarchical features, parties in these newer programme contracting areas are engaging in a more collaborative, or 'partnership' style of interaction.

Government workers in the USA are devoting growing portions of their time and resources to managing contracts instead of delivering services (Freundlich and Gerstenzang, 2002; Kettl, 2000), often in the context of diverse expectations such as reducing the size and cost of government, improving service delivery, and increasing accountability. Many of these shifts and reforms are adopted without much attention to accountability issues (Frederickson, 1997; Moe 1984) because of prevailing assumptions that contracting will ensure effective contractor performance, greater clarity and transparency regarding performance responsibilities and easy recourse when contractor performance fails to meet expectations (Light, 2000; Sclar, 2000).

For governments adopting these strategies, designing accountability relationships for partnerships and contracts has become a fundamental objective of programme management. Accountability issues are particularly challenging when government contracts are for services rather than goods, because services require more ongoing managerial attention from government administrators. Furthermore, when contracts for services involve programmes with outcomes that are difficult to define and/or measure, the accountability challenges increase significantly.

There is substantial evidence that, especially in the area of social services, contract managers often fall short (Johnston and Romzek, 2004; Romzek and Johnston, 2002; Fossett et al., 2000; Wright and Perrotti, 2000; McDonald, 1997; US GAO, 1997). This chapter attempts to explain this dynamic, drawing on insights from our work in just such an area – government contracting with nonprofit and for-profit entities for provision of social services in the State of Kansas. We followed an approach similar to that used by Milward and Provan (2000), who propose explanations of effective governance by looking for common patterns across a small number of cases (Yin, 1989).

In our previous research on some of these cases, some of our observations were unexpected. For example, we discovered that the adoption of new information technologies – often touted as essential to contract success – sometimes tended to impede accountability in these cases. We also found that, contrary to other findings (Milward and Provan, 2000), higher levels of risk shifting could reduce contractor accountability. And we observed that in a more competitive, market-like environment with multiple contractors and networks of service deliverers, accountability was especially difficult to achieve, despite the expectations of conventional contracting theories that multiple providers enhance accountability. Our objective here is to explore these patterns in greater detail to better understand when and why government was more effective in securing contractor accountability – that is, when and why government was a 'smart buyer' or 'prudent purchaser' (Fossett et al., 2000; Kettl, 1993).

EFFECTIVE CONTRACT ACCOUNTABILITY

The widespread use of contracts manifests itself in a broad range of approaches to contracting. In the USA, traditional market models of contracting – models that influence many government contracting decisions – rest squarely on the conviction that contractors will be disciplined by market forces such as competition, ease of seller access to the contract market, and ready and inexpensive availability of relevant contractor performance information. The implicit assumption is that nongovernmental organizations are more effective, particularly when they operate in market environments. Accountability under such conditions relies on the market to ensure desirable behaviour (Savas, 2000). Because this ideal contracting setting rarely exists, governments more often engage in 'incomplete' contracting, characterized by frequent transactions among contractual parties and high levels of uncertainty about future situations covered by the contract and about product and/or process (Sclar, 2000a; Hart, 2003). Incomplete contracts are vulnerable to problems of information scarcity, the information asymmetry embedded in principal–agent relationships (McDonald, 1997; Stoker, 1997), adverse selection, and moral hazard.

There is a third approach to public–private engagement – what has been referred to as a relational model (Sclar, 2000) or a corporatist governance model (DiGaetano and Strom, 2003). The relational model appears to be the prevailing model in state social service contracts in the USA. Relational contracting is based upon partnerships and trust between principals and agents in recognition of the absence of market competition and impossibly high information costs. It is in each party's interest in relational contracting to adjust flexibly to the concerns of the other party, regardless of the formal stipulations of the contract (Campbell and Harris, 1998). Teisman and Klijn (2001) make a similar argument based on their research in the United Kingdom, Western Europe and the United States, rejecting the notion of any hierarchy in PPPs and suggesting that joint decision-making replaces the principal–agent relationship envisioned by many contracting theorists. Because of these adjustments and joint decision-making, relational contracting tends to be less susceptible to uncertainty about product and processes, transaction costs, and moral hazards than incomplete contracting. Accountability under this type of contract tends to emphasize articulation and fine tuning of performance expectations through negotiation and mutual experience – what Sclar refers to as 'muddling through' (Sclar, 2000; Lindblom, 1959).

Effective accountability requires adapting structures to institutional strategies or mission (Romzek, 2000; Brown and Moore, 2001). We rely here on Sclar's framework, as well as others provided in the literature on contracting, to explore potential determinants of effective contractor accountability. Effective contractor accountability occurs when the state is able to design, implement, manage and achieve accountability for its social service contracts. This includes obtaining timely and accurate reporting from the contractor and using that reported information to evaluate performance and correct deficiencies. In other words, effectiveness exists when the relevant government agency has achieved the capability to assess contractor performance and the potential to hold the contractor accountable for that performance.

IDENTIFYING POTENTIAL DETERMINANTS OF ACCOUNTABILITY EFFECTIVENESS

As we reviewed our data for previous work on these cases, we had detected patterns of accountability effectiveness that suggested key roles played by a number of contextual factors. This study extends our analysis of those factors, and attempts to probe the observed patterns in greater depth, explain them, and articulate their contribution to contract accountability. All five cases are built around sets of contracts for social services between the State of Kansas and several nongovernmental organizations, most of which are nonprofit. Two of the cases involve components of Medicaid: Medicaid managed care (MMC) for low-income clients (served primarily through health maintenance organizations, or HMOs), and Medicaid funded Home and Community Based Services (HCBS) for the low-income elderly. Jointly financed and administered by the federal government and the fifty states, Medicaid is the largest health programme for the poor in the USA. Two additional cases are related to the delivery of employment preparation services (EPS) under the 1996 federal welfare reform (the Personal Responsibility and Work Opportunity Reconciliation Act). Finally, we include the case of state foster care and adoption (FCA) contracts. The FCA contracts have put Kansas on the 'cutting edge' of foster care/adoption reform, and have generated substantial controversy within and outside the state (Gurwitt, 2000; Freundlich and Gerstenzang, 2002).[2]

We identify several potential determinants of accountability effectiveness, organizing them somewhat arbitrarily into three categories: contract specifications, contract design and accountability design. We briefly review relevant research about each of these factors and our expectations of their impacts on contractor accountability.

Contract Specifications

An important feature of any contract is a clear and mutually understood specification of each party's contract obligations and of how the contractor's performance will be assessed. We focus here on contract specifications as they are manifested in the clarity of accountability relationships and the suitability of performance measurement criteria.

Clarity of accountability relationships

The logic of accountability under contracting requires advance specification of mutual expectations, responsibilities, and obligations of the contracting parties. One challenge of accountability for public managers is the presence of multiple, competing and shifting expectations for performance held by diverse, legitimate, and often conflicting sources of expectations (Klingner et al., 2000; Hayes, 1996; Romzek and Dubnick, 1994; Herman and Heimovics, 1991; Wilson, 1989). Similarly, contractors often face tradeoffs between responsiveness to the principal or purchaser (government) and their own organizational autonomy (Brown and Moore, 2001; Frumkin, 2001; Herman and Heimovics, 1991). Because nonprofits are particularly sensitive to the fact that both funders and clients are 'customers', it is especially important in such situations to be clear about the contractor's responsibilities and the state's expectations. We expect that contracts with clearly articulated responsibilities and reporting relationships are likely to enhance accountability effectiveness.

Suitability of performance measures, obligations and deliverables

Performance measures and deliverables embedded in a contract must provide the state with the information it needs to determine whether and how well the contractor is performing. Parties must agree that the performance measures and deliverables are suitable to the objectives of performance assessment. For example, Heracleous (1999), who studied privatization in Singapore, emphasized the need for clear policy objectives of what privatization is expected to achieve for the state.

Yet the development of suitable performance measures may not be straightforward, particularly for social service programs (Lynn et al., 2000; Behn and Kant, 1999). Grants and contracts to nonprofits have traditionally relied on inputs, process and output indicators, emphasizing staffing loads, funding compliance, and caseload headcounts. Outcome based measures present formidable new challenges, including political disagreements about performance standards (Radin 2003). Other problems relate to the time lag between the program intervention and the desired outcomes and the fact that for social services, contractors are rarely in total control of outcomes (Johnston and Romzek 1999). These issues must be carefully considered when the contract is structured. We expect that accountability effectiveness will be enhanced when contract performance measures and deliverables are suitable for realistic performance assessment.

Contract Design

Several different facets of contract design appear to exert substantial impacts on the effectiveness of contractor accountability. These include the ease of collecting performance data, the autonomy of contractors (or conversely, the extent to which contractors depend on other organizations as they deliver services), the degree of risk retained by the state, and the introduction of new technologies associated with the service delivery and performance measurement.

Ease of performance data collection

Accountability presumes the availability of performance data, whether qualitative or quantitative. In addition to designing suitable performance measures, the state must actually be able to obtain that information in order to evaluate and improve programme effectiveness. Governments often expect performance data to be more readily available than it is in reality (Fossett et al., 2000).

We observed that the capacity of the state to collect performance information may be related to external factors, including the political environment and the extent to which contractors might pressure elected policy makers to reduce reporting burdens. But if the state cannot collect accurate and timely performance data, the source of the difficulty – whether internal or external – is of secondary importance from the perspective of effective policy. Without good performance information, the government is simply unable to adequately assess contractor performance or to make sound decisions about the allocation of resources to maximize programme effectiveness. For example, despite the relatively well developed performance measures available in the field of health care – measures which most observers agree are suitable for assessing health service quality – managed care performance data, sometimes called 'encounter data', have proven to be problematic in most states. This is due to limits in states' capacity to collect the data, incentives in managed care that work against individual provider data submission, and the quality of the data (Landon et al., 1998; Fosset et al., 2000). We expect that accountability effectiveness is enhanced when barriers to obtaining performance information are minimal.

Autonomy of contractor
Social service contracts often require managing accountability through networks of multiple nongovernmental service providers. Just as theorists and government contractors have had to adjust to the phenomenon of multiple principals (Moe, 1984), now scholars and government contract managers must broaden their thinking to accommodate the phenomena of multiple agents, horizontal contractual partnerships, and the accountability challenges of networks (Brown and Moore, 2001; Kettl, 2000). Today's administrators must function in a '"hollow state" with a core of public management surrounded by an array of cross-institutional, primarily extra-governmental ties' (O'Toole and Meier, 1999:99; Milward and Provan, 2000; Milward, 1994; O'Toole, 2000).

The management of networks is not yet well understood, but we know that networks confront public managers with 'wicked problems,' complex coordination tasks and unclear accountability systems (Agranoff and McGuire, 1998; Van Bueren and Klijn, 2003). Yet most government contract managers have been trained in and are experienced with more hierarchical systems (Frederickson, 1997; Kettl, 2000). Traditional bureaucratic hierarchical systems are inherently more stable and conducive to management, while networks, which are more 'fluid', and which provide weaker buffers to external 'shocks', are far more difficult to manage (Milward and Provan, 2000; O'Toole and Meier, 1999).

O'Toole and Meier (1999) use the term 'environmental complexity' to explain the impact of the sheer numbers of organizations and actors in the networks that increasingly characterize social service delivery. Multiple actors threaten 'structural stability,' and instability can reduce the effectiveness of network management (Milward and Provan, 2000). Network 'teams' devoted to solving social problems are less cohesive as the network becomes larger and more diverse, and the capacity of the centralized contract manager declines due to an expanding span of control (Agranoff and McGuire, 1998).

In addition, a contractor may find it difficult to meet performance expectations if a subcontractor or some other actor in the delivery network has failed to do its part (Johnston, 2000). Dependence on other contractors or subcontractors for data collection and analysis will affect not only the ability of the contractors to measure and improve performance, but also the state's ability to understand and evaluate performance. The state's control over information declines as the number of contracting agents grows. We expect that contractor accountability will be enhanced when contractors are relatively autonomous regarding their contractual obligations (or conversely, will be diminished when complex networks of providers are used to deliver services).

Risk retention by the government
Risk shifting is an increasingly common component of government contracts and PPPs (Linder and Rosenau, 2000). In the risk shifting scenario, the contractor is expected to bear some of the burden of identifying strategies that can reduce service costs (Sclar, 2000), creating an incentive for administrative efficiency. In contrast to the Milward and Provan (2000) proposition that risk shifting enhances the governance of networks, our earlier research suggests the opposite (Johnston and Romzek, 2000). Some Kansas social service contractors and subcontractors were exposed to financial instability and/or loss because conditions originally anticipated during contract negotiations sometimes changed substantially (Johnston and Romzek, 2001). In such situations, the contractor may have incentives to reject expensive clients (despite state requirements for service for all eligible clients), or to cut back on staff. These developments can compromise the capacity of the contractor to meet performance expectations and to provide required reports to contract managers or to other contractors. When government sheds risk, the contractor may face incentives to 'game' the system and subvert accountability.

Of course, the allocation of risk must be examined in light of whether contract reimbursement rates are sufficient. Milward (1994:75) notes that contracting offers government the opportunity 'to export its uncertainties'. The contractor must be compensated through a system that is adequate and timely.[3] We expect that accountability effectiveness is enhanced when government retains most of the financial risk associated with programme delivery.

Ease of introduction of new technologies

As nongovernmental agencies take on new and broader social service programmes under contracts, they must often adopt new technologies to handle the breadth and complexity of service delivery and reporting requirements. Because states and other government purchasers strive increasingly to connect funding streams to measurable outcomes, technological capacity has become essential for nongovernmental contractors' organizational survivability and adaptability (Alexander, 2000). Governments see information technology as facilitating accountability by increasing and standardizing both fiscal and programmatic reporting. Yet observers note that, while government and nongovernmental agencies need to develop computer capacity to store, analyse, report and track outcome data, 'few have the software and skills needed to manage outcome data usefully' (Plantz, Greenway and Hendricks, 1997:28).

Our previous research on one social service contract case suggests that the introduction of new technology may interfere with the state's capacity to hold the contractor accountable (Romzek and Johnston, 1999). New technologies and/or information systems were often cited by the government and contractors as major sources of difficulty and friction. This was especially true when the contractors had limited experience with complex information systems or with data driven performance evaluation. We expect that the more complex the new technologies embedded in a contract, the greater the chance that the technological changes will undermine accountability effectiveness.

Accountability Design

Beyond contract specification and design, explicit accountability strategies embedded in contracts can also play a significant role in facilitating the evaluation of contractor performance. Western political democracies have produced webs of accountability relationships that reflect different types of accountability (Bovens, 1998; Romzek, 2000). The USA has relied on four different types: hierarchical, legal, professional and political (Romzek and Dubnick, 1987). While hierarchical accountability is likely to be operative within a contracting agency and can be affected by the presence of a contract, it is not typically part of a contractual relationship. The stability offered by traditional hierarchical models of governance is also lacking in the network systems increasingly used to deliver social services (Lynn et al., 2000; Milward and Provan, 2000; O'Toole and Meier, 1999). As a result, accountability mechanisms employed in managing contracts require varied approaches, especially with networks of providers (Brown and Moore, 2001). Legal, professional and political accountability are critically important to the contracting milieu; each can inform government agencies about contractor activities and thus enhance contract accountability. More importantly, the intensity of each type of accountability may be dictated by the institutional contracting context. Thus, the alignment of the accountability mechanisms must be tailored for each contract situation:

- *Legal accountability* involves detailed external monitoring of performance for compliance with established standards and mandates, typically through formal state oversight and external performance and financial audits (Gregory, 1998; Bardach and Lesser, 1996; Light, 1993; Uhr 1993).
- *Professional accountability* relationships are reflected in work arrangements that afford high degrees of autonomy to individuals or agencies, deference to expertise, ongoing consultation, and emphasis on performance that supports best practices. The traditional Whitehall model, with the dependence of ministers on a professional, nonpartisan civil service for advice (Campbell and Wilson, 1995), is an example of professional accountability. In contracting, this type of accountability is often manifested as acceptance of professional judgments about best strategies for achieving specified outcomes.
- *Political accountability* emphasises discretion in pursuit of responsiveness to key stakeholders, such as the state purchaser of services, state legislators, peer service provider networks, and clientele. Responsiveness to key stakeholders is a common survival skill for nonprofits because of their historic dependence on donors and government grants and contracts for financing (Milward and Provan, 2000; Smith and Lipsky, 1993; Herman and Heimovics, 1991). In a contracting context, this type of accountability relies on external stakeholders' judgments about contractor performance. Stakeholders can use a variety of indicators of performance including output measures such as programme products, donor and client satisfaction, and caseload ratios (Behn and Kant 1999; Light 1993, 2000).
- *Accountability alignments*: while the conditions of accountability are rarely ideal, it is possible to discuss accountability configurations

reflecting an appropriate alignment between managerial strategy and core contract task. Managerial strategies tend to reflect different emphases, including inputs, processes, outputs and/or outcomes (Campbell, 2001). The nature of the core contract tasks can range from routine to complex, the former lending themselves to standardization and rules, the middle ground often involving a mix of routinization and discretion, and the most complex tasks requiring nonroutine responses based upon individual discretion and expertise.

When performance expectations are cast in terms of inputs and tasks are routine, hierarchical accountability, with its emphasis on limited discretion and close supervision, is most appropriate. When performance standards emphasize processes and the tasks are relatively routine, legal accountability relationships can be the most effective. If managerial strategies emphasize outputs and agency tasks are less routine, political accountability relationships, with their emphases on responsiveness to key stakeholders (including clientele) may be most appropriate. Finally, contract performance specified in terms of outcomes, combined with complex agency tasks, tends to require professional accountability relationships. The shaded cells in Figure 7.1 reflect these idealized relationships.

Core task

		Routine			Nonroutine
	Inputs	Hierarchical			
	Process		Legal		
Managerial strategy	Outputs			Political	
	Outcomes				Professional

Source: Romzek and Dubnick, 1994.

Figure 7.1 *'Ideal' accountability alignments: managerial strategy and core task*

In a contracting environment, the presence of several simultaneous accountability relationships is commonplace, as are the less than ideal blended configurations of accountability. The question for this analysis is whether the alignments of accountability types structured into the various contracts are well suited to the managerial strategies and core tasks, bearing in mind that one type of accountability is not necessarily appropriate for each and every circumstance (Romzek and Dubnick, 1994; Brown and Moore, 2001). We expect that accountability effectiveness is enhanced by accountability alignments that are suitable for the institutional environment, managerial strategy, and contracting tasks.

DESCRIBING THE PROPOSED DETERMINANTS OF ACCOUNTABILITY EFFECTIVENESS

The analyses reported here reflect the coauthors' independent and joint assessments of these cases. Our intent is to discern which, if any, of the examined factors play a noteworthy role in accountability effectiveness.[4] We established possible effectiveness scores of low, moderate or high in a comparative sense – that is, a high rating would indicate high relative to the other cases included in the analysis. The bottom row of Table 7.1 displays these scores for each of the five cases.

We then conducted independent assessments of the data (interviews and document reviews) to assign similarly comparative scores to each of the identified determinants – low (1), moderate (2), or high (3) – for each case (see rows in Table 7.1). For example, we concluded that the ease of performance data collection was lowest for the MMC case (a score of 1), and highest for the EPS cases (a score of 3).[5] For the most part, our assessments are based on comparing the cases to one another, but the implicit standard for this comparison is the level of accountability we might expect in an ideal contracting environment. We next provide some detail on how the scores were derived for each of the identified determinants.

Contract Specifications

Clarity of accountability relationships
For the most part, the data from these cases indicate moderate to high levels of clarity regarding reporting relationships. In cases with the highest levels of clarity, the state and its direct contractors were quite clear about their responsibilities to one another. Two cases exhibited less clarity (MMC and HCBS); in these instances, although contractors were fairly well versed in their responsibilities and their relationships to other parties in the program,

Table 7.1   Contract accountability effectiveness: factors affecting accountability in social services contracts

Suggested determinants of accountability effectiveness	Home and community based services (HCBS)	Foster care and adoption (FCA)	Medicaid managed care (MMC)	Employment preparation services–comprehensive (EPS-COMP)	Employment preparation provider agreements
Contract specifications					
Initial clarity of accountability relationships	2*	3	2	3	3
Suitability of performance measures, obligations, and deliverables	2	2	3	3	3
Contract design					
Ease of performance data collection	2	2	1	3	3
Autonomy of contractor	2	1	2	3	3
State retention of risk	2	1	1	2	3
Ease of introduction of new technologies	1	2	2	3	3
Accountability design					
Appropriate accountability alignment	2	3	3	3	2
Column scores (sums of scores)	13	14	14	20	20
Contractor accountability effectiveness**	M	M	M	H	H

Notes:
* Scores are assigned as follows: 1 = low, 2 = moderate, 3 = high.
** Effectiveness ratings (bottom row) are derived from independent assessments, based on interviews and document review.

Table 7.1a   Use of range of accountability strategies in contracting cases

Accountability strategies***	HCBS	FCA	MMC	EPS-COMP	EPS-PA
Legal accountability (compliance)	M	H	H	M	L
Professional accountability (deference)	L	H	H	H	H
Political accountability (responsiveness)	M	M	M	M	H

Note: *** Scores are assigned reflecting intensity of use as follows: L = low; M = moderate; H = high. These scores (described in detail in Appendix 1) were used to determine the appropriate accountability alignment scores in Table 7.1 above.

they reported confusion over contractor obligations and inconsistency between the state's expectations and contract provisions.[6]

Suitability of performance measures, obligations and deliverables

Performance measures and obligations in these cases exhibited moderate to high levels of suitability. Cases with high scores had high levels of understanding and agreement about appropriate performance measures, obligations, and deliverables. The two cases with lower scores (FCA and HCBS) relied upon performance measures that were less well developed.[7]

Contract Design

Ease of performance data collection

The ability of the state to obtain timely and accurate performance data varied substantially across these cases, and was not always directly related to the clarity of the contract with regard to required data or to the suitability of the data. In the two cases that exhausted the most successful performance data collection patterns (both EPS), parties to the contracts were satisfied with the data collection process and with the quality and accuracy of the data; they worked together very closely to fine tune the process and the information. Data were harder to collect in the other cases. The challenge in the FCA case was related to frequently altered performance requirements; nonetheless, the state typically was able to collect the information on the schedule agreed on by all parties. For the HCBS contract, data collection problems stemmed from incompatible data systems. The MMC case presented the most difficulties, featuring the data collection problems typically encountered in other states. Kansas has faced the additional challenges of managing in an environment devoid of competition; hence the state's ability to enforce the performance data requirements of this contract was weakened (Johnston, 2000).

Autonomy of contractor

These cases reflect a range of autonomy levels among contractors. The contractors with the highest levels of autonomy (both EPS), were relatively unencumbered by relationships or dependencies on other organizational entities to fulfill their obligations. The cases with moderate autonomy (MMC and HCBS) involved some interdependencies with other service provides over whom the contractors had no control.

The case characterized by the highest levels of diversity and complexity of relationships among the contractors, the state, and various subcontractors (FCA), best exemplifies the challenges of using networks to deliver services. We scored it lowest on autonomy. The state let contracts to five principal contractors for foster care services; each in turn contracted extensively with a variety of subcontractors for various programme services (foster care residence – institutional or individual, counselling and mental health services, and so on). These interdependent and overlapping networks of service providers blurred the lines of accountability.[8]

Risk retention by the government

These five cases exhibited a range of risk shifting to contractors, typically combined with inadequate reimbursements. The case where the state retained most of the financial risk, the EPS provider agreements, reimbursed providers on a 'head count', or process basis. The moderate risk cases (HCBS and EPS COMP) involved contractors sharing some risk with the state wherein the contractors bore the risk that their costs could be contained within the reimbursement rate.

The high risk cases, MMC and FCA, shifted significant levels of financial risk to the contractors. Using a capitated, or prepaid managed care model, the state required contractors to deliver all required services to all eligible clients, regardless of the costs. In the FCA situation, mental health costs, most of which were provided through subcontracts with mental health organizations throughout the state, exceeded expectations; many contractors experienced significant financial problems as a result.[9] The range and cost volatility of the services provided in the MMC and FCA cases far exceeded those embodied in the comprehensive EPS contract, resulting in substantially higher levels of risk.

Ease of introduction of new technologies

The design of the social service contracts in these cases was often based on the assumption that new technology would facilitate accountability, especially for the reporting and monitoring functions. Yet the cases varied in terms of the ease of introduction and reliance on new technology. The highest scoring cases, both EPS, encountered few requirements for or complications from technologies (new or old). The impact of technology was relatively minor for these cases, when compared to the complications generated for the MMC, FCA and HCBS contractors. For the FCA contractors, the introduction of new technologies varied substantially due to the diversity of contractors' pre-existing technological capacities. Several of the contractors were relatively well equipped to assume the data and reporting requirements associated with the new programme, while others that exhibited low levels of technological capacity were generally able to adapt. Complex new technologies were incorporated into the contracts for both MMC and HCBS. Because both of these programmes are funded through the federal Medicaid program, the contractors had to communicate frequently with the state's fiscal agent, Blue Cross and Blue Shield of Kansas (BCBS), the entity responsible for managing portions of the state's Medicaid information systems, and for client and provider enrollment management. As a result, all contractors in the MMC and HCBS programs had to learn to 'talk' to the BCBS system. This communication requirement was often cumbersome at best, especially in the early stages of the contracts. The impact of new technology was greatest in the HCBS case because the limited nature of the contractors' mission had previously required relatively low levels of technological capacity. As a result, the contractors had to devote substantial resources (financial, staff and time) to upgrading their computer and communications systems to meet their new contractual obligations.

Accountability Design

To better understand whether the accountability strategies embedded in these contracts were aligned with the contract contexts, one must have some understanding of the underlying components of this alignment factor. Since these components determine the accountability alignment, they are not included as separate determinants of contract accountability effectiveness. Table 7.1a summarizes the use of the various accountability strategies in these contracting cases. The scores (low, moderate and high), within the columns reflect the relative intensity of use of the particular accountability strategy for each case. This grid presents a base from which to evaluate the degree to which accountability alignments are appropriate for the various cases, and it provides background for the alignment scores in Table 7.1.

Legal accountability

These cases reflect a range of reliance on monitoring and oversight strategies for accountability. The two cases with the greatest risk shifting, MMC and FCA, exhibited the highest levels of legal accountability, with emphases on auditing and external monitoring based on explicit standards; often these standards are specified in the contract.[10] The comprehensive EPS contract had a strong element of legal accountability at the outset but this was subsequently relaxed, and we therefore assigned a moderate rating to this case. For the HCBS case, moderate levels of legal accountability were manifested through requirements for prior approval for all case plans of care and external audits by state staff who reviewed 100 per cent of case management records annually. In contrast to these other contracts, EPS provider agreements featured low, almost nonexistent levels of legal accountability.

Professional accountability

Four of these five contracting cases manifest a high reliance on professional accountability, with its emphasis on deference to contractor expertise. For these cases, contractors had a great deal of latitude regarding how they accomplished their tasks; contractors had established records of service provision in the contract programme areas and were presumed to know best how to deliver services. Accountability focused on benchmarks and outcomes, such as client health, supportive and permanent home placements for foster care children and sustained employment for welfare recipients. In the low professional accountability case, HCBS, the state was less comfortable deferring to the expertise of the contractor due to concerns about the capacity of the nonprofit contractors to assume responsibilities for the contract. The state designed training and technical assistance programmes to upgrade contractor capacity and offered financial assistance in the form of bridging loans during the first year.

Political accountability

Political accountability, with its emphasis on responsiveness to the contract principal and clientele using predetermined outputs and benchmarks, was most evident in the case of the EPS provider agreements where performance was based on caseloads and client participation. State administrators relied on personal feedback from clients to judge how valuable and effective the services were. The remaining four cases exhibited moderate levels of political accountability, relying on service benchmarks, such as client contact and caseload measures, to evaluate contract performance. Client contact and satisfaction measures were collected, but they were given less emphasis in the overall evaluation of contractor performance.

Appropriate Accountability Alignment

The question of interest with these data is the extent to which the observed accountability approaches are aligned with the managerial strategies and tasks of the contract. The contracting environment, administrative tasks, and managerial strategies in these cases lend themselves to blends of multiple accountability approaches. For the most part, the data suggest that the contracts encompass appropriate alignments with a mix of accountability strategies well suited to the performance expectations. As Table 7.1 indicates, three of the five cases were given high alignment ratings because they use blends of accountability that were compatible with the managerial emphases and contract tasks. (For additional detail regarding how alignment scores were assigned, see Appendix 1.)

ASSESSING THE RELATIONSHIP BETWEEN THE DETERMINANTS AND ACCOUNTABILITY EFFECTIVENESS

The final step in our process represents an attempt to establish whether the observed patterns suggested a relationship between the identified determinants and accountability effectiveness across the five cases. The 'column' scores at the bottom of Table 7.1, which reflect sums of the scores for each determinant in the case, suggest an association between high ratings for the identified determinants and high levels of effectiveness. The highest total column scores for the potential determinants are associated with the highest accountability effectiveness scores – the two EPS cases. In the remaining three cases, the determinants generated lower scores, and overall effectiveness was rated lower, relative to the two EPS cases.

These patterns yield insights into the nature of the relationships between those determinants and effectiveness. Future research is necessary to ascertain whether the patterns we observe hold up in other settings, especially for the more surprising findings. We know, for example, that Milward and Provan (2000) find a positive relationship between risk shifting and the success of mental health contracts in Arizona. That research is at odds with what we observed, and it will be important to better understand that conflict. Similarly, we conclude that when contracts deliver services through networks, accountability is seriously complicated. This seems inconsistent with the notion that a more commercial environment – one that offers a relatively large supply of providers and more closely resembles a competitive context – fosters accountability.[11] And although government reforms often adopt new information technologies with the intent to better manage information and assess contractor performance, our findings suggest that public managers may underestimate the capacity of government and nongovernmental organizations to adapt to technological changes. In view of these findings and their incongruence with research on this topic, independent settings should be used to attempt to verify the patterns reported here.

CONCLUSION

While none of the five contracting cases analysed in this study were problem-free regarding accountability, our data lead us to conclude that for two of the cases, accountability effectiveness was relatively high, with the other three cases exhibiting moderate effectiveness. It appears that in Kansas, state administrators have performed well in terms of specifying social service contracts: that is, constructing contracts for effective accountability. Public managers specified contracts so that they could discern whether contractors were meeting their obligations. Managers of both government and contract agencies used accountability strategies appropriate for the contracting context as defined by contract tasks, managerial emphases and institutional environments.

In the area of contract design, state administrators had less success. Contract managers were often unable to design effective strategies for performance data collection, despite specifying suitable performance measures in the actual contracts. Contract and accountability management were compromised when the state designed contracts around networks of providers and their inherent interdependencies, and when risk was shifted to contractors. Traditional contracting theories predict that relying on networks of providers and shifting risk (both elements that simulate a more commercial environment) should enhance contract and accountability effectiveness. In these cases, those predictions were not borne out. The sheer complexity of the most 'networked' case – the FCA case – hindered accountability and contract management despite the potential benefits of provider competition. Finally, new information management technologies were intended to enhance accountability. In fact, they served as a drag on accountability effectiveness because they sometimes hindered implementation and coordination among contractors and state agencies.

In related research, we have found that, despite differences in the contracting contexts and constraints across the American federal system of governments, the patterns are remarkably similar (Johnston et al., 2003). Whether for local refuse collection or ambulance services, for state social services, or for federal space or transportation security programmes in the wake of the attacks on the World Trade Center on 11 September 2001, effective contract structures and management of contract accountability are elusive goals. The tendency at all levels in the US federal system is to under-invest in several dimensions of contract management: staff numbers, management resources, and monitoring and evaluation activities. This, in turn, leads to difficulties in holding contractors accountable.

While some of the lessons learned from accountability for state social service contracts may not transfer directly to other levels of government in the USA, or to other federalist or unitary systems in the international community, it seems clear that public managers must be prepared to construct accountability strategies that will enhance the management of contracts and PPPs in environments that are often less than ideal. In a contracting system dependent on the 'partnership' concept – collaboration and cooperation – accountability requires relatively complex management techniques (US GAO, 1997).

Contracts represent one significant form of the broader phenomenon of PPPs. The findings reported here suggest several factors that help determine the effectiveness of accountability in a contracting context. Even in fairly straightforward contracting environments, contract management becomes very complicated. For other, more encompassing examples in the range of PPPs, such as joint ventures, even greater management complexity is likely. The task for public managers is to prepare for the appropriate context, and to be ready for the unforeseen developments that typify PPPs, contracts, and other new forms of governance.

NOTES

1. This research has been funded in part by the PricewaterhouseCoopers Endowment for the Business of Government, the Kellogg Foundation through the Rockefeller Institute of Government, and the University of Kansas.
2. The five cases actually incorporate many contracts, primarily because of the relatively large number of FCA contracts and the hundreds of provider agreements the state social service agency maintained for welfare EPS. There are five primary FCA contracts with the state, and dozens of subcontracts between the primary contractors and a wide variety of private organizations. In fact, Kansas was in the process of attempting to build a system to determine the numbers of social service contracts while we were collecting our data.
3. It is very possible that risk shifting could exert different effects for contracts that are outside the social service realm or that generate adequate reimbursements. For example, recent government investigations of Department of Defense overpayment of Halliburton, a company with exclusive and noncompetitive contracts for postwar reconstruction and related services in Iraq, suggest that the cost-plus format used for these contracts, in which government bears all financial risk, have led Halliburton to over-bill the government at best, and to ignore least-cost-purchasing standards (Brinkley, 2004; Center for Public Integrity, 2003).
4. To begin the process of understanding patterns, both coauthors independently assigned overall accountability effectiveness scores to each of the five contracting cases. These scores were based on individual qualitative judgments of administrative processes and outcomes for each of the cases – judgments derived from assessments of data gathered during in-depth interviews with elected officials, state administrators, contracting agency administrators, and case workers, as well as documentary reviews, reviews of administrative histories and various external audits and evaluations of the contracted programmes. We conducted over 80 interviews across the five cases, and several of the interviews included more than one respondent. Using semi-structured personal interviews, we asked officials to respond to a standard list of questions designed to identify key issues in the cases. To supplement the interview data, we obtained and reviewed a number of relevant administrative and legislative documents, and press reports. The use of both types of data enabled us to better understand the impetus for the actual contracting decision, as well as its implementation.
5. Our scores for each determinant were assigned independently – each of the two authors derived ratings separately. We then compared ratings, most of which were compatible. In those instances where we disagreed, we discussed the rating, our judgements, and reconciled our differences. Note that the range of scores varies. For example, there was less variation in contract specification scores than for contract design scores. Each determinant was expected to exert a positive impact on accountability effectiveness. For example, we focused on the autonomy of the contractor – expected to have a positive influence on effectiveness – as opposed to the contractor's dependence on other agencies and

organizations, which we would expect to inhibit effectiveness. This was done in order to derive the column scores in the table (that is, the positive impacts of the determinants), which are discussed later in the paper.

6. The MMC case involved three primary contracts – the HMO that delivered managed health care services, and two others related to administration and oversight, including client and provider enrollment, consumer complaints administration, provider performance reports and quality reviews. The two administrative contractors relied on information submitted by the HMO contractor(s). (For most of Kansas's MMC history, the state has been able to solicit only one HMO contract, despite its attempts to generate competition and multiple providers.)

7. The state, in collaboration with the contractors, frequently altered the FCA performance measures, as well as the schedule and form of deliverables. In the HCBS case, the capacity of the contractors to meet their performance reporting obligations was compromised in part by the challenge of adapting their operations to the larger, more complex, and highly regulated Medicaid program. Performance data varied from case to case. For the EPS comprehensive contract, the performance data included client outcomes: number of clients placed in employment, levels of pay and availability of employment benefits associated with the employment. For the EPS provider agreements, performance data were based on more traditional contact (or process) data, such as the number of clients who attended job training sessions, were counselled about job search strategies and so on. Performance data for the HCBS contracts included number of clients served, level of services provided, and assessments of appropriateness of client plans of care. For the MMC case, performance data consisted of the widely used 'encounter data,' which simulate insurance claims – contact, diagnosis, and so on. These were to be incorporated into outcome reports that tied the encounter data to such benchmarks as reductions in emergency room use and reduced asthma inpatient admissions. FCA performance data included number of clients, number of foster home placements per client, timeliness of foster home placements, stability of placements, and timeliness of permanent adoption placement.

8. When FCA subcontractors disagreed with payment authorization decisions made by primary contractors with the state, they tended to appeal directly to the state for relief, effectively going over the head of the organization with which they contracted and to which they were directly accountable. In some instances, there was disagreement between contractors and subcontractors over whether the contractor had authorized services.

9. At least two FCA contractors threatened bankruptcy, and several subcontractors settled for fractions of their scheduled reimbursements. In fact, one widely respected contractor, Lutheran Social Services, lost its adoption contract with the state in the latest round of contract bids, and only avoided bankruptcy when its subcontractors agreed to accept $0.74 on each dollar owed them (Associated Press, 2000).

10. The MMC programme also entailed extensive auditing and reporting to the state welfare agency and its two administrative contractors, mostly because of strict compliance required by federal regulations. State courts and state oversight agencies are significant actors in the legal accountability associated with the FCA contracts. Scrutiny of FCA contractor decisions occurs when the courts rule on child custody issues, in periodic monitoring by the state's Division of Legislative Post Audit, and in licensing decisions made by the state agency responsible for monitoring group foster homes.

11. Rosenau (2000) argues that PPPs work best when competition is minimized so that collaboration can flourish.

REFERENCES

Agranoff, Robert and Michael McGuire (1998), 'Multinetwork management: collaboration and the hollow state in local economic policy', *Journal of Public Administration Research and Theory*, **8** (1), 67–91.

Alexander, Jennifer (2000), 'Adaptive strategies of nonprofit human service organizations in an era of devolution and new public management', *Nonprofit Management and Leadership*, **10** (3), 287–303.

Associated Press (2000), 'Adoption pact puts Lutheran back in picture: network stable, SRS maintains', *Lawrence Journal World*, 23 September.

Bardach, Eugene and Cara Lesser (1996), 'Accountability in human services collaboratives: for what? And to whom?', *Journal of Public Administration Research and Theory*, **6** (2),197–224.

Behn, Robert and Peter A. Kant (1999), 'Strategies for avoiding the pitfalls of performance contracting', *Public Productivity and Management Review*, **22** (4), 470–89.

Bovens, Mark (1998), *The Quest for Responsibility: Accountability and Citizenship in Complex Organisations*, New York: Cambridge University Press.

Brinkley, Joel (2004), 'Halliburton likely to be a campaign issue', *New York Times*, 14 February.

Brown, L. David, and Mark H. Moore (2001), 'Accountability, strategy, and international nongovernmental organizations', *Nonprofit and Voluntary Sector Quarterly*, **30** (3), 569–87.

Campbell, Colin (2001), 'Juggling inputs, outputs, and outcomes in the search for policy competence: recent experience in Australia', *Governance*, **13** (2), 253–82.

Campbell, D. and D. Harris (1993), 'Flexibility in long-term contractual relationships: the role of co-operation', *Journal of Law and Society*, **20** (2), 166–91.

Campbell, Colin and Graham Wilson (1995),*The End of Whitehall: A Comparative Perspective*, Cambridge, MA: Blackwell.

Center for Public Integrity (2003), 'Winning Contractors: US contractors reap the windfalls of post-war reconstruction', October 30.

DiGaetano, Alan and Elizabeth Strom (2003), 'Comparative urban governance: an integrated approach', *Urban Affairs Review*, **38** (3), 356–95.

Fossett, James W., Malcolm Goggin, John S. Hall, Jocelyn M. Johnston, Richard Roper, L. Christopher Plein, and Carol Weissert (2000), 'Managing Medicaid managed care: are states becoming prudent purchasers?', *Health Affairs*, July/ August, 39–49.

Frederickson, H. George (1997), *The Spirit of Public Administration*, San Francisco: Jossey Bass.

Freundlich, Madelyn and Sarah Gerstenzang (2002), *An Assessment of the Privatization of Child Welfare Services: Challenges and Successes*, New York: Children's Rights.

Frumkin, Peter (2001), *Managing for Outcomes: Milestone Contracting in Oklahoma*, Arlington, VA: PricewaterhouseCooper's Endowment for The Business of Government.

Gregory, Robert (1998), 'Political responsibility for bureaucratic incompetence: tragedy at Cave Creek', *Public Administration*, **76**, 519–38.

Greve, Carsten and Graeme Hodge (2004), 'Introduction', in Graeme Hodge and Carsten Greve (eds), *The Challenge of Public–Private Partnerships – Learning from International Experience*, Cheltenham UK and Northampton, MA, USA: Edward Elgar.

Gurwitt, Rob (2000), 'The lonely leap', *Governing*, July, 38–44.

Hart, O. (2003), 'Incomplete contracts and public ownership: remarks and an application to public–private partnerships', *The Economic Journal*, **113**, C69–76.

Hayes, Treasa (1996), *Management, Control and Accountability in Nonprofit/ Voluntary Organizations*, Ipswich, Suffolk: Ipswich Book Company.

Heracleous, Loizos (1999), 'Privatization: global trends and implications on the Singapore experience', *The International Journal of Public Sector Management*, **12** (5), 432–44.

Herman, Robert D. and Richard D. Heimovics (1991), *Executive Leadership in Nonprofit Organizations*, San Francisco: Jossey-Bass.

Hodge, Grame A. (2000), *Privatization: An International Review of Performance*, Boulder, CO: Westview Press.

Johnston, Jocelyn M. (2000), *Implementing Medicaid Managed Care in Kansas: Politics, Economics and Contracting* (Case Studies in Medicaid Managed Care Series), Albany, NY: The Rockefeller Institute of Government.

Johnston, Jocelyn M. and Barbara S. Romzek (1999), 'Contracting and accountability in state Medicaid reform: rhetoric, theories, and reality', *Public Administration Review*, **59** (5), 383–99.

Johnston, Jocelyn M. and Barbara S. Romzek (2000), *Implementing State Contracts for Social Services: An Assessment of the Kansas Experience*, May, Washington, DC: PricewaterhouseCooper's Endowment for the Business of Government.

Johnston, Jocelyn M. and Barbara S. Romzek (2001), 'Examining the stability hypothesis: comparing stable and dynamic systems in social service contracts', paper presented at the 6th National Public Management Research Conference, Bloomington, IN, October.

Johnston, Jocelyn M. and Barbara S. Romzek (2004), 'Contracting and accountability: a model of effective contracting drawn from the US experience', in Christopher Pollitt and Colin Talbot (eds), *Unbundled Government: A Critical Analysis of the Global Trend to Agencies, Quangos and Contractualisation*, London: Routledge.

Johnston, Jocelyn M., Barbara S. Romzek and Curtis H. Wood (2003), 'The challenges of contracting and accountability across the federal system: from ambulances to space shuttles', paper presented at the National Public Management Research Conference, 9–11 October, Washington, DC.

Kettl, Donald F. (1993), *Sharing Power: Public Governance and Private Markets*, Washington, DC: Brookings Institution.

Kettl, Donald F. (2000), 'The transformation of governance: globalization, devolution, and the role of government', discussion paper prepared for the Spring meeting presented at the National Academy of Public Administration, Albuquerque, NM, 1–3 June.

Khademian, Anne M. (2000), 'Is silly putty manageable? Looking for the links between culture, management, and context', in Laurence O'Toole, Jr and Jeffrey L. Brudney (eds), *Advancing Public Management: New Developments in Theory, Methods, and Practice*, Washington, DC: Georgetown University Press, 33–8.

Klingner, Donald, John Nalbandian, and Barbara S. Romzek (2002), 'Politics, administration and markets: conflicting expectations and accountability', *American Review of Public Administration*, **32** (2),117–44.

Landon, Bruce, Carol Tobias and Arnold Epstein (1998), 'Quality management by state Medicaid agencies converting to managed care', *JAMA*, **279** (3), 211–16.

Light, Paul (1993), *Monitoring Government: Federal Inspectors General and the Search for Accountability*, Washington, DC: Brookings Institution.

Light, Paul (2000), *Making Nonprofits Work: A Report on the Tides of Nonprofit Management Reform*, Washington, DC: Brookings Institution.

Lindblom, Charles E. (1959), 'The science of muddling through', *Public Administration Review*, **19** (Spring), 79–88.

Linder, Stephen H. and Pauline Vaillancourt Rosenau (2000), 'Mapping the Terrain of the Public–private Policy Partnership', in Pauline Vaillancourt Rosenau (ed), *Public–Private Policy Partnerships*, Massachusetts Institute of Technology, 1–18.

Lynn, Laurence E., Carolyn J. Heinrich, and Carolyn J. Hill (2000), 'Studying governance and public management: challenges and prospects', *Journal of Public Administration Research and Theory,* **10** (2) 233–61.

McDonald, Catherine (1997), 'Government, funded nonprofits, and accountability', *Nonprofit Management and Leadership*, **8** (1), 51–64.

Milward, H. Brinton (1994), 'Nonprofit contracting and the hollow state', *Public Administration Review*, **54** (1), 73–7.

Milward, H. Brinton and Keith G. Provan (2000), 'Governing the hollow state', *Journal of Public Administration Research and Theory*, **10** (2), 359–79.

Moe, Terry M. (1984), 'The new economics of organization', *American Journal of Political Science*, **28**, 739–77.

O'Toole, Laurence J., Jr (2000), 'Research on policy implementation: assessment and prospects', *Journal of Public Administration Research and Theory*, **10** (2), 233–62.

O'Toole, Laurence J., Jr and Kenneth J. Meier (1999), 'Modeling the impact of public management: implications of structural context', *Journal of Public Administration Research and Theory*, **9** (4), 505–26.

Plantz, Margaret C., Martha Taylor Greenway and Michael Hendricks (1997), 'Outcome measurement: showing results in the nonprofit sector', in Kathryn E. Newcomer (ed.), *Using Performance Measurement to Improve Public and Nonprofit Programs*, San Francisco: Jossey-Bass.

Pollitt, Christopher and Colin Talbot (eds) (2004), *Unbundled Government: A Critical Analysis of the Global Trend to Agencies, Quangos and Contractualisation*, London: Routledge.

Radin, Beryl A. (2003), 'A comparative approach to performance management: contrasting the experience of Australia, New Zealand and the United States', presented at the 2003 National Public Management Research Conference, Washington DC, 9–11 October.

Reidenbach, Michael (1997), 'The Privatization of Urban Services in Germany', in Dominique Lorrain and Gerry Stoker (eds), *Privatization of Urban Services in Europe,* London: Pinter, 79–104.

Romzek, Barbara S. (2000), 'Dynamics of public sector accountability in an era of reform', *International Review of Administrative Sciences*, **66** (March), 19–42.

Romzek, Barbara S. and Melvin J. Dubnick (1987), 'Accountability in the public sector: lessons from the Challenger tragedy', *Public Administration Review*, **47** (May/June), 227–38.

Romzek, Barbara S. and Melvin J. Dubnick (1994), 'Issues of accountability in flexible personnel systems', in Patricia W. Ingraham and Barbara S. Romzek (eds), *New Paradigms for Government: Issues for the Changing Public Service*, San Francisco: Jossey-Bass.

Romzek, Barbara S. and Jocelyn M. Johnston (1999), 'Reforming Medicaid through contracting: the nexus of implementation and organizational culture', *Journal of Public Administration Research and Theory*, **9** (1),107–39.

Romzek, Barbara S. and Jocelyn M. Johnston (2002), 'Contract implementation and management effectiveness: a preliminary model', *Journal of Public Management Research and Theory*, **12** (3), 423–53.

Rosenau, Pauline Vaillancourt (2000), 'The strengths and weaknesses of public–private policy partnerships', in Pauline Vaillancourt Rosenau (ed.), *Public–Private Policy Partnerships*, Cambridge, MA: MIT Press, 217–42.

Salamon, Lester M. (1999), *America's Nonprofit Sector: A Primer*, Foundation Center, Revised Edition.

Savas, E.S. (2000), *Privatization and Public–Private Partnerships*, New York: Chatham House Publishers.

Sclar, Elliott D. (2000), *You Don't Always Get What You Pay For: The Economics of Privatization*, Ithaca, NY: Cornell University Press.

Smith, Steven Rathgeb and Michael Lipsky (1993), *Nonprofits for Hire: The Welfare State in the Age of Contracting*, Cambridge, MA: Harvard University Press.

Stoker, Gerry (1997), 'Conclusion: privatization, urban government, and the citizen', in Dominique Lorrain and Gerry Stoker (eds), *Privatization of Urban Services in Europe*, London: Pinter, 204–12.

Teisman, G.R. and E.H. Klijn (2001), 'Public–private partnerships in the European Union: official suspect, embraced in daily practice', in Stephen P. Osborne (ed.), *Public–Private Partnerships: Theory and Practice in International Perspective*, London: Routledge.

US General Accounting Office (1997), 'Privatization: Lessons Learned by State and Local Governments', *GAO-97-48*, June.

US General Accounting Office (2002), 'Welfare reform: federal oversight of state and local contracting can be strengthened', *GAO-02-661*, June.

US General Accounting Office (2003), 'Military operations: a report to the Subcommittee on Readiness and Management Support, Committee on Armed Services, US Senate', *GAO-03-695*, June.

Van Bueren, Ellen M. and Erik-Hans Klijn (2003), 'Dealing With wicked problems in networks: analyzing and environmental debate from a network perspective', *Journal of Public Administration Research and Theory*, **13** (2), 193–214.

Wilson, James Q. (1989), *Bureaucracy: What Government Agencies Do and Why They Do It*, New York: Basic Books.

Wright, Vincent and Luisa Perrotti (2000), 'Institutional framework for privatization', in Vincent Wright and Luisa Perrotti (eds), *Privatization and Public Policy: Volume II*, Cheltenham, UK and Northampton, MA, USA: Edward Elgar Publishing, 149–203.

Yin, Robert (1989), *Case Study Research: Design and Methods*, Newbury Park, CA: Sage.

APPENDIX 1

Scoring the Alignment of Accountability Strategies in Kansas Social Service Contracts

To better understand whether the accountability strategies embedded in these contracts were aligned with the contract contexts, one must have some understanding of the underlying components of this 'alignment' factor (see Table 7.1). Table 7.1a describes the use of the various accountability strategies in the five contracting cases. The scores (low, moderate and high), within the columns reflect the relative intensity of use of the particular accountability strategy for each case. This grid presents a base from which to evaluate the degree to which accountability alignments are appropriate, based on the management emphases and core tasks associated with each case, and it provides background for the alignment scores in Table 7.1.

As Table 7.1 indicates, three of the five cases were given high alignment ratings because they use blends of accountability that emphasize alignments compatible with the managerial emphases and contract tasks. In the comprehensive EPS contract, the managerial strategy emphasizes outcomes, with performance payments explicitly tied to successful placements and additional bonuses for sustained employment. The task is fairly complex: to provide welfare clients with job skills necessary to make a successful transition to sustained workforce participation. We place this task three-quarters of the way toward the non-routine end of the task complexity continuum (Figure 7.1). The blend of political and professional accountability is well suited to the performance emphases of the contract, resulting in a high score for accountability alignment.

In the MMC case, the contracts reflect multiple managerial emphases: processes (treatment of clients, intake procedures, etc), outputs (reimbursement based on client enrolment), and outcomes (a goal of improved access and health status for welfare clients). The core task is highly complex and involves substantial professional judgment. Given these facets of the programme, the accountability alignment should be a blend of legal, political and professional strategies; in fact, all three types are in evidence.

The FCA contracts embody several managerial emphases: processes (quickly taking custody of the child, a 'no reject' policy) outputs (number of cases, benchmarks regarding length of time in the foster care system) and outcomes (reimbursement schedule based on client movement through the system). The dozens of benchmarks listed in the original contracts were subject to renegotiations when initial targets proved to be unrealistic. The nature of the contract management task reflects a range of complexity. Some tasks require compliance with legal mandates, others represent complex professional judgments of highly individualized cases, and somewhere in the middle of the range of complexity is the challenge of case management, mental health counselling, and long-term placement of children from abusive homes. The mix of tasks and managerial emphases indicates that a blend of accountability types would be well suited to these contracts. We find a suitable blend of legal (in the sustained role of courts and audits), political (extensive periodic outside evaluations of contractor performance) and professional accountability (reimbursements based on 'success' finding permanent child placements).

For the EPS provider agreements, the tasks involve discrete activities (resume preparation, job search) and the managerial strategy for such contracts emphasizes outputs, such as the numbers of clients who attend job training sessions. The core task is about mid-way on the routine–nonroutine continuum, so political accountability would be the best alignment because it relies on the contractor's discretion to decide which job preparation programmes to offer. The state evaluates contractor performance based upon head count and contact hours, reflecting an outputs approach. Political accountability strategies are the ones most frequently in evidence. Yet the presence of professional accountability, as reflected in deference to contractors to decide how best to improve client job readiness, is an example of complementary accountability strategy that is less than ideal in its alignment. It is complementary because professional strategy still affords discretion needed for the task. It is less than ideal because it does not emphasize or measure employment outcomes. As a result we rate this case as moderate on accountability alignment.

In the HCBS case, managerial emphases reflect a combination of inputs, process and outputs. Multi-faceted tasks under the contract reflect some routine tasks, like forms and documentation, and there are other fairly complex tasks requiring professional judgments, such as developing plans of care that allow the frail elderly to continue living independently. As a result of the range of tasks, a blend of accountability types is appropriate: legal for the process items such as eligibility, professional for the complex judgments about mental acuity and physical independence, and political accountability emphasizing billing by client caseload. In practice the contract relies mostly on legal and political, with very little professional deference; we rate it as moderate on accountability alignment.

8.   United States: human services

Lawrence L. Martin

INTRODUCTION

In the United States (USA), most human services are provided by the 50 states. The US federal government provides substantial funding, frequently with matching or cost sharing requirements, but actual service delivery is generally delegated to the states. The states have three major options in terms of how human services are delivered: (1) direct state provision, (2) subvention to county governments,[1] or (3) private sector delivery. In the United States, the term 'private sector' includes both non-governmental organizations (NGOs) as well as for-profit business firms (Martin, 2000; 1999a).

The involvement of the private sector in the delivery of human services has a long history in the USA. For reasons perhaps unique to the USA, this relationship has primarily involved the use of contracting. This chapter argues that over the last 25 years two major models (the market model and the partnership model) have competed for dominance in human service contracting. In recent years, however, a new 'tool' of human service contracting (performance-based contracting) has appeared on the scene. While it is too early to say with confidence, PBC may be the mechanism that will lead to more public–private partnerships in human service contracting (Martin, 2005, 2004b, 2002; Thomson, 2002).

THE MARKET MODEL AND PARTNERSHIP MODEL OF HUMAN SERVICE CONTRACTING

Human services contracting in the USA has been influenced by two competing paradigms, the market model and the partnership model (Kettner and Martin, 1998, 1987, 1986). In the market model, the role of US state and county governments is viewed as one of promoting competition in the delivery of human services. The relationship between the public and private sectors is viewed as one of buyer and seller. When selecting contractors, little or no distinction is generally made between NGOs and for-profit business firms. Short term (generally one year) contracts are preferred and cost and price considerations tend to drive the decision making process. The tenets of the market model are compatible with the basic arguments advanced by pro-privatization adherents (such as Savas, 2000).

The alternative model of human service contracting is one of public–private sector partnership. In the partnership model, US state and county governments view the public and private sectors as constituting one comprehensive human service system. When making choices between private sector partners, the stability and sustainability of the human service system is the paramount consideration (Kettner and Martin, 1996, 1986). In the partnership mode, long term stable relationships with private sector entities, preferably NGOs, are preferred.

Fast forwarding to the present day, contracting continues to be the major mode of human service delivery in the USA. Some researchers speculate that by the year 2010 as much as 80 per cent of all human service funding in the USA will involve contracts (Martin, 2001a; Lauffer, 1997). Today, there is also more discussion in the USA about partnership contracting than in the past (Agranoff, 2003; Lawther, 2002; Salamon, 2002). However, many US state and county government human service agencies still must operate under traditional public procurement laws and regulations predicated upon the existence of a buyer/seller relationship, not a partnerships relationship (Martin and Miller, 2005). The lack of an appropriate contracting tool (Salamon, 2002) that can operate within traditional public procurement laws and regulations has hindered the ability of many US state and local governments to create true public–private partnerships. Consequently, the success of recent experiments with performance-based contracting (PBC) has attracted considerable attention. PBC may be the solution to creating public–private partnerships within the framework of a buyer/seller legal relationship.

PERFORMANCE-BASED CONTRACTING (PBC): THE NEW TOOL

Performance-based contracting (PBC) can be defined as 'an approach that focuses on the outputs, quality and outcomes of service provision and may tie at least a portion of a contractor's compensation as well as any contract extension or renewal to their accomplishment' (Martin, 1999b:1, 8). PBC is one of the hottest topics in human service contracting today (Martin, 2002). For example, the US federal government has established a goal of transitioning 50 per cent of its service contracts to PBC by fiscal year 2005 (US GAO, 2001).

The difference between PBC and more traditional human service contracting in the USA is perhaps best understood by resort to what can be called the 'expanded systems framework'. As Figure 8.1 illustrates, inputs involve what goes into a human service including: client characteristics, staff qualifications, facilities, equipment, funding and so on. Process issues involve how the human service is delivered in terms of service definitions, treatment modalities, service tasks and other considerations.

Outputs, sometimes referred to as 'units of service,' are measures of the amount of service provided. Quality is concerned with the various dimensions of service quality (e.g. timeliness, reliability, conformity, etc.) from the perspective of service recipients (quality management), professionals (quality assurance) or both. Outcomes are the results, impacts or accomplishments of service provision attributable at least partially to the service or programme. In the human services, outcomes are usually measured by quality of life changes in service recipients (Martin and Kettner, 1996). In theory, PBC suggests that *input* and *process* accountability should be replaced with *output*, *quality* and *outcome* performance accountability.

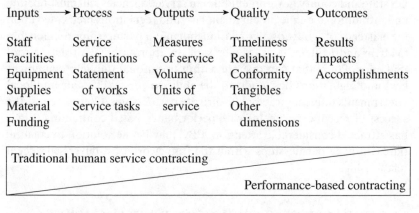

Figure 8.1   The expanded systems framework and PBC

THE BENEFITS OF PERFORMANCE-BASED CONTRACTING (PBC)

As a new tool of human service contracting, PBC has several major advantages. First, and perhaps foremost, PBC provides a mechanism for US state and county governments to create more public–private partnerships.

PBC enables US state and county governments and contractors to more closely align their interests by focusing on a few jointly agreed upon and precisely defined output, quality and outcome performance measures. The specification of valid outcome performance measures is frequently referred to as the 'Achilles' heal' of PBC. However, US state and county governments have made significant progress in recent in years in the development of generally agreed upon output, quality and outcome performance measures for human service programmes (see Arizona DES, 2003; Florida DCF, 2000; Oklahoma DRS, n.d.).

Second, PBC provides a way of reducing the transactions costs associated with the administration and monitoring of human service contracts. The cost of producing any service is comprised of both production costs and transaction costs (Martin and Miller, 2005; Martin, 2003; Williamson, 1985, 1975). Applied to human services contracting, production costs represent the reimbursements or payments governments make to contractors for providing services. Transaction costs are the costs incurred by governments in conducting the procurement or tendering process, administering contracts and monitoring contractor service delivery. Because PBC focuses on a few precisely defined output, quality and outcome performance measures, and not on detailed inputs and process measures, contract administration and monitoring is less complicated, less time consuming and less costly. US state and county governments benefit from reduced contract administration and monitoring costs associated with the change in focus from inputs and process to a focus on performance. Human service contractors benefit from the increased flexibility that comes with less government emphasis on, and control over, inputs and process.

Third, in keeping with guidance provided by the Office of Economic Cooperation and Development (OECD, 1999), PBC provides a risk sharing mechanism for performance failure. In any partnership, the risks as well as the rewards should be shared by the partners. The question is, to what extent? PBC for human services is not a single approach, but a collection of approaches. Each approach has different risk sharing implications for governments and contractors. In some PBC approaches, the risk of performance failure is shared equally. In other approaches, more of the risk for performance failure is allocated to governments or to contractors.

Fourth, PBC has the potential to significantly increase the volume and quality of human services provided by US state and county governments as well as the numbers of client outcomes achieved. Assessments of US state PBC human service efforts to date report significant increases in all three of these performance areas (eg. Martin, 2001b; Commons et al., 1997; Paulsell and Wood, 1999; Vinson, 1999).

In the following section, the PBC approaches of some selected US state human service agencies are reviewed. The discussion is restricted to state contracting for job training and child welfare services which have made the most use of PBC.

STATE APPROACHES TO PBC FOR JOB TRAINING AND CHILD WELFARE SERVICES

This section looks at the application of PBC by a small purposeful sample of state human service agencies. The five case examples are introduced in the order of their complexity with an emphasis on how the risk for performance failure is allocated between governments and contractors. The point should be stressed that the case examples represent a 'snap shot' of various state PBC approaches at a particular point in time. US state human service agency approaches to PBC are constantly changing and evolving as more experience is gained and more lessons are learned.

Massachusetts Department of Social Services

The Massachusetts Department of Social Services (Massachusetts DSS) has used PBC for permanency services for adolescents as part of a programme called 'Massachusetts Commonworks'. Contractors are compensated based on a case rate (a fee per child per month) that covers the cost of care. Contractors are also eligible to receive incentive, or bonus, payments for achieving certain process, output and outcome performance objectives. For example, contractors can earn incentive payments for closing a case (output) and achieving a permanent placement for six months (outcome) (Sahonchik, 1999:4).

In addition to earning incentive payments, contractors also incur some financial risk for cost overruns. If actual expenses on a per child basis are greater than the sum of the case rate payments plus any incentive payments, the contractors are responsible for those costs up to 103 per cent (Sahonchik, 1999).

In this approach to PBC for human services, the greatest proportion of the risk for performance failure is allocated to the government with only a small proportion being allocated to contractors.

Kansas Department of Social and Rehabilitative Services

The Kansas Department of Social and Rehabilitative Services (Kansas SRS) uses PBC for several child welfare services including family preservation, foster care and adoption (Kansas SRS, 2001; Gurwett, 2000; Martin 2001b). The original Kansas SRS approach to PBC was one of the boldest such initiatives ever undertaken by a US state human service agency (Johnston and Romzek, 2000; Petr and Johnson, 1999; Eggers, 1997). The original Kansas SRS approach can be thought of as PBC for outcomes within a managed care environment. This approach to PBC for human services essentially allocated the bulk of the risk for performance failure to contractors.

Neither the Kansas SRS, nor its contractors, had extensive experience with PBC. This inexperience, combined with the contractors' general lack of valid and reliable service utilization and cost data, significantly increased their financial risk. With the benefit of hindsight, it becomes clear that neither the Kansas SRS nor its contractors fully understood or appreciated the financial risks involved. As one might expect, several contractors found themselves in financial difficulty (Gurwett, 2000; State of Kansas, 2000). As a result, the Kansas SRS abandoned its managed care approach and changed to a 'milestone' approach to PBC.

Under a milestone approach to PBC, individual service recipients are treated as individual projects. Each service recipient has a definable start point (entrance into service), end point (exit from service) and major milestones along the way. Milestone contracting can involve any combination of inputs, process, outputs, quality or outcomes. Milestone contracting is perhaps best explained by the use of an illustration. Table 8.1 shows the Kansas SRS approach to milestone PBC for adoption services. A case rate (a fee per child) is established for each contractor. The contractor is paid a proportion of the case rate every time a specific milestone is accomplished for an individual child. For example, when a contractor achieves a permanent placement for a child (an outcome milestone), it receives 25 per cent of its case rate. The remainder (75 per cent) of the contractor's case rate is tied to input and process milestones.

Table 8.1   Kansas SRS milestone PBC

Milestone	Type of milestone	Case rate (%)
1. Child referred to contractor	Input	[25]
2. Contractor sends first 60-day report to Kansas SRS	Process	[25]
3. Contractor sends formal 180-day case plan to Kansas SRS	Process	[25]
4. Contractor achieves permanent placement for child	Outcome	[25]

Source: Adapted from NCWRCOI (1999).

The proportion of the risk for performance failure allocated to contractors is considerably less under the new Kansas SRS approach to PBC, then under the older approach. Contractors can earn 75 per cent of their case rates by accomplishing three non- performance milestones. Nevertheless, 25 per cent of their case rate is directly tied to outcome performance. This approach to PBC for human services is more in keeping with the notion of partnership and takes into consideration the contracting sophistication of contactors as well as how much risk for performance failure contractors can, and should, be asked to assume.

Oklahoma Department of Rehabilitative Services

The Oklahoma Department of Rehabilitation Services (Oklahoma DRS) also uses milestone PBC to provide job training and job placement services for persons with disabilities (Oklahoma DRS, n.d.; Frumkin, 2001). Table 8.2 illustrates the Oklahoma DRS approach to milestone PBC.

Table 8.2   Oklahoma DRS milestone PBC

Milestone	Type of milestone	Case rate (%)
Determination of need	Process	10
Vocational preparation	Process	10
Job placement	Output	10
Job training	Process	10
Job retention	Quality/outcome	15
Job stabilization	Quality/outcome	20
Case closure (client rehabilitated)	Outcome	25

Source: Adapted from Oklahoma DRS (n.d.); Obrien and Cook (n.d.) and Frumkin (2001).

The Oklahoma DRS approach to milestone PBC is similar to the Kansas SRS approach in that contractors are paid a proportion of their case rate for achieving a mixture of process, output, quality and outcome milestones. The Oklahoma approach is qualitatively different in that a substantial proportion (70 per cent) of a contractor's case rate is directly tied to performance (output, quality and outcome).

The proportion of risk for performance failure allocated to contractors under the Oklahoma DRS approach is high (70 per cent). If a particular contractor fails to accomplish all performance milestones for a service recipient, there is no apparent way that the contractor can escape losing money on that client. On the up side, most of the private sector partners have several years of reliable service utilization and cost data and consequently are able to forecast their performance and costs with a high degree of accuracy.

Pennsylvania Department of Welfare

The Pennsylvania Department of Welfare (Pennsylvania DW) has used yet another variation of milestone PBC to implement an experimental jobs programme called 'Community Solutions'. The purpose of the programme is to transition individuals from welfare to work. Again, the Pennsylvania DW pays contractors for the accomplishment of specific milestones. The Pennsylvania DW approach is illustrated in Table 8.3.

As Table 8.3 demonstrates, the Pennsylvania DW's approach to milestone PBC is not based on a case rate, like those of Kansas and Oklahoma, but rather on a fixed fee. Contractors are paid a fixed-fee for the accomplishment of specific milestones. For example, contractors receive a fixed fee payment of $1000 for placing a service recipient in an unsubsidized job, an additional fee of $400 if the job includes medical benefits, and yet another fee of $1600 if the service recipient remains employed for at least 12 months (Paulsell and Wood, 1999:7).

Table 8.3   Pennsylvania DW milestone PBC

Milestone	Type of milestone	Fee
1. Participation (client completes an assessment)	Output	$1000
2. Placement (client obtains unsubsidized employment)	Output	$1000
3. Medical benefits (the job includes medical benefits)	Quality	$400
4. Job Retention (client remains employed for 12 months)	Outcome	$1600

Source: Adapted from Paulsell and Wood (1999:7).

The Pennsylvania DW approach is qualitatively different from both the Kansas and Oklahoma approaches in that contractors receive no payments for the accomplishment of input or process milestones, only output, quality and outcome performance milestones. Because the Pennsylvania approach to milestone PBC ties all contractor compensation directly to performance, the proportion of the risk for performance failure allocated to contractors is substantial. However, along with this increased performance accountability comes greater service delivery flexibility and freedom in terms of inputs and process.

North Carolina Division of Social Services

The North Carolina Division of Social Services (North Carolina DSS) is an operating unit within the North Carolina Department of Health and Human Services. The North Carolina DSS approach is another example of milestone PBC for, but in this instance the service is adoptions and only outcome performance milestones are used. Under the North Carolina DSS approach (see Table 8.4), contractors are paid a percentage of their 'average placement cost' when any of three outcome performance milestones are achieved for a child.

Table 8.4   North Carolina DSS milestone PBC

Milestone	Type of milestone	Average placement cost (%)
1. Child placed for adoption	Outcome	60
2. Decree of adoption finalized	Outcome	20
3. Adoption intact for 12 months	Outcome	20

Source: Adapted from Vinson (1999:3)

As Table 8.4 illustrates, contractors receive 60 per cent of their average placement cost when a child is placed for adoption, another 20 per cent when the decree of adoption is finalized and a final 20 per cent when the placement has been intact for 12 months (Vinson, 1999:3). Because the North Carolina DSS approach to milestone PBC directly ties 100 per cent of a contractor's compensation to outcome performance milestones, all risk for performance failure is essentially allocated to contractors. The allocation of 100 per cent of the risk for performance failure to contractors might appear at first blush to violate the spirit of partnership between the North Carolina DSS and its contractors. However, adoption agencies in North Carolina have years of experience and consequently have valid service utilization and cost data. These adoption agencies simply insure that they do not contractually obligate themselves to performance and payment levels they cannot meet.

PUBLIC–PRIVATE SECTOR RISK SHARING

As the case examples above make clear, risk sharing arrangements for performance failure between US state and county governments and contractors is an important element of PBC for human services. However, it is important to note that the degree of risk for performance failure assumed by contractors can be affected by other factors outside the actual requirements of the contracts. For example:

- Contractors that rely on others (either the government or third parties) for service recipient eligibility determinations and referrals place themselves at greater financial risk. The number of referrals may not translate into sufficient revenues to enable contractors to reach their break-even points (the point at which revenues and expenses balance).
- The time lag between when contractors provide service and incur expenses and when they receive reimbursements or payments increases. As contractor compensation moves from being tied to outputs, to quality and particularly to outcomes, the time lag can increase significantly. Some human service outcomes can take six to twelve months to achieve. In such situations, contractors must have sufficient working capital to carry them until full reimbursement or payment is received.
- When contractor payment is tied to performance, the performance itself becomes auditable. While US state human service agencies have a long and somewhat notorious history of not adequately monitoring their contractors (Kettner and Martin, 1985), the same behaviour is not necessarily reflective of the audit function. Contractors must be able to demonstrate and document that the billings submitted and the payments received are based on actual observable and verifiable performance. If the performance cannot be objectively verified by auditors, contractors may encounter audit exceptions, questioned costs and demands for the repayment of monies.

OTHER PRIVATE SECTOR RISK SHARING STRATEGIES

In attempts to better manage the risk for performance failure, NGOs are not only becoming more sophisticated about the need for valid and reliable service utilization and cost data, they are also entering into new partnerships in attempts to minimize and diversify their risk exposure. Two such new strategies are: (1) the creation of lead agencies and (2) NGO/for-profit partnerships.

Lead Agencies

When it comes to information technology capabilities and financial management expertise, some NGOs are simply more sophisticated than others. The lead agency approach enables NGO contractors to further manage their risk exposure through what amounts to US state and county government sponsored public–private partnerships based on a division of labour.

Programmatically and fiscally sophisticated NGOs become lead agencies and concentrate on administration and financial management thereby enabling the other NGOs in the partnership to concentrate on service delivery. The lead agency concept involves US state and county governments identifying and contracting with small numbers of these more sophisticated lead agencies to serve as umbrella organizations for given communities and given clusters of NGO service providers (Kamerman and Kahn, 1998). These lead agencies essentially become 'prime contractors' and in turn subcontract part or all of the actual service delivery to other NGOs.

Florida is an example of one US state that has embraced the lead agency concept and is currently implementing the approach statewide. Family Services of Metro Orlando (FSMO) is one such designated lead agency. The state of Florida has contracted with FSMO to serve as the lead agency for Orange county (Orlando, Florida) and is charged with providing or contracting for state supported child welfare services (case management, foster care, foster parent recruitment, permancy placements and other services (Kurth et al., 2003).

NGO/For-profit Partnerships

For-profits also have a long history in the provision of contracted human services in the USA, but generally in relatively narrowly defined service areas. For example, the first major involvement of for-profits in US state and county government contract services occurred in the late 1960s and early 1970s when the US federal government decided to subsidize child day care services for welfare mothers (Kettner and Martin, 1988). US state and local governments decided to contract with both NGOs and for-profits in order to ensure the statewide availability of child day care services. A similar phenomenon occurred in the 1970s when US state and county governments first began contracting for in-home services for the elderly (Kettner and Martin, 1988).

The recent, and much publicized, involvement of for-profits in government contracting for 'welfare-to-work' services is more related to lead agency type issues than to any conscious US state and county policies to encourage for-profit involvement in human services. For-profits generally have better access to information technology and capital markets. Consequently, some NGOs have learned that by partnering with a for-profit, they gain a competitive advantage over other NGOs. Two examples serve to illustrate how this new form of NGO/for-profit partnership works:

- In Miami, Florida, Lockheed/Martin, a for-profit better known for its defence contracting, assumed responsibility as the lead agency for welfare-to-work services. In turn, Lockheed/Martin sub-contracted with about 30 NGOs to actually provide services. Lockheed/Martin handled the contract administration and financial management tasks and also provided needed information technology and working capital to the NGOs (Ryan, 1999).
- In Milwaukee, Wisconsin, the Milwaukee YWCA wanted to become involved in a welfare-to-work contract to be awarded by the state of Wisconsin. However, handling the administrative and financial management requirements of a $40 million contract was deemed too risky. The Milwaukee YWCA formed a new for-profit business called 'YW Works' that included itself plus two venture capital partners. The YWCA eventually won the contract (Ryan, 1999).

DOES PBC IMPROVE CONTRACTOR PERFORMANCE AND CLIENT OUTCOMES?

In attempting to answer this question, the point needs to be stressed that data on the results of PBC are hard to access and comparable data for comparable time periods are virtually impossible to access. Additionally, it is unclear in the following PBC examples if the results were accomplished with constant resources or if additional resources might explain some, but probably not all, of the performance increases. Nevertheless, the following reports and studies do shed at least some light on the extent to which PBC improves contractor performance and client outcomes. The discussion is again restricted to the PBC efforts of a select group of states.

Maine Department of Human Services

Commons et al. (1997) conducted an evaluation of the Maine Department of Human Services's (Maine DHS) use of PBC for substance abuse services.

The study reported two major findings: (1) the achievement of output and outcome performance increased when tied to contract renewal, and (2) the greater the proportion of a contractor's operating budget that came from PBC, the greater the performance.

The study findings confirm the basic premise of PBC: that contractor behaviour can be changed to focus more on performance. More importantly, the study suggests that contractor behaviour can be changed to focus more on performance even without directly linking compensation to performance.

Oklahoma Department of Rehabilitation Services

A self-assessment of 13 performance-based contracts awarded by the Oklahoma Department of Rehabilitation Services (Oklahoma DRS) between fiscal years 1992 and 1997 reported that the time clients spent waiting to receive services declined 53 per cent, case closures increased 100 per cent and contractor costs decreased 35 per cent (Oklahoma DRS, n.d.).

Minnesota Department of Human Services

For several years now, the Minnesota Department of Human Services (Minnesota DHS) has used PBC for job placement services for refugees (Vinson, 1999). As Table 8.5 illustrates, the Minnesota DHS reports some impressive results with PBC. Over a five-year period (between fiscal year 1995 and fiscal year 1999), total statewide full-time job placements increased over 240 per cent.

Table 8.5   Minnesota DHS PBC for job placement services

Assessment of performance-based contracts			
Fiscal year	1995	1998	1999
No. of job placements (outcomes)	591	1136	1423

Source: Adapted from Minnesota DHS (2000) and Vinson (1999).

Illinois Department of Children and Families

As Table 8.6 illustrates, the Illinois Department of Children and Families (Illinois DCF) reports a significant increase in adoptions as the result of changing to PBC. Based on Illinois DCF data, adoptions increased from 2220 in fiscal year 1997 to over 7000 in fiscal year 1999. The Illinois DCF reports that more adoptions were achieved during fiscal year 1999 then for a seven year period between fiscal year 1987 and 1994 (Illinois DCF, 2000).

Table 8.6   Illinois DCF PBC for child permanency placements

Fiscal year	1997	1998	1999
No. of adoptions	2229	4293	7315

Source: Adapted from Illinois DCF (2000).

Independent external reviews consider the Kansas Department of Social and Rehabilitative Services (Kansas SRS) experience with PBC to be both a success and a failure. On the success side of the equation, an evaluation conducted by the US General Accounting Office (US GAO, 2000) found that the outcomes achieved by the contractors equalled or exceeded the contract requirements. On the failure side of the equation, the Kansas state legislature (State of Kansas, 2000) found that the funding arrangements created severe financial problems for contractors, pushing some to the brink of bankruptcy.

In a personal discussion with the author, a representative of one Kansas SRS contractor reported that despite the 'turmoil' created by the transition, those child welfare agencies still functioning as contractors today prefer operating under PBC. The stated reason is the increased discretion over service delivery (inputs and process) that PBC affords contractors.

WHAT ABOUT CREAMING?

One of the most frequent criticisms levelled against PBC is that it will inevitably lead to contractor 'creaming'. The argument is made that once you begin requiring contractors to focus on performance they will seek out those clients that are the easiest to serve and avoid those clients that are the hardest to serve. While this criticism has been vocalized for some time, little research bearing on the issue exists. Recently, however, two studies have specifically addressed this subject. What makes these two studies particularly interesting is not only their findings, but the fact that they were both sponsored by Canadian research organizations looking at PBC for human services in the USA.

The first study, conducted by three researchers at the University of Calgary, looked at PBC for substance abuse services in the State of Maine (Lu et al., 2001). The study analyzed data on 18 972 clients served by contractors between 1989 and 1995, examining referrals between contractors. If creaming was taking place, the researchers reasoned that harder-to-serve clients would be referred between contractors more frequently than easier-to-serve clients. What the researchers found was that referrals between contractors did increase, but clients with more severe substance abuse problems were referred to and treated in more intensive programmes, while clients with less severe substance abuse problems were referred to and treated in less intensive programmes. Rather than using referrals to cream, the researchers concluded that the contractors were using referrals in order to specialize in the types of clients served.

The second study, funded by the Social Science and Humanities Research Council of Canada, involved a meta-analysis of other studies of PBC under the US federal Job Training Partnership Act (JTPA) (Heckman et al., 1999). The researchers found little evidence of creaming. In summarizing their findings, the researchers stated that, 'The literature has devoted too much attention to cream-skimming given the weak evidence of its existence' (ibid.:50).

SUMMARY AND CONCLUSION

PBC is a new emerging tool in human services contracting in the USA. By decreasing the traditional concern with input and process accountability and by focusing instead on output, quality and outcome performance accountability, PBC is said to create a community of interest between US state and local governments and their human service contractors.

PBC involves the allocation of the risk for performance failure between governments and contractors. As is the case with any true partnership, in PBC the partners share in both the rewards and the risks. However, the devil is in the detail. What proportion of the risk for performance failure should be shouldered by governments and what proportion should be allocated to contractors? Historically, the guiding principal in the allocation of risk for performance failure in US human service contracting has been to allocate the most risk, if not all the risk, for performance failure to governments. The problem with this approach is that contractors then have little or no incentive to focus on issues of performance. The result is that less service may be provided than might otherwise be the case, lower quality services may be provided than might otherwise be the case, and fewer client outcomes may be achieved than might otherwise be the case.

Initial experiments with PBC for human services demonstrate significant increases in contractor performance. The result is a win–win partnership situation for governments, contractors for service recipients. US state and county governments get better performance along with decreased administration and monitoring costs. Contractors get more freedom and flexibility in the design and implementing of human service programmes. And service recipients get more service, better quality service and achieve more outcomes.

NOTE

1. The 50 state human service systems in the USA are classified as either 'state administered' or 'state supervised/county administered.' Only 11 states are classified as state supervised/county administered. In these 11 states, the state governments have opted to decentralize responsibility for human services to their county governments. In state supervised/county administered systems, counties make the decisions to either provide a human service directly or to contract with the private sector. While representing only a small proportion of the 50 states, state supervised/county administered systems operate in two of the largest states, California and New York. In the other 39 states, the states themselves make the service delivery decisions (Martin, 2000).

REFERENCES

Agranoff, R. (2003), *Leveraging Networks: A Guide for Public Managers Working Across Organizations*, Washington DC: IBM Center for the Business of Government.

Arizona Department of Economic Security (Arizona DES). (2003), *Arizona Taxonomy of Human Services*, http://www.de.state.az.us/taxonomy, 10 December 2003.

Commons, M., T. McGuire and M. Riordan (1997), 'Performance contracting for substance abuse treatment', *Health Services Research*, **32** (December), 631–50.

Eggers, W. (1997), 'There is no place like home', *Policy Review*, **83** (May/June), 1–7.

Florida Department of Children and Families (DCF) 2000), *Model Contract Performance Measures fy 00/01*, Tallahassee, FL: DCF.

Frumkin, P. (2001), *Making Public Sector Mergers Work: Lessons Learned*, Arlington, VA: IBM Center for the Business of Government, www.businessofgovernment. org, 2 August 2003.

Gurwett, R. (2000), 'The lonely leap', *Governing*, **13** (10), 38–42.

Heckman, J., C. Heinrich and J. Smith (1999), *Understanding Incentives in Public Organizations*, Social Science and Humanities Council of Canada.

Illinois Department of Children and Families (Illinois DCF) (2000), *Harvard University Innovations in American Government Grant Application*.

Johnston, J. and B. Romzek (2000*), Implementing State Contracts for Social Services*, Arlington, VA: IBM Center for Business of Government, www. businessofgovernment.org, 10 December 2003.

Kamerman, S. and A. Kahn (1998), *Privatization, Contracting and Reform of Child and Family Social Services*, Washington DC: Finance Project.

Kansas Department of Social and Rehabilitative Services (SRS) (2001), *Statewide Assessment: Child and Family Services Review*, Topeka: Author.

Kettner, P. and L.L. Martin (1985), 'Developing monitoring systems for purchase of service contracting', *Administration in Social Work*, **9**, 8–11.

Kettner, P. and L.L. Martin (1986), 'Making decisions about purchase of service contracting', *Public Welfare*, **44**, 30–37.

Kettner, P. and L.L Martin (1987), *Purchase of Service Contracting*, Thousand Oaks: Sage Publications.

Kettner, P. and L.L. Martin (1988) 'Purchase of service contracting with for-profits', *Administration in Social Work*, **12**, 47–60.

Kettner, P. and L.L. Martin (1996), 'The impact of declining resources and purchase of service contracting on private non-profit agencies', *Administration in Social Work*, **20**, 21–38.

Kettner, P. and L.L. Martin (1998), 'Accountability in purchase of service contracting,' in Margaret Gibelman and Harold Demone (eds), *The Privatization of Human Services: Policy and Practice Issues*, New York: Springer Publications, 83–204.

Kurth, G., J. Vermillion and B. Mawoussi (2003), *Community-Based Care in Orange County*, Orlando, FL: Family Services of Metro Orlando.

Lauffer, A. (1997), *Grants, Etc.* Thousand Oaks: Sage Publications.

Lawther, W. (2002), *Contracting for the 21st Century: A Partnerships Approach*, Washington DC: IBM Center for the Business of Government.

Lu, M., C. Ma and L. Yuan (2001), *Risk Selection and Matching in Performance-based Contracting*, monograph, Department of Economics, University of Calgary.

Martin, L.L. (1999a), *Contracting for Service Delivery: Local Government Choices*, Washington DC: International City/County Management Association.

Martin, L.L. (1999b), 'Performance contracting: extending performance measurement to another level', *Public Administration Times*, **22** (January), 1, 8.

Martin, L.L. (2000), 'Administration and management of state human service agencies,' in John Gargan (ed.), *Handbook of State Government Administration*, New York: Marcel Dekker, 461–82.

Martin, L.L. (2001a), *Financial Management for Human Service Administrators*, Boston: Allyn and Bacon.

Martin, L.L. (2001b), 'Performance-based contracting for human services: lessons for public procurement?', *Journal of Public Procurement*, **2**, 55–71.

Martin, L.L. (2002), *Making Performance-Based Contracting Perform: What the Federal Government Can Learn From State and Local Governments*, Arlington, VA: IBM Center for the Business of Government, www.businessofgovernment. org, 10 December 2003.

Martin, L.L. (2003), *Performance-based Contracting for Human Services: A Review of the Literature*, Orlando, FL: Center for Community Partnerships, University of Central Florida, www.centralfloridapartnershipcenter.org/projects/workingpaper. pdf, 10 December 2003.

Martin, L.L. (2004a), 'Bridging the gap between contract service delivery and public financial management: applying theory to practice', in Aman Khan and W. Bartley Hildreth (eds), *Financial Management Theory in the Public Sector*, New York: Greenwood Press, (in press).

Martin, L.L. (2004b), 'Performance-based contracting for human services: Does it work?', *Administration in Social Work*, (in press).

Martin, L.L. and P.M. Kettner (1996), *Measuring the Performance of Human Service Programs*, Thousand Oaks, CA: Sage.

Martin, L.L. and John Miller (2005), *Contracting for Public Sector Services*, Herndon: National Institute of Governmental Purchasing (forthcoming).

Minnesota Department of Human Services (DHS) (2000), 'Request for proposals to provide social services to refugees in the state of Minnesota,' St. Paul, MN: DHS.

National Child Welfare Resource Center for Organizational Improvement (NCWRCOI) (1999), 'Practice form: performance-based contracting for out of home care,' *Managing Care*, **2**, 1–11, www.muskie.usmedu/helpkinds/mcII_3.html, 5 September 2003.

O'Brien, D. and B. Cook (n.d.), *Oklahoma Milestone Payment System*, www.onenet. net/~home/milestone/mlstjrnl.heml, 5 September 2003.

Organisation for Economic Co-operation and Development (OECD) (1999), *Lessons from Performance Contracting Case Studies: A Framework for Public Sector Performance Contracting*, Paris: OECD.

Oklahoma Department of Rehabilitative Services (Oklahoma DRS) (n.d.), *Milestone Payment System*, www.onenet.bet/home/milestone, 5 September 2003.

Paulsell, D. and R. Wood (1999), *The Community Solutions Initiative: Early Implementation Experiences*, Princeton, NJ: Mathematica Policy Research, Inc. (MPR Reference No. 8465–800).

Petr, C. and I. Johnson (1999), 'Privatization of foster care in Kansas: A cautionary tale,' *Social Work*, **44**, 263–7.

Ryan, W. (1999), 'The new landscape for nonprofits', *Harvard Business Review*, **12**, 103–36.

Sahonchik, L. (1999), 'Rate setting: Innovations in paying for out-of-home care', *Managing Care*, **2**, 1–11.

Salamon, L. (2002), *The Tools of Government*, New York: Oxford University Press.

Savas, E.S. (2000), *Privatization and Public–Private Partnerships*, New York: Chatham House.

State of Kansas (2000), minutes of the joint meeting with the SRS Oversight Committee and Children's Issues Committee of the Kansas State Legislature, September 26 2000.

Thomson, S. (2002), *Report on US Milestone Based Disability Employment Assistance Programs*, Canberra: Department of Family and Community Services.

US General Accounting Office (US GAO) (2000), *Major Management Challenges and Program Risks*, Washington DC: GAO.

US General Accounting Office (US GAO) (2001), 'Current condition of federal contracting,' presentation to members of the Commercial Activities Panel, www. gao.gov/a76panel/meeting.html, 28 August 2001.

Vinson, E. (1999), *Performance Contracting in Six State Human Service Agencies*. Washington DC: The Urban Institute.

Williamson, O. (1975), *Markets and Hierarchies: Analysis and Antitrust Implications*, New York: Free Press.

Williamson, O. (1985), *The Economic Institutions of Capitalism*, New York: Free Press.

9. North American infrastructure P3s: examples and lessons learned

Anthony E. Boardman, Finn Poschmann and Aidan R. Vining[1]

INTRODUCTION

This chapter summarizes the experience with infrastructure public–private partnerships (P3s) in Canada and the USA, which we call North America for convenience. While projects with partnership characteristics began to emerge in the late 1980s, it was not until the mid-1990s that P3s really began to take hold. Since that time P3 infrastructure projects have taken root in many areas.

A range of public–private relationships have been labelled as P3s.[2] For our purposes, a classic infrastructure P3 requires an explicit contract – between a government entity and one or more private sector firms, under which the private sector entity agrees to finance, build and operate some facility for a specific period of time after which ownership is transferred to the public sector.[3] Such projects are frequently referred to as a BOT. The public sector entity is sometimes the (intermediate) customer for the project's output. For example, in prisons and some wastewater projects, the government itself pays the user fees. In other cases, toll roads for example, the public partner negotiates the contract and specifies unit prices, but users pay directly.

Perhaps the critical distinguishing feature of a P3 is that it is a partnership – that is, an ongoing contractual relationship between a public sector entity and a private sector entity with some degree of joint decision-making and risk-sharing. As in marriages, the allocation of decision-making and risk-sharing in P3s can vary widely. But if decision-making authority and risk-bearing are not reasonably matched, incentives will be misaligned and effective outcomes will be unlikely.

Why do North American governments adopt infrastructure P3s rather than more traditional means of public provision? Stated broadly, governments want to reduce financial risk and political risk. Specifically, five major reasons appear to motivate them; they are not necessarily mutually exclusive. Governments usually argue that a main reason is to provide infrastructure at lower cost, resulting primarily from superior private sector technical efficiency, also called X-efficiency. A second reason is financial risk reduction. This pertains to both the cost of the project and the future revenue stream. Government infrastructure projects often cost far more than anticipated or budgeted (Boardman et al., 1994; Flyrberg et al., 2002). Furthermore, future revenue streams are often uncertain. A third reason is governments' desire to avoid up-front capital costs – private capital may be more readily accessible than additional tax revenue. A fourth reason is to keep public sector budget deficits down. Most US states have constitutional or legislative requirements to balance budgets, and while Canadian provincial governments can run deficits, there are political benefits to keeping large capital projects off the balance sheet or 'off-budget'. Fifth, private sector provision of financing means that it is easier to impose user fees – while voters sometimes accept that the private sector needs to raise revenue to repay its debt, they are often reluctant to accept the argument that the public sector needs to do so.

There are many reasons to expect that infrastructure P3s could lower construction and operating costs – in other words, lower production costs in aggregate. Private sector firms often enjoy advantages of economies of scale and are able to draw on a specialized knowledge base accumulated through experience. They may have more efficient operations, better project management skills, as well as more flexibility and innovativeness, implying superior dynamic technical efficiency.[4] They may also have lower wage costs, possibly due to hiring non-union labor, and a more effective incentive structure.

Ultimately, the ability of a P3 to provide the project at lower cost and meet the necessary social goals depends on the private sector partner having the appropriate incentives. Firms are interested in profit maximization, not cost minimization. Even if they can lower costs, they have no intrinsic desire to pass on lower costs as lower prices. They are especially wary of prices that do not fully compensate for all risks they assume. Contracts must be structured to account for this. If contracts are written so that incentives are compatible with private sector goals while simultaneously ensuring delivery of the desired product, then the outcome can be a 'win–win' situation.

Although the above reasons favour the private sector, it is often thought that the cost of financing may be lower for the public sector. US tax policy generally favours the public sector because state and local governments may issue bonds that are exempt from state and federal taxes. Canada does not provide such tax benefits, but provincial bonds generally carry a lower interest rate than corporate bonds. However, after a comprehensive review of the issues, de Bettignies and Ross (2004:31) conclude:

[I]t is not at all clear that the government will be able to borrow at a lower cost than the private sector. A full evaluation of the relative costs will have to consider such factors as: (i) the credit-worthiness of the private borrower and the protections offered in its contract with the public sector partner; (ii) the extent to which tax savings may come from other levels of government; and (iii) the degree to which the supply of funds to the public sector is upward sloping.[5]

Concerning the third reason – keeping the project off the balance sheet – the government will normally account for the project in accordance with public sector accounting principles. However, it is important to recognise that the accounting will not usually reflect the underlying economic reality. For example, a government or health care provider that constructs a new hospital using a P3 will have to pay for it at some point in time via a rent charge or user charge. The present value of this payment is likely to be equivalent to the cost of constructing the hospital or even higher. Thus, while there is a political benefit, it does not offer a fundamental rationale for P3s: 'you pay now or you pay later'.

The critical issue in evaluating the success of a P3 is whether the total cost of the P3 is lower than the total cost of the counter-factual of government provision. Total cost equals production cost plus transaction costs (Williamson, 1975). Transaction costs include the cost of negotiating, monitoring and, if necessary, re-negotiating the contract.[6] Many of these costs are not captured in traditional budgeting. Private sector proponents of P3s have made optimistic pronouncements about the ability of P3s to deliver projects at lower cost than can government, but they typically use measures of P3 'success' that are often narrow and even self-serving, for example, whether a project was completed on time or on budget. These are not comprehensive measures of success as they do include transaction costs and do not consider what costs might have been under alternative provision. Independent studies of North American infrastructure P3 performance that use comprehensive measures of performance are rare.

The second section of this chapter presents an overview of P3s in the USA and Canada. The third section contains five short case studies intended to draw out core lessons. We focus on highway projects and water and wastewater treatment as most North American P3s are of these types. We selected better-known projects for which independent information was available on the basis of apparent success or failure. As it turns out, none of these projects was a resounding success. In the fourth section we present some reasons why we think these P3s did not do very well. Many of these lessons are probably generalizable. The fourth section concludes the chapter.

OVERVIEW OF US AND CANADIAN P3s

There has been a long history of private sector provision of various kinds of public infrastructure in North America. For example, the first private turnpike in the United States was chartered by Pennsylvania in 1792. In aggregate, between 2500 and 3200 companies successfully financed, built, and operated toll roads (Klein and Majewski, n.d.; see also Engi et al., 2002). 'In 1825, Kentucky became the first (US) state to employ a private contractor to manage its entire correctional facility system, and by the end of the Civil War the majority of southern states had followed suit' (Pozen, 2003:257). Franchise contracts were introduced in New York City in the 1820s for gas and in the 1830s for street railway transportation. Over the years, cities extended such contracts to virtually all municipal services including gas, electricity, water, sewer, street railways, telegraph, telephone, subways, railroad terminals, ferries, private bridges, tunnels and toll roads (Priest, 1993:302).

While many of these arrangements might not meet our definition of infrastructure P3s, they have some partnership-like elements. As Priest (ibid.:294) notes, 'the interaction between the regulator and the regulated firm or industry is difficult to distinguish from long-term contracting, dominated by predictable problems of unilateral or mutual adjustment over time in response to changing conditions'.

P3s took off in Canada and the US in the mid 1990s. North American governments, like those in Europe and Australia, have been attracted to P3s in the areas of transportation, water and wastewater, and for other technologically complex infrastructure projects. 'The most dominant area, both in number of projects and total dollar volume of business, is in water and wastewater facilities' (Norment, 2002:27).

Tables 9.1 and 9.2 catalogue the major P3s in the US and Canada. Although this is not a comprehensive list, it is intended to include all of the largest and most well-known P3s. Some of these projects are very large; for example, the Toronto Pearson International Airport, Ontario, cost CA\$4.4 billion, and the new International Air Terminal at John F. Kennedy Airport, NY, cost US\$1.4 billion. Less than half of these projects include significant private-partner financing roles. Nonetheless, many do involve private finance roles and, as we shall see in the cases below, the finance role is an important one in assessing the success of a partnership. It does not appear there are marked or important differences between P3s in Canada and the US.

Table 9.1 P3s in the United States

Project	Start year	Operating period	Design	Build (or purchase)	Operate	Finance	Size (cost or contract amount)	Public partner	Private partner
Transportation Roads									
Pocahontas Parkway – Virginia[1,2]	1998		Y	Y		Y	Total project value was $318 million.	Virginia DOT	Fluor Daniel/Morrison Knudsen (FD/ MK)
NM Corridor 44 Highway Construction – New Mexico[3,4]	1998		Y	Y			First bond issue was $105 million.	New Mexico State Highway & Transportation Department	Mesa Development Corporation
Massachusetts Route 3 North Project – MA[5]	1999	30 years	Y	Y	Y	Y	Approx $100 million	Commonwealth of Massachusetts Executive Office of Transportation and Construction/ MassHighway	Route 3 North Transportation Improvements Project
Virginia 228 – Virginia[6,7]	1995		Y	Y			Contract $236 million	Virginia DOT	APAC-Virginia, Inc., CH2MHill Koch Performance Roads
NJ Turnpike Exit 13A Interchange – New Jersey[8]			Y	Y			Contract $85 million	New Jersey DOT	Slattery Skanska Inc.
San Joaquin Hills Transportation Corridor – CA[9,10]	1985		Y	Y	Y		$790 million in design/ construction	California DOT	Kiewit; Granite
Dulles Greenway Toll Road – Virginia[11,12]			Y	Y	Y		Contract $145 million	Virginia DOT	Bryant/Crane family, AIE, L.L.C., and Kellogg Brown & Root, Inc.

Project	Year	Duration			Contract	Authority	Contractor
SR-91 Express Lanes – California[13,14]		35 years	Y		Contract $60.4 million	California DOT	California Private Transportation Company (CPTC)
Southern Connector Toll Road – South Carolina[15]			Y	Y	Contract $191 million	South Carolina DOT	Interwest Carolina Transport Group (Thrift Brothers, Florence & Hutcheson)
Conway Bypass – South Carolina[16]			Y		Contract $386.3 million	South Carolina DOT	Fluor Daniel
Eastern Toll Road – CA[17]			Y		Contract $780 million	California DOT	Flatiron; Ways $ Freitage; Sukut; Obayashi
Carolina Bays Parkway – South Carolina[18]		3 years	Y		Contract $226 million	South Carolina DOT	Flatiron
Hudson Bergen Light Rail – New Jersey[19,20]	1996	15 years	Y	Y	Contract $1.12 billion	New Jersey DOT	Washington Group (70%), Kinkisharyo and Itachu (30%)
Winghaven Research Park – O'Fallon, Missouri[21,22]		15 years	Y	Y	Contract $9.5 million		Koch Performance Roads and Koch Financial Services
Pavement Rehabilitation, City Streets, Aspen, CO[23,24]		15 years	Y		Contract $2.7 million	The City of Aspen	Koch Performance Roads

Airports

Project	Year	Duration			Contract	Authority	Contractor
Intntl. Air Terminal 4 at John F Kennedy Airport – NY[25]			Y	Y	$1.4-billion terminal	Port Authority of New York and New Jersey	LCOR Incorporated

Project	Start year	Operating period	Design	Build (or purchase)	Operate	Finance	Size (cost or contract amount)	Public partner	Private partner
Stewart Airport – NY	1998	99 years		(Lease)	Y	Y	Payment $35 million plus percentage of revenues	New York State	National Express
Los Angeles County General Aviation Airport – CA[26,27]	1990	20 years		(Lease)	Y			Los Angeles Country	COMARCO
Other Transportation									
Union Station – Washington, DC[28]			Y	Y		Y	$170 million	U.S. Department of Transportation	Benjamin Thompson Associates, Jones Lang LaSalle, William Jackson Ewing, Inc.
Grand Central Terminal – New York[29]	1993		Y	Y		Y	Construction cost: $259 million	Metropolitan Transit Authority	Jones Lang LaSalle & Williams Jackson Ewing Inc
Water & wastewater									
Water Treatment (population 5 000–50 000)									
Bessemar Water Filtration Facility – Alabama[30]	1995	20 years	Y	Y	Y		Construction cost: $36 million	City of Bessemar, AL	Covanta
El Paso County Water Treatment – Texas[31]	1999	20 years	Y	Y	Y	Y	Capital cost: $6.7 million	EPCWA, Municipal District in El Paso, TX	ECO Resources

Water treatment (population > 250,000)

Project	Date	Duration			Value	Public entity	Private operator
Dr. Antonio Santiago Vazquez Water treatment plant – Puerto Rico[32]	1996	5 years	Y	Y	Contract $300 million	Puerto Rico Aqueduct and Sewer Authority (PRASA)	Dick Corporation and Thames Water Puerto Rico
Surface water treatment plant, Tampa Bay – Florida[33]	Mar-00	20 years	Y	Y	Contract $131 million	Tampa Bay Water, FL	US Filter (now Veolia North America)
Tampa Bay seawater desalination plant – Florida[34]	2000	30 years	Y	Y	Design–construction $75.1 million	Tampa Bay Water, FL	Covanta

Wastewater

Project	Date	Duration			Value	Public entity	Private operator
Springfield wastewater system – Massachusetts[35]	2000	25 years	Y	Y		Springfield, MA	United Water

Power/energy

Project	Date	Duration			Value	Public entity	Private operator
The University of Maryland College Park Energy & Utility Infrastructure Program – Maryland			Y	Y	Contract $469 million	The University of Maryland College Park	Trigen–Cinergy Solutions
Educational facilities James F. Oyster Bilingual Elementary School – Washington, DC[36]	1995		Y	Y		District of Columbia Public Schools and 21st Century School Fund	LCOR Inc

Table 9.2 P3s in Canada

Project	Start year	Operating period	Design	Build (or purchase)	Operate	Finance	Size (cost or contract amount)	Public partner	Private partner
Transportation *Roads*									
Highway 407 – ON[37]	1999*	99 years	Y	Leased	Y		$3.11 billion	Province of Ontario	407 International Inc
Cobequid Pass – NS[38,39]	1997*	30 years	(manages)	(manages)	(manages)	(manages)	Construction cost: $112.9 million.	Province of Nova Scotia	The Highway 104 Western Alignment Corp.
Bridges									
Confederation Bridge – NB and PEI[40]	1997*	35 years	Y	Y	Y	Y	Direct construction costs were $730 million.	Federal Government	Strait Crossing Development Inc
Charleswood Bridge – MAN[41]	1995*	30 year	Y	Y	Y	Y	Capital costs: $10 million (part one) and $5 million (part two).	City of Winnipeg	DBF Ltd
Airports									
Toronto Pearson International Airport – ON[42]	1996*	60 years; renewal term of 20 years		Leased	Y		$4.4 billion	Federal Government	GTAA – Greater Toronto Airports Authority

Facility	Year	Term				Notes	Public authority	Operator
Vancouver International Airport (YVR) – BC[43]	1992*	60 years, renewal term of 20 years	Leased	Y		$350 million	Federal Government	Vancouver Int'l Airport Authority
Hamilton International Airport (YHM) – ON[44]	1996*		Leased	Y			City of Hamilton	TradePort Int'l Corporation
Seaports and Harbours								
St Lawrence Seaway – Quebec and ON[45]	1996*	20 years		Y	Y	SLSMC spent $23.4 million on asset renewal 1999/2000.	Federal Government	St Lawrence Seaway Management Corporation
Goderich Harbour Revitalization – ON[46]	1996						Town of Goderich	Sifto Canada Inc/ Goderich Port Management Corporation
Water and Wastewater Wastewater treatment & delivery								
Alberta Capital Treatment Wastewater Treatment Plant – AL[47]	1998	8 years		Y			City of Edmonton	OMI Canada
Halifax Harbor Solutions – ON[48]		30 years	Y	Y	Y		Halifax Regional Municip.	Onedo (water division of Suez)

Project	Start year	Operating period	Design	Build (or purchase)	Operate	Finance	Size (cost or contract amount)	Public partner	Private partner
Norfolk Wastewater Treatment – ON[49]	Jan 98	5 years plus 5 year option			Y			Town of Norfolk	US Filter Operating Services
Water and wastewater treatment									
Canmore Water & Wastewater Treatment – AL[50]	May 00	10 years			Y			Town of Canmore	EPCOR
Goderich Water & Wastewater Services – ON[51]	Dec 00	5 years plus 5 year option			Y			Town of Goderich	USF Canada Inc
Hamilton-Wentworth Water & Wastewater Treatment – ON[52]	1995	10 years			Y			Region of Hamilton-Wentworth (now the City of Hamilton)	Philip Utilities Management Corporation (PUMC)
Hamilton-Wentworth Water & Wastewater Treatment – ON[53]	May 99			Y	Y	Y		Region of Hamilton-Wentworth	Azurix
Port Hardy Water Treatment Facility – BC[54]	1999	20 years	Y	Y	Y	Y	Plant construction cost was $3.67 million.	Region of Port Hardy	EPCOR (then Aqualta)

Water treatment and delivery

Project	Date	Term			Details	Public entity	Private company
London & Area Water Treatment Facilities – ON[55,56]	Sep 01	10 years plus 5 year option	Y	Y		City of London	Azurix
Moncton Water Treatment Facility – NB[57]	Jun 05	20 years	Y	Y	Total construction and operations contracts is $85 million	City of Moncton	USF Canada Inc.
Seymour Filtration Project – BC[58,59]	May 03	20 years	Y	Y	Consuction cost of plant: $135 million.	GVWD	EPCOR
Winnipeg Water Treatment – MAN[60]			Y	Y		City of Winnipeg	TBD (2003)

Power/energy
Nuclear power

| Bruce Nuclear Power Facility – ON[61] | Jul 2000 | 18 years | Y | (lease) | The total liability is approximately $3.1 billion. | Ontario Power Generation (ON Government) | Bruce Power (95% owned by British Energy) |

Green Power

| Waterloo Landfill Gas Power Plant – ON[62] | 1998 | Long-term | Y | Y | Capital cost of $7.5 million | Regional Municipality of Waterloo | Toromont Energy |

Hospital facilities

| Centracare Psychiatric Care Facility – NB[63] | | 25 years | Y | Y | Capital cost was $6.4 million | Government of New Brunswick | Cardinal Pomerleau Inc. |

Project	Start year	Operating period	Design	Build (or purchase)	Operate	Finance	Size (cost or contract amount)	Public partner	Private partner
William Osler Health Centre – ON[64]	2001		Y	Y	Y	Y		Provincial Government of Ontario	The Healthcare Infrastructure Co.
Royal Ottawa Hospital – ON[65]	2003	25 years	Y	Y	Y	Y	The new facility will cost $100 million.	Provincial Government of Ontario	TBD
Educational facilities									
Aurora College Family Student Housing – NWT[66]	2000	20 years		Y (Lease)	Y		Capital costs $4.7 million	Government of the NWT	Aurora Building Developers
O'Connell Drive Elementary School – NS[67]							Project cost $8 million.	Provincial (Nova Scotia) Government	Nova Learning Inc.
Auguston Elementary School, BC								Abbotsford School District	
Housing facilities									
Bloomfield Gardens Housing Project[68]	1994							Vancouver Resource Society	TDM Group Inc.
Technical facilities									
BC Online – BC[69]	1999	10 years		Y	Y	Y	$55 million	BC Assets and Land Corp.	MacDonald Dettveiler & Associates

Notes:

* Start year refers to the start of the lease and/or operation.

1. http://www.ncppp.org/cases/pocahontas.html
2. http://www.virginiadot.org/projects/constrich-895facts.asp
3. http://ncppp.org/cases/index.html
4. http://www.nmshtd.state.nm.us/general/depts/planning/pdf/US_550_WAR-RANTY_MONITORING/Project_Overview.pdf
5. http://ncppp.org/cases/index.html
6. http://www.ncppp.org/resources/papers/battellereport.pdf
7. http://www.route288.com/abouttheproject.htm
8. http://www.ncppp.org/resources/papers/battellereport.pdf
9. http://www.ncppp.org/resources/papers/battellereport.pdf
10. http://www.city.newport-beach.ca.us/Boardmanual/SanJoaquinHillsTransJPA.htm
11. http://www.ncppp.org/resources/papers/battellereport.pdf
12. http://www.dullesgreenway.com/cgi-bin/dghome.cfm
13. http://www.ncppp.org/resources/papers/battellereport.pdf
14. http://gridlock.calpoly.edu/sr91/sr91.htm
15. http://www.ncppp.org/resources/papers/battellereport.pdf
16. http://www.ncppp.org/resources/papers/battellereport.pdf
17. http://www.ncppp.org/resources/papers/battellereport.pdf
18. http://www.ncppp.org/resources/papers/battellereport.pdf
19. http://www.ncppp.org/resources/papers/battellereport.pdf
20. http://www.bayonnenj.org/lightrail3.htm
21. http://www.ncppp.org/resources/papers/battellereport.pdf
22. http://www.performanceroads.com/projectportfolio_winghaven.htm
23. http://www.ncppp.org/resources/papers/battellereport.pdf
24. http://www.performanceroads.com/projectportfolio_aspen.htm
25. http://ncppp.org/cases/index.html
26. http://www.privatization.org/database/policyissues/airports_local.html#8
27. http://www.privatization.org/database/policyissues/airports_local.html#8
28. http://ncppp.org/cases/index.html
29. http://ncppp.org/cases/index.html
30. http://www.waterpartnership.org/casestudies.htm
31. http://www.waterpartnership.org/casestudies.htm
32. http://www.waterpartnership.org/casestudies.htm
33. http://www.waterpartnership.org/casestudies.htm
34. http://www.waterpartnership.org/casestudies.htm
35. http://www.waterpartnership.org/casestudies.htm
36. http://ncppp.org/cases/index.html
37. Canadian Council for Public–Private Partnerships (2001).
38. Canadian Council for Public–Private Partnerships (2001).
39. http://www.gov.ns.ca/tran/Projects/cobequid_pass.stm#ThePartners
40. Canadian Council for Public–Private Partnerships (2001).
41. Canadian Council for Public–Private Partnerships (2001).
42. Canadian Council for Public–Private Partnerships (2001).
43. Canadian Council for Public–Private Partnerships (2001).
44. Canadian Council for Public–Private Partnerships (2001).
45. Canadian Council for Public–Private Partnerships (2001).
46. Canadian Council for Public–Private Partnerships (2001).
47. Canadian Council for Public–Private Partnerships (2001).
48. http://www.suez-lyonnaise-eaux.com/finance2/english/news/detail.php?id=863&pg=arch
49. Canadian Council for Public–Private Partnerships (2001).
50. Canadian Council for Public–Private Partnerships (2001).
51. http://www.pppcouncil.ca/aboutPPP_photoCredits.asp
52. Canadian Council for Public–Private Partnerships (2001).
53. Canadian Council for Public–Private Partnerships (2001).
54. Canadian Council for Public–Private Partnerships (2001).
55. http://www.watersupply.london.ca/Notice/NRF_WaterAwardSept20.pdf
56. http://www.waterindustry.org/New%20Projects/azurix-america.htm
57. Canadian Council for Public–Private Partnerships (2001).
58. Canadian Council for Public–Private Partnerships (2001).
59. http://www.nsnews.com/issues01/w021201/news/top-stories/09-news-01.html
60. Canadian Council for Public–Private Partnerships (2001).
61. Canadian Council for Public–Private Partnerships (2001).
62. http://www.canren.gc.ca/renew_ene/index.asp?CaID=47&PgID=1110
63. Canadian Council for Public–Private Partnerships (2001).
64. http://www.williamoslerhc.on.ca/Redevelopment/redevelopment_main.htm
65. http://www.royalottawahospital.com/P3_Qs_and_As_as_of_Sept_2003.htm
66. Canadian Council for Public–Private Partnerships (2001).
67. Canadian Council for Public–Private Partnerships (2001).
68. http://www.landcentre.ca/lcframedoc.cfm?ID=1992
69. http://www.mda.ca/news/pr/pr90429A.html

175

NORTH AMERICAN INFRASTRUCTURE CASE STUDIES

We have chosen the following five case studies because of information availability, their local significance and the generic lessons they offer for P3 contract design and implementation. Here we summarise the main elements pertaining to two high-profile P3s in the USA: the Dulles Greenway toll road in Virginia and the Tampa Bay Seawater Desalination Plant in Florida, and three in Canada: the Alberta Special Waste Management System, Highway 407 in the Greater Toronto Area and the Confederation Bridge linking Prince Edward Island (Canada's smallest province) with the Canadian mainland in New Brunswick.[7]

Dulles Greenway

Although private toll roads were common in the United States in the 19th century, no new road involving private sector operation was built until the end of the 20th century. Two major recent projects are the Dulles Greenway toll road in Virginia and Orange County State Route 91 express lanes.

The Dulles project is a fourteen-and-a-half mile toll road that runs from Dulles International Airport to Leesburg in Virginia. Apart from $3.5 million in state funds, its owner, the Toll Road Investors Partnership II (a partnership of a Virginia family, the profitable Italian toll road operator Autostrade SpA. and Texas's Kellogg, Brown and Root), raised $360 million in private capital to finance the startup. This financing preceded Virginia's Public–Private Transportation Act and, therefore, did not qualify as a tax-exempt bond issue (Taliaferro, 1997). The highway opened in September 1995, a number of months ahead of schedule. However, early ridership was lower than projected, and the project went into default in July 1996, within a year of its opening.

A subsequent refinancing did qualify for tax-favorable treatment and thus lower carrying costs for the partnership. Economic growth drove up ridership, which increased over six years from about 10 000 per weekday to about 60,000 (Brumback, 2003). Nonetheless, the partnership's losses have been about $30 million per year, and sustainability will naturally depend on future revenue growth outstripping capital and operating costs.[8]

The Dulles Greenway case illustrates the potential vicious cycle that sometimes confronts toll projects: tolls are set high in an attempt to cover financing and operating costs, demand is overestimated at the prospective toll price (it is assumed that demand will be not much lower than it would be at zero price), high tolls discourage usage and thus total revenues are not high enough to cover financing and operating costs. Tolls are lowered, as a result demand increases, but total revenues do not increase substantially and still do not cover financing and operating costs; the builder/operator requests some form of bailout by government and if it does not get them then the firm slides into technical default.

The potential for such an unhappy cycle is perhaps less following incremental reforms to highway procurement contracts that introduce some greater degree of incentive-compatibility between government and highway construction firms. Various forms of performance-based contracting do seem to improve highway procurement (Battelle, 2003).

Tampa Bay Seawater Desalination Project

The Tampa Bay region decided in the mid-1990s to attempt to partially solve a looming water shortage by constructing a major water desalination plant. The plant was projected to process 25 million gallons a day, or approximately 10 per cent of the volume that West Coast Regional Water Supply (now Tampa Bay Water), the region's water supplier, provided to the cities of Tampa Bay, St Petersburg and New Port Richey as well as surrounding counties. At the time, the technology was still an emerging one and was expected to be considerably more expensive than incremental conventional groundwater sources (Johnson, 2003). However, the Southwest Florida Water Management District was putting pressure on jurisdictions to reduce groundwater pumping and was prepared to provide subsidies for desalination. No other utility in the United States provided water by desalination on a regular basis.

The water utility wished to proceed with a P3 that protected it from financial risk. The project was divided into two separate components: an engineering–procurement–construction project and a 30-year operations and maintenance contract. Initial bids were to provide water at $2 to $3 per 1000 gallons. This quote was considerably below the price the water utility expected to pay. Firms appeared to have come in with low bids in the hope of gaining an early lead in the desalination market. Covanta Tampa Construction was selected for both the construction contract and the 30-year operations and maintenance contract. However, the relationship between the utility and the firm appears to have been fraught with mistrust, partly brought about by constant delays in completing the plant. Eventually, Covanta filed for bankruptcy (in October 2003) with the operations and management contract, worth approximately $350 million, as its only asset.

One reason for the bankruptcy filing was to prevent Tampa Bay Water from terminating Covanta's contract and replacing it with another firm. The plant was completed in 2003. Although the plant has begun producing water, Tampa Bay Water refused to approve the plant during a 14-day acceptance test, claiming major deficiencies (Wright, 2003). The main problem appeared to be that the costly purification membranes clogged easily and needed replacement on a much more frequent basis than forecast. Without this approval, Covanta was blocked from beginning the operations and management contract. In November 2003, a US Court ordered the two parties into mediation, but by 2004 the relationship was terminated with Tampa Water paying Covanta $4.4 million of the $7.9 million it had retained from the construction contract.

At the time of writing, the plant was producing 22.4 million gallons a day, not far off its projected volume of 25 million gallons, albeit at higher-than-projected costs. Tampa Bay Water is negotiating with a number of firms concerning repairs to the filters and other problems. These repairs are forecast to cost somewhere between $8 million and $20 million (Pittman, 2004). The St. Peterburg Times concludes: 'The dumbfounding part of the troubled odyssey in opening this important desal plant is that the contract arrangement was designed to limit the public's financial liability' (*St Petersburg Times*, 2003, 14A).

The Alberta Special Waste Management System

The Alberta Special Waste Management System (ASWMS) was created in 1987. It was jointly owned by the Alberta Special Waste Management Corporation (ASWMC), a provincial Crown corporation (40 per cent), and BOVAR Inc., a private firm (60 per cent).[9] ASWMS built an integrated hazardous waste-treatment facility at Swan Hills, Alberta. BOVAR was to collect 60 per cent of the profits, and all of the net earnings of the operator (Chem-Security).

Under the agreement, BOVAR also received a guaranteed minimum return on capital linked to the current prime rate plus four percentage points (with tax adjustments), regardless of the profitability of the venture. Furthermore, the Government of Alberta provided debt guarantees for BOVAR, as well as indemnity against any future remediation or insurance liabilities in excess of $1 million. This arrangement followed from the government's belief that a private sector entity could build and operate the plant more efficiently than the public sector, although the plant would not be commercially viable without subsidies.

The parties later modified the agreement to permit a large capacity expansion. Partly as a result of this expansion, the subsidy turned out to be considerably larger than expected – approximately $445 million between 1986 and 1995 (Mintz, 1995:17). Also, the additional capacity turned out to be excessive.[10] The plant has operated at about 50 per cent of its capacity through most of its life. In 1995, the Alberta government bought out BOVAR's ownership interest for $150 million. In 2000, in exchange for $1, BOVAR returned the facility to the province, as permitted under the agreement. The cash drain on Alberta's finances for fiscal 2001/2002 was about $11 million. Subsequently, a partnership agreement was negotiated with another private operator that assumed plant operation in April 2001.

The contract's return-on-capital provisions provided a clear incentive for overcapitalization (Averch and Johnson, 1962). BOVAR's profits did not depend on revenue exceeding costs: earnings were a function of capital investment, rather than efficiency or profitability.[11] The contract also meant that BOVAR had no incentive to encourage cost reductions by the plant operator. As a result, BOVAR received a high, guaranteed rate of return.[12] High returns are justifiable when they are compensation for risk-taking. However, the debt guarantees meant that BOVAR was exposed to little risk. Because there was no useful sharing of risk and reward, it is hard to classify Swan Hills as a successful P3. The result was a waste treatment facility with capacity that exceeded Alberta's needs, having been built and operated under terms very costly to provincial taxpayers.

The Highway 407 Express Toll Route

Highway 407 is a controlled-access 108-kilometre highway that crosses the north side of the Toronto metropolitan area. The request for proposals (RFP) was announced in the fall of 1993, when the province of Ontario was emerging from a recession that had left it in a weak financial position. The recession and the province's high debt provided the economic backdrop that made a toll road politically viable. The 407 project was launched through a special-purpose entity that the Ontario government created to manage the procurement process.

The original RFP required the selected private partner to provide financing and operation. In addition to requiring a plan for debt and equity, the proposal had to guarantee a maximum construction price. The financier–operator would be paid from toll revenues. The province would be responsible for land assembly and related costs, but did not guarantee traffic levels or toll revenues. Thus the private partner would bear the financing risk. The RFP specified few highway characteristics, facilitating private-sector innovation and providing the opportunity to profit from relevant technical skills and management ability.

In responding to the RFP, the two qualified consortia sought extensive provincial backing for the debt. Credible private partners were reluctant to assume financing risks on top of construction and operating risks. Without a toll-revenue guarantee to help a private company achieve an investment-grade rating for its debt, a private firm would have had to pay at least 75 basis points more for debt than would the province (SG Hambros, 1999): this was the reason the province gave for eventually assuming the financing.[13]

Subsequently, one consortium would be responsible for the DBO phases, as well as highway maintenance, while another would manage the toll system. The removal of financial risk fundamentally transformed the project. The province found that both consortia faced higher borrowing costs than it did. If it did not assume the risk, it would face higher financing costs. Taxpayers would pay one way or another, either through higher tolls or higher provincial debt.

With the financing split off and the bulk of the capital cost and financial risk shifted to the province, the project necessarily lost much of its P3 quality. The private partner was now tendering a fixed-price contract. Although the private firm shared the design and quality assurance risks, the province assumed ownership and operational risk. Risks to the province, however, were reduced when the province sold the highway's operating concession to a Canadian–Spanish–Australian consortium for $3.1 billion after it had been operating for 18 months (Mendoza et al., 1999). The term of the concession is for 99 years, after which ownership of the asset reverts to the government. This sale is essentially a privatization, although the highway eventually returns to the province – its net proceeds will depend in part on the condition of the asset when ownership reverts.

It is difficult to make an overall assessment of the success of this project. There are clearly a number of positives, but also some important negatives. The 407 project has been successful to the extent that the highway was built quickly. The highway generates more than 300 000 daily vehicle trips, and the gross number of kilometres travelled that it has lifted from untolled public highways is about 200 million per month.[14] Given that each vehicle kilometre is billed to users and that no part of the highway exercises an effective monopoly, these figures suggest there is significant demand for the road.

The 407 design process appears to have saved substantial provincial money in the initial construction phase, perhaps in the order of $300 million (SG Hambros, 1999). Some of these savings were not realized, however, because design changes were needed before the highway opened. These changes were charged to the province because the parties agreed they were not part of the initial price-guaranteed contract. The full extent of savings is therefore unclear. And while innovative design features such as short entrances and short radius ramps certainly reduced land assembly and construction costs, any negative safety impacts will only be revealed over the highway's life.

Overall, then, it is clear the 407 does not stand out as an exemplary P3 model, owing to the failure to share financing risks effectively.

The Confederation Bridge to Prince Edward Island

Prince Edward Island joined the Canadian federation in 1873 under a constitutional agreement which guaranteed ship service to the island in perpetuity.[15] Beginning in the 1880s, and for more than a century following, there was debate over whether to substitute a fixed link for a weather-dependent ferry. In early 1988, a plebiscite approved such a link. Later in that year, the federal government selected three bids out of seven proposals for further development. Strait Crossing Development Inc. (SCDI), a consortium of Canadian, Dutch, French and American interests submitted the winning bid.

The selected bid was essentially a build–operate–transfer agreement. The contract specified a $41.9 million (1992 dollars) annual payment from the federal government to the operator, notionally representing the avoided cost of ferry operation. SCDI was entitled to all toll revenues for 35 years, after which bridge operation and ownership of its revenue (and cost) stream would revert to the federal government. The government provided an annual $13.9 million revenue guarantee. SCDI initially took on most of the construction and operational risk, as well as toll revenue risk beyond the $13.9 million level. The federal government agreed to bear a number of the residual risks from enemy attack, nuclear catastrophe, earthquake and environmental injunctions and regulatory risk. The federal payment to SCDI was to begin whether or not the bridge was in service in 1997, but if the bridge was not substantially completed, SCDI was required to pay the ferry subsidy. SCDI was required to post performance bonds and guarantees for specific contingencies.

Principal financing was secured in 1993 through the sale of $640 million in real return bonds by Strait Crossing Finance Inc. (SCFI). SCFI was established as a special purpose Crown Corporation of the province of New Brunswick. Its bonds were guaranteed by the federal payment stream and received high credit ratings, providing a financial structure sufficiently durable to survive the 1996 pullout of the American partner, Morrison Knudsen. Fabrication began in late 1993 and the bridge opened on 1 June 1997. Initial tolls were set at the ferry price for comparable vehicles and passengers. Annual increases were, and are, permitted at 75 per cent of the rate of consumer price inflation. The federal government estimated its incremental costs for project management to be $46.0 million.

This P3 is clearly a success to the extent that it delivered a functioning bridge on time. While there have been weather closures and some unexpected repairs owing to excessive pier scouring caused by storms, the bridge itself is functioning as expected, entirely supplanting the prior ferry service. The federal government claims that the Confederation Bridge entailed no incremental cost to government and required no direct funding from government. The basis for the claim is the argument that the guaranteed payments to the SDCI are the same as the avoided cost of ferry provision, which the government was constitutionally required to pay anyway. The accuracy of this particular argument depends on the cost of (hypothetical) future ferry service provision.

As to financial risk, recall that the SCFI's bonds are guaranteed by statutory federal payments. Therefore the financial risk has remained largely in federal hands. The bonds were sold at a 4.5 per cent interest rate, at a time when similar federal issues were priced at 4.1 per cent. Moreover, SCFI paid a sales commission of 1.75 per cent, as compared with a typical rate of 0.6 per cent for federal real return bonds. SCFI's higher rate and fees would not be an issue if the federal government had extinguished equivalent risk (in other words, if the federal government had acquired a put-option against the risk of project default) or if the consortium's capital requirement had imposed on the private partners an incentive to minimize project capital. However, because the money was raised by the special purpose Crown Corporation and was guaranteed by the federal taxpayer, there was no net reduction in risk exposure. It is difficult to escape the conclusion that the structure was primarily chosen in an effort to achieve off-balance sheet financing.[16]

The project was completed and put in service very quickly. Again, however, it is not clear if the federal government laid off risks that matched its financial exposure, making this build–operate–transfer agreement an imperfect P3.

Lessons from the Case Studies

These case studies illustrate many of the difficulties of implementing effective or 'successful' P3s that deliver services at lower total costs than direct government provision or traditional contracting out. As described in the introduction, a major expected benefit of P3s is the private sector's ability to generate lower production costs due to economies of scale, more experience, better incentives and better ability to innovate. However, as we also pointed out, the critical test is whether P3s have lower total costs, including production costs and all the transaction costs associated with managing an external supplier of services.

The case studies illustrate that contracting difficulties make it difficult for the public sector actually to realize lower total costs. This is not really surprising. P3s are usually complex contracting situations with high transaction costs. Indeed, one way of thinking of P3s is simply government contracting out under relatively unfavourable conditions. Following

Williamson (1975), Globerman and Vining (1996) and Boardman and Hewitt (2004), contracting out theory suggests that contracting costs are likely to be high when there is asset specificity, complexity/ uncertainty, low *ex ante* competitiveness, and poor contract management skills. In these circumstances, after the contract has been signed, contestability will be low, the risk of hold-up will be high and thus the aggregate contracting costs are likely to be high. Many infrastructure P3s are likely to have these characteristics.

It is useful to consider the factors that are likely to raise costs in the context of the five case studies we have described. First, consider the issue of complexity/uncertainty. (Complexity and uncertainty are conceptually different, although in practice they are often treated as a single variable.) Many highway projects are relatively predictable from a construction cost perspective, but are highly uncertain from a usage perspective. For example, there was relatively little problem in constructing the Dulles highway on schedule. However, use levels on the toll road were significantly lower than anticipated (10000 per day during its initial month versus 34000 per day projected). This P3 essentially involved bundling a relatively standard highway construction project with a much more uncertain (and complex) business that involved demand estimation and pricing expertise. Bundling the two projects resulted in a relatively complex project. In contrast, construction of the Tampa Bay water project was complex, while usage demand (and price) was guaranteed. Construction was complex because large-scale desalination was an emerging technology. High complexity of construction resulted in costs that were far higher than expected.

It is generally thought that it is sensible to specify contracts in terms of outcomes or outputs rather than inputs. P3s have special merit in infrastructure provision because imperfect information and the reality of incomplete contracts make it difficult to specify *ex ante* the best design, construction techniques, or even the optimal investment in physical plant as opposed to later operational and servicing costs. In these circumstances, leaving design and investment choices to a private partner can be optimal (in providing incentives for innovation and parsimonious allocation of capital) if the public partner can adequately specify the desired service level. However, the Highway 407 case study illustrates how complexity can be increased by specifying performance in terms of outcomes rather than inputs. The lack of specification on the 'how' in the RFP was presumably intended to draw our private sector innovation, but it increased complexity substantially. In turn, this had the effect of reducing *ex ante* competitiveness, as indicated by the fact that there were only two qualified bidders.

Second, consider asset specificity. Many infrastructure P3s have high asset specificity which is to say their value is low in any alternative use.

Another critical issue is whether the government is in effect the sole buyer or not. In the Tampa Bay desalination plant, the plant was characterized by locational asset specificity and the government was the sole buyer. The city would not approve the plant and the contractor could not sell the water to any other customers due to its location. Here, the contractor was subject to government holdup. A highway also has locational asset specificity as it cannot be used as anything other than a highway in that location. One might think that this would lead to a potential problem and indeed it is a problem during the construction phase – either side runs the risk of hold-up. On the government's side, it is generally a lot cheaper for the initial contractor to finish the job than to bring in a new contractor because it has a great deal of specific knowledge about the particular project, i.e. there is considerable human capital asset specificity. However, once the infrastructure has been constructed (and approved), the potential problem of asset specificity is reduced because there are many users; in effect, there is a fundamental re-transformation where the situation switches from one of bilateral monopoly to one that is not.

Third, the lack of contract management skills is common. Contract management effectiveness may pertain to contracting expertise or to subject matter expertise. Subject matter expertise should not really be a problem. Contracting expertise is an historical problem for governments with limited P3 experience and many municipalities have been learning-by-doing. In these circumstances, lack of transparency may have tended to encourage opportunism by private sector firms and perhaps political favouritism as well. In the Alberta Special Waste Management System project, BOVAR, the private partner, received a very high guaranteed return on capital. Taxpayers essentially paid twice for the project. Furthermore, the project capacity was too large, having operated at about 50 per cent of capacity most of the time. Here, lack of government contract skills led to a contract where the public sector partner had an incentive to raise, rather than lower, costs. It is tempting for a firm to be opportunistic in these circumstances.

Opportunism can harm contract management effectiveness in many other ways. If governments want P3s to succeed, they will be less likely to 'pull the plug' on projects. Indeed, there may be an escalation of commitment (that is, a tendency to throw good money after bad). It is very hard politically for governments to stop P3 infrastructure projects in the middle – the bigger the project, the harder it is to stop. Of course, this is also true for pure public sector projects (Boardman et al., 1993). Again, if the private sector firm knows the public sector is committed to continuing the project regardless of escalating cost, it has an opportunity to behave opportunistically.

In sum, during the construction phase of infrastructure P3s, there may be problems of complexity, asset specificity and low contract management effectiveness, which would lead to high risk of opportunistic hold-up. During the operating phase of infrastructure P3s, there are almost always problems of uncertainty. These factors alone are not too bad. Contestability is often reasonably high and the risk of hold-up quite low. If one operator fails, government can bring in another. The greater risks relate to incentive design and the matching of risks and returns; therein rests the case for openness and transparency in the contracting process: 'sunshine' is likely to highlight potential contracting conflicts and failures.

4. CONCLUSION: CAVEAT EMPTOR

In North America almost any project involving the public and private sectors might be referred to as a P3. However, we believe that the term P3 should be reserved for build–operate–transfer projects. In this chapter we have provided a catalogue of the largest and most well-known infrastructure P3s in the USA and Canada. They occur most frequently in the areas of transportation (roads, airports and bridges), water and wastewater, power and energy, and for hospital and other facilities. Infrastructure P3s took off in the mid-1990s and are quite common in some jurisdictions.

This chapter has also discussed the main reasons why governments are drawn to P3s – lower cost provision, lower financial risk, avoidance of up-front capital costs, keeping the budget deficit down, and the ability to impose user charges. Even if these reasons are valid, it is important to realize that from a social perspective the key issue is whether the total cost of the P3 is lower than the total cost of the government provision, including production costs and all transaction costs. To investigate this issue we examined five case studies of North American infrastructure P3s.

There has been a tendency in some quarters to suggest that P3s are a holy grail that can reduce public sector costs and transfer various categories of risk to private sector actors. But the sobering reality that 'there are no free lunches' appears to apply to P3s as much as it does to everything else. The evidence from North America is perhaps not surprising: it suggests that profit-making private sector entities, whether they be construction firms, operating entities or whatever, are adept at making sure, one way or another, that they are fully compensated for risk-taking. In practice, there has been considerable variation in the degree to which financial risk has been shifted to the private sector. In some cases, in spite of the initial intentions of the public partner, projects have ended up largely or completely financed by the public sector. This fact alone should not necessarily stop the public sector from engaging in P3s, but it is does suggest that caution and realism are the appropriate attitudes.

Private sector participants will frequently go to considerable lengths to *avoid* risk, especially those associated with usage, even when that was the primary motivation for the public sector to utilize the P3 form. At the extreme, this means that the private sector will tend to establish 'stand-alone' operating firms when carrying out P3 contracts that entail large risks from technological or demand uncertainty. These stand-alone entities can avoid large losses by the parent when things go badly wrong by declaring bankruptcy or even by threatening to go bankrupt. The case studies suggest that the public sector has difficulty in recognizing and anticipating this form of strategic behaviour (perhaps because it is something the public sector – with its taxing power – rarely has to deal with).

Unless public sector managers recognize that they must design contracts that both compensate the private sector for risk and then ensure that they actually bear it, P3s will not improve allocative efficiency (make society better off). Hopefully, this chapter will help foster appropriate institutional design.

NOTES

1. We would like to thank Caroline Burns and Amber Lannon for research assistance.
2. For example, the US General Accounting Office (GAO) includes conventional contracting out of government services and even privatization – the complete withdrawal of government provision and financing – as P3s (GAO, 1999).
3. Specifically, we think it does not make sense to include the following relationships as P3s: (1) service contracts or other forms of contracting-out by the public sector; (2) privatization in the form of the sale of public assets; (3) regulation (including franchise contracting) by public sector entities of privately owned natural monopoly facilities, or (4) the construction of facilities by the private sector and the leasing or sale of those facilities to the public sector based upon fixed, certain terms (including lease/purchase or turn-key agreements).
4. Input costs may also be lower in a P3 if the private-sector firm manages procurement better than the public-sector counterpart. This is possible (in imperfectly competitive markets) because the private sector managers derive benefits from cost control that are normally not available to public sector managers.
5. The last point means that governments cannot borrow infinite amounts without affecting their credit rating. Raising funds for a P3 project may raise the cost borrowing for subsequent projects. Analysts should include these additional costs in the 'full' cost of the P3.
6. Vining and Weimer (2005) distinguish between *ex ante* transaction costs, which can be called governance costs, and *ex post* transaction costs, which can be called opportunism costs or hold-up costs.
7. The first two case Canadian studies draw extensively on Poschmann (2003).
8. Hall (1998) quotes the Chief Financial Officer of the private firm that operated the road as saying: 'We haven't made any debt payments in so long I've forgotten how much we owe now'.
9. This discussion draws extensively on Mintz (1995).
10. Chem-Security said the reasons for this included generators' pursuit of lower-cost options for waste disposal. These included immediate management, waste minimization

and on-site treatment or disposal, postponement of site clean-ups, an increase in the waste-treatment options available to Alberta generators, including recycling and resource-recovery options and out-of-province disposal options, as well as regulatory changes that mandated upstream reductions in waste production (NRCB, 1994:6–8).

11. Of course, if Chem-Security and BOVAR could actually have earned profits higher than the guaranteed rate of return, they would have had an incentive to control costs. However, Mintz (1995) shows that even with some positive probability of profit, the companies would have an incentive to over-invest (p. 33 and appendix).

12. Mintz (1995) estimates a weighted return on equity of 15.9 per cent for the period 1989–94, far above the risk-free return. Also see Poschmann (2003) for further details, Figure 2.

13. Note that the logic is deeply imperfect. The province's taking on the financing necessarily brought risks and costs not featured in the government's analysis, such as the issues raised by de Bettignies and Ross (2004).

14. See: www.407etr.com, accessed 16 August 2005.

15. This discussion borrows liberally from Loxley (1999).

16. This was the Auditor General's conclusion, and the government did not ultimately succeed in keeping the structure off-book. The 1994–5 Public Accounts read 'the Government is obligated to pay an annual subsidy of $41.9 million (1992 dollars) to SCFI (to) begin on May 31, 1997 and continue for 35 years. The amount of annual payments is subject to escalation in accordance with the Consumer Price Index ... there are no conditions related to these payments ... The Government has recorded a liability of $726 million which is the estimated present value of the subsidy payments. In addition, deferred subsidies of an equal amount have been included in other loans, investments and advances' (Receiver General for Canada, 1995).

REFERENCES

Averch, H. and L.L. Johnson (1962), 'Behavior of the firm under regulatory constraint', *American Economic Review*, **52** (5), 1052–69.

Battelle Corporation (2003), *Performance-Based Contracting for the Highway Construction Industry: An Evaluation of the Use of Innovative Contracting and Performance Specification in Highway Construction*, February.

Boardman, A.E. and R. Hewitt (2004), 'Problems with contracting out government services: lessons from orderly services at SCGH', *Industrial and Corporate Change*, **13** (6), 917–29.

Boardman, A.E., A.R. Vining and W.G. Waters, II (1993), 'Costs and benefits through bureaucratic lenses: example of a highway project', *Journal of Policy Analysis and Management*, **12** (3), 532–55.

Boardman, A.E., W.L. Mallery and A.R. Vining (1994) 'Learning from *ex ante/ex post* cost-benefit comparisons: the Coquihalla Highway example', *Socio-Economic Planning Sciences*, **28** (2), 69–84.

Brumback, T. (2003), 'SCC weighs toll road rate ceiling', *Leesburg Today*, 4 December.

de Bettignies, J.E. and T.W. Ross (2004), 'The economics of public–private partnerships', *Canadian Public Policy*, **30** (2), 135–54.

Canadian Council for Public–Private Partnerships (2001), *100 Projects: Selected Public–Private Partnerships Across Canada – 2000 Edition*, Toronto: Canadian Council for Public–Private Partnerships.

Engi, E., R. Fischer and A. Galetovic (2002), 'A new approach to private roads', *Regulation*, **25** (3), 18–19.

Flyrberg, B., M.S. Holm and S. Buhl (2002), 'Underestimating costs in public works projects: error or lie?', *Journal of the American Planning Association*, **68** (3), 279–93.

Globerman, S. and A. Vining (1996), 'A framework for evaluating the government contracting-out decision with an application to information technology', *Public Administration Review*, **56** (6), 40–46.

Hall, T.C. (1998), 'Red ink floods greenway', *Washington Business Journal*, **17** (18), 1–2.

Johnson, N. (2003), 'As seawater desalination plant readies for day 1, eyes turn to Tampa', *Knight Kidder Tribune Business News*, 6 January.

Klein, D.B. and J. Majewski (n.d.), 'America's toll roads heritage: the achievements of private initiative in the 19th century', working paper, Santa Barbara, CA: University of California.

Loxley, S.J. (1999), *An Analysis of a Public–Private Sector Partnership: The Confederation Bridge*, a report prepared for the Canadian Union of Public Employees.

Mendoza, E., M. Gold, P. Cater and J. Parmar (1999), 'The sale of Highway 407 express toll route: a case study', *Journal of Project Finance*, **5** (3), 5–14.

Mintz, J.M. (1995), *An Evaluation of the Joint Venture Agreement Establishing the Alberta Special Waste Management System*, mimeo, Toronto: University of Toronto Faculty of Management.

Natural Resources Conservation Board, (1994), *Receipt of Hazardous Waste from Other Canadian Jurisdictions by the Alberta Special Waste Management System*, Decision Report: Application #9301, Chem-Security (Alberta) Ltd, Calgary: Natural Resources Conservation Board.

Norment, R. (2002), 'PPPs – American style', *The PFI Journal*, **39**, 26–7.

Pittman, C. (2004), 'Contractors differ over cost to fix desal plant', *St. Petersburg Times*, 16 March, 1B.

Poschmann, F. (2003), *Private Means to Public Ends: The Future of Public–Private Partnerships*, Toronto: C.D. Howe Institute.

Pozen, D.E. (2003), 'Managing a correctional marketplace: prison privatization in the United States and the United Kingdom', *Journal of Law and Politics*, **19**, 253–84.

Priest, G.L. (1993), 'The origins of utility regulation and the "theories of regulation" debate', *Journal of Law and Economics*, **36** (1), part 2, 289–323.

Receiver General for Canada (1995), 'Public Accounts of Canada, 1995, volume 1', Ottawa: Canadian Government Publishing.

SG Hambros (1999), *Public–Private Partnerships for Highways: Experience, Structure, Financing, Applicability and Comparative Assessment. Objective One: Final Report*, report to the Council of Deputy Ministers Responsible for Transportation and Highway Safety, March, Ottawa: Transport Canada.

St. Petersburg Times, (2003), 'A troubled water odyssey', editorial, Friday, 31 October.

Taliaferro, R., Jr (1997), 'Greenway runs into financial troubles', *Richmond Times Dispatch*, 28 September, A-17.

US General Accounting Office (GAO) (1999), 'Privatization: lessons learned by state and local governments', GAO/GGD–97–48, report to the chairman, House Republican Task Force on Privatization.

Vining, A.R. and D.L. Weimer (2005), 'Economic perspectives on public organizations', forthcoming in Donald L. Ferrin, Larry Lynn and Michael Pollitt (eds), *Oxford Handbook of Public Management*, Oxford and New York: Oxford University Press, 209–33.

Williamson, O. E. (1975), *Markets and Hierarchies: Analysis and Antitrust Implications*, New York: Free Press.

Wright, A.G. (2003), 'Desalination dispute leaves a bitter taste; judge orders Tampa Bay Water and Covanta to name a mediator to work out plant dispute', *ENR*, **251** (23), 12.

10. The Private Finance Initiative or the public funding of private profit?

Jean Shaoul

As with many public policies, the rationale for the British government's Private Finance Initiative (PFI) and Public Private Partnerships (PPP), known elsewhere as design, build, finance and operate (DBFO), build, own, operate and transfer (BOOT), build operate and transfer (BOT), partnerships or concessions, has changed so much over time that even its proponents have described it as 'an ideological morass' (IPPR, 2001). It was originally justified as providing the capital investment that the public sector could not afford, the macroeconomic argument. Later, the UK government claimed that PFI would deliver greater value for money (VFM) over the life of the projects because the private sector firstly is more efficient than the public sector and secondly assumes some of the financial risks (and costs) that the public sector would otherwise carry, the microeconomic argument. More recently, the government has justified PFI on the basis that it delivers assets to, for example, time and budget (Treasury, 2003). The shifting rationale may imply that, like the various justifications given for the war against and occupation of Iraq, the promises may prove to be a chimera.

Introduced by the then Conservative government in 1992 (Treasury, 1993), PFI was revitalized and rebranded as Public Private Partnerships (PPP), an umbrella term that includes PFI, by the incoming Labour government in 1997. While privatization was the preferred policy measure for reform of the state owned trading enterprises, partnerships are playing a key role in the transformation of those public services that can not be privatized for political or financial reasons. Partnerships have taken different forms in each of the public services and there are differences in their mode of operation. They nevertheless all share certain common features. Services remain publicly funded and subject to a regulatory framework set by government, and the core professional or frontline services as in health and education are provided by the public agency: this is the 'public' aspect. The ancillary services are provided by the private sector as is the physical infrastructure to support both the professional and ancillary services: these are the 'private' and 'finance' aspects of the partnership arrangement.

The purpose of this chapter is to examine the development, control and scope of PFI/PPP in public services, which includes health, education, IT in administrative departments and the criminal justice system, review the outcomes in terms of the claims of value for money and risk transfer, and consider some of the wider implications of this policy for service delivery, control and accountability.

The chapter is organized in four sections. The first section explains the development, control and scope of the policy. The second section reviews the evidence as it relates to *ex ante* value for money that lies at the heart of the government's case for PFI/PPP. The third section examines the outcomes of PFI projects. The final section concludes by drawing out the implications for the various stakeholders, explains the significance of the value for money rhetoric and private finance, and why accountability is so poor.

THE DEVELOPMENT, CONTROL AND SCOPE OF PFI

Initially applied to the transport sector for roads, bridges and rail services, and later to prisons and IT provision in administrative services that had low public visibility, PFI was slow to get off the ground in frontline human services such as health and education. There were several reasons for this: the policy was deeply unpopular with the public[1] and the trade unions,[2] the projects were complex and the relatively small scale of the desired refurbishment (in the case of schools and hospitals) and even new builds in the case of education was unattractive to the private sector, as the following examples show. The 1994 proposal to refurbish Pimlico School, the first under PFI, became a new build in 1995 because no private sector company was interested in bidding for the contract (Edwards and Shaoul, 2003). In more than one hospital case, the move from refurbishment to total new build was because as the hospital Trust acknowledged, reburbishment was unappealing to bidders, 'There is considerable evidence that very large schemes are more attractive to the private sector' (WNHT, 1998). It was also unclear that the National Health Service (NHS) had the legal power to enter into PFI contracts. Furthermore, unlike roads, prisons and administrative IT projects, where the purchaser was central government with established procedures, the Trusts did not have a proven financial track record.

In 1997, the incoming Labour government resuscitated the policy and got PFI projects off the ground. In the case of hospitals, it removed a number of obstacles and introduced legislation[3] to persuade potential bidders and their financial backers that NHS Trusts not only had the power to enter into such contracts but their payments to the consortia were effectively underwritten in the event of a financial crisis within the Trust, as Standard and Poor's, the credit ratings agency, acknowledged (2003). In the case of education and other local authority projects, the government made PFI 'credits' available to cover some of the capital costs. Small schemes, particularly in education, were later 'bundled' together to make them larger and more attractive to the private sector.

There are several financial criteria that must be met if a PFI project is to proceed. Firstly, the scheme must be affordable and secondly, VFM must be demonstrated (Treasury, 1997). Affordability is crucial if services to be provided under PFI or elsewhere are not to be jeopardized. However, it is a flexible term that defies precise measurement. While value for money is a colloquial term that has intuitive appeal, its substantive meaning is ambiguous. It is usually associated with the three 'Es': economy, efficiency and effectiveness. In practice, for a variety of conceptual and methodological reasons, VFM audits, as carried out by the National Audit Office, have focused on economy rather than efficiency and effectiveness. Its meaning in the context of PFI is no more precise and is similarly based upon economy.

VFM is demonstrated by identifying and discounting the whole life costs of the project as financed under conventional procurement methods and compared against the discounted costs of the PFI option. The scheme with the lowest cost is assumed to offer the greatest VFM. The comparison also includes the costs of some of the risks associated with the construction and management of the asset. Since some of the risks are to be transferred to the private sector, the PFI option will (it is argued) provide greater VFM than a publicly financed alternative where the public sector bears all the risks. Thus all the risks associated with design, construction, finance, maintenance and operation of the asset over the life of the project must be identified. Probabilities of their occurrence must be assigned and financial values attributed to their outcomes so that the value of the risk to be transferred to the private sector can be included as a cost in the public sector comparator (PSC). The greater the value of the risk transferred, the more expensive the PSC becomes relative to the PFI option.

It is believed that market forces will provide VFM through the requirement to put the contract out to competitive bidding. This is because an identifiable market of private sector bidders, prepared to consider competing for the opportunity to design the services to be provided, undertake the financing and delivery of the project, should create a competitive tension and innovative solutions that will help to deliver a more economical service and thus provide the best assurance of VFM (Treasury Private Finance Panel, 1995).

But none of this should obscure a number of important issues. First, the VFM case is necessarily based on *estimates* of future costs and operates only at the point of procurement. Second, risk transfer is the crucial element in delivering whole-life economy since under PFI private sector borrowing, transactions costs and the requirements for profits necessarily generate higher costs than conventional public procurement. Thirdly, the public sector retains the ultimate responsibility of essential and often statutory services for which there is usually no alternative. Fourthly, where central government or its agencies are the purchaser, the government underwrites the payments. Elsewhere, government commitment to the policy means that the revenue streams are assured as the capital markets recognize (Standard and Poor's, 2003). Thus the ability to transfer risk in practice remains very limited as the rescue of failed PFI/PPP projects such as National Air Traffic Services, the Channel Tunnel Rail Link, the Royal Armouries Museum and so on demonstrate. This, plus the commitment to future payments over a long period, in turn means that the government is building up long term liabilities for the future. Finally, just three corporations now account for the overwhelming majority of the UK government's IT systems (Dunleavy et al., 2001) and major hospital and IT schemes have attracted only one qualified bidder. This means that the corporations are now in a position to exert the monopoly power that undermines the VFM argument and thus to control the direction of future policy in ways that privilege the few at the expense of the many.

But neither the appraisal methodology nor the control process is neutral. Firstly, this highly technical VFM appraisal methodology, established by the Treasury, is not neutral but is itself biased in favour of the private sector option and has important wealth distributional implications (Shaoul, 2005). Secondly, the key government department, the Treasury, both champions and controls the PFI process. The Treasury's projects division was initially established in 1997 with a two-year life, largely with staff on secondment from the private sector. This was later itself reconstituted as a public–private partnership, Partnerships UK (PUK), whose mission is to help the public sector deliver fast and efficient development and procurement of PPPs; strong PPPs that build stable relationships with the private sector; savings in development costs; and better value for money (Partnerships UK, 2003). The majority shareholding of 51 per cent is held by private sector institutions, including financial services companies that have been involved in financing PFI projects, and others that have PFI contracts. Furthermore, the majority of the board members come from the private sector, with the public sector represented by only two non-executive directors and the public interest represented through an Advisory Council. The structure, ownership and control of PUK is important because it sets the PFI agenda and reflects the conflict between policy promotion and policy control acknowledged by government (Timms, 2001) and noted elsewhere (Freedland, 1998; Edwards and Shaoul, 2002). It means that the control process is dominated by parties which have a vested interest in the policy's expansion.

It is however impossible to see, let alone understand, how these processes operate to control PFI. Firstly, even the most basic data showing the number, size and cost of PFI projects is difficult to collect. For example, numerous government sources produce information in ways that do not reconcile, as evidenced by the Education and Home Office projects in Table 10.1. Secondly, it has been impossible for the purpose of this chapter to produce a table showing the amount of PFI and non-PFI expenditure on a departmental basis for each year since the policy was introduced. Thirdly, it is almost impossible to ascertain the proportion of PFI to total public capital expenditure because although the Treasury produces a list of all signed deals, dates and their capital values on a departmental basis, it does not produce a comparable list of non-PFI or even total capital expenditure on a departmental basis. In addition, it is not clear that the government records all IT PFI projects as PFI capital expenditure since it maintains it is purchasing services, not assets. Certainly, the Treasury list was not complete; for example, the Home Office did not show the problematic Criminal Records Bureau project. Furthermore, PFI will not be scored as government expenditure if the underlying asset is off the government's balance sheet. But since the statistics do not identify whether the asset is on or off the government's balance sheet, the ratio of public to non-public capital expenditure is impossible to calculate. Fifthly, it is impossible to find out on a systematic basis the public sector's expected annual payments on a project basis (since the full business cases setting out the financial costs are not in the public domain for reasons of 'commercial confidentiality') or even on a departmental basis, although the Treasury does produce aggregated data that suggest that future commitments now constitute about 3 per cent of departmental expenditure (excluding welfare payments). Finally, and even more worryingly, despite the fact that central government is known to underwrite the Highways Agency's payments in the case of roads (Standard and Poor's, 2003) and presumably its other contracts, there is no mention in the departmental accounts of such contingent liabilities.

While the use of parliamentary questions has elucidated some information (Health Select Committee, 2000), this is a cumbersome route that provides data on an *ad hoc* basis only and has limited visibility. Thus it only serves to highlight, rather than to resolve the problem. In short, there is a lack of consistent and useful data about the extent of private finance in public

Table 10.1   PFI signed projects list as at July 2003 (all projects)

Functional area	Department	Number of signed projects	Capital value (£m)
Administrative	HM Customs and Excise	1	14
	Constitutional Affairs	11	263
	Work and Pensions	7	930
	HM Treasury	1	563
	Inland Revenue	8	391
	Office of Government Commerce	1	10
	Public Records Office	1	–
Health	Health	117	3 162
Education	Higher Education *	At least 6	278
	Further Education *	At least 8	113
	Schools *	At least 6	1 000
	Total education and skills	96	1 979
Criminal Justice system	Home Office prison projects *	At least 14	613
	Home Office IT projects **	At least 6	677
	Total Home Office	36	1 633
	Local authority police projects in England and Wales *	21	300
	Local authority probation service* projects in England and Wales	6	14
Other	Culture, media and sport	5	60
	Environment, food and rural affairs	11	346
	Transport	37	20 496
	Trade and industry	8	180
	Foreign and Commonwealth office	2	91
	GCHQ	1	330
	Defence	46	2 492
	Northern Ireland	29	416
	Office of the Deputy Prime Minister	42	549
	Scotland	78	2 136
	Wales	26	502
Total		593	36 413

Notes:
* DoT *Construction Statistics Annual*, 2002.
** PFI Signed projects list – July 2003, at www.pppforum.com/signedprojectshub/ho.html, 10 February 2004.

Sources: PFI Signed projects list – July 2003, at www.hm-treasury.gov.uk/media//D6678/ pfi_signed_list.xls, 10 February 2004. See also above.

services making it difficult to analyse the use of private finance and its wider implications, as Australian researchers have also noted (Walker and Con Walker, 2000).

EVIDENCE OF THE *EX ANTE* VFM CASE

The very first investigations into PFI came from the National Audit Office, which has produced more than 20 reports on PFI, including some that have reviewed specific projects, examining the *ex ante* value for money case and other issues arising out of the procurement process. Its evidence and conclusions on the VFM case are mixed. Although its evidence about the early PFI bridge, roads, prisons and hospital schemes showed that the margin of anticipated VFM was small and less than the public agencies had estimated and there were problems with individual projects (NAO, 1997a, 1997b, 1998, 1999a), it generally concluded that projects demonstrated VFM in terms of the prescribed methodology (NAO, 1999b). However it questioned the reliability of the complex financial modelling required for VFM appraisals (NAO, 2000a). But while useful, since the National Audit Office reports provided little in the way of financial information to permit an informed debate or financial critique, it was difficult for the public to verify or otherwise the government's financial case for individual PFI projects.

In contrast, PFI in hospitals and schools have been particularly important for a wider public understanding of PFI. The first wave schemes, typically involving capacity reduction to make them both PFI-able and affordable, were deeply unpopular and some of their full business cases (FBCs) entered the public domain, albeit without other supporting documentation and after financial close. Crucially, the contracts were not released due to reasons of 'commercial confidentiality', which makes it difficult to assess the actual degree of risk transfer. These limitations not withstanding, PFI hospitals and later schools were crucial because the publication and/or leaking of their FBCs made it possible for the first time to examine systematically the financial case and the wider issues raised by PFI. In other words, the policy has been subject to detailed and independent scrutiny only after deals were signed, rather than before, and in the context of specific projects rather than the policy or programme as a whole.

In health, a number of studies have examined the business cases used to support new hospital builds and have questioned both the ability of the methodology to measure VFM in an unbiased way and the degree to which they demonstrate VFM (Gaffney and Pollock, 1999a; Price et al., 1999; Pollock et al., 2000). Other work in the health service (Hodges and Mellett, 1999; Gaffney and Pollock, 1999b; Gaffney et al., 1999a, 1999b, 1999c; Pollock et al., 1999) showed that the high cost of PFI projects led to affordability problems, an issue that the emphasis on VFM downplays, and led to hospital downsizing in order to bridge the affordability gap. The evidence showed that the VFM case rested upon risk transfer but in almost all cases, the amount of risk transferred was almost exactly the amount required to bridge the gap between the cost of PFI and conventional procurement. At the very least, this indicates that the risk assessment methodology is somewhat arbitrary and that the value of the risk transfer was calculated in such a way as to close the gap between the Public Sector Comparator (PSC) and PFI. Indeed, it is difficult to avoid the conclusion that the function of the 'risk transfer' motif was to disguise the true cost of PFI (Pollock et al., 2002). A study of the appraisal process in hospitals concluded that that there were numerous flaws in the process that raised doubts as to whether the PFI proposals that were accepted demonstrated either that they were economically sound or affordable, raising questions about service provision and the conflict between policy promotion and regulation (Froud and Shaoul, 2001).

The National Audit Office review of the Dartford and Gravesham PFI hospital project (NAO, 1999a) found that there might be no savings under PFI as a miscalculation in the PSC had overstated estimated savings by £12.1m and the sensitivity analysis indicated that a 10 per cent reduction in costs in real terms would lead to PFI being more expensive than traditional public procurement. However the NAO reported that, despite the extra financial support of £4m a year required to pay for the scheme, the health authority and the NHS Executive were satisfied that the scheme still remained good VFM. It did not comment on their optimism or itself explicitly draw any conclusions about the overall VFM of the project based upon its own work.

In the context of education, studies have suggested that the policy is no less problematic (Ball, Heafey and King, 2001, 2003; McFadyean and Rowland, 2002; Pollock and Rowland, 2002; Edwards and Shaoul, 2002). The evidence suggests that as in hospitals, the number and size of schools may be rationalized to make them more PFI-able. In other words, as in hospitals, the PFI tail wags the planning dog. Scotland's Accounts Commission (2002) was unhappy about the VFM methodology and concluded that it was not possible to draw overall conclusions on VFM by comparisons of the costs and benefits involved.

Although the business cases demonstrating VFM for IT projects and other administrative services are not in the public domain, it is likely that they are similarly flawed. For example, the leaked Passport Agency's business case, entitled 'Private sector involvement in the issue of the British Passport', was a self serving document clearly written to justify a decision already taken. It cited as one of its five objectives private sector involvement which necessarily precluded the conventional public procurement option that was cheaper than the PFI solution at a higher and more realistic volume level (UKPA, 1997). In the case of the Benefits Agency's NIRS2 project, the government accepted such a low bid from Andersen Consulting which retained ownership of the software – a factor it was later to rue – that there was little point in producing a fully worked up Public Sector Comparator (NAO, 1997c).

The National Audit Office reviewed the first two prisons built under PFI (NAO, 1997b) and its conclusions indicated some doubts as to the expected VFM. For example, the Fazakerley PFI solution was more or less the same as the PSC, which in any case was not a precise forecast, and there was some doubt as to how the risks were to be allocated between the PFI partners.

Two reports that collated secondary evidence have been widely cited as demonstrating the case for PFI. Firstly, the Andersen report, commissioned by the Treasury, is particularly important (Arthur Andersen/LSE, 2000) because it shows that the *ex ante* case for PFI rested upon the transfer of risk. But a closer examination shows that this was dependent upon just a handful of projects, and one project, NIRS2, which it did not explicitly identify by name, that failed disastrously, accounted for more than 80 per cent of the risk transfer (Pollock and Vickers, 2000). Thus its wider *ex ante* case largely disappears when set against the outcomes. Secondly, the think tank, the Institute for Public Policy Research (IPPR, 2001), concluded that PFI demonstrated VFM in some sectors but not universally. It was particularly concerned about health and education.

One of the most useful sources of information about PFI in general and hospitals in particular comes from a surprising source: the corporate sector itself. Firstly the corporate and trade press such as *Project Finance International* and the credit ratings agencies taking the perspective of the capital markets provide information not available elsewhere. Secondly, the credit ratings agency, Standard and Poor's (2003), makes a useful assessment of PFI from the corporate perspective. After reviewing a number of projects, it concluded that PFI provided a relatively stable income stream and limited operational risks for the private sector consortium, typically structured as a Special Purpose Vehicle (SPV) and made up of a bank and construction and facilities management companies. This plus the ability of the SPVs to structure the deal in ways that push risk down to the subcontractors meant that the SPVs carried little effective risk. Nevertheless, the high level of debt, low debt service coverage and the single asset nature of PFI projects means that most PFI projects fall within the low investment grade of BBB+ (ie more risky to investors) unless they are insurance wrapped (Standard and Poor's, 2003).

It is therefore instructive to look at one just such low grade bond.[4] The Meridian Hospital Company, a UK SPV, issued a bond of £100m, which provided £91m after fees, at about 4.5 per cent interest rate. This favourable interest rate was not surprising since Meridian noted that investors were partly protected by a 'letter of support' from the Health Secretary, which provided bondholders with 'additional comfort' and the deal was structured in such a way as to provide 'little inherent risk' to investors (Barclays Capital, 1998). Of the £20m annual fee income from Greenwich Hospital Trust, Meridian anticipated that after paying operating costs to run the hospital, there would be £10–11m a year to support debt servicing, dividends and future growth. The project would be able to pay dividends to the parent companies by 2007 and this was set to increase. In reality, Meridian's accounts show that it has made a post-tax profit ever since the hospital started operating in 2001.

Two important points follow from this. Firstly, even a low grade project is very profitable and more profitable than expected. Secondly, more useful information is made available to the capital markets than to the public at large, which refutes the government's 'commercial sensitivity' argument used to justify the lack of disclosure to the public since the capital markets themselves require this information to be made available to potential investors.

POST IMPLEMENTATION EVALUATION OF PFI

As PFI projects have only recently come on stream, there is as yet little in the way of systematic empirical research as to how PFI is working in practice, with some of the evidence gleaned as 'snippets' from the press.

The construction phase of PFI projects have usually but not universally been built to budget and on time (NAO, 2003b). But given that most of the extra cost of PFI is justified in terms of risk transfer, this indicates that the public sector is paying a huge premium to ensure the underlying asset is built to time and budget and only begs the question why conventional contracts cannot be written in such a way as to ensure that the contractor builds to time and budget. This and the generally low risk for the operational phase of the contract is confirmed by the refinancing of PFI deals after completion of the construction phase. But this carries with it the potential, as in the case of the refinancing of Fazakerley prison[5] (NAO, 2002), for the companies to increase their profits in ways that serve to increase the risk to the public sector.

While the NAO reported that the aims of PFI had been met in the construction and design of 70 per cent of the 11 hospitals built to date (NAO, 2003a), this must be qualified by the absence of user satisfaction surveys and the widespread criticism of at least one hospital (it has corridors too narrow to permit more than one trolley) and problems in other hospitals.[6] 'Other more strategic criticisms have been made of their design (Worthington, 2002; Appleby and Coote, 2002). In the context of schools, the Audit Commission's review of PFI schools found that PFI did not guarantee better buildings despite their higher cost (2003).

Although there have been numerous adverse press reports in the UK of poor service delivery in hospitals under PFI contracts, some of which are documented in evidence to the Health Select Committee (2002), there have been few deductions and these have been small (Standard and Poor's, 2003). There have been similar press reports of concerns about poor performance in schools projects. In many cases, the original contract negotiation team has moved on making it difficult to know the assumptions and intentions underlying the contract. Monitoring has turned out to be more costly than anticipated, performance indicators have been difficult to operationalize, due to the subjective nature of the outcome, and contracts changes have been time consuming and complex.

There is as yet only one study that has systematically compiled empirical evidence as to the way PFI is operating in practice in the roads and hospital sectors (Edwards et al., 2004). In the context of hospitals, it found that the financial reporting of the 13 operational or partly operational PFI hospitals, despite capital costs of about £1.4bn, total costs of about £6bn over the 30-year life of the projects, and their combined annual cost of about £230m, was limited and opaque. In a number of cases, the actual payments to the private sector turned out to be considerably higher than originally estimated. This could be due to volume increases, inflation, contract changes and failure to identify and/or specify the requirements in sufficient detail: for example, the failure to specify that marmalade should be included in patients' breakfast led to an increased charge. But at the very least, this suggests that forecasting the cost of PFI payments, and hence its anticipated VFM, is not straightforward. The hospital Trusts' cost of capital, including the capital element of PFI and capital charges on their existing assets, rose from about 3 per cent of income pre-PFI to 9 per cent of income post-PFI. Despite an increase in funding, of which a third was accounted for by the increased cost of PFI, six of the 13 Trusts had a very substantial deficit, much higher than the national average. Four of these six were paying more than expected for their PFI contracts.

The private sector companies, organized as SPVs that are little more than shells, operate in a complex and opaque web of subcontracting to their sister companies that increases the costs and complexity of monitoring and enforcing the contract, and makes it impossible to assess the parent companies' total returns. After paying interest on their debt, which was higher than the total construction cost and rising, of about 7 per cent, the SPVs reported a post-tax return on shareholders' funds of 86 per cent. The SPVs' high effective cost of capital means that the PFI is expensive and considerably higher than the cost of conventional procurement. All this raises questions about both the VFM, the affordability of PFI in practice, and future service provision.

In the case of criminal justice contracts, court service projects have escalated in price, refuting the claim that PFI contracts deliver fixed prices (Centre for Public Services, 2002). HMP Altcourse at Fazakerley, the first PFI prison, has been controversial from the start because of its poor planning, lack of scrutiny of costs, a flawed savings assessment, operational performance failures and lastly the refinancing scandal that saw the private sector refinance the deal in a way that generated extra £11m for itself while at the same time increasing the risk to the public sector (NAO, 2000b). A report on prison performance noted that prisoners were confined to their rooms for longer periods and that their cells contained 'substantial ligature points' that 'rendered the cells unfit for use at all' (Chief Inspector of Prisons, 2000). In a report of operational performance of PFI prisons, the NAO reported that performance against contract had been mixed (2003b).

But PFI contracts, even when 'successful', have hidden costs to the rest of the public sector. For example, the Centre for Public Services (2002) shows that the private sector paid lower wages to its prison staff than did the public sector and some of its workforce were paid such low wages that they qualified for working family tax credits, in effect a low wage subvention by the state to the private sector.

PFI has been conspicuously unsuccessful in IT projects. But these failures are important because they demonstrate the fallacy of risk transfer argument: risk was transferred in unanticipated ways. Consider just two of the most well known IT project failures. When the Passport Agency's new system was rolled out before being adequately tested, prospective travellers experienced such delays in receiving their passports that they went in person to collect them, resulting in the passport equivalent of a run on the bank and more than 500 missing their travel dates. While the Passport Agency largely waived the penalties in the interests of partnership, the £12.6m resultant costs to hire extra staff led to an increase in the passport fee (NAO, 1999c). The much vaunted risk transfer was therefore not from the public sector to the private sector but to the public as individuals. The Contributions Agency's NIRS2 system was late and poorly tested. This led to incorrect and lost records, late and wrong welfare payments, additional costs to both the Contributions and the Benefits Agencies and an estimated £5bn in 'lost' taxes to the Inland Revenue as a result of the incorrect and lost records since recipients could not be assessed or were under-assessed for tax. This shows that when things go wrong, costs may be diffused well beyond the purchasing agency. Again, the limited penalties were waived, and when there was a need to renegotiate the contract, the agency found that it was locked in due to the private contractor owning the copyright on the software (Edwards and Shaoul, 2003).[7] Indeed, the outcomes of IT projects in the benefits recording and payments systems, the criminal justice system and other administrative services have been so poor that even the government has had to admit that PFI may not be the best means of procuring IT services (Treasury, 2003).

To what extent are these results generalizable? Firstly, the nature and context of public services means that they are typically difficult to define and measure. As statutory services, there are usually no substitutes. Despite the now fragmented nature of the public sector, such services are often interdependent. This inevitably makes PFI in IT more problematic than PFI in physical infrastructure. But the latter have not been without problems as the collapse of the National Air Traffic Services PPP, the Channel Tunnel Rail Link, and recent press reports of problems on the London Underground PPP demonstrate. Secondly, the 'successful' use of private finance in roads was and is a consequence of very high payments to the private sector that mean that the initial construction costs were paid for in just three years and that the private sector is making a 68 per cent operating profit per year on a 30-year contract (Edwards et al., 2004). Thus success comes at the expense of affordability, value for money and service cuts elsewhere. Finally, it is unlikely that these results are a purely British phenomenon, as the evidence on the hospital sector in Australia shows (Senate Community Affairs References Committee, 2000; Auditor General Western Australia, 1997; New South Wales Auditor General, 1996).

CONCLUSION

The evidence shows that the outcomes are inconsistent with the claims. At best, PFI has turned out to be very expensive with the inevitable consequences for service provision. But when things went wrong, and this was not infrequent, the costs were diffused throughout the public sector and onto the public at large, a travesty of risk transfer. Thus while the VFM argument rested upon risk transfer, the real significance of the VFM methodology has been the transfer of wealth from the public at large to the corporate sector. It is policies such as PFI that have played such a crucial role in the ever greater social inequality that is the hallmark of Britain today.

The lack of even the most basic statistical information makes scrutiny, control and accountability all but impossible. The concept of accountability in the context of public expenditure on essential services implies first that citizens, or at least their political representatives, the media, trade unions, academics and so on, can see how society's resources are being used and second that no members of that society are seen to have an explicitly sanctioned unfair advantage over others in relation to how those resources are used. At the very least, the lack of accountability to the public means that it is difficult if not impossible to learn from past experience. In the absence of public scrutiny, these projects may burden government with hidden subsidies, diversion of income streams and implicit loan guarantees whose impact on public finance may not become apparent for many years. More importantly, in so far as the information is made available to the capital markets, albeit unknown to a wider audience, this suggests that the government and the private sector are only reluctant to disclose the information to the public at large. Could this be because these are policies that enrich the few at the expense of the majority and for which no democratic mandate can be secured?

NOTES

1. As the government readily acknowledges with phrases such as 'policy as yet to win over all the stakeholders'.
2. See for example, Unison's website: www.unison.org.uk/pfi
3. NHS (Private Finance) Act 1997.
4. There are very few PFI bond documents that provide financial information since most are insurance wrapped and thus have high ratings (low risk) and this is the only one we have be able to obtain. But since the underlying risk to investors of the insurance wrapped (AAA) PFI hospital projects is of a similar nature (BBB+), the assumption must be that this deal is not atypical.
5. Because the private sector's debt repayment profile is restructured, the public sector could find itself exposed to additional termination liabilities, should the contract be terminated for any reason. This increased exposure would occur when the private sector had received most of the benefits and be facing additional costs associated with long term maintenance, thereby tempting the private sector in adverse circumstances to cut and run.
6. The NAO observed that it was not possible to determine whether the same results could have been achieved with alternative forms of procurement.
7. While conventional government procurement has not been without problems, the point is that under PFI the government has paid extra to ensure that the private sector carries the risk – to no avail.

REFERENCES

Accounts Commission (2002), *Taking the Initiative: Using PFI contracts to renew council schools*, Audit Scotland.

Appleby, J. and A. Coote (2002), *Five Year Health Check: A Review of Health Policy 1997–2002*, London: The Kings Fund.

Arthur Andersen and Enterprise LSE (2000), *Value for Money Drivers in the Private Finance Initiative*, report commissioned by the Treasury Taskforce, January, available from the Treasury's website: www.treasury-projects.gov.uk/series_1/andersen.

Audit Commission (2003), *PFI in Schools: The Quality and Cost of Buildings and Services Provided by Early Private Finance Initiative Schemes*, London: Audit Commission.

Auditor General Western Australia (1997), *Private Care for Public Patients: the Joondalup Health Campus, Report No 9*, Perth, Australia: WA Government.

Ball, R., M. Heafey and D. King (2001), 'The Private Finance Initiative', *Policy and Politics*, **29** (1), 95–108.

Ball, R., M. Heafey and D. King (2003), 'Some lessons from using PFI for school building projects', local government study.

Barclays Capital (1998), *Meridian Hospital Company Plc,* initial public offering circular, London: Barclays Capital.

Centre for Public Services (2002), *Privatising Justice: the Impact of the Private Finance Initiative in the Criminal Justice System*, Sheffield.

Chief Inspector of Prisons for England and Wales (2000), *HM Prison Altcourse, Report of a Full Inspection*, 1–10 November 1999, London: Home Office.

Department of Transport (DoT) (2003), *Transport Statistics Great Britain*, London: DoT.

Dunleavy, P., H. Margetts, S. Bastow and H. Yared (2001), 'Policy learning and public sector information technology: contractual and e-government change', paper presented at the American Political Science Association's annual conference, August, San Francisco.

Edwards, P. and J. Shaoul (2002), 'Controlling the PFI process in schools: a case study of the Pimlico project', *Policy and Politics*, **31** (3), 371–85.

Edwards, P. and J. Shaoul (2003), 'Partnerships: for better, for worse?' *Accounting, Auditing and Accountability Journal*, **16** (3), 397–421.

Edwards, P., J. Shaoul, A. Stafford, and L. Arblaste (2004), 'Evaluating the operation of PIF in roads and hospitals,' ACCA research report no. 88, London.

Freedland, M. (1998), 'Public law and private finance – placing the Private Finance Initiative in a public law framework', *Public Law*, **288**, 307.

Froud, J., and J. Shaoul (2001), 'Appraising and evaluating PFI for NHS hospitals', *Financial Accountability and Management*, **17** (3), 247–70.

Gaffney, D., and A. Pollock (1999a), 'Downsizing for the 21st Century', a report to Unison Northern Region on the North Durham Acute Hospitals PFI scheme, School of Public Policy, University College, London.

Gaffney, D. and A. Pollock, (1999b), 'Pump priming the PFI: why are privately financed hospital schemes being subsidised?' *Public Money and Management*, **17** (3), 11–16.

Gaffney, D., A. Pollock, D. Price and J. Shaoul (1999a), 'NHS capital expenditure and the Private Finance Initiative – expansion or contraction?' *British Medical Journal*, **319**, 48–51.

Gaffney, D., A. Pollock, D. Price and J. Shaoul (1999b), 'PFI in the NHS – is there an economic case?' *British Medical Journal*, **319**, 116–19.

Gaffney, D., A. Pollock, D. Price and J. Shaoul (1999c), 'The politics of the Private Finance Initiative and the new NHS', *British Medical Journal*, **319**, 249–53.

Health Select Committee (2000), *Public Expenditure on Health and Personal Social Services 2000*, memorandum received from the Department of Health containing replies to a written questionnaire from the committee, HC 882, Session 1999–2000, London: Stationery Office.

Health Select Committee (2002), *The Role of the Private Sector in the NHS*, HC 308, Session 2001–2, London: Stationery Office.

Hodges, R. and H. Mellett (1999), 'Accounting for the Private Finance Initiative in the United Kingdom National Health Service', *Financial Accountability and Management*, **15** (3/4), 275–90.

Institute for Public Policy Research (2001) '*Building Better Partnerships: The Final Report of the Commission on Public Private Partnerships*', London: IPPR.

McFadyean, M., and D. Rowland (2002), *PFI vs Democracy? School Governors and the Haringey Schools PFI Scheme*, London: Menard Press.

National Audit Office (1997a), *The Skye Bridge*, report of Comptroller and Auditor General, HC 5, Session 1997–8, London: Stationery Office.

National Audit Office (1997b), *The PFI contracts for Bridgend and Fazakerley Prisons*, report of Comptroller and Auditor General, HC 253, Session 1997–8, London: Stationery Office.

National Audit Office (1997c), *The Contributions Agency: The Contract to Develop and Operate the Replacement National Insurance Recording System*, report of Comptroller and Auditor General, HC 12, Session 1997–8, London: Stationery Office.

National Audit Office (1998), *The Private Finance Initiative: The First Four Design, Build, Finance and Operate Roads Contracts*, report of Comptroller and Auditor General, HC 476, Session 1997–8, London: Stationery Office.

National Audit Office (1999a), *The PFI Contract for the New Dartford and Gravesham Hospital*, report of Comptroller and Auditor General, HC 423, Session 1998–9, London: Stationery Office.

National Audit Office (1999b), *Examining the Value for Money of Deals under PFI*, report of Comptroller and Auditor General, HC 739, Session 1998–9, London: Stationery Office.

National Audit Office (1999c), *The Passport Delays of Summer 1999*, report of Comptroller and Auditor General, HC 812, Session 1998–9, London: Stationery Office.

National Audit Office (2000a), *The Financial Analysis for the London Underground Public Private Partnership*, report of Comptroller and Auditor General, HC 54, Session 2000–2001, London: Stationery Office.

National Audit Office (2000b), *The Refinancing of the Fazakerley PFI Prison Contract*, report of Comptroller and Auditor General, HC 584, Session 1999–2000, London: Stationery Office.

National Audit Office (2002), *PFI Refinancing Update*, report of Comptroller and Auditor General, HC 1288, Session 2001–2, London: Stationery Office.

National Audit Office (2003a), *PFI: Construction Performance*, report of Comptroller and Auditor General, HC 371, Session 2002–3, London: Stationery Office.

National Audit Office (2003b), *The Operational Performance of Prisons*, report of Comptroller and Auditor General, HC 700, Session 2002–3, London: Stationary Office.

New South Wales Auditor General (1996), *Report for 1996; Volume I*, Sydney: NSW Parliament.

Partnerships UK (2003), 'What is partnerships UK?', www.partnershipsuk.org.uk/puk/index.htm.

Pollock, A., M. Dunnigan, D. Gaffney, D. Price, and J. Shaoul (1999), 'Planning the "new" NHS: downsizing for the 21st century', *British Medical Journal*, **319**, 179–84.

Pollock, A., D. Price, and M. Dunnigan (2000), *Deficits Before Patients: A Report on the Worcestershire Royal Infirmary PFI and Worcestershire Hospital Configuration*, School of Public Policy, University College, London.

Pollock, A. and N. Vickers (2000), 'Private pie in the sky', *Public Finance*, 14 April, 22–3.

Pollock, A. and D. Rowland (2002), 'Credit where it's due?' *Public Finance*, 5–11 July, 26–7.

Pollock, A., J. Shaoul and N. Vickers (2002), 'Private finance and "value for money" in NHS hospitals: a policy in search of a rationale?' *British Medical Journal*, **324** (18), 1205–8.

PPP Forum (2003), PFI signed projects list – July 2003, accessed at www.pppforum. com/signedprojectshub/ho.html.

Price, D., D. Gaffney and A. Pollock (1999), *The Only Game in Town: A Report on the Cumberland Infirmary Carlisle PFI*, report to Unison Northern Region, London: Unison.

Senate Community Affairs References Committee (2000), *Healing our Hospitals*, Canberra: Commonwealth of Australia.

Shaoul, J. (2005), 'A critical financial appraisal of the private finance initiative: selecting a financing method or reallocating wealth?', *Critical Perspectives on Accounting*, **16**, 441–71.

Standard and Poor's (2003), *Public Finance/Infrastructure Finance: Credit Survey of the UK Private Finance Initiative and Public–Private Partnerships*, London: Standard and Poor's.

Timms, S. (2001), 'Public Private Partnership, Private Finance Initiative', keynote address by the Financial Secretary to the Treasury to Global Summit, Cape Town, 6 December.

Treasury (1993), *The Private Finance Initiative: Breaking New Ground Towards a Partnership Between the Public and Private Sectors*, London: HM Treasury.

Treasury Private Finance Panel (1995), *Private Opportunity, Public Benefit: Progressing the Private Finance Initiative*, London: HM Treasury.

Treasury (1997), *Step by Step Guide to the PFI Procurement Process*, London: HM Treasury.

Treasury (2003), *PFI Meeting the Challenge*, London: HM Treasury.

Walker, B. and B. Con Walker (2000), *Privatisation: sell off or sell out? The Australian experience*, Sydney: ABC Books.

Walsgrave Hospital NHS Trust (1998), *Walsgrave Hospital NHS Trust Strategic Outline Case*, Coventry.

Worthington, J. (2002), *2020 Vision: Our Future Healthcare Environments*, report of the Building Futures Group, London: Stationery Office.

UKPA (1997), *Private Sector Involvement in the Issue of the British Passport*, business case summary, London: UKPA.

11. Learning from UK Private Finance Initiative experience

Michael Pollitt

The UK has been one of the leading countries in reforming the role of the state in the economy since 1979. The pervasive and long-running nature of the reforms in the UK make them an important source of case studies for the rest of the world.

In the early 1990s the Conservative government launched the Private Finance Initiative (PFI) in an attempt to attract private-sector support for a wide range of government projects in such sectors as health, prisons, transport and defence. To December 2004 this initiative has raised around £43 billion of capital investment from the private sector and typically raises 15–20 per cent of the government's capital budget each year. Total government commitments to future payments under around 670 contracts are estimated at £141 billion over 26 years.[1]

The current Labour administration has enthusiastically continued with policies aimed at increasing the involvement of the private sector in the economy, albeit with the occasional setback.[2] At the beginning of its second term in office (in mid-2001) the government announced plans for an extension of private-sector involvement in the provision of government-funded health and education services.[3] Indeed between the beginning of 2002 and July 2003 the total amount of PFI capital expenditure doubled.[4] More radical forms of competition to provide public services are being experimented with, such as allowing foreign clinical teams to bid for contracts to provide hospital services and the PFI has become so mainstream that it is no longer thought of as 'an initiative' but as part of the government's policy of public–private partnerships (PPPs).

In this chapter we will discuss the general lessons from the UK PFI but concentrate on infrastructure-related PFI (such as roads) in our discussion of specific cases. We begin by briefly discussing the history of the UK PFI and the theory of private finance for public goods.[5] We go on to outline the recurring themes in the UK experience. Next we review overall assessments of the success of the UK PFI programme and provide details of five PFI case studies based on independent National Audit Office reports.

THE DEVELOPMENT OF THE UK PRIVATE FINANCE INITIATIVE (PFI)

The PFI is 'one of the main mechanisms through which the public sector can secure improved value for money in partnership with the private sector. Through PFI, the private sector is able to bring a wide range of managerial, commercial and creative skills to the provision of public services, offering potentially huge benefits for Government' (HM Treasury Task Force 1997:2).

PFI projects involve the government in purchasing services from private companies where the private sector retains substantial ownership and control of the productive assets involved and the public sector pays for the delivered product. The associated PFI contract is awarded through a lengthy competitive tendering process which may end up in significant negotiation and re-specification with the winning bidder. Until 1989 the development of PFI schemes was restricted by Treasury rules which did not allow risk premia to be paid to the private sector on government projects. The PFI scheme formally began in 1992 (see HM Treasury, 1993) and became the preferred option for the funding of government capital projects in November 1994. After this and in spite of initial problems the annual amount of projects began to rise.

Since 1997 there have been a number of the reviews of the PFI. A 1997 review under Malcolm Bates, chairman of Pearl Assurance, led to the establishment of a Treasury Task Force to oversee and advise on PFI projects across contracting government departments. A second Bates review completed in March 1999 (Bates, 1999) led to the creation of Partnerships UK, which employs City experts to help the private sector get the best deal from the PFI and other forms of public–private partnerships.[6] In July 1999 the UK Treasury published guidelines on the accounting treatment of PFI payments and liabilities in response to the UK Accounting Standards Board's concern about way that government accounts were not properly reflecting PFI liabilities.[7] Partnerships UK succeeded the Treasury Task Force and became a partnership with a minority government stake (49 per cent) in March 2001. Similar expertise is offered to local government bodies through 'the 4ps' of the Public–Private Partnership Program, an agency set up by local authority associations in April 1996.[8]

In a parallel development, the government instituted a review of government procurement policy in 1999 led by Peter Gershon, the CEO of BAE Systems. His report led to the merger in April 2000 of several agencies previously involved in procurement into the Office of Government Commerce, a new Treasury department.[9] With respect to PFI projects, the new office is responsible for overall contract strategy and the spread of best practice within the public sector. Partnerships UK provides hands-on implementation, skills to bear on individual PPP projects.[10]

THE THEORY OF PRIVATE FINANCE FOR PUBLIC PROJECTS

The theoretical basis for the increasing private involvement in infrastructure projects considers the effects of liberalization – the introduction of market-based incentives into industries where they did not exist previously (see Pollitt, 1997). On balance, these effects seem to favour moves toward privatisation of state-owned assets. Hart et al. (1997) go as far as to suggest that state ownership is superior to private ownership only under a narrow range of circumstances: when opportunities for cost reductions that lead to non-contractible deterioration of quality are significant, when innovation is relatively unimportant, when competition is weak and consumer choice is ineffective and when the reputation mechanisms affecting private firms keen to win additional government contracts are also weak.

The PFI projects usually amount to a special type of privatization which separates the ownership and operation of the asset from the payment for the service. The government may wish to continue to pay for services where there are significant positive externalities in consumption, public goods considerations or significant distributional effects.

The introduction of the private sector into the production process for government services usually involves the transfer of some key elements of the project to the private sector such as project management, design of the delivery, operation of created assets, and significant financial risks. The private sector can improve efficiency by involving specialist project managers, designers, operators and financial risk managers, which may not be available within the public sector. This process is facilitated by bidding for projects by different private-sector contractors who 'compete for the field' (Demsetz 1968).

ISSUES THAT PFI PROJECTS MUST ADDRESS

Given the theoretical context outlined above there are a number of issues that individual PFI projects must address (see Brealey et al., 1997; Grout, 1997; Hall, 1998; Spackman, 2002). These issues have been confronted time and again during the course of the UK PFI programme and are listed below:

1. *Measurement.* The PFI can work only if the outputs and inputs specified in a contract can be measured accurately. This is problematic for public services because they are often multi-dimensional and quality is difficult to assess. Thus the 'output' of a prison or hospital represents a measurement challenge. Similarly it is not easy to assess a created asset's quality (as distinct from the service that it provides).
2. *Incentives.* The most desirable aspect of the PFI is that it introduces private incentives into areas of public-service delivery where they did not exist previously. However the extent to which this occurs depends on how well the terms of the contract are written. In transport projects making payments dependent on volume would seem sensible, however it does give rise to the incentive to be over-optimistic in volume projections in order to win contracts (we note this was a feature of the winning NATS PPP bid discussed later).
3. *Public-sector comparator.* An important issue in evaluating PFI contract bids is the comparative cost of doing the project in the public sector. Decisions on whether to go ahead with a PFI project or a government procurement option depend on this value being calculated accurately. However the basis of such measures is increasingly unclear. For instance, Froud and Shaoul (2001) find that some PFI hospital projects have arbitrarily assumed longer construction periods and shorter asset lives for the public sector comparator than was warranted by the evidence.
4. *Risk transfer.* A number of different risks are associated with PFI projects, and these need to be efficiently allocated between the parties (see NAO, 1999a, Appendix 2). Risks associated with building an asset, such as strikes, technical problems and poor management, can affect cost. Normally the government should seek to transfer as much of the risk outside its control to the private sector (that is, operational risks rather than risk of policy change).
5. *Residual departmental budget risk and affordability.* An interesting effect of the certainty of PFI contract payments is the effect on the ability of departments to handle other shocks to their expenditure. In the absence of the PFI departments had complete flexibility to transfer expenditure between ongoing capital projects and operational expenditure. Dunnigan and Pollock (2003) suggest that in the Scottish NHS the PFI has encouraged hospital trusts to over-commit to large capital projects which will have to be repaid over a long period and which will distort patterns of expenditure for decades.
6. *Mortgaging the future.* A major advantage of the PFI is that it allows the fiscal-deficit implications of large infrastructure projects to be smoothed, but this comes at the cost of transferring claims to future governments. While the current total value of these claims in the UK

is currently only 1.2 per cent of total government expenditure on PFI projects, the figure is nearer 50 per cent for the transport budget. What is an acceptable level of PFI commitments? The degree to which future budgets should be pre-allocated by earlier administrations is clearly an important political issue.

7. *Transparency of contracting and monitoring.* One of the major problems with the PFI is that contracting authorities may find it easier to get some projects off the ground than others. There may be conflicts between good monitoring of projects and the ability to attract private sector interest. In many cases some of the contract terms are not made public and hence monitoring is weaker than it could be and the scope for learning from experience is reduced.

8. *Safety and security.* There has been significant use of the PFI in transport and defence projects. In transport, questions have been raised about incentives to compromise safety that may be present in the private sector, as highlighted by the debates around the partial privatization of the National Air Traffic Control System and the failings of the rail industry. In defence, the government signed a PFI contract to undertake the building of a new top-secret intelligence-gathering centre (GCHQ) at Cheltenham.

9. *Competence and system wide optimization.* While some government departments seem to have learnt much from their early projects and benefited from lessons learned (eg transport), this may not be possible for smaller contracting authorities, particularly educational authorities and NHS trusts. Associated with the potential for lost economies of scale and scope there is the related problem of the loss of system-wide benefits. If each individual public authority is free to make use of the PFI this may lead to a non-optimal portfolio of government contracts. This is a recognized area of weakness in recent NAO (2001) and Audit Commission (2003) reports.

UK PFI EXPERIENCE

In this section I draw together some of the main observations to arise from the PFI program as a whole, noting both positive and negative aspects. Among the positive outcomes are the lifting of financial constraints, the enthusiastic response of the private sector to the PFI, and stimulation of innovation. On the negative side, the bidding process under PFI can be very lengthy, bidding costs are high, there are often only a small number of bidders and there seem to be particular problems in hospital PFIs. In addition, PFI contracts often have questionable risk properties, and cost overruns can be substantial.

Positive Experiences

The PFI has been successful in lifting financial constraints by attracting significant amounts of private-sector capital spending. While the overall figures show that PFI expenditure by the private sector is ahead of PFI payments by the government, it is possible to identify several large projects that probably would have been seriously delayed if they had not been financed by the PFI. These include the Channel Tunnel Railways Link and the Skye Bridge (see NAO, 1997a). The PFI seems well suited to handle the high up-front capital costs of transport projects that yield extended streams of benefits. If conventionally financed, these projects would have absorbed a large percentage of their relevant budgets while they were being built.

The private sector has responded enthusiastically to the PFI. As experience with the PFI process has grown, private contractors have come forward to provide services to the government. These companies include significant numbers of foreign companies, which can bring new ideas and technology into the UK public sector.

Innovation has been substantial as well as varied, from the types of contracts private-sector bidders have offered to the physical assets that have been installed. The NAO (1997b) noted the innovation in design and operation of prisons in the winning bidders' plans for the new Fazakerley and Bridgend prisons. There have also been financial innovations with development of extended maturity bank loans for PFI projects and uninsured PFI bond issues.[11] With respect to the operational performance of PFI prisons the NAO (2003b) noted that there is much to be gained by the sharing of experiences between the public and private (representing 7 per cent of total prisoner numbers) parts of the prison service. PFI Prisons seemed to be better monitored and prisoners surveyed were happier in them. This observation strongly suggests the benefit of the PFI in external learning to conventional publicly owned and managed facilities even when PFI schemes are in a minority.

A particularly important part of the success of PFI is in its potential to improve construction performance on capital projects which make up 25–30 per cent of the total value of the contract. The NAO (2003a) compared construction performance between the 37 PFI contracts and 66 arrangements under conventional government procurement. The NAO found that 73 per cent of government projects came in above cost and 70 per cent were delivered late, compared with 22 per cent and 24 per cent under PFI. PFI projects earned favourable assessment for quality and design. It is an open question, however, as to whether conventional procurement could not be improved to match the PFI performance.

Negative Experiences

The bidding process under PFI can be very lengthy. The initial phase of public-sector assessment leading to the signing of a contract takes up to two years. The process of inviting, preparing, assessing and refining bids and negotiating contracts is complex and procedural. This process certainly delayed the initial flow of signed contracts (see Cutler, 1997 and Gaffney and Pollock, 1999 for experience in the NHS). A survey of investors and non-investors in urban regeneration (Royal Institution of Chartered Surveyors, 1998) revealed criticism of the PFI as speculative, time consuming and overly bureaucratic, with too high a risk transferred to the private sector. Recently, the length of time in commissioning PFI projects has been blamed for the relatively low levels of public-sector investment in 1999 and 2000 and the failure to meet targets for PFI investment.[12]

The bidding costs are high. The detailed and lengthy nature of the bidding process naturally implies increased transaction costs under the PFI (Hewitt, 1997), and these can be substantial for each bidder. Initial bids may cost £0.5 million per bidder to prepare; the final bid costs for a winning hospital-building project may total £3 million (Kerr, 1998). Wilkins (1998) estimates the tendering costs for all PFI projects in the pipeline in 1998 may finally total £500 million. These costs are eventually reflected in the cost of contracts signed and are significant for most projects.

There are often only a small number of bidders for PFI projects, and the statistics on which companies are actually involved in PFI deals reveal that a small number of firms act as legal advisors, financial advisors, contractors, funders, technical advisors, property advisors and facilities managers to PFI projects.[13] This has given rise to the suspicion that competition is more apparent than real in the bidding process. On large individual projects there may be, even initially, only two or three serious bidders. For example, the Dartford and Gravesham Hospital (NAO, 1999b) had only one bidder at the final bid stage.

Cost overruns can be substantial for PFI projects, and there is often considerable scope for cost inflation through the bidding process. The initial evaluation of the viability of PFI funding may be based on calculations that are massively exceeded by the final contract stage. Even after the contract has been signed, contract terms may leave much of the cost risk with the government, which leaves considerable scope for cost inflation. The initial project to computerize payments at post offices, a £1.5 billion project dating from 1996, has now been partially abandoned at a cost of £620–940 million to the government.[14] According to the British Medical Association (1997) capital costs for 14 prioritized hospital had increased 72 per cent by the tender stage.

PFI contracts often have questionable risk properties. On the one hand it is not clear to what extent the government can shift risk to the private sector, given the fact that its policies can affect the returns to contractors. Thus the government may have ended up paying for the high price of financing investments that its actions make more risky. In this case it may be suboptimal for the private sector to bear the risk. On the other hand it may have proved too easy for the private sector to argue that it needed to be compensated for potential risks at the same time as ensuring that those risks remained with the government. The private sector's relative advantage in risk management may have facilitated this. A significant issue related to this has been the sharing of the benefits of refinancing of PFI projects following successful start-up of the operation phase of the project. Early contracts provided for no or minimal sharing of refinancing benefits. The government has now changed its guidelines to state that PFI contracts should include provision for sharing of at least 50 per cent of the gains from refinancing with the public sector (NAO, 2002b).

Several authors have discussed problems with Hospital PFIs (see Froud and Shaoul, 2001) and some of their points referred to above. These PFI projects seem to be the most problematic due to the complex nature of the goods that that private sector is providing. It does seem to be the case that the separation of private ownership of the assets and public operation of the clinical services does create contractual problems (as theory suggests it might). It does seem to be the case that either new hospitals should be funded under conventional design, build and transfer contacts or that private management should be given more freedom to innovate in the organization of clinical services (Nicholson, 2000).

More recently evidence has begun to come through about the performance of school PFIs. The Audit Commission (2003) compared 25 new PFI schools with 12 conventionally procured schools. It found the quality of PFI school buildings was lower than traditional schools. However there was risk transfer, no evidence of higher costs and long term funding in place for maintenance. These findings raise the issue of whether local authorities are currently competent enough to handle school PFI projects.

OVERALL ASSESSMENTS OF THE PFI

The government view of the PFI since 1992 has been extremely positive. This is striking because there have been high-profile problems with individual projects such as the Skye Bridge and a series of reviews of the PFI under both Conservative and Labour administrations. Yet the view taken has been to streamline the process and to expand its size and scope. The willingness of the Labour administration to embrace 'privatization' of public services can be seen in the wider context of its willingness to accept most of the pro-market policies of the previous Conservative administration. In general this enthusiasm seems to extend to all government contractors: central government departments, local government and hospital trusts.

One obvious explanation of this government enthusiasm for the PFI stems from the experience under the previous system of government procurement. A National Audit Office report on the price of road contracts (NAO, 1992a) showed that the Department of Transport was paying an average of 28 per cent more than the originally agreed price. A major problem was the unwillingness of the department to transfer project risks to the contractor, something which the PFI aims to do. The National Audit Office also unearthed problems with contracting out by the Ministry of Defence (NAO, 1992b). The ministry was accused of failing to keep records over the 13 years of the contracting-out process and of not having the expertise to assess contractors' bids. Serious problems with government procurement *before* the PFI put isolated problems with the PFI in context. This view is expressed clearly in HM Treasury (2003) which notes that: on timing, over 85 per cent of PFI projects were delivered on time or early against only 30 per cent for previous non-PFI projects; on value for money, only 21 per cent of PFI projects experienced cost rises against over 70 per cent for non-PFI projects.

Unions have been critical of the PFI. In 1996 the public-sector trade union Unison called on Scottish councils to boycott the PFI because it was a way of making 'cash strapped councils open up to public services for exploitation and commercial gain' (see Kerr, 1998). The 1998 Trade Union Congress backed a motion against the PFI to reinstate 'proper capital funding to ensure the future infrastructure of the public services in a way which does not damage jobs and services' after the GMB union (a large general union) changed its previous policy of supporting the PFI.[15] The British Medical Association, the doctors' union, recently stepped up its opposition to the PFI in the NHS following evidence that PFI schemes are costing more than traditional schemes.[16]

In January 2000 a report commissioned by the Treasury Task Force (Arthur Anderson and Enterprise LSE, 2000) analysed the outcome of 29 PFI projects with a net present cost of £5 billion[17] and found a cost saving relative to the public-sector comparators of just over £1 billion. This figure was dominated by two large projects, but the unweighted average saving was 17 per cent, with individual savings varying between 0.7 and 45 per cent. These figures are estimates and the true value to the public sector depends on the value of risks transferred and on actual future payments. The report recommended more sharing of experiences, more centralized monitoring of

PFI project performance, transfer of experienced staff between departments, use of ongoing benchmarking to ensure continuing value for money from existing projects and more careful assessment of the value of the risks transferred to private sector.

An influential report from the Institute for Public Policy Research (IPPR, 2001) concluded that the PFI had been successful with prisons and roads but of limited value to date in hospital and school projects. The report further noted that value-for-money calculation was sensitive to the choice of discount rate, with higher discount rates (6 rather than 5 per cent) favouring PFI schemes over public-sector comparators because costs are shifted into the future by PFI. The report highlighted the work of Boyle and Harrison (2000) in hospitals. They found that gains from 11 PFI hospitals were positive but small and more than explained by the valuation of risk transfer.

The National Audit Office has assessed a number of large PFI projects in terms of value for money. On the basis of this ongoing experience, NAO (1999a) highlights four key aspects of successful PFI projects: clear objectives, application of proper procurement processes, getting high-quality bids, and ensuring that the final deal either makes sense or is dropped or re-tendered. The NAO (2001) reviewed 121 projects contracted before 2000. For 98 of the projects it records the public authority's perception of value for money at the time of the survey. Six per cent of the projects were rated as excellent, 46 per cent as good, 29 per cent as satisfactory, 15 per cent as marginal and 4 per cent as poor. For a further 20 large projects the NAO found that they were mostly good value-for-money relative to the public sector alternatives.

As Spackman (2002) suggests it may be too early to assess the PFI definitively as most of the assessments are based on early perceptions (or comparisons to hypothetical public sector comparators) rather than on actual performance over a significant time period. It also seems clear that the major current problems seem concentrated in hospitals and schools PFI where there has been a relatively shorter learning time and the contractual environment is less favourable to PFI.

CASE STUDIES OF FIVE PFI PROJECTS

The Skye Bridge (NAO, 1997a)

This project involved building a toll bridge to the Isle of Skye, off the Scottish coast, to reduce congestion and delays associated with the existing ferry service. The project needed to take account of the sensitivity of the environment, the cost of the existing ferry crossing, and value for money.

The Scottish Office Development Department first advertized the competition to design, build, finance and operate the Skye Bridge in October 1989, before the formal start of the PFI. The department did not assess a public-sector comparator because they had no intention of funding the project except through private finance. There were six initial bidders with ten designs. Three preferred bidders were chosen, and two submitted qualifying bids. The contract was awarded in April 1991 to Skye Bridge Limited, a joint venture between Miller Civil Engineering, Dyckerhoff and Widman AG and Bank of America Financial Corporation. The nature of the original contract allowed the company to recover a fixed discounted sum of £24 million from users before the contract is terminated, over a maximum 27-year period, subject to increasing the price by a maximum of 30 per cent in real terms.

The bridge was completed after a local public enquiry that resulted in delays and design changes costing £3.8 million (to protect a local otter population). The total cost of the project was £39 million (constant 1991 prices discounted at 6 percent): £24 million to be paid by users of the bridge, £12 million paid to Skye Bridge Limited by the department (this was paid during the course of construction) and £3 million counted as the department's direct cost of advice and staff costs. The out-turn departmental contribution to Skye Bridge Limited was 48 per cent higher than originally expected because of compensation for delays and extra costs.

The bridge opened in 1995 with charges of £5.40 for a single car trip in high season and £4.40 in low season. Ten tickets averaging £2.51 could be purchased in bulk. This compared with £1 for the Dartford Bridge and £3.90 return for the Severn Bridge.

The NAO identified gains to the users from (1) relatively low tolls since all but one of the categories of fare were lower in real terms than with the ferry, (2) improved reliability and (3) the expectation of complete elimination of charges when the contract terminates after 14–18 years. The department gained by reducing its peak financing requirements and by transferring risks in building and operation to the developer. The NAO's advisors were satisfied that the project finance terms obtained by the developer were competitive.

The tolls for the Skye Bridge have proved controversial. In 1997 the Secretary of State for Scotland announced that the tolls would be cut by up to 50 per cent, with the reductions to be financed by the taxpayer. This is estimated to have cost the government another £3 million. It now appears that the PFI has proved expensive as a way to borrow for a public project.[18]

Bridgend and Fazakerley Prisons (NAO 1997b)

The Prison Service sought private finance for two facilities: an 800-place prison at Bridgend, South Wales, and a 600-place prison at Fazakerley, Merseyside. These were to be designed to accommodate prisoners on remand, awaiting sentence, serving short sentences or awaiting transfer to another prison (Category B prisoners) and also for a small number of Category A (maximum security) prisoners. After a 17-month process the contracts to design, build, finance and maintain the prisons were awarded in 1995 to Securicor/Costain for Bridgend (Parc) and Group 4/Tarmac for Fazakerley (Altcourse).

An engineering firm monitored construction performance, and each prison has a Prison Services' Controller who will monitor service provision against the contract, with financial penalties for lapses. There were ten initial pre-qualification bidders, six were invited to tender bids and five submitted bids for both prisons. Three of the five bidders had overseas partners in their consortia. The Prison Service decided against awarding both contracts to the same bidder even though the Securicor/Costain bid was the lowest combined bid by 10 per cent. They did this to stimulate competition in the sector and because of worries about the consortia's ability to handle two prison projects at once.

The contract transferred the risk of time and cost overruns to the contractors. The contract payment mechanism gives no payment until the prisons are operational. The contractors are paid for availability rather than actual usage. The contract price contains a fixed element relating to construction costs, some operating costs (non-salary costs) are fixed in real terms and further costs (relating to salaries) are indexed to 2 per cent above the RPI (retail price index) The contract, which runs for 25 years, allows for some risk sharing of cost increases beyond the contractors' control, some benefit sharing if contractors' profits are higher than anticipated, and additional fees are payable if the specified number of prisoners is exceeded. An identified shortcoming in the pricing is a lack of benchmarking of costs against other prisons at periodic intervals.

The NAO estimated that the prison contracts represented good value for money. Bridgend is expected to cost £266 million over its contract life (against £319 million in the public sector); Fazakerley is expected to cost £247 million (against £248 million). The contract-letting costs were £1.55 million (more than 140 percent over the original estimate). There has been significant risk transfer, additional funding was secured and there was innovation in building, design and operational methods. The prisons are now operational, having been built 45 per cent faster than the average for public prison projects.

The companies involved in the deal recently caused controversy by subsequently refinancing their debts associated with the projected savings of £9.7 million after the prisons opened. This saving was added to the direct gains of £3.4 million from opening the prisons ahead of schedule. Only £1 million of this gain was returned to the public sector. This has allowed firms to increase their projected rate of return from 12.8 per cent to 39 per cent and has led to calls by the National Audit Office to require sharing of refinancing windfalls on PFI projects through contract terms (NAO, 2000). The reason for the significant saving on financing costs is attributable to the decline in perceived risk of PFI-backed bond and debt issues.[19] It seems reasonable that private firms should benefit from refinancing gains due to their own good performance and the risks they took with early PFI contracts. However it is also the case that if these gains arise partly from government policy and actions (in facilitating the rapid delivery of the project and demonstrated commitment to honouring the contract) it is efficient to share the benefits with the government more equally as is the case with current PFI contracts. Indeed such benefit sharing increases the commitment of the government to its contractors and may increase the benefits to the private sector in the long run.

The NAO (2003b) investigated the operational performance of both the Bridgend and Fazakerley prisons as part of a report on all PFI prisons. It noted that while Bridgend had had initial problems it had had a good Chief Inspector of Prisons (HMCIP) report in 2000 (HM Inspectorate of Prisons, 2000) and was now performing well against contract. Fazakerley was given a more positive report noting that a 1999 HMCIP report (HM Inspectorate of Prisons, 1999) had described it as 'the best local prison that we have inspected'.

The First Four Road Schemes (NAO 1998)

Between December 1993 and March 1996, the Highways Agency sought and negotiated four contracts for designing, building, financing and operating roads. The contracts were awarded for 30 years and involved government payment of a shadow toll based on actual road use. These tolls would be based on two classes of vehicles – those over 5.2 metres long and all others – and there would be a cap on total contractor revenues. Table 11.1 shows roadway features and gives the estimated contract price and the price of a traditionally financed public road. The public-sector comparator cost is the sum of the NPV (net present value) of the construction cost plus the operation and maintenance costs plus the NPV of the risk transferred to the consortia discounted over the 30-year period at a real interest rate of 8 per cent. As shown in Table 11.1, all but one of the roads is expected to yield considerable benefits.

Table 11.1 The first four PFI roads

	Type	Length (km)	Expected net present value of shadow tolls	Public-sector comparator
M1-A1 Link (Yorkshire)	2 to 5-lane dual carriageways	30 plus 22 side roads	£232 million	£344 million
A1(M) Motorway (Alenbury/Peterborough)	all motorway	21	£154 million	£204 million
A419/A417 (Swindon/Gloucester)	single/dual carriageway	52	£112 million	£123 million
A69 (Carlisle/Newcastle)	single/dual carriageways	84.3 with 3.2 bypass	£62 million	£57 million

Note: All monetary values are excluding value-added tax.

Source: NAO (1998).

The NAO was critical of the cost of the bidding process, which was delayed because of the complex information required. Bidding costs were reckoned at more than £11 million for the four winning bidders, and unsuccessful short-listed bidders incurred substantial costs as well. The NAO pointed out that the wrong discount rate had been used in comparing the bidders' prices with the public-sector comparator cost – if the correct figure (6 per cent) had been used, the A419/A417 assessment would have yielded negative benefits for a PFI project but the overall benefits would still have been positive. It was also not clear that transferring volume risk to the contractor is efficient given that this is largely outside their control (Debande, 2002).

The Highways Agency can terminate the contract if performance criteria are not met, and a department representative monitors the operation and maintenance of each road. The roads must revert to the public sector in good condition. The residual life of a road is ten years for 85 per cent of the pavement on hand-back. Payments are based on complex audits of traffic flows, and there are clauses that allow for additional payments if a road is upgraded. As Debande (ibid.) points out, final assessment of PFI road projects must include information on performance during the operational phase but there is very little evidence on this.

Government Communications Headquarters (GCHQ): New Accommodation Programme (NAO, 2003c)

GCHQ is the intelligence gathering facility of the central government. It is responsible for monitoring foreign broadcasts and providing specialist intelligence information to the government as part of its national security strategy. Since 1952 it has developed on two sites on opposite sides of Cheltenham. Ministerial responsibility rests with the Foreign Office but its main customers include the Ministry of Defence. In 1997 it was decided to redevelop its Cheltenham accommodation which houses its 4500-strong staff, and in June 2000 a contract was signed under the PFI with IAS Limited, a company owned by a consortium of construction and specialist firms. The deal was to provide serviced accommodation in a new building for a period of 30 years.

The net present value of the contract with IAS is £489m payable via an annual fee of £46m to start on completion of the new building. In addition to the PFI contract GCHQ had to move its large and complex computer systems into the new facility. This is known as 'technical transition'. This project is to be managed by GCHQ, though coordinated with IAS. Originally the technical transition was costed at £40m; the latest estimate is £450m, phased in such a way as to reduce the cost to a net present value of £300m.

The combined programme is together known as the 'New Accommodation Programme'.

This PFI project combines the typical building type of PFI with associated expenditure by the government. It is further made interesting by the complex nature of the project and the questions raised by ongoing private involvement in security-sensitive projects.

The PFI project was initially advertised in June 1997. This led to 149 expressions of interest. Even though the project was exempt from normal European procurement rules it followed a procurement process based on the EU's Negotiated Procedure in common with other PFI deals. This lead to nine bidders reaching the pre-qualifying stage. Eventually four consortia were short-listed and invited to tender, which they did in April 1998. The IAS consortium (consisting eventually of Carillion (40 per cent), a construction firm, Group 4 (40 per cent), a security firm, and British Telecommunications (20 per cent)) presented the best bid on a combination of price and quality. IAS bid £328m, more than £100m less than the second cheapest bid. IAS proposed an innovative doughnut shaped design for the main building and consolidation of GCHQ on one site.

Negotiations with the two cheapest bidders continued over the scope of the project, which was increased to include physical security, logistics and waste disposal. In September 1998 IAS was selected as the preferred bidder with net present value of payments at £404m. Negotiations continued as GCHQ reviewed the specifications of the project. In particular IAS was required to add a logistics building to their plan for a single doughnut shaped main building; specification changes were required for the designs of the supercomputer halls, office floors and laboratory space; and IAS had to upgrade its blastproofing plans. These changes resulted in the size of building increasing by 30 per cent, partly as a result of the fact that GCHQ increased its requirements for workspaces from 3750 to 4025 due to increasing demand for its services. The final result was that the net present value of the payments due to IAS increased to £489m.

The technical transition part of the move to a new building was never envisaged as part of the PFI. Originally this was costed at £41m on the basis of a 'box move' – shutting down each system, moving it to a new building and restarting it – and was envisaged to take two years. However by 1998 this cost had risen to £60m and the PFI negotiations were well advanced. It was only in late 1999 was it reported that the technical transition could only be done for £450m without unacceptable damage to the continuity of services in the light of millennium computer compliance. Rescoping and staging over a longer period brought the cost down to the final figure of £300m. However a May 2000 report on the costs identified failure to coordinate the development of the PFI deal and the technical transition as a strategic weakness of the project management (among several other problems).

The NAO's assessment of the project was that the IAS deal did offer substantial benefits. GCHQ estimated that a public sector comparator would have cost £71m more. Significant risks were transferred, in particular construction and running cost risks, and there were incentives to complete ahead of schedule. Site security is the responsibility of the consortium but security policy remains the responsibility of GCHQ. After 15 years there will be five yearly benchmarking reviews of services costs and there are clawback arrangements for additional profits on land sales from the existing GCHQ sites. The NAO report's conclusion was that the deal did make sense, the procurement process was competitive until the selection of a preferred bidder and the right partner had been chosen. However it is interesting to note the nature of the public sector procurement alternative.

Table 11.2 GCHQ: Treasury comparison between PFI bid and public sector comparator

| | Net present value (£ million) | |
	IAS deal	Public Sector Comparator
Building, refurbishment and services	489	600 (Basic cost) 156 (Risk adjustment)
Technical transition	264	68
Total	753	824

Source: NAO (2003c:25)

These figures compiled by the Treasury in 2000 indicate that the building costs are lower under the PFI deal but the costs of technical transition are much higher. This seems to indicate that coordination between the PFI deal and the government-managed technical transition (or indeed the more radical alternative of including much of the technical transition in the original PFI advertizement) would have yielded substantial overall savings. The nature of the difference is that this assumes that the public sector comparator would have retained two sites, which would limit the potential savings from better coordination. It is important to note that risk transfer benefits are substantial and that these (as in many PFI projects) are the crucial part of the benefit of a PFI deal.

IAS successfully issued a £407m bond to finance 75 per cent of the deal costs in June 2000 (one of the largest associated with a PFI project). The new GCHQ building was completed, seven weeks ahead of schedule, in July 2003.

National Air Traffic Services Ltd (NAO, 2002a, 2004)

National Air Traffic Services Limited (NATS) was part-privatized in July 2001. This is neither a conventional PFI deal, nor a conventional privatization. The NATS part-privatization is classed as a PPP, however it has many of the features of the PFI in that it does involve substantial up-front investment by the private sector and significant project management by the government.

NATS is responsible for air traffic control for aircraft flying over the United Kingdom and jointly responsible, with its Irish counterpart, for aircraft over the North East Atlantic. It provides services at most large airports in the UK and charges airlines for its services. It was fully owned by the Civil Aviation Authority (CAA) which regulates it. The CAA is the responsibility of the Department of Transport. In 1997 it became clear that NATS would need an additional £100m of capital expenditure per year to meet its obligations. This would have had to have been financed through the public sector borrowing requirement and compete with other demands for public expenditure.

In order to give NATS greater freedom to raise capital and invest in expansion the decision was taken to part-privatize NATS. The Airline Group, a consortium of seven UK based airlines, was given operational control and a 46 per cent share holding in NATS for a payment of £800m and a commitment to undertake the necessary investment (the government retained 49 per cent and employees got 5 per cent). The PPP almost immediately ran into trouble following the collapse in air traffic following the events of 11 September 2001. En route revenue fell 14 per cent in six months following this date and the viability of the investment programme was threatened. Eventually the government was forced to come up with a rescue package whereby it injected £65m, BAA bought a 4 per cent stake for £65m, cost savings were identified and charges were allowed to rise above originally agreed levels.

By the standards of the PFI programme various elements of the deal did not make sense (Shaoul, 2003). In particular, the original bidding process involved two consortia and no attempt to undertake an assessment of the alternatives to privatization. There was no public sector comparator. In terms of risk transfer the deal was very poor. The company was sold to its customers who would face exactly the same risks and financing problems as NATS in the light of events such as 11 September 2001. In order to mitigate their risks the new airline owners of NATS proceeded to issue debt to pay the government for most of their stake in the company (only £65m of the sale price came from the Airline Group directly). A debt free commercial entity was converted into a highly leveraged company, vulnerable to fluctuations in its income.

The NAO (2002a) took a favourable view of the competitiveness of the tendering process, though it noted that the bidding costs and financial advice (as is usual with privatization) was expensive at around £77m. The process took 17 months to complete. There was much discussion about the setting up of a not-for-profit alternative to NATS based on the NAV Canada model. However this was assumed to have led to capital expenditure remaining as part of the PSBR and would not have yielded either sales revenue or the degree of financial freedom required by the Treasury. The House of Commons Public Accounts Committee (2003) was highly critical of the NATS PPP. It noted that the not-for-profit Network Rail was classified by the Office for National Statistics as a private company in late 2002, weakening the case for a PPP. It also concluded that the Airline Group's original revenue forecasts were over-optimistic and took insufficient account of the past history of downturns in air traffic; and that the government put undue emphasis on maximizing the sales revenue from NATS even when this largely came from the NATS balance sheet.

The NAO (2004) concluded that with respect to the refinancing of NATS the government did get a fair deal and that subsequently the company was able to refinance its original debt and is now on a sound financial basis. However the process of transacting a refinancing deal was onerous and time consuming (September 2001 to March 2003) and created a longer period of disruptive uncertainty than that experienced by NATS peers in other countries, who in most cases simply raised their prices. It is worth noting that NAV Canada required comparable refinancing arrangements to help it to deal financially with the aftermath of 11 September 2001, but it had re-established its financial position within five months as against 18 in the UK. It is difficult to conclude that the NATS PPP was anything other than a poorly conceived attempt to combine privatization with the PPP concept without proper application of the value for money principle and its associated risk assessment analysis.

CONCLUSION

The UK Private Finance Initiative will remain a rich source of learning for other countries seeking to increase the involvement of the private sector in public–private partnerships for some time to come. This is because the deal flow seems set to continue for the foreseeable future under governments keen to improve delivery of public services and because of the lessons from the ongoing observation of the performance of existing PFI contracts.

The use of the PFI is well established in the UK public sector and accounts for around 20 per cent of net capital expenditure, though a very small part of total government expenditure. It is focused on capital related construction projects in transport, health, education, prisons, defence and central government departments. Much of the expenditure is on hard assets and their associated maintenance (e.g. in transport) but there have been many projects focused on soft services such as in education and IT support for central government. It is still the case that PFI schemes are a small minority of total public sector provision in most sectors and that it is early days to make judgements about the long term contribution of the PFI. Clark et al. (2002) find that the PFI only makes a minimal impact on the sharply declining overall trend in public investment as a percentage of GDP since 1985.

What are the lessons of the UK PFI experience for other countries in the area of hard assets? It seems difficult to avoid a positive overall assessment. The UK PFI seems to have been generally successful relative to what might have happened under conventional public procurement. Projects are delivered on time and to budget a significantly higher percentage of the time. Construction risks are generally transferred successfully and there is considerable design innovation. Where the private sector also manages the asset subsequently, the scope for greater benefits is increased (for example, in roads and prisons). There is also the added benefit of allowing better management of departmental budgets and scheduling of expenditure (such as for the Skye Bridge).

Procurement processes can, of course, be improved. In particular, integrated assessment of all available options needs to be carefully undertaken. Assessment of PFI projects depends on correct valuation of public sector comparators and a fair assessment of risks. There needs be much more transparency and guidance on how to assess this. Our case study of GCHQ and of the NATS PPP clearly indicate that PFI projects should not be considered in isolation for associated departmental expenditure or without regard to proper risk assessment and consideration of alternative PPP vehicles (such as not-for-profit companies).

It is possible that 'many of the assumed benefits of the PFI would appear to be available to better managed and controlled conventional procurement'.[20] However it also seems clear that without the benefit of some PFI projects such conventional procurement cannot be improved. Indeed the UK experience seems to suggest strongly the benefit of some PPP projects as a vehicle for learning for the conventional public sector (such as

PFI prisons). The ongoing UK experience also exhibits much continuing learning within the PFI programme.

The continuing and increasing success of the UK PFI (and indeed any national PPP programme) in the sectors we have highlighted will depend on a number of factors. First, the ability to define clearly the role of the private sector in projects where public policy is essential. This is most clearly the case where issues of defence or public safety are important. Successful prison and defence PFIs have had to address these issues. Second, there need to be mechanisms for spreading best practice procurement across government. PPPs need to be managed well from within government departments and trouble needs to be taken to build capacity within the civil service to do this. Third, PFI financial contracts need to be entered into responsibly. Such deals can lead to over-expansion of commitments to future payments. In general this has not happened in the UK but could happen for cash-strapped departments or local governments. The UK took steps early on to monitor overall PFI payment commitments across government. Fourth, there is the capacity to separate the financing issue from the issues of design, build and operate (Palmer, 2001). In this context it is important that the benefits from financial re-engineering are not disproportionately captured by the private sector (as they seem to have been in the NATS part-privatization and early prison PFIs). Financial windfalls to private investors detract from the non-financial benefits of PPPs and can be easily catered for within appropriately specified contracts.

ACKNOWLEDGMENTS

The author would like to thank David Newbery, Yuri Biondi, Jean Shaoul, Graeme Hodge and Veronica Vecchi and participants at an IDE-JETRO workshop in Tokyo for helpful comments. The IDE-JETRO provided the original financial support and Ronald Bachmann the original excellent research assistance. All errors are the responsibility of the author.

NOTES

1. See Table C19 of HM Treasury (2005) and 'PFI Signed Project List – December 2004', available at www.hm-treasury.gov.uk.
2. Only one previously private enterprise has been de-privatized – the Railtrack infrastructure company was put into special administration in October 2001 and resurrected as a not-for-profit enterprise in October 2002.
3. *Financial Times*, 22 June 2001.
4. Source: OGC (2003).
5. For an expanded discussion of these two themes see Pollitt (2002).

6. See www.partnershipsuk.org.uk/puk/index.htm.
7. See Kirk and Wall (2001).
8. www.4ps.co.uk/the4ps/what.htm.
9. See www.ogc.gov.uk.
10. OGC press release, 13 June 2000.
11. Warner (1998).
12. Robinson (2000).
13. For details of the most successful firms involved in the PFI, see 'The PFI report database: Leading players', *PFI Report*, November, 18, 2000.
14. Timmins, 'An explosive mixture: Britain's attempts to involve the private sector in designing and operating technology for public services have resulted in some costly failures' (1999b).
15. 'PFI gets the thumbs down from trade unions', *Supply Management* 3(19), 24 September 1998,
16. Nicholas Timmins, *Financial Times*, 5 July (1999).
17. Arthur Andersen and Enterprise LSE (2000).
18. Buxton (1997), and Timmins (1999c).
19. See Timmins (June 2000).
20. House of Commons Treasury Committee (1996).

REFERENCES

Arthur Andersen and Enterprise LSE (2000), 'Value for money drivers in the Private Finance Initiative', January, London: HM Treasury Task Force.

Audit Commission (2003), *PFI in Schools*, London: Audit Commission.

Bates, M. (1999), *Second Review of the Private Finance Initiative*, London: HM Treasury.

Boyle, S. and A. Harrison (2000), 'PFI and health: the story so far', in G. Kelly and P. Robinson (eds), *A Healthy Partnership: The Future of Public Private Partnerships in the Health Service*, London: Institute for Public Policy Research (IPPR).

Brealey, R.A., I.A. Cooper and M.A. Habib (1997), 'Investment appraisal in the public sector', *Oxford Review of Economic Policy*, **13** (4), 12–28.

British Medical Association (1997), *Can the NHS Afford the Private Finance Initiative?* London: BMA.

Buxton, James (1997), 'Skye Bridge toll cuts will be subsidised', *Financial Times*, 5 July, 4.

Clark, T., M. Elsby and S. Love (2002), 'Trends in British public investment', *Fiscal Studies*, **23** (2), 305–42.

Cutler, P. (1997), 'Can use of the PFI be healthy?' *New Economy*, **4** (3), 142–6.

Dawson, D. (2001), 'The Private Finance Initiative: a public finance illusion?', *Health Economics*, **10**, 479–86.

Debande, O. (2002), 'Private financing of transport infrastructure: an assessment of the UK experience', *Journal of Transport Economics and Policy*, **36** (3), 355–87.

Demsetz, H. (1968), 'Why Regulate Utilities?' *Journal of Law and Economics*, **11**, 55–65.

Dunnigan, M.G. and A. M. Pollock (2003), 'Downsizing of acute inpatient beds associated with private finance initiative: Scotland's case study', *British Medical Journal*, 26 April, **326**, 1–6.

Financial Times (2001), 'Private finance, public gain', lead editorial, 22 June.

Froud, J. and J. Shaoul (2001), 'Appraising and evaluating PFI for NHS hospitals', *Financial Accountability and Management*, **17** (3), 247–70.

Gaffney, D., and A. M. Pollock (1999), 'Pump-priming the PFI: why are privately financed hospital schemes being subsidised?' *Public Money and Management*, **19** (1), 55–62.

Grout, P. A. (1997), 'The economics of the Private Finance Initiative', *Oxford Review of Economic Policy*, **13** (4), 53–66.

Hall, J. (1998), 'Private opportunity, public benefit?' *Fiscal Studies*, **19** (2), 121–40.

Hart, O., A. Shleifer and R. W. Vishny (1997), 'The proper scope of government: theory and application to prisons', *Quarterly Journal of Economics*, **112** (4), 1127–58.

Hewitt, C. (1997), 'Complexity and cost in PFI schemes', *Public Money and Management*, **17** (3), 7–9.

HM Inspectorate of Prisons (1999), *Report on a Full Announced Inspection of HM Prison Altcourse*, 1–10 Novermber 1999, London: Inspectorate of Prisons.

HM Inspectorate of Prisons (2000), *Report on a Short Unannounced Inspection of HM Prison and YOI Parc*, 5–7 September 2000, London: Inspectorate of Prisons.

HM Treasury (1993), *Breaking New Ground: The Private Finance Initiative*, London: HMSO.

HM Treasury (2003), *PFI: meeting the investment challenge*, London: HMSO.

HM Treasury (2005), *Financial Statement and Budget Report, Chapter C: The Public Finances*, London: HM Treasury.

HM Treasury Task Force (1997), *Partnerships for Prosperity – The Private Finance Initiative*, London: Stationary Office.

House of Commons Committee of Public Accounts (2003), *The Public Private Partnership for National Air Traffic Services Ltd.*, HC80, Session 2002–3, London: HMSO.

IPPR (2001), *Building Better Partnerships: The Final Report of the Commission on Public Private Partnerships*, London: Institute for Public Policy Research.

Kerr, D. (1998), 'The PFI miracle', *Capital and Class*, Spring (64), 17–28.

Kirk, R.J. and A.P. Wall (2001), 'Substance, form and PFI contracts', *Public Money and Management*, July–September, 41–6.

National Audit Office (1992a), *Department of Transport: Contracting for Roads*, London: HMSO.

National Audit Office (1992b), *Ministry of Defense: Competition in the Provision of Support Services*, London: HMSO.

National Audit Office (1997a), *The Skye Bridge*, HC 5, Parliamentary Session 1997–8, London: HMSO.

National Audit Office (1997b), *The PFI Contracts for Bridgend and Fazakerley Prisons*, HC 253, Parliamentary Session 1997–8, London: Stationery Office.

National Audit Office (1998), *The Private Finance Initiative: The First Four, Design, Build, Finance and Operate Roads Contracts*, HC 476, Parliamentary Session 1997–8, London: Stationery Office.

National Audit Office (1999a), *Examining the Value for Money Deals under the Private Finance Initiative*, HC 739, Parliamentary Session 1998–9, London: Stationery Office.

National Audit Office (1999b), *The PFI Contract for the New Dartford and Gravesham Hospital*, HC 423, Parliamentary Session 1999–2000, London: Stationery Office.

National Audit Office (2000), *The Refinancing of the Fazakerley PFI Prison Contract*, HC 584, Parliamentary Session 1999–2000, London: Stationery Office.

National Audit Office (2001), *Managing the Relationship to Secure a Successful Partnership in PFI projects*, HC54, Parliamentary Session 2001–2, London: Stationery Office.

National Audit Office (2002a), *The Public Private Partnership for National Air Traffic Services Ltd.*, HC 1096, Parliamentary Session 2001–2, London: Stationery Office.

National Audit Office (2002b), *PFI Refinancing Update*, HC 1288, Parliamentary Session 2001–2, London: Stationery Office.

National Audit Office (2003a), *PFI: Construction Performance*, HC 371, Parliamentary Session 2002–3, London: Stationery Office.

National Audit Office (2003b), *The Operational Performance of PFI Prisons*, HC 700, Parliamentary Session 2002–3, London: Stationery Office.

National Audit Office (2003c), *Government Communications Headquarters (GCHQ): New Accommodation Programme*, HC 955, Parliamentary Session 2002–3, London: Stationery Office.

National Audit Office (2004), *Refinancing the Public Private Partnership for National Air Traffic Services*, HC 157, Parliamentary Session 2003–4, London: Stationery Office.

Nicholson, C. (2000), 'The PFI in health: how could it be made to work better', *New Economy*, **7** (3), 138–42.

Palmer, K. (2001), *Contract Issues and Financing in PPP/PFI (Do we need the 'F' in 'DBFO' Projects?)*, contribution to the IPPR Commission.

Pollitt, M.G. (1997), 'The impact of liberalisation on the performance of the electricity supply industry: an international survey', *Journal of Energy Literature*, **3** (2), 3–31.

Pollitt, M.G. (2002), 'The declining role of the state in infrastructure investments in the UK', in S.V. Berg, M.G. Pollitt and M. Tsuji (eds), *Private Initiatives in Infrastructure: Priorities, Incentives and Performance*, Cheltenham, UK and Northampton, MA, USA: Edward Elgar, 67–100.

Robinson, Peter (2000), 'Private finance comes up short', *Financial Times*, 29 November, 27.

Royal Institution of Chartered Surveyors (1998), *Accessing Private Finance – The Availability and Effectiveness of Private Finance in Urban Regeneration*, London: RICS.

Shaoul, J. (2003), 'A financial analysis of the National Air Traffic Services PPP', *Public Money and Management*, July, 185–94.

Spackman, M. (2002), 'Public–private partnerships: lessons from the British approach', *Economic Systems*, **26**, 283–301.

Supply Management (1998), 'PFI gets the thumbs down from trade unions', **3** (19), 24 September.

Timmins, Nicholas (1999a), 'Health service medical association to step up opposition to PFI', *Financial Times*, 5 July, 8.

Timmins, Nicholas (1999b), 'An explosive mixture', *Financial Times*, 27 July.

Timmins, Nicholas (1999c), 'The £84bn question', *Financial Times*, 15 December, 20.

Timmins, Nicholas (2000), 'Taxpayers should share fat PFI profits', *Financial Times*, 29 June, 2.

Warner, A. (1998), 'PFI spotting the PPP track', *The Banker*, **148** (871), September.

Wilkins, N. (1998), 'The Private Finance Initiative', *Business Economics*, **29** (1), 21–29.

12. Public–private partnerships in social services: the example of the City of Stockholm

Roland Almqvist and Olle Högberg

INTRODUCTION

The concept of public–private partnership (PPP) is based on the notion that the public sector can, over a long period, contract out public services to private providers. One reason for doing so is to make use of these private providers' competence in directing and managing activities; another is to permit financial risks to be transferred to these providers. PPP includes agreements and quasi-franchising deals whereby private providers assume responsibility for performing the public service by, for example, administering, improving or constructing new, necessary infrastructure. The concept is also based on the public sector retaining responsibility for the requirements, volume and funding of the services to be performed. The public sector also remains in charge of setting and monitoring performance levels and quality, and is still obliged to act in the event of services being inadequate in terms of volume or quality.

In European municipal activities, a range of tools are used to run PPP arrangements (Torres and Pina, 2001). One option is to create an organization in which the municipality and the private service provider are jointly responsible for the commitment. Another is full outsourcing of service delivery to a private provider, while the municipality retains primary responsibility for the manner in which the work is carried out, and also control over the strategic decisions involved. The latter approach includes contracting-out, but franchising assured for private providers and the use of voluntary organizations to deliver municipal services are also found.

Provision of municipal services by organizations other than the municipalities and, by the same token, cooperation with external providers have long been topical in Scandinavia. There are, for example, extant documents showing that, back in the 1770s, the City of Stockholm signed a contract with a private firm whereby it was engaged to carry out street cleaning in the city. Accordingly, tradition and experience of contracting out technical services are long and solid. Nevertheless, in recent years there has been a marked increase in municipalities' interest in cooperating with private providers with respect to social services as well. Of the Scandinavian capitals, Stockholm is where this interest seems to have been especially strong.

The tool used for this form of cooperation has been initial competitive procurement, in which the municipality performs the role of purchaser and finally signs a contract, or cooperation agreement, with the provider (often private) that wins the tender and thereby obtains the right to deliver the service concerned during the agreed period. It thus does not involve competition in the usual sense of the word, with actors competing for customers on an open market. Rather, it is a matter of what is termed '*ex ante* competition', i.e. competition for a market itself. This is a common form of competition when social services are procured through competitive bidding (Jonsson, 1993). In this case, the market is defined by means of the purchaser's tender documentation.

One purpose of inviting private actors to engage in competitive bidding to provide public services has been to devise methods of boosting efficiency and developing activities. Private companies' ways of organizing themselves and managing their activities, and their working methods, have been seen as interesting subjects for study and cooperation by public organizations (see, for example, Stevens, 1978; Uttley, 1993; and Torres and Pina, 2001). There have also been expectations of competitive procurement and cooperation agreements resulting in cheaper, better management of public activities (Walsh, 1995). A great deal of research has also been devoted to the outcomes of competitive procurement, and one conclusion consistently reached in these studies has been that it may bring about more efficient production by means of improved resource allocation and more effective organization (see e.g. Thordarson, 1994; Bailey and Davidson, 1996; Boyne, 1998; Hodge, 2000).

The research affords no unanimous answer, on the other hand, to the question of whether public services should be provided by the public or the private sector. According to one school of thought, it is the competition as such – rather than whether the work is done by public or private actors – that boosts efficiency (see Bishop and Kay, 1988, and Harrison et al., 1990). Other research findings substantiate the view that both the existence of competition and the identity of the principal are important (see Stevens, 1978; Szymanski, 1996) while other researchers also put forward the view that the 'threat' of competition, rather than competition itself, is the spur (Baumol et al., 1988; Dodgson and Topham, 1988; Sorensen 1993; Uttley, 1993; Ellwood, 1996). Irrespective of which of these theories is the most convincing they are thus all based on the notion that inviting private companies to engage in competitive bidding for public services affords new opportunities for finding methods of economizing and improving efficiency.

Accordingly, it falls to the lot of the public organization – which may be seen as a purchaser – to plan, define and evaluate the services to be performed by the provider. Here there are, broadly speaking, two approaches to specifying this kind of relationship. The first involves the purchaser defining *what* may be expected to ensue from the task to be performed or, specifically, the anticipated outcome of the provider's actions.[1] This also means that the provider is entirely responsible for deciding on the method, or *how* to perform the task. In less complex activities, establishing outcomes is relatively easy. In more complex ones, such as healthcare and social care, this is likely to be less simple, and this paves the way for the second approach. When purchasers have no idea how the outcomes are to be determined, they can instead refer to the methods that providers must use in production processes (Walsh, 1995).

If the purpose of the cooperation is to devise methods of saving money and improving efficiency, the first of the above-mentioned approaches should apply. Responsibility for resources and processes in the contracted-out activity rests entirely, in this case, on the provider. The purchaser's responsibility is to manage and monitor the work to ensure satisfactory performance and outcomes of the contracted-out activity. The ideal therefore stipulates that clear guidelines and social objectives must be laid down in the contract. It must also be possible to monitor and measure fulfilment of objectives (Bailey, 1999). Somewhat simplified, the approach thus involves the purchasers saying to potential providers: 'This is the performance, and these are the outcomes and objectives, you are to attain. Now you find some efficient method of attaining them.'

To fulfil the aim of enhancing understanding of PPPs, it is therefore crucial to study financial and qualitative outcomes of cooperation, but also how the parties' cooperation is organized, managed and monitored. Another key subject of study is whether a functioning market exists, that is, whether there are private actors interested and willing to embark on cooperative, contractual relationships with public organizations. Finally, it is also vital to study how the public purchaser's and private provider's relationship is shaped and developed over time.

There are several alternative approaches to elucidating these aspects. One chosen here is to examine a few individual cases in order to clarify in greater depth the requirements, nature and outcomes of collaboration between the public and the private actor. This approach permits in-depth studies and analysis of key documents in the cooperative relationship, and also interviews with people involved. The case we have chosen to study in detail is the City of Stockholm. This is because this municipality has progressed far in cooperating with private companies with respect to social services and, over time, succeeded in obtaining ample experience in this field. The City of Stockholm's chosen tool for this form of cooperation has been competitive bidding, and the services involved have included nursing homes, service buildings, senior citizens' and group residential homes and open home-help services. We have studied these procurement processes, including the contracts signed, which thus regulate the relationships between the City of Stockholm and the providers who have won contracts through competitive bidding. We have also included procurements won by the municipality's in-house management, in order to explore whether the contracts with in-house actors differ in form from those with private providers.

Our study is longitudinal, covering the three strategies for opening up social services to competition that the City of Stockholm implemented, at various times, between 1993 and 2002. From each of these strategies, some ten procurement processes have been selected for more in-depth analysis of the documents included in the procurement process. These have been the tender documentation, the tender and the contract. The study is also based on material from previous investigations of the municipality's strategies for exposing various activities to competition (Alexandersson and Ölvestad, 1998; City of Stockholm, 2000a and 2000b; PLS, 2001; KOMrev, 2002a and 2000b), and also empirical evidence recently collected from a number of interviews conducted with city of Stockholm purchasers and with providers in both categories – those under municipal management and private companies.

Below, we present the three strategies for introducing competition; the financial and qualitative outcomes thereby attained; and an account of the market conditions under which these strategies have been implemented.

FINANCIAL AND QUALITATIVE OUTCOMES OF THE CITY OF STOCKHOLM'S PROCUREMENT STRATEGIES AND MARKET TRENDS, 1993–2002

As mentioned above, three strategies for opening up municipal activities to competition were devised during the period in question. The first, known as the 'Competition Programme', was applied under a non-Socialist majority during 1993 and 1994. Under this strategy all services, except governance and voucher-financed activities, were to be procured competitively over a five-year period. These activities represented 20 per cent of the remaining social services (nursing homes, service homes, senior citizens' and group residential homes and open home-help services). The actor who, in this competitive situation, submitted the best tender in terms of price and quality, would be allowed to conduct the activities during the agreed period. The purpose of the strategy was twofold: to attain a long-term cost saving of 10 per cent and to bolster quality development (City of Stockholm's Executive Office, 1992).

After the election of autumn 1994, this programme was stopped by the leftwing majority that came to power and an outcome evaluation was initiated. The Institute of Local Government Economics (IKE) presented the results of this evaluation early in 1996. The evaluation showed that exposure to competition had brought about an increase in cost-effectiveness. Altogether, this outcome in the activities procured competitively was estimated at SEK 48 million or 12 per cent gross (Högberg, 1996). There were major variations in the cost reductions, and also cases in which costs were allowed to rise (in the hope that quality would thereby be enhanced). The outcome of the 'threat to competition' was also investigated and found to lie in the range of 4–6 per cent (Almqvist, 1996a and 1999). Here, too, there were major variations in the material, but the overall outcome was estimated at a total of some SEK 120 million. The researchers at IKE also attempted to estimate the impact of competitive bidding on quality in the activities concerned, and the fact that private providers had taken over. Overall, the results of this study afforded no evidence for any deterioration in the quality of the services concerned due to the Competition Programme (Jonsson, 1996).

In May of the same year, a new strategy, 'Procurement '96', was presented. In it, competition was put forward as an alternative means of developing services, and one that was voluntary for the social service districts concerned. After the 1998 election, this strategy was superseded by the non-Socialist majority's 'Policy for procurement, freedom of choice and competition'. This policy, adopted in April 1999, laid down that all activities, excluding governance and strategic management functions, were to be procured by competitive means. Now the City of Stockholm has once more imposed a temporary freeze on competitive procurement, pending a decision on future strategies. Evaluations of 'Procurement '96' and 'Policy for procurement, freedom of choice and competition' show, however, that the savings outcome has had a tendency to decrease. In the latter strategy, savings were estimated at 7.8 per cent (gross) for activities procured competitively, while the 'threat of competition' was deemed to have non-existent financial effects. The purchasers and providers interviewed also agree with this picture of developments. Prices were 'harmonized', and profitability and the profit margin for companies that win tender contracts are currently perceived as low: margins of 2–4 per cent at best are mentioned. One contractor expressed the view that 'these days, savings are a matter of chasing risk premiums'.

In both the evaluations, attempts were also made to estimate quality effects, if any. However, no clear conclusions could be drawn regarding differences either between municipally and privately managed activities conducted or between activities facing and not facing direct competition. In both evaluations, however, it was concluded that the procurement procedure had helped to bring quality aspects of activities to the fore. Below, we return to the question of what specific manifestations of this there have been.

A close look at the trends of market conditions over the ten-year period studied reveals certain clear patterns. Overall, the market is moving from many (and a larger number of small) actors with a large number of tenders submitted in most procurements to a situation of few (and large) actors and a small number of tenders in each procurement process. During one interview with a purchaser this was, moreover, confirmed. The interviewee also related that:

> There's been a change from many actors to few. In the early 1990s there were numerous actors, but the hived-off companies have gradually been bought up. Today, there are some ten private actors in Stockholm. Having just a few actors on the market may be advantageous, though – for example, that they occupy different niches.

According to purchasers and providers alike, there are various factors that exclude minor actors from the market. One mentioned is the growing size of contracts procured, which tends to bring about fewer actors. Another example is the terms of payment, involving payment in arrears, which requires a financial strength that only major actors can muster. In our data we have also observed that, over time, procurements have entailed ever increasing sums. Another purchaser related that in the 'packaging' discussions (when suppliers tender for the whole 'package', i.e. the whole of a major contract, or for parts of it), suppliers have expressed wishes for larger contracts. Moreover, this purchaser related, split procurements had been discontinued because, within the framework of a single contract, comparing the tenders received was too difficult.

When asked directly about the optimal size of a procurement contract, many contractors stated the opinion that size obviously affected interest in bidding for it. To be interesting the contract should, in the contractors' view, comprise at least 25–30 places (or SEK 8–10 million). The fact that the actors have become fewer and larger is due mainly to the small companies being bought up by the larger ones. One purchaser expressed this as follows:

It's a strange market, with few purchasers, and we've created this market ourselves. The small actors are being swallowed up by the big ones – who, what's more, don't want competition. The situation is ideal for cartel formation.

More actors are therefore needed on the market, above all if we want to avoid a kind of oligopoly situation in the future. This need is also emphasized by private providers, who think diversity (i.e. numerous actors) in turn results in improved quality in services purchased.

As for contract periods, these have remained the same over time, with a median of three years. In interviews with contractors it has emerged that they call for longer contracts, preferably lasting five years, and with an extension clause. In their opinion, longer-term contracts can afford incentives for investments and capacity-building work, which may generate favourable effects. They are also interested in getting a chance to own the premises where activities are carried out. The current situation, with its short-term agreements combined with non-existent ownership of premises or equipment, entails disincentives for suppliers' own investments and initiatives, according to several contractors. It was also argued that longer contract periods create continuity for users and a more stable situation for staff and businesses alike. Our own interviews confirm this, and it also emerged that the purchasers understand the contractors' wish for contracts of longer duration. One purchaser reflected on this, describing the three-year contract period as follows:

The first year is one of unease. In the second year everything settles down. Then in the third everything is uneasy again, because extension or a new procurement is looming.

Nevertheless, some purchasers also expressed the view that contract periods exceeding three years pose difficulties, since they involve a risk of the purchaser becoming tied up in the long term in a relationship that may not, perhaps, be particularly good.

The past ten years of competition in the City of Stockholm's social care services have also added new financial aspects to the issue of whether to retain activities under municipal management or outsource them. If the City of Stockholm is forced into cutting costs, it can do so only in activities that are managed in-house. The more that is tied up in contracts, the more difficult it is to meet demands for savings during the fiscal year. One representative of the purchaser side expressed this as follows:

Hopeless cycles – one-year budgets, three-year contracts and four years between elections. The City hadn't considered the whole picture properly before starting. [. . .] Contract terms are unconnected with the rest of local government.

At the same time, perceptions of an imbalance in the parties' risk-taking were also expressed during the interviews. For example, it was mentioned that the contractor must often assume responsibility for changes due to a change in political leadership in the city. One purchaser also related that:

> Requirements and risks tend to be transferred to the provider when it comes, for example, to premises or empty beds. This isn't always the best strategy.

In a labour-intensive activity like elderly care, indexing – which now compensates for only a portion of salary increases during the contract period – causes the financial values in a written agreement to be eroded over time. The substantial price competition between participating tenderers observed at the outset of the period of exposure to competition has slackened considerably in recent years. Nowadays, the private tenderers seek full coverage for their costs, which in several cases has resulted in procurement being interrupted because no tender fulfils the stated budgetary requirements at cost level: the 'reference prices', as they are called. One reason for this development is that the contractors are aware of what good quality means for their reputation: they do not wish to risk their companies being associated with 'poor' care. Another reason prices are high is the now well-developed evaluation criteria that are applied in the selection of the 'best tenders'. These criteria apply to quality aspects in particular, and the tenderers know that they must submit their tenders in such a way as to fulfil the quality criteria. This exerts upward pressure on prices.

Table 12.1 below illustrates changes in financial aspects and market trends in the period between the City of Stockholm's first and third competition strategies.

In the next section, we examine in more detail how the quality aspects were dealt with in the procurement documents during the study period.

THREE COMPETITION STRATEGIES IN THE CITY OF STOCKHOLM: WHAT DO THE DOCUMENTS SAY?

An Analytical Model

As a practical means of observing how quality aspects have been dealt with in the actual procurement documents, we have used results from two previous studies and carried out a new investigation of the City of Stockholm's latest competition strategy. This work plan has enabled us to follow the development of relationships and cooperation agreements between purchasers and providers over nearly ten years. In the first study, we analysed the quality requirements applying to ten procurements in

Table 12.1 Comparison of the 'Competition Programme' and 'Policy for procurement, freedom of choice and competition' in terms of financial aspects and market trends

Aspects	Competition Programme, 1993–1994	Policy for procurement, freedom of choice and competition, 1999–2002
No. of procurements	25	41
No. of tenders (median) per procurement	7 tenders (max. 17)	4 tenders (max. 5)
Scale of procurement contracts in SEK (spread)	SEK 2–72 million	SEK 3–99 million
Average (volume, 1994 prices)	SEK 16.3 million	SEK 31 million
Contract periods (median)	3	3
Saving effect of procurements (gross)	12%	7.8%
Saving effect of competition threat	4–6%	No financial effects

1993–4 (Almqvist, 1996b and 2001). In the second, Alexandersson and Ölvestad (1998) followed up Almqvist's survey of 12 current procurements in the years 1997–8. We carried out the third investigation, relating to ten procurements, in autumn 2003. The selection criteria in the third survey were, first, to select procurement contracts as recent as possible that had been included in the previous surveys and, secondly, to obtain a spread between district administrations and winning tenders (private companies or municipal management). The ten that were finally selected cover the period from 1999 to 2003.

Analysis of the documents is based on our own model (Almqvist, 1996b and 2001). Initially, the quality criteria found in the procurement documents are identified (regarding tenders, only the winning tender is included in the analysis), as are their content: resources, processes and outcomes attained, in the form of result quality. 'Resources' – or in this case the term used should, perhaps, be 'resource quality' – relates to resource characteristics, such as personnel strength, employees' educational level, equipment, and so on. 'Process quality' is, rather, a matter of the working approach or method in the actual treatment and care provided. 'Result quality', finally, relates to the outcome of performance on health: examples may be quality of life, frequency of side-effects, and so on (Donabedian, 1979; Jonsson, 1993). The quality criteria found in the tender documents were, in the subsequent stage, assessed according to a four-grade scale (0 to 3; 3s criterion does not appear in procurement documents), depending on their specificity. In some cases they can be highly specific and even *measurable* (level 3), while in others they are couched in *general* terms (level 1). The former are more or less quantified and a standard, or level, of attainment is specified. The generally defined quality criteria indicate, instead, a particular emphasis or broadly discuss what the providers should seek to achieve. In a further portion of cases, it is doubtful whether the quality criteria can be labelled one way or the other. In other words, it is questionable whether they can be measured, but they are still specific to some extent. If wished, compliance or non-compliance with them can be more or less checked: they may be described as *checkable (level 2)*.[2]

When the quality criterion in question is assessed in all the documents according to the above-mentioned scale, a mean is worked out. This mean makes it possible to determine at an aggregate level which quality criterion or criteria have developed well and/or been neglected. This also affords scope for comparison of contracts with the tender documents and tenders, and for obtaining an overall picture of the quality discussion in the procurement documents.

The analytical model is thus based on two dimensions. One dimension is a matter of what the quality criterion in question concerns. The other describes how specific it is:

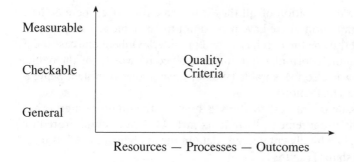

Figure 12.1   The two dimensions of the analytical model: content of the quality criteria and degree of specification

Competition Programme

When we analysed the ten procurement cases within the framework of the City of Stockholm's first strategy for introducing competition, 12 quality criteria stood out as particularly frequent. Table 12.2 below illustrates these quality criteria, divided according to resources, processes and outcomes.

Table 12.2   Quality criteria in the procurement documents, divided into resources, processes and outcomes (Competition Programme)

Resources	Processes	Outcomes
Competence	Competence development Availability Continuity Freedom of choice User modification Information/communication Monitoring/evaluation Safety Cooperation Transparency	Quality objectives regarding outcomes of social care services

In 1993–4, quality criteria relating to processes in the procurement documents predominated: competence development, availability, continuity and so forth. Result quality, in the form of social-care outcomes attained, have been summarized as 'quality objectives regarding outcomes of social care services' (outcome objectives) in Table 12.2. The reason for not presenting the formulation of all these 'outcome objectives' here is that, on closer examination, these have proved not to be viable as such, despite being labelled thus by the purchasers and providers. Only in one case did a purchaser genuinely formulate an outcome objective worthy of the name, and one that was also measurable (the objective in question then being a matter of user satisfaction).

The next issue of interest to study is how far the quality criteria that featured in the procurement documents in 1993–4 can be monitored or verified. When we finally entered our data in the analytical model, it took the following shape (Figure 12.2):

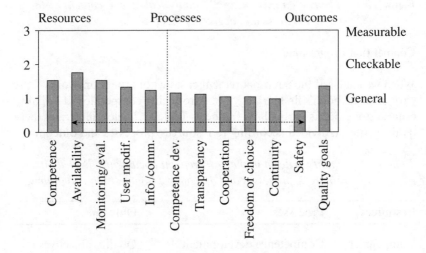

Figure 12.2   Quality criteria analysed at aggregate level on the basis of the two dimensions in the analytical model (Competition Programme)

Figure 12.2 includes all the quality criteria in the tender documentation, tenders and contracts studied. As reported above, most of the quality criteria in the purchasing documents are known to concern process quality. What Figure 12.2 further illustrates is that, at an aggregate level and in terms of the whole purchasing process, no quality criterion attained the mean value of 2. That is, no quality criterion maintained the specification level defined as *checkable* or *measurable* throughout the procurement of the activity. The aggregate mean value is 1.4. Figure 12.2 also shows that *availability*, *competence* and *monitoring/evaluation* were the quality criteria for which the highest means were obtaind and, accordingly, those specified in the greatest detail throughout the procurement process. Here, it may also be mentioned that in our comparison of procurements won by private and municipal actors respectively, we found that private tenderers had satisfied the purchasers' requirements to a considerably higher degree than the municipal ones.

Procurement '96

All the procurements in elderly care that took place in 1998 were analysed using the analytical model described above (Alexandersson and Ölvestad, 1998). In this investigation, no comparisons were made between the procurement documents. Our analysis was thus not as detailed as that of the Competition Programme and that was presented above. Table 12.3 below illustrates the most central quality criteria applied under Procurement '96.

Table 12.3   Quality criteria in the procurement documents, divided into resources, processes and outcomes (procurements in 1996)

Resources	Processes	Outcomes
Competence	Competence development	
	Availability	
	Continuity	
	User modification	
	Environmental programme	
	Information/communication	
	Monitoring/evaluation	
	Client respect	
	Rehabilitation/activation	
	Transparency	

In a comparison with the first competition strategy, the 'Competition Programme', we note that a couple of quality criteria have been added to the actors' documents: *rehabilitation/activation* and *client respect*. We can also see that four quality criteria have now been removed: *safety, cooperation, freedom of choice* and, perhaps most important of all, *quality objectives regarding the outcomes of social care*.

The other overall observation from the analysis of Procurement '96 is illustrated in Figure 12.3. In a comparison with the results from the Competition Programme analysis (Figure 12.2), a minor tendency towards growing measurability of the quality criteria is discernible.

Figure 12.3 includes all the quality criteria in the tender documents studied. It shows that, at an aggregate level and with reference to the

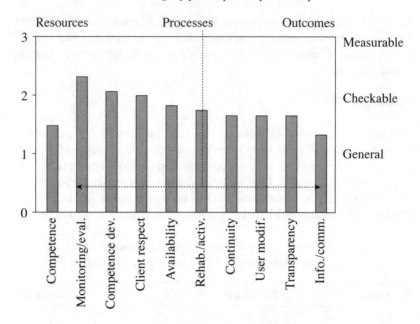

Figure 12.3   *Quality criteria analysed at aggregate level on the basis of the two dimensions in the analytical model (Procurement '96)*

whole procurement process, more quality criteria (*monitoring/evaluation, competence development* and *client respect*) attained the mean value of 2, the specification level defined as *checkable*. The aggregate mean is 1.7.

Policy for Procurement, Freedom of Choice and Quality

Our analysis of the ten selected cases from the City of Stockholm's third competition strategy may be summarized in three general observations. First, the quality criteria are now more numerous. Secondly, just as in the two previous strategies, the dominant quality criteria are those that relate to processes in the procurement documents: *competence development, availability, continuity* and so on. Thirdly, the degree of specification is higher than before. Table 12.4 illustrates the first of the three overall observations.

As we see, some entirely new quality criteria have come into being within the scope of this third strategy: *leadership, security, complaint management, integrity/self-determination*. A few new types of outcome goal (the rates of bedsores and fall injuries) have been devised. Various quality criteria have been reincorporated into the procurement process: *safety, cooperation* and *freedom of choice*.

Table 12.4   *Quality criteria in the procurement documents, divided into resources, processes and outcomes (policy for procurement, freedom of choice and quality)*

Resources	Processes	Outcomes
Competence	Competence development	Outcome goals
Leadership	Availability	
	Continuity	
	Freedom of choice	
	User modification	
	Information/communication	
	Monitoring/evaluation	
	Safety	
	Cooperation	
	Transparency	
	Client respect	
	Activation/rehabilitation	
	Security	
	Complaint management	
	Integrity/self-determination	

Figure 12.4 illustrates the second general observation, and shows the distribution of the criteria over time among resources, processes and outcomes. A study of all three competition strategies makes it clear that the dominance of the process criteria has remained stable over time. Between 80 and 90 per cent of all the quality criteria have continuously related to processes in the three strategies, as Figure 12.4 shows.

The third general observation was that the degree of specification has risen slightly over time. If the mean is used, an increase in measurability may be noted in each strategy: from 1.4 (in 1994) to 1.7 (1998) and 1.8 (2002). This is illustrated in Figure 12.5, which shows the results for all quality criteria in the three competition strategies.

The figure also prompts the observation that the number of criteria has risen over the past ten-year period. New criteria have been added to the old, and in the last survey as many as 18 criteria were noted.

We shall now analyse and interpret these results and this trend on the basis of the relationship between purchaser and provider. The purpose of this analysis is to generate understanding of the contractual relationship between these parties. With reference to social services, three general approaches to the contractual purchaser-provider relationship are distinguishable: 'non-contractibility', 'trust-based' and 'control-based'.

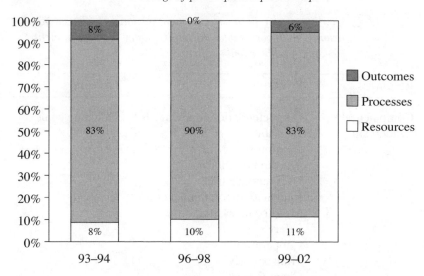

Figure 12.4   Distribution of quality criteria among the three categories of resources, processes and outcomes

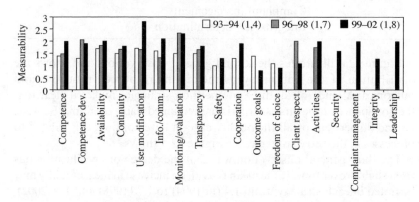

Figure 12.5   All quality criteria, with their degree of specification in the three surveys

PUBLIC–PRIVATE PARTNERSHIP IN SOCIAL SERVICES: THREE APPROACHES

Non-contractibility

The results of the documentary study reported above show that the City of Stockholm's three competition strategies to date have not lived up to theoretical claims in terms of controlling and regulating quality through contracts with external parties. The contracts may not be said to be designed to control performance outcome (result quality), regarded in terms of a quality perspective on activities. Nor, within the framework of the first two strategies, were they generally designed in such a way as to enable any quality criteria to be measured or monitored. The quality criteria found in the procurement documents were discussed largely in terms of general features, and were mainly oriented towards processes in activities. A tendency towards a larger number of measurable quality criteria is discernible within the framework of the third strategy, but the focus is still on processes, rather than outcomes.

One viable approach to the purchaser–provider relationship relates to regulation of the quality aspects of activities. This is what Domberger (1998) terms 'non-contractibility'. Here, the approach means that quality in certain activities is primarily a matter of judgment. In these activities it is difficult – not to say impossible – to specify quality requirements in a manner that permits measurement of work outcomes. In these circumstances, it is easier to specify the resources and processes used, rather than the outcomes expected to ensue from the activities. This approach is thus based on the assumption that the contractual purchaser–provider relationship never needs regulating with respect to the outcomes the provider is expected to attain. The reason for this is that it is, quite simply, not possible. This kind of explanation is also accepted by one of the purchasers interviewed, who said:

> It's difficult to define good outcome requirements, and that's why we talk about what the *nature* of the work processes should be [our emphasis].

The problems of regulating quality in the manner advocated by the theorists have had particular repercussions on the purchaser–provider relationship. Over time, we can also see a change in these repercussions. In our empirical analysis of the City of Stockholm's three competition strategies, we found that the number of quality criteria and the proportion of checkable quality criteria had risen over time in the procurement documents, and that process-related quality criteria had predominated throughout. These developments may be summarized thus: contractual regulation has, over time, come to involve stricter regulation of processes with respect to activities procured. Moreover, we noticed a marked change in the actors' statements regarding the purchaser–provider relationship over time. Below, we emphasize two further approaches to the relationship that appear highly relevant.

Trust-based Approach

This view is based on the notion that purchasers and providers have, by signing the contract, embarked on close cooperation. The view emphasizes the need for mutual trust and establishment of long-term client relationships (Lind, 1995). Sanctions are seen as an ineffective means of correcting failures. In the event of problems the parties should, instead, sit down and jointly work out how to attain certain objectives in activities, or how to overcome difficulties.

This approach to the contractual relationship may be reasonable when activities, such as social services, entail difficulties in terms of management and control of performance and fulfilment of objectives. One way of strengthening the relationship with a provider is then to seek to connect the provider with the purchaser's organization and adopt an attitude more reminiscent of the relationship with other employees in the organization than of one with an 'outsider' that the purchaser attempts to control at arm's length. This kind of attitude lays more emphasis on confidence and building up good relationships than on rights and obligations in accordance with a written contract. Referring to the contract is thus, so to speak, a last resort (Walsh, 1995). Research carried out by Ouchi (1979) and others also shows that management through the setting-up of detailed measurement and monitoring systems tends to reduce enthusiasm for the work and impair trust between parties involved in economic or social transactions. This approach means deliberately refraining from designing the contracts in such a way as to permit measurement and monitoring of specified quality indicators, since this may be deleterious to trust between the parties.[3]

During an interview with a senior purchasing manager, within the framework of the evaluation of the Competition Programme, this aspect was, moreover, emphasized. In the manager's view, the part of the purchasing process that is documented is indeed important, but even more important is what results from the parties meeting at the negotiating table. This is where trust and a foundation of good relationships start to be established, according to the manager. The fact that certain quality criteria are not specified in the contracts in accordance with the purchasers' original requirements may possibly reflect what happened at the negotiating table. If the situation is perceived as favourable and trust is emerging between the parties, they may perhaps simultaneously 'feel' that certain aspects, quite simply, do not need to be specified in the contract.

Generating trust between two parties includes having, or establishing, common values. According to Walsh (1995), there are three ways for purchasers to ensure that providers are performing well even when the activity concerned is difficult to measure and it is virtually impossible to follow up whether the service has been delivered efficiently or not. First, purchasers can introduce mechanisms that afford an assurance that providers' commitments are credible. Secondly, purchasers can assure themselves that the providers share their own values and that they support, and feel obliged to pursue, a notion of providing good services. Finally, purchasers can exert pressure on providers to do a good job by issuing threats of sanctions if there is any suspicion of their not doing so. Burns et al. (1994) emphasize the importance of the second of these attitudes, and is of the view that relationships set up through contracts require the kind of confidence that rests on common values, the sense of being a family and honest exchange of information between the parties.

With respect to the City of Stockholm's first competition strategy, the content of the procurement documents may be readily interpreted as being formulated in a spirit of discussion or reasoning concerning the quality aspects of activities. In this discussion, a number of quality criteria have proved particularly salient. Generally speaking, however, they were neither focused on outcomes nor specified in measurable or checkable terms. Within the scope of the Competition Programme the purchasers' intention appears, rather, to have been to present a quality viewpoint or image of the values concerning quality that prevailed in the organization and was based on the quality criteria identified. From the purchasers' point of view, achieving common values and approaches was thus considered more important and a better way of getting activities to develop in the desired direction than seeking to control them through sophisticated measuring and monitoring systems.

Control-based Approach

When we analyse the form of procurement documents and actors' statements within the scope of the City of Stockholm's latest competition strategy – the policy for procurement, freedom of choice and competition – the picture of the purchaser-provider relationship that emerges is different, however, from that presented above. Our interview material describes in depth a striking change in the relationship between the parties. The actors' latest descriptions and statements are readily explainable in terms of what may be called a 'control-based approach'.

With this approach, the contractual relationship is seen as an impersonal process in which the parties agree on their formal mutual commitments. This approach is also based on the notion that purchasers and providers have divergent interests, and that contracts serve to allocate risks, responsibilities and rewards. The parties' relationship is thus, under the contract, specified in detail, and if the aspects regulated in the contract are not fulfilled by the provider it is possible for the purchaser to apply the sanctions prescribed in the contract (Walsh et al., 1997).

We have observed that the tender documentation in recent procurements appears stereotyped and has been adapted to the standardized forms designed by the purchasers concerned. In the interviews, viewpoints have emerged that indicate a certain uniformity in tender documents, tenders and contracts alike. This prompts the view that the tender documentation contains insufficient information both about the purchaser's intentions and hopes in contracting out the activity concerned, and regarding staff, activities and change requirements at the time of the invitation to tender. In addition, several contractors consider that the tender documents are excessively oriented towards healthcare and too detailed in terms, for example, of the tenderer's organization, way of working and quality systems. They perceive rigidity with respect to work procedures and resource levels, such as availability of nurses or staff density. One purchaser also confirmed this during an interview, stating the following opinion:

> Some companies say that the requirements we impose are much too controlling. They think they have become increasingly regulated over time. The requirements must certainly be clear, but still provide scope for companies' own concepts and ideas. Companies like to see some degree of development work in the assignment [...] Demands for a certain staffing level, for example, should be avoided. There must be some flexibility when it comes to staffing.

Our consequential question raised the matter of whether this development towards stricter and more detailed control of processes is a matter of reduced trust in the contractors. Several interview statements from the purchasers indicated that this may perhaps be the case, but at the same time they tried to describe the situation in more subtle terms and explain why trust in the contractors may have decreased. A series of healthcare scandals over the years was, for example, cited as a key factor. One purchaser related that:

> Trust in the parties hasn't improved. But this doesn't really have anything to do with the development of the actual contracts. Other parameters are involved. Healthcare scandals, media pressure and price competition have, for example, resulted in more rigorous examination of contractors, and things like this are bound to impair trust.

Another purchaser was slightly clearer than this with respect to the parties' roles, but also cited external factors as part of the reason why trust between the parties is not always the best:

> We purchasers see the contractors at a distance – and that's the way we want it! Ours is a wait-and-see attitude: we don't want to get too close. The contractor is

often perceived as an 'opposite party' rather than an 'associate'. But the Public Procurement Act has a lot to do with making this happen. Sometimes I went to check up on the contractors that I'd let win the competitive procurement. It was quite a cloak-and-dagger act! Quite simply, one doesn't have the same trust in them as in municipal in-house management.

The same purchaser expanded on the ways in which he felt that the Public Procurement Act was creating problems:

One problem in procurement processes is that you're not allowed to depart from the specification. If you do, you have to start negotiating all over again – that is, a new procurement. This causes a conflict between the regulations and the purpose of procurement. Tenderers aren't, for example, allowed to lower their prices or come up with a good idea – 'Let's do it like this instead – we've got a good idea!' Then we take the idea and carry out a new procurement instead. The outcome is that, next time, they don't come up with any new ideas about how the work should be run: they don't say anything.

The repercussion on the management and attitudes described above is that the contractors perceive the assignment as one of administration, rather than fully developed contracting. Detailed management is seen as hampering the contractors' scope for new, high-quality and resource-efficient solutions. The contractors get the feeling that the emphasis seems to be on their continuing to carry out the work along the same lines as before, but at lower cost and preferably with higher quality. The level of detail in the tender documentation is seen as preventing the tenderers from showing new, interesting solutions of their own for meeting the demands of the Health and Medical Care Act, the Social Services Act, residents and their relatives: that is, demand or encouragement for alternative solutions or innovation is, in the contractors' view, insufficient.

One purchaser's description is particularly telling when it comes to the relationship being something of a deadlock:

Uncertainty on both sides – the purchasers', what with the Public Procurement Act and healthcare scandals, and the providers', what with healthcare scandals and our misuse of the providers' ideas – mean that the desire to experiment in submitting a tender is eliminated. Threats of damages also inhibit the wish to experiment.

PUBLIC–PRIVATE PARTNERSHIPS IN SOCIAL SERVICES – A FUTURE PERSPECTIVE

As mentioned in the introduction, one purpose of inviting private actors to join in competitive bidding for public services is to identify means of raising efficiency and developing activities, that is, to generate innovation. Our study shows that, over time, situations have arisen that impede such development. All three approaches to the purchaser–provider relationship presented above have proved relevant to the form of procurement used. However, a tendency is discernible: a trust-based approach in the parties' relationship is giving way to one that is more control-based, despite certain obvious features of 'non-contractibility' in the activities. This shift in approach has proved to cause adverse repercussions on the relationship between the parties. Nevertheless, in our empirical material, we have observed ample opportunities for developing PPPs in the future, thereby circumventing the problems revealed in this study. Below, we discuss these opportunities.

First, both purchasers and providers describe a need to develop the existing market for social services. When the City of Stockholm introduced its first competition strategy, a smoothly functioning market was created: new private contractors arose, municipal employees formed their own 'spin-off' companies, and in-house management, which was always invited to join in the competitive bidding, competed for operation of activities. Plenty of tenders were submitted in each procurement, and the financial impact in the form of substantial savings was evident. After ten years with the three competition strategies in the City of Stockholm, all the parties involved now agree that few, if any, additional savings are attainable through procurement procedure. In time, the companies with the most capital also bought up the small contractors, and the market has progressively come to resemble an oligopoly. The current risk of insufficient competition and emergence of, for example, cartel arrangements is substantial, and this means that there is a need to develop the market. Aspects that have emerged during our interviews, and which could be one way of solving this problem, are what the respondents call 'packaging' of the activities procured. The problem is that the ever growing size of procurements is bringing about a reduction in the number of actors on the market. One solution thus appears to be, in the future, to reduce the scale of activities procured in order to attract smaller, and accordingly more, actors to the market. This may be done by, for example, allowing tenderers to bid not only for the whole, but also for parts ('packages'), of a major procurement.

Other ways of attracting more actors to the market are to facilitate investment opportunities and balance risk-taking between the parties. In the interviews, contractors expressed their wish for longer-term agreements: in their opinion, these can yield incentives for investments and expansion, which may generate favourable outcomes. They are also interested in getting a chance to own the premises where the work is conducted. Accordingly, it might perhaps be feasible to manage in a more reasonable manner what the contractors perceive as the imbalance in risk-taking among the parties with respect to premises and empty beds.

The parties should conduct a continuous dialogue about the above aspects. During one interview, a purchaser stated that this is not done in a systematic way and the contractors have no one to consult about aspects of this kind. The interviewee proposed the creation of a 'development forum' for all municipally funded activities, where the parties could meet and discuss work development in depth. The purchaser compared this 'development forum' with the building meetings that are held concerning technical services in the municipality.

Something should also be done about the nature of the contracts. Previously in this section, we have summarized development during the period studied as follows: that contractual management has, over time, come to involve stricter control of processes with respect to the activity procured. In general, conditions for competitive procurements have been increasingly dictated from above. Nowadays, tenders must often be written according to a set model, with given headings. As the providers have grown steadily in size, their tenders have also been increasingly often worded in general terms and professionally written, and less often adapted to the specific activities procured. Simultaneously, purchasers in the City of Stockholm have imposed detailed management through, for example, demands for staffing and transparency, partly to avoid 'healthcare scandals' in the mass media. Healthcare-oriented and highly detailed tender documentation contributes to assignments being seen, from the contractors' point of view, as administrative functions rather than independently developed contracting operations with scope for unconventional alternative solutions and innovation.

We have, moreover, observed a shift in the basis of the purchaser–provider relationship from trust to control. The tendency has also been for requirements and risks to be increasingly transferred to providers. Today, a future characterized by stagnating municipal finances, and a labour market in which skilled staff are in short supply and have higher pay claims than before, awaits purchasers and providers alike. If no further savings can be made; if the market for social services cools down; if elderly care proves unsuited to procurement; and if the aim is to go on running activities along the same lines as to date, procurement no longer appears a particularly advantageous option.

If, on the other hand, forms of cooperation can be developed in a more confidence-inspiring way, perhaps through a joint development company; if risk management can be more reciprocal; if incentives for improving outcomes can be implemented; and if the value of agreements can be secured over the contract period, procurement processes may remain a key feature of development of the PPP concept, in social services as in other areas.

NOTES

1. This is also advice put forward by some people with practical experience of competitive procurement. In a study by Bryntse (1992), interviews were conducted with reprsentatives of five municipalities in the UK. One reply to the question of what advice they would give their Swedish colleagues was 'It's more important to specify the *result* to be attained from the activity than *how* it is to be done'.
2. Christopher Hood (1995) thinks that one dimension of change in the reforms that now characterize the public sector concerns the development of measurable targets – or at least checkable – standards of performance.
3. But there is also an underlying argument of a financial nature in this reasoning. It may thus impair the parties' mutual confidence if too much time and energy are devoted to specification and monitoring of contracts. Another risk is that it may result in high transaction costs for the client (Coulson, 1998). In all probability, well specified contracts require extra work of a proactive nature during the outlining phase. At the same time, they require additional work of a reactive nature when it is time to start monitoring compliance with the contract. Oliver Williamson (1985) distinguishes between *ex ante* and *ex post* types of transaction costs. Transaction costs of the *ex ante* type involve such phases as outlining of contracts, negotiating with agents and securing agreements. Transaction costs of the *ex post* type may be related to, for example, extra costs of checking compliance with the contract and also costs of setting up and administering management structures capable of dealing with disputes between the parties. These transaction costs can thus be kept in check if a more confidence-based approach is adopted when the parties enter into contractual relationships.

REFERENCES

Alexandersson, L. and J. Ölvestad (1998), 'Konkurrensutsättning av äldreboende i Stockholms stad – en kritisk granskning av utvärderingsprocessen' ['Introducing competition in the City of Stockholm's elderly care – a critical examination of the evaluation process'], Stockholm University, School of Business, master's thesis.

Almqvist, R. (1996a), 'Effekter av konkurrenshotet – en studie av egen regis resultatenheter inom äldreomsorgen i Stockholms stad' ['Effects of the threat of competition – a study of profit centres under municipal management in the City of Stockholm's elderly care'], IKE 1996: 58, Stockholm University, School of Business.

Almqvist, R. (1996b), 'Vilka kvalitetskrav ställs i anbudshandlingar?' ['What are the quality requirements in procurements?'], IKE 1996: 56, Stockholm University, School of Business.

Almqvist, R. (1999), 'Measuring the threat of competition – services for the elderly in the City of Stockholm', *Local Government Studies*, 25 (1), 1–16.

Almqvist, R. (2001), 'Management by contract – a study of programmatic and technological aspects', *Public Administration – an International Quarterly*, 79 (3), 689–706.

Bailey, S.J. and C. Davidson (1996), 'Did quality really increase for UK local government services subject to compulsory competitive tendering?' discussion paper no. 33, Glasgow Caledonian University: Department of Economics.

Bailey, S.J. (1999), *Local Government Economics – Principles and Practice*, Macmillan Press Ltd.

Baumol, W.J., J.C. Panzar and R.D. Willig (1988), *Contestable Markets and the Theory of Industry Structure*, New York: Academic Press.

Bishop, M. and J. Kay (1988), *Does Privatisation Work? – Lessons from the UK*, London: London Business School.

Boyne, G.A. (1998), 'Public services under New Labour: back to bureaucracy?', *Public Money and Management*, **18** (3), 43–50.

Bryntse, K. (1992), 'Erfarenheter av entreprenader och privatisering i engelska kommuner' ['Experience of outsourcing and privatization in British local authorities'], KEFU's [Council for Local Government Research and Education] series of labour reports, 1.

Burns, D., R. Hambleton and P. Hogget (1994) *The Politics of Decentralisation – Revitalising Local Democracy*, Basingstoke: Macmillan.

City of Stockholm (2000a) 'Fyra avbrutna upphandlingar inom äldreomsorgen – en processtudie' ['Four interrupted procurements in elderly care – a process study'], City of Stockholm's report series, 17 August.

City of Stockholm (2000b) 'Intervjuer med vårdgivare – en sammanställning av utförda intervjuer med sex stycken vårdgivare inom äldreomsorgen verksamma inom Stockholms stad' ['Interviews with care providers – a summary of interviews with six elderly care providers in the City of Stockholm'], City of Stockholm's report series, May.

City of Stockholm's Executive Office (1992), 'Stadens verksamhet i konkurrens, ['The city's activities in competition'].

Coulson, A. (1998), 'Trust and contract in public sector management', in A. Coulson (ed.) *Trust and Contracts – Relationships in Local Government, Health and Public Services*, British: Polity Press.

Dodgson, J.S. and N. Topham (1988), *Bus Deregulation and Privatisation*, Aldershot, UK: Athenaeum Press.

Domberger, S. (1998), *The Contracting Organization*, Oxford: Oxford University Press.

Donabedian, A. (1979), 'The quality of medical care: a concept in search of a definition', *The Journal of Family Practice*, **2** (2), 277–84.

Ellwood, S. (1996), *Cost-based Pricing in the NHS International Market*, The Chartered Institute of Management Accountants, Birmingham: University of Aston.

Harrison, S., D.J. Hunter and C. Pollitt (1990), *The Dynamics of British Health Policy*, London: Unwin Hyman.

Hodge, G. (2000), *Privatization: An International Review of Performance*, Boulder, CO: Westview Press.

Hood, C. (1995), 'The New Public Management in the 1980s: variations on a theme', *Accounting, Organizations and Society*, **20** (2/3), 93–109.

Högberg, O. (1996), 'Kostnadseffekter av konkurrensutsättning – en studie av Stockholms stads äldreomsorg' ['Cost effects of introducing competition – a study of the City of Stockholm's elderly care'], IKE 1996:59, Stockholm University: School of Business.

Jonsson, E. (1993), 'Konkurrens inom Sjukvården – vad säger forskningen om effekterna?' ['Competition in healthcare – what effects does research show?'], SPRI [Swedish Institute for Health Services Development] report no. 350.

Jonsson, E. (1996), 'Konkurrensutsättning och kvalitet – en studie av Stockholms stads äldreomsorg' ['Competition and quality – a study of the City of Stockholm's elderly care'], IKE 1996:60, Stockholm University, School of Business.

KOMrev (2002a), 'Prisanalys och prisutveckling inom den entreprenaddrivna äldreomsorgen' ['Price analysis and price trends in contracted-out elderly care'], Öhrlings PriceWaterhouseCoopers.

KOMrev (2002b), 'Studium av prisnivåer m m i Stockholms stads entreprenaddrivna äldreomsorgen' [Study of price levels etc in contracted-out elderly care'], Öhrlings PriceWaterhouseCoopers.

Lind, J.I. (1995), 'Att konkurrensutsätta eller inte – en modefråga? Tolkningar och lärdomar från några systemskiftesförsök' ['Introducing competition – a matter of fashion? Interpretations and lessons from some system-change trials'], KEFU's [Council for Local Government Research and Education] publication series, 1995:1.

Ouchi, W.G. (1979), 'A conceptual framework for the design of organizational control mechanisms', Management Science, 25 (9), 833–48.

PLS Ramboll Management (2001), 'Utvärdering av konkurrensutsättning inom Stockholms stad – sammanfattning' ['Evaluation of competition in the City of Stockholm's services – summary'], PLS Ramboll Management A/S.

Sorensen, R.J. (1993), 'The efficiency of public service provision', in K. Eliassen and J. Kooiman (eds), Managing Public Organizations – Lessons from Contemporary European Experience, London: Sage Publications.

Stevens, B.J. (1978), 'Scale, market structure and the cost of refuse collection', The Review of Economics and Statistics, 60 (3), 438–48.

Szymanski, S. (1996), 'The impact of compulsory competitive tendering on refuse collection services', Fiscal Studies, 17 (3), 1–19.

Thordarson, B. (1994), 'Privatisering av kommunal verksamhet – en granskning av de teoretiska argumenten för privatisering och kommunernas val av verksamhetsform' ['Privatization of municipal activities – an examination of the theoretical arguments for privatization and municipalities' choice of enterprise form'], KEFU's [Council for Local Government Research and Education] publication series 1994:2, Lund, Sweden.

Torres, L. and V. Pina (2001), 'Public–private partnership and private finance initiatives in the EU and Spanish local governments', The European Accounting Review, 10 (3), 601–19.

Uttley, M. (1993), 'Contracting-out and market-testing in the UK defence sector: theory, evidence and issues', Public Money and Management, 13 (1), 55–60.

Walsh, K. (1995), Public Services and Market Mechanisms – Competition, Contracting and the New Public Management, Basingstoke: Macmillan.

Walsh, K., N. Deakin, P. Smith, P. Spurgeon and N. Thomas (1997), 'Contracting for change', in Health, Social Care and other Local Government Services, Oxford: Oxford University Press.

Williamson, O.E. (1985), The Economic Institutions of Capitalism – Firms, Markets, Relational Contracting, New York: The Free Press.

13. Public–private partnerships for infrastructure in Denmark: from local to global partnering?

Carsten Greve and Niels Ejersbo

INTRODUCTION

Public–private partnerships (PPPs) are currently the subject of much debate and discussion in the fields of public policy and public management in Scandinavia, including Denmark. While there is much talk about partnerships for infrastructure, there is little action on the ground in Denmark. PPP's can be understood as 'co-operation of some durability between public and private actors in which they jointly develop products and services and share risks and services which are connected to these products and services' (Van Ham and Koppenjan, 2001:598). What is striking about most commentaries about PPPs is their assumption that PPPs represent something 'new'. The argument in this chapter is that partnership-like arrangements have been with us for some time. PPPs are not new. To help us develop this argument further, we take our theoretical point of departure in historical–institutional theory (Thelen and Steinmo, 1992; Thelen, 1999). Historical institutionalism puts 'emphasis on how institutions emerge from and are embedded in concrete temporal processes' (Thelen, 1999).

This chapter explores a particularly interesting case for exploring the evolution of partnerships during a longer time perspective. The case is about the relationship between a private sector company (Falck), responsible for ambulance driving and fire fighting in Denmark, and Danish local and regional governments. The case highlights a nearly century-old relationship that enables it to show how partnerships develop and how they change during various critical junctures in history. In the absence of any real PFI-like or other types of new PPP-type arrangements as yet, it could be interesting to examine a case in an area where partnering has been an institution for a long time.

Falck[1] has been a family owned company that contracted with local governments in Denmark for fire fighting and ambulance driving services and is today listed on the stock exchange. In the years since the company's establishment in 1906, the company developed a partnership arrangement. This was disturbed by a fierce competition with another private company after a few decades. In the 1970s, the competition was quashed and Falck and the Danish public sector renewed their partnership. In the 1990s, Falck was listed on the stock exchange and merged with an English-based company to form a new company, Group 4 Falck,[2] that immediately announced its global market ambitions.

Since the merger, Group 4 Falck has followed a strategy of acquiring companies in different countries, for example Wackenhut Corporation in the USA. The question is whether local partnering is possible at the same time as the company is pursuing global partnering? The challenge for Group 4 Falck is now to establish global partnerships with governments all around the world. In February 2004, Group 4 Falck merged with the British based company Securicor to become the world's second largest company for security services. The new name of the company is Group 4 Securicor[3] – and the Falck company is a subsidiary company in the global business of Group 4 Securicor. The relationship between Falck and the Danish public sector can therefore be characterized as moving from 'local partnering to global partnering'. The interesting question to be explored then is, how is it possible to sustain 'global partnering' in the long run?

The chapter is divided into three parts. The first part introduces the themes of the PPP debate in Denmark. The second part briefly mentions concepts from historical institutional theory before tracing the relationship between the Falck company and the Danish public sector. The third part discusses explanations for the move from local partnering to global partnering in a historical institutional perspective. Concluding remarks make up the fourth part of the chapter.

THE PUBLIC–PRIVATE PARTNERSHIP DEBATE IN DENMARK

Denmark (with a population of 5.3 million people) has been in discussion about market-based governance of services since the 1980s. Contracting out and the sale of assets in state owned companies have been dominant themes. The privatization of state owned companies has progressed steadily with the Danish government privatizing companies in telecommunications, airports, and transport. The largest sale was the sale of the telecom company to an American-based firm fetching 31 billion DKK (roughly 310 million GBP).

Contracting out has been another story. The general verdict is that there has been too much talk and too little action. Contracting out is primarily a local government issue since Denmark's 13 regions and 271 local governments enjoy extended autonomy from central government and are responsible for much service provision and infrastructure and levy their own taxes. Local governments still only contract out between 11 and 13 per cent of their service functions while the percentage has been much higher (80 per cent) historically in infrastructure. The PPP debate in Denmark follows on from the contracting-out debate in particular. The government and private companies have begun to talk in terms of 'partnerships' instead of contracting out. One private company has openly declared an interest in the language of partnership in order to be able to break the deadlock that the term 'contracting out' had effectively caused in Danish policy debates. The language about partnerships is confusing in the present Danish context, especially as the various parts of government tend to use different definitions in their documents on partnerships.

The talk about partnerships, however, has mostly concentrated on infrastructure. Mostly the infrastructure debate is centered around the question of financing. The British Private Finance Initiative appears to be the main inspiration for this debate. The important government departments are the Danish Ministry of Finance, the Ministry of Transport and the Ministry for Economics and Industry, including their various agencies. There is as yet no single PPP unit in central government, although a common inter-ministerial working group has been established. Partnerships for infrastructure are mentioned in the Danish government's 'Action plan for public–private partnerships' (Danish Ministry of Finance et al., 2004) from January 2004, and the areas include transport, housing and prisons.

On the ground, not much has happened yet, although local governments have done a little experimentation. There have been attempts at establishing partnerships in some regional hospitals, and a handful of local governments have experimented with sale-and-lease-back models. In particular, partnerships had a bad name for a while because they were associated with a scandal in a NPM-oriented local government where the former mayor now faces prosecution (Greve and Ejersbo, 2005).

The lack of any solid partnership experience in Denmark in infrastructure so far has led to the examination of older and more institutionalized public–private cooperation in Denmark: the provision of ambulance and fire fighting that could be said to be a crucial part of any country's infrastructure. While ambulance driving and fire fighting often are considered to be essential public functions, responsibility for arranging ambulance driving and fire fighting has been left to private companies in many parts of Denmark. The private involvement is so common, and goes back so many years, that most Danish people do not even think about a partnership with the private sector in this essential area.

GROWTH OF A PUBLIC–PRIVATE PARTNERSHIP IN DENMARK

This chapter examines the evolution of the public–private partnership between the private sector company Falck, and the Danish regional and local governments. First a brief note on historical institutional theory is required. Historical institutionalism is considered one of the three new institutionalisms in political science (Hall and Taylor, 1996). There are two key concepts that have been associated with historical institutionalism which are relevant to our purpose here: path dependency and critical juncture (Thelen and Steinmo, 1992). Path dependency has usually been described as the mode where organizations find themselves 'locked in', which prescribes a certain way forward where alternatives cannot readily be chosen, or where alternatives are too costly to choose because of high transaction costs. Path dependency can be explained as follows: 'Technology, like politics, involves some elements of chance (agency, choice), but once a path is taken, then it becomes "locked in", as all the relevant actors adjust their strategies to accommodate the prevailing pattern' (Thelen, 1999).

Critical junctures are 'about crucial founding moments of institutional formation that send countries along broadly different development paths' (ibid.). The question is whether these paths are 'locked in' for good, and if so, how can they progress? Other analysts have argued that one reason is the prospect of 'increasing returns' as in economic theory (Pierson, 2000). The main idea is that when a new path is emerging, it does not necessarily mean that the old path disappears completely. Instead, one can imagine concurrent tracks that run along a railway line. Because a train runs on set of tracks, another set of tracks can be in place beside it, and at junctures, trains can switch tracks. The same applies to policy paths: The rejection of one path at one moment in time does not mean that the path is dead forever: it can be reinvigorated at a later point in time. Especially in times of internationalization and globalization, it becomes important to understand how paths in the local or national level intersects with paths at the global level (Thelen, 1999). This implies a need to look both at paths as they occur and the critical junctures that shape the paths in their local, national or global setting. The main argument is that there are two paths that the relationship between Falck and the private sector can take; a competition path and a partnering path.

The company Falck was founded by Sophus Falck in Copenhagen, Denmark in 1906. The Falck company developed a partnership with the Danish public sector almost from the beginning of the company's existence. That was the first critical juncture. From the beginning in 1906, Falck delivered fire fighting to the public sector. Falck filled a vacuum that local governments were not able to fill. Many local governments were not professionally capable of delivering effective fire fighting because the local governments were small. Furthermore, local governments that were on the outskirts geographically had difficulty arranging an effective fire fighting service. Falck was seen as a partner in providing an essential form of public service. The 'market' was shared between public providers and Falck as a private provider. In some cities, like in the capital Copenhagen, local governments made other arrangements for fire fighting. But in other places, the cities contracted with Falck for this service. In 1926, a law on fire fighting was passed in Parliament, which contained a clause that mandated local governments to enter into contractual relationships for fire fighting as they saw fit. Falck soon decided it was time to branch out. The company invested in ambulances and became the preferred provider for ambulance services for a number of local governments in Denmark.

When the Falck company held its 25th anniversary the founder Sophus Falck wrote in an anniversary publication if the Falck company shouldn't rather be a public organization? He answered the question himself by saying that the way Falck was organized, it could stand up to rescue companies in other countries and that it combined the advantages of a public organization with the value of a private initiative. Sophus Falck saw the company as combining the responsibility as a public organization with the private initiative secure process and improvement' (Zone-Redningskorpets Venner, 2002).

The second critical juncture was when the competition logic was sharpened as a new company, Zonen, was formed to compete against Falck. Falck had divided its operations in Denmark into different 'zones' with a local manager in charge of each 'zone'. In the 1930s, a local zone manager formed his own company. He called it Zonen ('The Zone') and it became Falck's main competitor during the next decades. Zonen was a highly innovative company. It pioneered the use of small aeroplane ambulances that could be used on the outskirts of the country. It made all kinds of innovations. Falck felt that its position as the number one choice for private provision of fire fighting and ambulance services was threatened. The competition became fierce as the power of Zonen grew. There are tales of ambulances from one company arriving first at a scene of action blocking the way of ambulances from the other company to deliver the services. In this period there was strong competition between the companies, which challenged the partnership between Falck and the purchaser organizations in the public sector. Both Falck and Zonen tried to establish partnerships with the local governments they were serving. In the end Falck was the strongest of the two companies. Zonen could not uphold its level of services. In the 1960s, Falck prevailed and acquired the Zonen company. The new merged company was renamed Falck–Zonen.

This was the third critical juncture when the partnership between the Falck and Danish local governments were strengthened. The new path from the end of the 1960s was one of partnering. From that time onwards, there was Falck and the public sector, and nobody else apart from some local governments who provided their own ambulance and fire fighting infrastructure.

In the 1960s and 1970s, Falck consolidated its position in the Danish market for fire fighting and ambulance services. After a while, the name Zonen was dropped, and the name Falck was used alone. The company strengthened its liaisons with the public sector in Denmark. The market was stable. A few places in the country had their own fire fighting organizations, notably Copenhagen and Roskilde. In most other parts of the country, Falck was the preferred partner for delivery of fire fighting and ambulance services. Gradually, Falck broadened the type of services the company could provide: for example, they developed transport between hospitals and people's homes. The contracts between Falck and the Danish public sector were slowly institutionalized. The result was a 'basic contract' negotiated between Falck and Danish Regions, an association organizing the Danish regions. In Denmark, the regional level of government is responsible for providing ambulance services. The contractual negations became institutionalized as negotiations over the 'basic contract'. The partners agreed upon the regulatory framework, the norms and values surrounding the contracts (providing essential services for the citizens of Denmark), and internalized the norms and values so that organizations as well as the general public would come to take Falck for granted as a provider of public services. The advantages have been that all problems and challenges were dealt with in the basic contract. Local governments could then negotiate the details that applied to each local area or region separately, but all contracts would build on the basic contract. The partnership reached its high point of institutionalization in the early 1990s.

In 1988, Falck ceased to be a family-owned company and was listed on the stock exchange. The new owners installed a new chief executive officer (Lars Norby Johansen). Then the company embarked on an expansionary strategy, which meant buying up companies in other countries as well as considering mergers with companies. Secand Denmark was one of the first companies to be bought by Falck. The international engagement was to be more prolific in the coming years. In the following years, the expansion continued through several takeovers of companies in Norway, Sweden, Germany, Finland, Poland, Estonia, Holland and Lithuania.

The next major event was the merger between Falck and the British based company, Group 4, in May 2000. Although based in Britain, Group 4 was owned by a Danish citizen whose father had started the original Securitas company in Copenhagen around the same time as Sophus Falck started his company in Copenhagen. The new company was called Group 4 Falck, and Lars Norby Johansen became chief executive officer while Group 4's owner became chairman of the board (see www.group4falck.com). The new company was the second largest security company in the world with operations in more than 50 countries. Not only did the new company have operations around the world, but also (for Falck) engaged in new services such as running prisons.

In March 2002, Group 4 Falck bought the American Wackenhut Corporation that operated a number of prisons in the USA. However, this acquisition only lasted for a short time. Group 4 Falck sold its shares in the Wackenhut Corporation in May 2003. The main reason was probably that Falck did not want to be associated with the often controversial prison industry in the USA.

From 2002 to the beginning of 2004, Group 4 Falck continued to expand its activities around the world. The company acquired part of the Israeli security company Hasmira, which was another controversial step to take. The acquaintance caused bad publicity for the company later. In late February 2004 Group 4 Falck merged with the British company Securicor and changed its name to Group 4 Securicor (see www.group4securicor.com). The headquarters have been moved to London. The CEO of Group 4 Falck, Lars Norby Johansen, is heading the new company. Group 4 Securicor has activities in 108 countries with a total of 340000 employees. The merger meant that the company was separated into several independent businesses, and Falck Denmark was once again established as a company operating mainly in Denmark.

EXPLAINING THE MOVE FROM LOCAL TO GLOBAL PARTNERING

The evolution from family-run to multinational companies has placed the companies with a number of key questions and the resulting dilemmas. The question revolves around the two dimensions: local vs global and competition vs partnerships. A closer look at the public debate[4] in the last phase of the company's growth illustrates some of the difficulties in acting according to both a competitive logic and a partnering logic in both a local and a global setting.

In the mid-1990s, Falck's image went through a transition in the public debate. From being considered a *semi-public* rescue company it was more often referred to as a *private* rescue company. It is also possible to detect a more critical attitude towards the company. However, the general positive image of Falck is still intact. During the following six to seven years the criticisms of Falck grew. Its partners started questioning its special position giving the company a near monopoly. Regional governments were dissatisfied with the quality of the service delivered by Falck and invited more competition. At the same time, Falck tried to improve its public image by hiring disabled personnel. By the beginning of 2000, Falck was increasingly gaining an image as a private company with special privileges. This was illustrated when a local government turned its fire fighting operations over to Falck and local fire fighters told a newspaper that they did not want to work for a private company.

Following the public debate, Falck has experienced an even more intense criticism during the past couple of years. The debate about Falck's monopolistic position on ambulance services continues and intensifies. Up to now ambulance services have been regulated through the 'basic contract' between Danish regions and Falck. Several regional governments have announced their intentions to put ambulance services up for public tendering. In addition, the Competition Agency in the Danish Government has begun to look into the 'basic contract' to see if it is prohibiting real competition among providers of ambulance driving and fire fighting.

During the same period, a number of incidents put the company in the firing line of newspaper reports. These included a controversial contract to do security patrolling in the Palestinian areas occupied by Israel. The Falck Company's connections to the Wackenhut Company means that the company was blacklisted by the Banco Investment Group, which is as investment group that only invests in companies with a sound ethical stance. In early 2004, Group 4 Falck was accused of neglecting employees' rights in its US operations. Discussions between Group 4 Falck and the unions will probably go on for some time yet. Many of the incidents question the ethical base of the company, which, a decade ago, was considered one of its assets. Now it could be viewed by some as the Achilles' heel of the company when trying to operate locally as well as globally and trying to balance between competition and partnering. By now, Falck's image has to some degree moved beyond being 'a partner 'or 'a semi-public organization'. It is seen more as a global company.

The situation regarding both Group 4 Falck and Falck Denmark can be said to be faced with a challenge: can the company find room for both a competitive strategy and a partnership strategy? The shifts between com-petition and partnering in much of the 20th century all took place within a known national boundary. The context has now changed into not only an international context but a global context. The new Group 4 Securicor company is be present in 108 countries on six continents around the world and compete with a number of local companies, but it will also compete on a global scale with its main competitor, the Swedish-based company, Securitas. There will still be a national-based company called Falck Denmark, which dominates the national market in Denmark, but its place in the global company structure gives it a very different position from before.

The question is whether 'global partnering' is possible at all? Or whether 'Global competition' is more likely? The implications of a global partnership can also be discussed in the light of the Danish experience with local partnering for the most part of the last century. The global strategy has not been Falck Denmark's strategy, nor has it been the Danish local governments' preferred strategy. Rather, the strategy has been the result of the globalization of public and private service provision identified by Roberts (2004) and others. It is not just a case of globalization mysteriously forcing the development. Group 4 Falck has been highly active in making the change and taking the company on to a new course. The strategy is the combined result of a more globalized market for public and private services and the strategic management initiatives taken by the management of the Group 4 Falck company. A critical juncture emerged because of a new situation with globalization, otherwise the partnership looked set to go on and on, or being disrupted at some point from a new private competitor. In the national setting, the critical junctures would mean changing from competition and co-operation. But as the latest developments in critical juncture theory has taught us, old strategies and logic are almost never defeated totally but will lie around dormant, ready at some juncture to jump back into the limelight again if new opportunities arise.

Partnering on a global scale will be very different from partnering on a national and local scale if it is possible at all. Group 4 Securicor will operate a number of crucial services and obviously have to do it in some form of cooperation with the governments of the country where they are operating. At the same time, Group 4 Securicor will be fighting for global market shares with their main global competitor, Securitas of Sweden, as well as a number of national and local companies around the world. A partnership strategy would have to adjust to many different institutional partnership settings around the world, and that would pose great challenges to such a strategy. The implication of the new global competition is that it puts the national and local partnership strategy between the Danish public sector and Falck Denmark at risk. There is also pressure from the European Union to open up markets and be more competitive. Both partners, the Danish local governments and the Falck Denmark company, must strive hard in the coming years to maintain and constantly to rebuild their partnership instead of taking it for granted.

What are the implications for partnership theory in the Falck case? The lessons we can learn are these: first, partnerships are to some extent dependent on the structure of the markets. Where competitive markets exist, no matter if the scale is local, national, international or global, partnerships will come under pressure. In other words, partnerships need secure and stable conditions to thrive. This is in line with the suggestions from Milward and Provan (2000) about networks for public service provisions that also emphasized stability. Second, a partnership strategy can be actively pursued but will need some years to build. The partnership between the Danish public sector and the Falck company has been built and nurtured since the beginning of the 20th century. Establishing trust-based relationships around essential services requires returning rounds of contractual negotiations where the partners get to know each other and the different views. In the contracts for fire fighting and ambulance services, both partners have agreed upon the basic concept and mission: to provide reliable and effective public service at a reasonable agreed-upon price. This is also in accordance with the partnership theory in which a negotiation climate established over long time based on shared norms and values seems to be a precondition for a successful partnership (Klijn and Teisman, 2003). It is also in accordance with the general Scandinavian approach to partnerships (Greve, 2003). Third, partnerships can be interrupted by external forces while partnerships are built and nurtured. In the Falck case, the emergence of global markets and the global strategies taken by the larger Group 4 Falck company, now Group 4 Securicor, have put pressure on the national and local-based strategy that the management of the strictly Danish company Falck Denmark must be expected to prefer. A new global partnership strategy does not seem likely to emerge in the near future, which means the national and local strategies are under pressure.

There were, in fact, two strategies in play in 2004, a global competition strategy and a national and local cooperative partnership strategy. While the partnership strategy has not disappeared, but continues to exist as Thelen's theoretical contribution suggests, it is under pressured from the global competition strategy striving for world domination of the market for particular types of services. Global markets do not seem to provide the stability under which partnerships seem to thrive best.

CONCLUDING REMARKS

This chapter has looked at public–private partnerships in a historical–institutional perspective, emphasizing critical junctures and path dependencies. Historical–institutional theory has been refined, thanks to the work of Thelen and others. Much of the public–private partnerships literature only deals with new organizational forms in a contemporary context. The chapter has discussed the developments of the Falck Company that have been responsible for developing infrastructure in fire fighting, ambulance services and security services. Falck has developed from a local provider of public services in Denmark to become part of a global provider of public services operating in more than 100 countries. The development has spanned a century.

The main question is how partnering is played out when a company is operating in both a local and a global context and at the same time must balance between competition and partnering. Recent years have meant a change of setting from local and national to a global context. Falck merged with the British based company Group 4 to become Group 4 Falck. The strategy for the Group 4 Falck was competition on a global scale. The headquarters were still in Copenhagen, Denmark and the chief executive officer was Danish. The strategy involved buying up other companies.

In early 2004, this strategy reached its climax when Group 4 Falck merged with another British based company Securicor to become Group 4 Securicor The competition is now on a truly global scale with the Swedish-based company Securitas as the main global competitor (Securitas is the world's largest security company while the new Group 4 Securicor is the second largest). Formally, the nationally-based partnership strategy in Denmark exists along side the global competition strategy, but as a global partnership strategy seems unrealistic with competition being so fierce, the global competition strategy seems likely to dominate the nationally-based partnership strategy.

The implications for partnership theory are three-fold. Partnerships thrive best under stability and do not function well in highly competitive surroundings. Stability has to be nurtured and prepared which takes several decades. And finally, partnerships are challenged by globalization. Partnerships between global companies and national or subnational governments are not likely to emerge. National or local partnership strategies will be potentially undermined by global service providers' competitive strategies for world markets. The historical–institutionalist perspective has shown how partnerships evolve throughout the decades, and the conditions in which they do so. Understanding the history of public–private partnerships enables a different analysis of how partnerships can exist now and in the future. Public–private partnerships are different in local and national contexts from the global context and serious doubts should remain as to whether global public–private partnerships will emerge in the future.

NOTES

1. See www.falck.com.
2. See www.group4falck.com.
3. See www.group4securicor.com.
4. The public debate is covered by tapping a database of all news articles in Danish newspapers and news magazines from 1 January 1993–20 February 2004. The search resulted in 1510 articles. The data collection has been done by student assistant Mette Fog, whose help is acknowledged.

REFERENCES

Danish Ministry of Finance, Danish Ministry of the Interior, Danish Ministry of Health, Danish Ministry for Transport and Danish Ministry for Economics and Business Affairs (2004), *Handlingsplan for offentlig–private partnerskaber – OPP* [Action plan for public–private partnerships – PPP], Copenhagen: Danish Ministry for Economics and Business Affairs.

Greve, C. (2003), 'Public–private partnerships in Scandinavia', *International Public Management Review*; electronic journal at www.ipmr.net, **4** (2), 59–68.

Greve, C. and N. Ejersbo (2005), *Contracts as Reinvented Institutions in the Public Sector. A Cross Cultural Analysis*, Westport, CT: Praeger.

Hall, P.A. and R.C.T. Taylor, (1996), 'Political science and the three new institutionalisms', *Political Studies*, **44**, 936–57.

Klijn, E.H. and G.R. Teisman (2003), 'Institutional and strategic barriers to public–private partnerships. An analysis of Dutch cases', *Public Money and Management*, **3** (23), 137–46.

Milward, H.B. and K.G. Provan (2000), 'Governing the hollow state', *Journal of Public Administration Research and Theory*, **10** (2), 359–79.

Pierson, P. (2000), 'Increasing returns, path dependency and the study of politics', *American Political Science Review*, **94** (2), 251–67

Roberts, A. (2004), 'Globalized service delivery systems: a new form of networked governance', in *The IBM Endowment for the Business of Government*, Washington, DC: IBM Center for the Business of Government.

Thelen, K. and S. Steinmo (1992), 'Historical institutionalism in comparative politics', in Sven Steinmo, Kathrine Thelen and Frank Longstreth (eds), *Structuring Politics. Historical Instiutionalism in Comparative Politics*, Cambridge: Cambridge University Press, 1–32.

Thelen, K. (1999), 'Historical institutionalism in comparative politics', *Annual Reviews of Political Science*, **2**, 369–404.

Van Ham, H. and J. Koppenjan (2001), 'Building public–private partnerships: assessing and managing in risk port development', *Public Management Review*, **3** (4), 593–616.

Zone-Redningskorpets Venner (2002), *Zone-Redningskorpset i Danmark*, Denmark: Museum for Zone-Redningskorpset.

14. German public–private partnerships in personal social services: new directions in a corporatist environment[1]

Maria Oppen, Detlef Sack and Alexander Wegener

In Germany, public–private cooperation is not fundamentally new. In fact, it has been fairly common over time. But whereas intersectorial cooperation may in retrospect appear to be a recurring phenomenon of technical infrastructures and of urban and regional development, a growing number of new partnerships are taking their place alongside familiar corporatist arrangements in Germany's sector for social services. What conditions have fostered the emergence of these new public–private partnerships (PPPs) in social services? What specific functions do they assume?

Unlike international developments of New Public Management (NPM), the general trend in Germany focuses squarely on the internal modernization of management, which used to be confined to local government. To be sure, there has been a good deal of dispute about the government's main responsibilities and the question of which tasks should be performed by government and which can be delegated (Gusy, 1998; Naschold et al., 1996). However, attempts at privatization and marketization have remained marginal, especially compared to efforts in Great Britain (Naschold et al., 1997; Pollitt and Bouckaert, 2000). Around the late 1990s, modernized bureaucratic hierarchy and elements of competition were complemented by new forms of social association and by an increasing orientation to networking (Klenk and Nullmeier, 2003). Mobilizing 'stakeholders' and their resources for the local provision of services – through PPPs, for example – can be regarded as a transition from the specifically German variant of NPM to a broader perspective on governance (Bovaird et al., 2002; Damkowski and Rösener, 2003; Oppen, 2002). NPM discussion of cooperation between the public sector and private business adopts the viewpoint of institutional economics, where the chief goal is efficiency and a reduction in the government's provision of services. By contrast, the governance approach integrates theoretical aspects of democratic participation and self-determination. Stressing the cooperative, or 'activitating', state and the voluntary engagement of citizenry, discussion at the national level in Germany has been expanded to include the incorporation of private actors, with special emphasis on new forms of sharing social responsibility. This change is pluralizing ways of organizing and guiding the provision of services in the public interest. Given the differing currents in Germany's various *Länder* (federal states) and policy fields, and given the correspondingly fragmented programmes for developing partnerships in specific areas, it is unclear how much public–private cooperation is becoming a quantitatively and qualitatively relevant element of present efforts to modernize.

Coupled with the absence of a widely accepted definition of PPP, this empirically confusing situation leads us to begin this chapter by adopting a 'broad' understanding of PPP, one largely compatible with the definition quoted by the editors of this book. Accordingly, PPP is 'cooperation of some sort of durability between public and private actors in which they jointly develop products and services and share risks, costs, and resources which are connected with these products (Ham and Koppenjan, 2001:598).

In our minds, PPP thus has specific characteristics. First, formal autonomous actors, each with his, her, or its own objectives and resources, decide whether they wish to provide certain services in exchange with other actors. Second, interactions between the participants are framed by specific forms of organization – whether contractual or rather informal – and are coupled by virtue of the resources. Complementary resources are combined to serve a jointly defined function. Third, what sets intersectorial cooperation apart is that the participating actors are tied into different institutional arrangements roughly described by the generic terms 'government', 'market', and 'society'. The actions of the cooperating actors are thus determined and guided by different rules and differing basic convictions. This circumstance can give rise to relatively unstable joint coordination and coupling of resources in comparison to intrasectorial output processes. It can, however, also explain the comparative advantage of cooperative arrangements: combining different material resources, skills, and ideas can develop new definitions of problems and new solutions to them.

In the following pages we explore the question of innovation by examining three instructive PPP case studies embedded in different institutional frameworks of their respective subsector of welfare-state services. We begin with an overview of the development of welfare corporatism in Germany.

DEVELOPMENT OF GERMAN WELFARE CORPORATISM

Discussion of PPPs has been infrequent and only very recent in Germany's sector for social services. Nonetheless, hybrid organizations linking entrepreneurial spirit with objectives in the public interest are definitely on the increase (Eichler, 2000; Evers et al., 2002). This step in public welfare seemed to occur later in social services than in other fields of public obligation, perhaps because legal changes enabling commercial service providers to gain a footing in various parts of social and health services did not come about until the 1990s. And corporate social investment has not been an issue in the welfare state. Up to then, nonprofit organizations and both governmental and public law agencies shared such duties. Negotiation, cooperation, and coordination between these actors therefore have a long tradition. What is known today as the corporatist system of negotiation between and interlinkage of public and nonprofit agencies took root in the Weimar Republic.

HISTORICAL ROOTS

From the outset, associations of civil society have had 'a major impact on the origins and development of the German system of social policy' (Inquiry Commission, 2002:496). The existence of the welfare associations was guaranteed by law in the 1920s with assurances that shape the collaboration between public and nonprofit organizations to the present day. The associations are granted 'conditional priority', and the public agencies must give assistance and guarantee that services are provided (ibid.:496). This combination constitutes the dual structure of German welfare work but does not release the family or individual from all responsibility. The principle of subsidiarity and solidarity is complemented by the duty to help oneself. Hence, the government is only one agent providing for welfare – the others are families and intermediary organizations (see Evers and Olk, 1996).

The expansion of the welfare state, particularly in the 1960s and 1970s, both enlarged the public sector and contributed to an 'outright explosion in the growth' of welfare associations. However, they also became increasingly tied into a regulated cooperative network for meeting public responsibilities (Inquiry Commission, 2002:498). They saw to a rising number of public programmes and social tasks, a service for which they received appropriate public funding.

The impact of this activity is reflected in the growth of employment. Whereas the number of jobs in the entire public sector about doubled (from 2.1 million to 4.3 million) between 1960 and 1990, it tripled in the nonprofit sector (from 380 000 to 1.25 million).[2] These soaring job rates are found in the health system and social services. In both these subsectors, the nonprofit sector also provides a large share of services overall.[3] In other words, more than 80 per cent of what nonprofit organizations do in the health system and social services depends on public funds. The subsidiarity principle and the legal guarantee of priority thus constitute the 'economic foundation' of these organizations.

These developments successively eroded the third sector's specific advantages over the provision of services solely by the government. Such advantages had derived primarily from welfare organizations' capacity for self-regulation and value commitments, which promised a more flexible and locally more appropriate and need-oriented service culture than the government did. With the centralization of the associations and with their ever closer integration into the system of public social services, processes leading to increased regulation, standardization and professionalization became established in the third sector, too, as in the public sector in general. The weak position that the client had within the 'total institution' attracted attention. Since the early 1970s, the spread of self-help groups, particularly in the health area, and of grass-roots initiatives for improving the quality of life, has been an expression of growing social criticism.

Meanwhile, segments of this social movement have developed into publicly recognized and partially funded partners cooperating with welfare-state agencies. At best, however, they have been accorded 'a place on the margins and in the niches' of the corporatist system of interlinkages (Inquiry Commission, 2002:502), which survived the changes relatively untouched. 'Institutionalized cooperation' (Heinze, 2000:36) between associations and government institutions still characterized Germany's system of social services in the 1990s, when programs were jointly formulated and implemented.

MODERNIZATION SINCE THE EARLY 1990s

The spread of modernization strategies based on NPM and its German variant, the New Steering Model (KGSt, 1993) in the international public sector, has exemplified social services developments that are often described as a paradigm change in social policy. As the internal administrative functions in the public sector are modernized with the tools of business management, their external relations are being redesigned according to principles of competition. The major welfare associations and other providers of social services have thereby come under immense pressure to adapt. They have tended to develop into social enterprises competing with each other for public contracts and/or for customers and beneficiaries of what they provide. To make their facilities and services 'fit' for competition, they have felt compelled to optimize their internal business operations, focus on their core competencies, and redefine their activities accordingly.

Four key mechanisms have marked the change of governance arrangements. First, emphasis has shifted from the hitherto prevailing public subsidies for nonprofit organizations to contract management, the prospective agreement on compensation for services. Second, the monopoly that the associations used to have on the supply of services has been dissolved. To sharpen competition, new laws and regulations[4] since the mid-1990s have placed commercial providers more and more on a par with nonprofit organizations. Third, measures to ensure standards of quality and service have increased[5] in response to the introduction of price competition, which exacerbated the already thinly veiled quality problem. Fourth, there is an effort to strengthen the primacy of the consumers by bringing their desires and freedom of choice to bear.[6]

In reality, however, the role of contract management and competition, which would predicate a clear separation between the government as the contracting agency and service providers as bidders, has not been great, let alone comprehensive. Although no fundamental abandonment of corporatist structures seems to be in the offing (see Heinze, 2000), there are observable processes of change in favor of decentralizing and pluralizing local service provision, not least with a view to increasing efficiency. Moreover, the trend is away from nonspecific, publicly subsidized services toward clearly defined services with calculated prices. These signs suggest that the structures of interlinkage are eroding.

The move towards contracting has been accompanied by a policy of network-building (Dahme, 2000), some of the initiative for which has come from legislation. The idea is to mobilize additional resources by actively including societal actors and to develop problem-solving skills by 'creating innovative milieus' (Heinze, 1998:33) and cultures of cooperation through which to pursue the redesign of social infrastructures. Sociopolitically motivated forms of networking 'aim to create boards, introduce discursive control, pool resources, and create more self-management and self-organization' (Dahme, 2000:56–7). In this context, one may ask whether interorganizational cooperation in the social services sector is an expression of an innovative problem-solving orientation or actually rather a means of selectively rationing services and solving cost issues by relying on voluntary instead of professional personnel.

NEW SOCIAL PARTNERSHIPS

Available empirical studies do not yet clearly indicate the balance between innovation and substitution; case-studies currently predominating (such as Evers et al., 2002; Hinte et al., 2003) point to both directions. Another difficulty is that the institutional conditions and specialized policy discussions to be considered vary from one subsystem to the next. Before examining selected cases, we shall point out some of the characteristics in the respective policy areas.

Cooperation in Child and Youth Welfare Policy

The law has long mandated that public and nonprofit agencies dealing with child and youth welfare cooperate in determining policy and in planning and harmonizing measures. In practice, nevertheless, work in this field is still dominated by bureaucratic logic within specialized, entrenched structures. There is social work with juveniles, broken down by target groups or concentrated on facilities (see Hinte, 2000); assistance with education, broken down into numerous individual measures stipulated by law; and 'general social services' as a contact and placement organ. Thinking in terms of functional areas and segmentation of services is reinforced by forms of financing that allocate funds to specific agencies or cases. Case-centered funding is particularly susceptible to dysfunctional effects of control. Cases are 'manufactured' (ibid., 2000) in order to secure financing, and in terms of social policy the system encourages a 'diagnosis-intervention scheme' that is out of touch with everyday reality and heavy on therapy (Peters, 2000:124).

Experts therefore reached broad consensus long ago that social work with young people needs to be completely reoriented. The aim is to develop flexible and integrated services and assistance relating to a specific social space and available from a single source if at all possible. Some of the principles underlying this work are that it must appeal to the interests of the users, promote the ability to help oneself, and address a variety of target groups and areas (Hinte et al., 2003; Koch, 2003). People are permitted to move easily from one form of help to another, organizations and professions must remain adaptable, and cooperation is sought. Contract management based on budgets for social spaces (see KGSt, 1998) is a specific and potentially sustainable variant now being tested in a pilot project.[7] A programme jointly run by the German federal and state governments, 'Development and opportunities for young people in social problem areas – D. and O.' (*Entwicklung und Chancen junger Menschen in sozialen Brennpunkten – E & C*), is a further initiative to disseminate the coordination and cooperation of social spaces. It funds the 260 'social city' programme areas in order to improve the opportunities available to disadvantaged children and youth and to halt the decline of urban quarters with social problems. The concept is to link funding for urban planning to youth welfare centered in particular social spaces, and the programme receives €11 million annually.

The federal initiative entitled 'Businesses: partners of youth' (*Unternehmen: Partner der Jugend, UPJ*) has taken another approach. Operating with support from some of Germany's *Länder* since 1997, it has launched and monitored projects promoting local cooperation between companies and social work with young people. Relating primarily to education, the world of work, and culture, the initiatives involved in this programme go well beyond sponsoring.

Computainer Vogelheim
An instructive example of this approach, albeit a case outside the UPJ, is *Computainer Vogelheim*,[8] a local service for children and young people in Essen, Germany's sixth largest city. Computainer consists of 32 former construction containers, which lend the project its name. Its objective is to improve the social, health, educational and economic situation in an especially disadvantaged part of the city. Computainer is conceived for children and young people from socially weak families and their parents. Computer training is combined under one roof with occupational counselling, monetary and other kinds of help in arranging for training, and support from the social department of the local district government. For socially disadvantaged children and young people, these services create meeting places that are open to groups from the neighbouring quarters. The idea is to promote sustained development of an infrastructurally weak region in the Ruhr District. The programme can succeed only by bringing together many of the locality's inhabitants and organizations. Corporate social involvement is a pillar of the entire concept.

The idea for a computer school came from the 'Fairnetzen' Foundation of BOV AG, a small IT-systems supply company in Essen. For this project it drew on experience with involvement in regional educational policy since the early 1990s in Brazil, where this idea was tried out. Essen agreed to cooperate through the Department of Youth and Social Affairs. The project is part of a three-year action plan by the City Quarter Conference for the area of Vogelheim.[9] The project is managed by the head of the local community's city quarter office. Personnel for social and occupational counselling and support services are drawn from public administration, the employment office and welfare agencies, and assigned to specific problems and situations.

Computer training is conducted mainly by voluntary 'trainers' from the city quarter. They, in turn, were taught this job and equipped with concepts by qualified BOV AG trainers schooled in holistic learning methods. A group of regional corporate investors contributes to the construction and operation of the building. These businesses also benefit from their involvement: coordinated through the 'Fairnetzen' Foundation, joint projects with young people have served the companies as human-resource measures for developing the social skills of their employees.

The Computainer project combines a number of services in a new way in one place (colocation). Various youth welfare programmes and approaches to occupational choice are integrated with new ways of using leisure time and learning opportunities. They are embedded in a network of participating local government administrations, third-sector organizations, and companies seeking to build reputations as good corporate citizens in the community as well as in the market.

Cooperation in Care of the Elderly

In 1994 Germany introduced mandatory insurance for nursing care. This law is predicated on cooperation but does not contain structural requirements and incentives for it. The underlying assumption is that all care-giving institutions share responsibility for 'guaranteeing efficient, regional, proximate, and mutually complementary outpatient and inpatient care for the population'.[10] This insurance for nursing care is conceived of as 'partial coverage for some needs' (Schmidt, 2000:217). Treatment for those needing hospitalization or rehabilitation services, for example, come under other jurisdictions and have to be coordinated to ensure humane care. 'Shared responsibility' also includes family members, volunteers, neighbours and self-help groups. It should be supported to develop a new culture of help and concern for others. In practice, however, this philosophy encounters serious problems partly because of the familiar dysfunctional dichotomization into inpatient and outpatient care. Innovative hybrids between the two extremes face formidable obstacles particularly because the two systems differ so much in the incentives and mentalities underlying them.

Change in the sector for care of the elderly has prompted legislation putting the administrative authorities responsible for funding nursing care (*Pflegekassen*) in charge of conducting pilot projects on the development of new high-quality ways to provide for people in need of care. In so doing, it has facilitated additional financing arrangements as well. In 2000 the German Federal Ministry for Families, Senior Citizens, Women and Youth launched a nationwide pilot program fostering approaches that help eliminate structural shortcomings, further develop the system of geriatric care, and try out new forms of networking and combining support services.[11]

These kinds of experiments with individual case management for dovetailing person-centered services and reducing the discontinuities of care-giving can be distinguished from structural cooperative alliances (regional work groups or conferences on nursing care). Such alliances pool available regional resources in order to solve problems jointly, coordinate or couple services, or avoid duplication of work. This sort of structural cooperation is also planned for the development of quality control and quality improvement in the network of funding agents and product suppliers.[12] Since the beginning of 2004, services and quality standards must be spelled out in agreements, and documentation measures taken to comply with those agreements must be submitted to independent review authorities. Because the attempts to establish uniform nationwide regulations for quality control have failed thus far, voluntary cooperative developmental strategies and pilot projects are all the more important. This point is illustrated by the Heilbronn Regional Quality Control Network of inpatient geriatric care (*Regionaler Qualitätssicherungsverbund stationärer Altenpflege Heilbronn*).

Heilbronn Regional Quality Control Network of Inpatient Geriatric Care
The Quality Control Network encompasses 11 nursing homes (six private, five nonprofit), which together account for 57 per cent of the region's beds in these institutions. Other members of this network are the responsible nursing-home funding authorities, the local agency for welfare assistance, the nursing-home supervisory authority, and the representatives of the residents and their family members. The network's foremost mission is to develop and conduct external quality control: peer review coupled with inspection by external experts and a review of agreed standards. If the agreed minimum standards are not met, a binding improvement plan is achieved through consensus, and its implementation is monitored. Repeated failure to meet the minimum standards can lead to exclusion from the network or a demotion to associate status and the loss of the seal of quality.

The chief duties of a quality control conference are thus collectively to formulate and continue developing binding standards, to prepare and evaluate reciprocal inspections, and to agree on specific measures to ensure and promote quality. This work also means implementing joint measures to train personnel, conducting hands-on projects, and continually evaluating inspection practices. It is based on rules of procedure, which regulate membership, the responsibilities of the network and the groups of visiting peers, work methods and the passing of resolutions. Each nursing home bears the costs of the external scientific consulting and facilitation involved in its own inspection. In addition, the facilities allocate 85 to 90 hours of their own resources for inspecting other facilities and participating in the quality-control conference and its work groups.

The network is, hence, a voluntary association of actors from heterogeneous, even opposing, interests and has been recognized by the *Land* government as a pilot project. It does not consist only of nonprofit and for-profit service providers competing with comparable products for clients in the same regional 'market segment' with fixed, negotiated prices ('scale alliance'). This network also includes local administration and semi-state actors who finance these services, conclude the necessary contracts, and check whether contracts are met both quantitatively and qualitatively. Given the fact that all the actors are highly uncertain about future legal requirements, one could call this strategy of development proactive. They have created for themselves a regional learning platform based on trust, with the participants regarding the development process itself as even more important than its output. In six years of experimentation as a pilot project, this partnership has generated expertise that it strives to bring, from the bottom up, into the state and federal political debates on quality control.

Cooperation in Health Care

In the health sector, too, competitive elements are strengthening and new forms of cooperation and networking are having an effect. As in youth welfare and geriatric care, there is structural experimentation with regional health conferences and roundtables. The goal of establishing them is to orient the planning of various services to the needs and wishes of the local inhabitants (see Badura, 2000). In some regions hosting these activities, self-help groups, representatives of patients, and all the actors involved in providing and financing services are invited to contribute under the aegis of the local authorities. Essentially, these parties jointly develop methods and instruments to improve cooperation, and they work out decisions whose implementation is based on the participant's own pledge to act on them.[13]

At present, many service providers are networking along American lines of case, care and disease management that start from the individual's course of care or structured programme of treatment. The kinds of arrangements being tried out are expected to solve a variety of problems caused by the system's well-known shortcomings and wrong turns – whose fundamental reform, however, has been repeatedly thwarted by complexly intertwined interests. Pilot projects typically aim to do three things (Schröder and Ratzeburg, 2002):

- To improve health care by systematically interlinking individual services, coordinating service providers, and thoroughly involving and activating the patients;
- To promote quality control and quality improvement by developing and testing treatment and care guidelines, documentation systems and training and compliance programmes;
- To reduce inefficiency by testing new forms of remuneration, namely, the combined budgets that bridge between the sectorial specifics of payment.

Integrated approaches to care, especially for chronically ill persons and complex clinical care, are to be tried out voluntarily by consortia of practices that have institutionalized their work with hospitals, therapeutic occupations, nursing services, and self-help groups/family members and that have thereby taken on the transsectorial management of treatment. Several organizational variations exist, with the necessary coordination coming from service providers, from neutral agencies, or, to borrow from the managed-care concepts practised in the United States, from case managers employed in health insurance companies. Yet another possibility is self-organization by local citizenry, which is the exceptional feature of our next instructive example of PPP, the Augsburg model for integrated post-hospitalization care (*Augsburger Nachsorgenmodell*).

Augsburg model for integrated post-hospitalization care

This model involves several levels of cooperative relations formed in order to develop and regularize the coordination of various levels and types of care, particularly during and after the transition from inpatient to outpatient treatment of young children (and their families) dealing with chronic or severe diseases or cancer. Methodologically, this model is a networked approach to care that dovetails existing services through case management centered on the families and their specific resources and needs for assistance. By interlinking medical, nursing, psychosocial and family inputs, the model strives to perpetuate successes of medical treatment, minimize recurring hospitalization, optimize the child's development, promote parent–child interaction, and enhance the family's quality of life.

Conceived at a roundtable discussion between personnel of the children's hospital, the hospital's chaplains, and parents from self-help groups, an association was created in 1994 (*Verein zur Familiennachsorge Bunter Kreis, e. V.*), and the first case manager was hired. The model for integrated post-hospitalization care has since grown to 70 employees from different professional backgrounds. Integrated post-hospitalization care was initially financed solely through donations and corporate sponsorship.

The fragmentation of jurisdictions between health insurance, insurance for nursing care, youth welfare, and care of persons with disabilities long delayed the ability to meet legal standards of public funding. Since 1996, however, grants from the Bavarian ministry responsible for social affairs have been directed to work with persons with disabilities. This funding has financed a small percentage of special educational services. The regional health funds recognized integrated post-hospitalization care in 1998, meanwhile making it possible for about a third of the annual €1.2 million in costs to be refinanced from public monies. Nevertheless, scientifically documented effectiveness is essential for steady long-term funding from the health insurance system.

This background explains the creation of the Augsburg model for research on integrated post-hospitalization care, which is a thematic platform and research network initiated by three actors: the self-help initiative Bunter Kreis, the generic pharmaceutical drugmaker betapharm, and the children's hospital in the city of Augsburg. The institutionalized nucleus is the 'beta Institute' for Sociomedical Research and Development, a nonprofit company founded by Bunter Kreis and betapharm. In cooperation with universities, the institute elaborates and researches holistic approaches to dealing with disease at the interface of institutional care-giving structures and family care.

The gist of the work consists of several interdisciplinary research projects.[14] To establish integrated post-hospitalization care as a standard part of the health-care system, a transfer and feasibility study is under way.[15] The case-management approach is also being tested and evaluated as a cross-sectorial form of care for other groups of patients as well. Part of the beta Institute's explicit strategy is to create organizations like Bunter Kreis throughout the Federal Republic of Germany. To this end, workshops on need analyses, financial planning, the marketing of social services, organizational and personnel development, and quality management are offered. In November 2002 a Bunter Kreis quality network was established to enable all integrated post-hospitalization care initiatives to share their experience, facilitate continued and advanced training and create a vehicle for certification. The pharmaceutical company takes over the funding of the beta Institute through social sponsoring in conjunction with a targeted marketing strategy. Specific projects receive public money from research grants. Volunteer work is mobilized as an additional resource, particularly through Bunter Kreis.

SOME TRENDS AND IMPLICATIONS

Taking stock of trends in public–private cooperation on the development and provision of social services in Germany, we can touch upon only some of the questions on the research agenda that the editors provided in their introduction. Before gauging the novelty that PPP represents historically, let us turn to the question of exactly what PPP is in the social sector. Lastly, we shall consider the performance and the managerial implications of new social partnerships that are spreading.

Intersectorial Collaboration

At the outset of this chapter, we deliberately opted for a broad definition of public–private cooperation. This choice facilitated the search for new partnership arrangements dealing with personal social services, an area in which discussion of PPP is only very recent and sporadic, unlike the case with projects on technical infrastructure or urban regeneration. Even the actors involved do not usually classify their respective community initiatives as PPP. When describing these activities, they are apt to use terms like network, consortium, project, or platform. This self-description is quite compatible with our 'second-order' observations. For two reasons, it seems necessary to adapt previous definitions of PPP in order to grasp the developmental dynamics in the sector for social services. First, the contexts in which PPP is used are ones in which the private partner tends to be associated with for-profit companies. Empirically, however, there is wide variety of partners in the private sphere. Beyond private companies, which are still gaining a foothold on this terrain,[16] the major players are large welfare associations, nonprofit foundations, grass-roots initiatives and user groups. And as our examples show, there are also freelance scientists, consultants, and independent research institutes that perform tasks of facilitation, knowledge transfer, and evaluation. In this sense, complex 'multi-stakeholder' or intersectorial partnerships exist, especially in the sector for social services.

Second, the PPP construct is burdened by a monetary 'bias'. In many large infrastructure projects – from the construction of airports to e-government – PPPs are preferentially treated as finance models by means of which the public sector hopes to overcome its lagging investment (see Gerstlberger and Sack, n.d.). A one-sided Private Finance Initiative (PFI) understanding of partnership has also gripped Germany. In the area of social services, though, the mobilization of private capital or of the resources of third-sector organizations tends to play a secondary role. The focus is on collaborating instead of cofinancing and on sharing of responsibility, visions and criteria of relevance instead of sharing risks and profits (which is not to say that 'investments' in social partnership projects are without risk or cost). Characteristically, transsectorial cooperation entails complex social problems that single organizations in fragmented supply systems are doing ever less to help solve. The pooling of intangible resources such as experience, competence, connections, ideas and commitment seems to be a factor critical to success in finding new, creative solutions surpassing the limited perspectives of individual actors (see Gray, 1985; Rod and Paliwoda, 2003).

Novelty

Cooperation between public institutions and nongovernment aid organizations has been the central element of Germany's dual welfare state since it began. However, the expanding corporatist structure of interlinkages outlined in this chapter has led to many dysfunctions and a proneness to rigidity. Since the mid-1990s, processes of restructuring in health and social policy have set a 'modernization of welfare corporatism' in motion (Heinze, 2000:44). New organizational patterns are emerging from the dynamic of competition and cooperation. From today's perspective, these diverse new social partnerships complement and undergird the institutionalized corporatist system of negotiation and interlinkage; they do not replace it.

The formerly twofold architecture of the system in the social sector is diversifying. The spectrum of actors is broadening, particularly to include private commercial service providers, business firms that take up the role of 'good corporate citizens', as well as the 'empowered' clients and users and the representatives of their interests. A new arena for the new social partnerships is the local level, where the development, planning, provision and evaluation of services takes place 'in the shadow of' basic contracts and formal agreements negotiated between state actors and welfare associations. Neither the obligation that goes with membership nor a received logic of interest representation serves as the motive. The motive is an explicit problem-solving logic. The 'symbiotic community of obligation' that exists between the government and associations is being loosened at least partially by elements such as price systems and competitive performance. The distinction between public authority as the contracting agency and the role of competing bidders is becoming clearer than it has been. In the transition from 'status to contract' (ibid.:37), divergence between interests is admittedly growing, but so is the latitude for autonomous action. This development is paving the way to emancipated partnerships based on the principle of free will and interdependent objectives and orientation.

Modern partnerships of this kind may be classified into two main types. The first consists of local and regional working groups, conferences or roundtables for planning and harmonizing service structures. These approaches are strategic partnerships, which reflect the modernized contours of Germany's welfare corporatism in that they are open to user groups and other interested local actors beyond the large established corporate organizations. The second type of modern partnership consists of the operative ones, more and more of which are forming in order to buffer the system's shortcomings in the everyday world of work and to develop and experiment with new solutions. The emphasis in enlightened professionalism is to examine each case or field and then pool resources and mesh or cluster separate services accordingly. However, the task of networking providers and combining component services is becoming increasingly relevant as users turn to holistic and customized service packages. For in a competitive environment, users affect demand through their decisions, and those decisions are increasingly determining the profitability and market position of the individual facility.

Performance

As we have seen, a high degree of fragmentation and entrenched structures for providing highly regulated personal services characterize all sociopolitical arenas. In addition to public and quasi-governmental institutions, there are many nonprofit, for-profit and self-help organizations offering both complementary and competing assistance. In many cases, both production and funding are distributed across several organizations. With NPM instruments such as pluralization of suppliers and performance-based compensation spreading an entrepreneurial mindset among public and nonprofit organizations, there is the obvious danger that producers will even more be single purpose-oriented than is already the case through their competition for dwindling financial resources. Increasingly, attempts to combat such perennial flaws and new risks of the system involve transsectorial cooperation.

Experimentation, which has been stimulated by pilot projects and rules on trying out new cross-sectorial forms of cooperation, has also widened the scope for bottom-up initiatives. The cases presented illustrate some of the possible advances. First, local services have been developed, some of them new. Second, a key to local innovation seems to be the integration and clustering spatially and procedurally of hitherto segmented services. In the Essen Computainer project, different existing services are recombined into a new kind of palette. In the Augsburg model for integrated post-hospitalization care, innovation and new problem-solving capacity is not so much about inventing a new service as about recombining existing services by bridging across ingrained subsystems and discernible gaps in care-giving. Third, the innovative character of these initiatives also lies in their explicit orientation to changed social needs, whether they be the growing importance of information technology in the lives of young people or customized health care. Citizens and user groups in our three examples of social partnerships bring to bear their fresh ideas to the developmental process, and new modes of co-production are brought to test. The fourth innovative dimension illustrated by the cases presented in this chapter is the long overdue development and spread of performance standards and quality control methods (see Oppen, 1997) of the kind aspired to in the Heilbronn Quality Control Network and the Augsburg model for integrated post-hospitalization care.

All these advances point to a potential social dynamization of such partnerships that goes beyond the service provision itself. The performance of the projects and models cited above is reflected in a win–win situation that is widely alluded to. In all cases the public or the user profits from improved services, the public sector has no appreciable increase in burdens, and companies can cash in on their social involvement to enhance their reputations and competitive positions.

Coordination

The problem-solving capacity newly acquired through cross-sectorial arrangements in personal social services are due chiefly to the type of coordination and the way it is achieved. Unlike many infrastructural PPPs, the social sector has hybrid arrangements that do not fit familiar classification schemes. However, we recognize many similarities with a type called 'the conceptual organization' (Sonnenwald, 2003). At its core lies the vision, the intention of which is to facilitate the way in which a complex and important problem is approached. It is about developing solutions as efficiently and effectively as possible, of 'meeting diverse stakeholder needs with minimum capitalization and start-up costs' (ibid.:262). This kind of concept is reified in the very names of the examples above. The motives of the different actors may differ: the calculus of business economics (say, the use of sponsoring and volunteerism as a marketing strategy, or quality-based positioning on the market); objectives that government actors set for policy implementation and standard-setting; and the specific interests that users and the service providers have in the quality of service provision.

The shared perception that a crisis exists (as in Essen), that the gaps in services are glaring (as in Augsburg), and that fewer and fewer problem-solving alternatives are emerging from conventional corporatist arrangements seem to motivate actors to act jointly. Squeezed by the perception of lock-in effects emanating from existing organizational structures and by the obvious pressure for reform, they are compelled to create new kinds of cross-sectorial cooperation. This purpose accounts for the mode of that cooperation, the sharing of competencies and influence, the definition of criteria for access and exclusion, and the acquisition of actors and resources.

The cases reported above illustrate what is now the parallel existence of quite different ways (and centres) for coordinating and regulating interaction. In Computainer's case the foundation is responsible for the computer school and the mobilization of volunteers; the city looks after the legal coordination of different public services. Sometimes, however, the forms of coordination supercede each other in the course of the partnerships. In the Augsburg model for integrated post-hospitalization care, for example, an informal roundtable has become an association with clear statutes and the authority to act as an employer. The more the model for integrated posthospitalization care became part of the standard health care system, the more necessary it became to found the beta Institute to generate the prescribed scientific documentation. The principle of 'form follows function' (understood both temporally and materially) has led to a bewildering array of approaches to institutionalization. Sydow (2001) gives reason to assume that the structuring of social partnerships is not a matter for specialists such as brokers or facilitators (though they do play an important role) but rather the responsibility of several other kinds of actors. Nor does the structuring of social partnerships seem to be a routine activity but rather a 'result of overlapping problem-solving processes' (ibid.:88).

CONCLUDING REMARKS

In the German welfare sector, central government sets the basic framework for the creation and spread of transsectorial partnerships. The political turn toward cultivating local problem-solving skills and cooperative structures is an attempt to foster comparable, even better, services with less public money. Temporary incentive programmes and funding of pilot projects are one way to secure 'political steering effects' (Evers et al., 2002:226). Such federal and state programmes have proven to be crucial to the advent of PPP in the three policy fields we selected for this contribution.

But as the case studies presented above illustrate, incentive programmes are not the only stimulus to the growth of PPP. In the field of personal social services there is also the trend toward deregulation and reregulation, which confronts service providers with shifting and diffuse demands but at the same time with new opportunities. A major motivation behind the participation of the different actors is the complex and all-but-incalculable quandary they face within a framework of increased competition for reduced resources whose main parameters and effects are still unclear.

On the whole, the new PPPs are caught up in top-down as well as bottom-up processes. The space for experimentation that the government has explicitly expanded or involuntarily opened up facilitates new forms of self-organization, discursive planning of services, and of debating quality and standards. At the same time, the innovations percolating up from these local PPPs can affect the general framework of service provision if they inform supraregional development strategies and political negotiations. An example is the Augsburg model for integrated post-hospitalization care where the partnership provided relevant evidence for the necessity and advantage of new legislation which already went into effect. But given the path dependencies of interlinked corporatist structures, the allegiance to the status quo among interest groups (for example, professional associations and large corporatist welfare providers), and associated dynamics of interaction, it is not clear under what conditions results and lessons of such experiments can contribute to debates over fundamental changes in basic institutions. And it remains to be seen whether collaborative ventures survive and spread as islands of innovation alongside conventional structures – thereby at least diversifying the range of problem solutions – or whether they fail in the absence of broader support.

NOTES

1. This article stems from the research project entitled 'Public–private partnership – Hybridvarianten der Dienstleistungsproduktion', an international comparative study conducted at the Wissenschaftszentrum Berlin für Sozialforschung and funded by the German Federal Ministry of Education and Research.
2. The statistics in this section are based on the results of the Johns Hopkins comparative Nonprofit Sector Project cited in Anheier (1999).
3. Nearly 33 per cent of all hospital employees, 66 per cent of all persons employed in nursing homes, homes for the elderly and day-care centres, and more than 80 per cent of the jobs assisting persons with disabilities fall into the nonprofit area.
4. See §78 a–g KJHG (*Kinder- und Jugendhilfegesetz*) and §93 of Germany's Federal Social Assistance Act (*Bundessozialhilfegesetz*, BSHG).
5. See §93 BSHG, §77, 78 a–g KJHG and §§80 and 112–118 SGB XI (*Sozialgesetzbuch*).
6. See §5 KJHG, §76 SGB V and §2 SGB XI.
7. Since 1998, a federal pilot project entitled INTEGRA (whose second phase ran from 2001 through 2003) has been funding and assessing such a structure of services in five regions in order to gain information relevant across these areas (Koch, 2003).
8. http://www.computainer.net.
9. The City Quarter Conference is a voluntary grouping of associations, institutions, and committed members of the public. They have been involved in developing and planning improvement in the quality of life in parts of the city since 1986.
10. §8 SGB XI.
11. The three-year pilot programme entitled 'Future structures for assisting the elderly' (*Altenhilfestrukturen der Zukunft*) has been running since 2000. There are 20 pilot projects, 13 of which concern structural development, cooperation and networking. Of those 13 projects, five focus on case-management concepts, and five others deal with the mobilization of additional potential for care and self-help.
12. This arrangement illustrates an element of cooperative control that is used in rehabilitation, AIDS prevention and other sociopolitical arenas (see Dahme, 2000).

13. Local health conferences are familiar in several of Germany's federal states, some of which have institutionalized them in law.
14. Some of this work deals with quality management in Bunter Kreis, which is helping develop a manual of guidelines for disease management for post-hospitalization integrated care. Another example is a socioeconomic study on the cost–benefit analysis of different profiles of post-hospitalization integrated care, including indirect costs (such as lost working hours, expenses borne by the family in delivering care, and quality of life).
15. Although the Augsburg model for posthospitalization integrated care is not a formally recognized pilot project as defined by the statutory health insurance system (§63 SBG V), the health funds require such efficiency studies on principle before they can recognize posthospitalization integrated care as a standard service.
16. And even the formerly clear boundary between private 'for-profit' organizations and 'not-for-profit' welfare corporations in successively eroding. Private companies, on the one hand, act as competitors to non-profit organizations in the newly established 'market' for social services. And, on the other hand, they collaborate as 'socially responsible corporations' with non-profit associations (and public agencies) investing resources in the common good.

REFERENCES

Anheier, H. (1999), 'Dritter Sektor, Ehrenamt und Zivilgesellschaft in Deutschland. Thesen zum Stand der Forschung aus internationaler Sicht', in E. Kistler, H.-H. Noll and E. Priller (eds), *Perspektiven gesellschaftlichen Zusammenhalts. Empirische Befunde, Praxiserfahrungen, Meßkonzepte*, Berlin: edition sigma, pp. 145–70.

Badura, B. (2000), 'Kooperation und Netzwerksteuerung in kommunalen Gesundheitskonferenzen', in H.-J. Dahme and N. Wohlfahrt (eds), *Netzwerkökonomie im Wohlfahrtsstaat: Wettbewerb und Kooperation im Sozial- und Gesundheitssektor*, Berlin: edition sigma, pp. 187–200.

Bovaird, T., E. Löffler and S. Parrado-Díez (eds) (2002), *Developing Local Governance Networks in Europe*, Baden-Baden: Nomos Verlagsgesellschaft.

Dahme, H.-J. (2000), 'Kooperation und Vernetzung im sozialen Dienstleistungssektor. Soziale Dienste im Spannungsfeld "diskursiver Koordination" und "systemischer Rationalisierung"', in H.-J. Dahme and N. Wohlfahrt (eds), *Netzwerkökonomie im Wohlfahrtsstaat: Wettbewerb und Kooperation im Sozial- und Gesundheitssektor*, Berlin: edition sigma, pp. 47–67.

Damkowski, W. and A. Rösener (2003), *Auf dem Weg zum Aktivierenden Staat. Vom Leitbild zum umsetzungsreifen Konzept*, Berlin: edition sigma.

Eichler, A. (2000), 'Strategische Allianzen im Non-profit-Bereich: Gefahr oder Chance? Ein Bericht aus der Praxis', in H.-J. Dahme and N. Wohlfahrt (eds), *Netzwerkökonomie im Wohlfahrtsstaat: Wettbewerb und Kooperation im Sozial- und Gesundheitssektor*, Berlin: pp. 289–99.

Evers, A. and T. Olk (1996), *Wohlfahrtspluralismus*, Opladen: Westdeutscher Verlag.

Evers, A., U. Rauch and U. Stitz (2002), *Von öffentlichen Einrichtungen zu sozialen Unternehmen. Hybride Organisationsformen im Bereich sozialer Dienstleistungen*, Berlin: edition sigma

Gerstlberger, W. and D. Sack (n.d.), 'Public Private Partnership and E-Government', in Bertelsmann Stiftung (ed.), Clifford Chance Pünder und Initiative D 21, available at http://www.begix.de.

Gray, B. (1985), 'Conditions of facilitating interorganisational collaboration', *Human Relations*, **38** (19), 914–36.

Gusy, C. (1998), 'Privatisierung als Herausforderung an Rechtspolitik und Rechtsdogmatik. Ein Tagungsbericht', in C. Gusy (ed.), *Privatisierung von Staatsaufgaben: Kriterien – Grenzen – Folgen*, Baden-Baden: Nomos Verlagsgesellschaft, pp. 330–51.

Ham, H. van, and J. Koppenjan (2001), 'Building public–private partnerships. Assessing and managing risks in port development', in *Public Management Review*, **3**, (4), 593–616.

Heinze, R.G. (1998), *Die blockierte Gesellschaft. Sozioökonomischer Wandel und die Krise des 'Modell Deutschland'*, Opladen: Westdeutscher Verlag.

Heinze, R.G. (2000), 'Inszenierter Korporatismus im sozialen Sektor. Politische Steuerung durch Vernetzung', in H.-J. Dahme and N. Wohlfahrt (eds), *Netzwerkökonomie im Wohlfahrtsstaat: Wettbewerb und Kooperation im Sozial- und Gesundheitssektor*, Berlin: edition sigma, pp. 31–46.

Hinte, W. (2000), 'Kontraktmanagement und Sozialraumbezug. Zur Finanzierung von vernetzten Diensten', in H.-J. Dahme and N. Wohlfahrt (eds), *Netzwerkökonomie im Wohlfahrtsstaat: Wettbewerb und Kooperation im Sozial- und Gesundheitssektor*, Berlin: edition sigma, pp. 151–67.

Hinte, W., G. Litges and J. Grope (2003), *Sozialräumliche Finanzierungsmodelle. Qualifizierte Jugendhilfe auch in Zeiten knapper Kassen*, Berlin: edition sigma.

Inquiry Commission [Enquête-Kommission] (2002), 'Zukunft des bürgerschaftlichen Engagements' des Deutschen Bundestags (2002): Bericht: 'Bürgerschaftliches Engagement: Auf dem Weg in eine zukunftsfähige Bürgergesellschaft', Berlin: Leske and Budrich.

KGSt (1993), *Das Neue Steuerungsmodell. Begründung, Konturen, Umsetzung*, Cologne: Kommunale Gemeinschaftsstelle für Verwaltungsvereinfachung.

KGSt (1998): *Kontraktmanagement zwischen öffentlichen und freien Trägern in der Jugendhilfe*, Cologne: Kommunale Gemeinschaftsstelle für Verwaltungsverein-fachung.

Klenk, T. and F. Nullmeier (December 2003): *New Public Governance als Reformstrategie*, Düsseldorf: Edition der Hans Böckler Stiftung.

Koch, J. (2003), 'Integrierte und sozialräumlich angelegte Erziehungshilfen. Zwischenbilanzen aus einem Bundesmodellprojekt', available on the Internet at http://http://www.lwl.org/LWL/Jugend/Landesjugendamt/LJA/jufoe/983524482/ik33/1041951105_3/Koch_Integrierte_und_sozialraeumlich_angelegte_Erziehungshilfen.pdf.

Naschold, F., D. Budäus, W. Jann, E. Mezger, M. Oppen, A. Picot, C. Reichard, E. Schanze and N. Simon (1996), *Leistungstiefe im öffentlichen Sektor. Erfahrungen, Konzepte, Methoden*, Berlin: edition sigma.

Naschold, F., M. Oppen and A. Wegener (1997), *Innovative Kommunen. Internationale Trends und deutsche Erfahrungen*, Stuttgart: Kohlhammer.

Oppen, M. (1997): 'Towards a New Client Orientation through Continuous Improvement', in A. Evers, R. Haverinen, K. Leichsenring and G. Wistow (eds), *Developing Quality in Personal Social Services: Concepts, Cases and Comments*, Aldershot: Ashgate.

Oppen, M. (2002), 'From "New Public Management" to "New Public Governance" – restructuring the public administration of tasks in Germany: an international comparison', in Friedrich Ebert Stiftung, (ed.), *Public Service Reform in Germany* pp. 25–38.

Peters, F. (2000), 'Auf der Suche nach reflexiven Institutionen. Integrierte, flexible Erziehungshilfen als strategische Antwort auf die ungeplanten Folgen fortschreitender Differenzierung und Spezialisierung', in H.-J. Dahme and N. Wohlfahrt (eds), *Netzwerkökonomie im Wohlfahrtsstaat: Wettbewerb und Kooperation im Sozial- und Gesundheitssektor*, Berlin: edition sigma, pp. 119–38.

Pollitt, C. and B. Bouckaert (2000), *Public Management Reform: A Comparative Analysis*, New York: Oxford University Press.

Rod, M.R.M. and S.J. Palliwoda (2003), 'Multi-sector collaboration: a stakeholder perspective on a government, industry and university collaborative venture', *Science and Public Policy*, **30** (4), 273–84.

Schmidt, R. (2000), 'Vernetzung unter den Bedingungen von Quasi-Markt- und Marktsteuerung in der Pflegeversicherung'. in H.-J. Dahme and N. Wohlfahrt (eds), *Netzwerkökonomie im Wohlfahrtsstaat: Wettbewerb und Kooperation im Sozial- und Gesundheitssektor*, Berlin: edition sigma, pp. 217–33.

Schröder, U. and E. Ratzeburg (2002), 'Modellprojekt Diabetes Sachsen-Anhalt – reif für Disease Management?', *Die Krankenversicherung*, **54** (5), 141–4.

Sonnenwald, D.H. (2003), 'The conceptual organisation: an emergent organisational form for collaborative R&D', *Science and Public Policy*, **30** (4), S. 261–72.

Sydow, J. (2001), 'Management von Unternehmensnetzwerken – auf dem Weg zu einer reflexiven Netzwerkentwicklung?' in P. Flocken, J. Howaldt and R. Kopp (eds), *Kooperationsverbünde und regionale Modernisierung – Theorie und Praxis der Netzwerkarbeit*, Wiesbaden: Gabler, pp. 80–101.

15. Using public–private partnerships to deliver social infrastructure: the Australian experience

Linda M. English

INTRODUCTION

Internationally, the past two decades have seen considerable changes in the mechanisms adopted by governments to deliver services to the public. The emergence of New Public Management (NPM) (Hood, 1995) has been characterized by a growing partnership between the public and private sectors to provide services that, in the past, were exclusively supplied by the public sector. The hallmark of traditional Westminster-style government is for hierarchical, vertically-organized, administrative functional units to supply discrete services and report to a responsible minister. Recently the silo approach has given way to linkages across departments and between the public and private sectors, known as 'joined-up government' (Barrett, 2003).[1] This chapter focuses on one aspect of 'joined-up government' in Australia, the growing dependence of governments on private-sector consortia to provide infrastructure and related services to the public.

My primary purpose is to provide an illustrative case study of the delivery of health and related services using the Public–private partnerships (PPPs) delivery option in the Australian state of Victoria. Accompanying analysis and commentary draws on the work of Broadbent and Laughlin (1999; 2002), and is framed using elements of the research agenda outlined in their 1999 paper. That agenda focuses on a number of research issues, underpinned by a need to 'consider whether and how the context of the "macro" economic and other requirements impinge upon the expression of Public Finance Initiative (PFI)[2] at the "micro" (organisational level)' (1999:107).

Broadbent and Laughlin's (1999) five research questions are:

1. Is PFI a form of privatization of the public sector?
2. What is the nature of PFI and who is regulating its application?

3. How are definitions of PFI in terms of value for money and risk transfer derived and operationalized?
4. How are PFI decisions made in different areas of the public sector and what are the effects of these decisions?
5. What is the merit and worth of PFI?

In relation to the Australian experience, English and Guthrie (2003) explored the second research question. This chapter primarily focuses on the third research question, which relates directly to the accounting treatment of PPPs, and also on the nature or purpose of PPPs (the first part of the second research question).

The paper is structured as follows. Section 2 introduces the institutional context. Section 3 focuses on the delivery of health services in Victoria, with particular reference to the use of Build–Own–Operate (BOO) and Build–Own–Operate–Transfer (BOOT) arrangements. Section 4 introduces the Latrobe case study. The analysis presented in Section 5 is framed around Broadbent and Laughlin's (1999) research agenda, with particular reference to risk transfer and the achievement of value for money (VFM). The final section provides a summary and conclusions.

PPPs WITHIN THE CONTEXT OF PUBLIC SECTOR

Australia is a federation of six states and two federal territories and includes three levels of government – federal, state and local. Each state has its own parliament, executive government and judiciary, and has the power to set laws on matters relating to the state. This is the second level of government. The third level of government is local government at the city, town, municipal or shire levels. Several factors have been associated with the growing popularity of PPPs in Australia (WWG, 2001). These include the size of the continent relative to its population; the expectations of citizens for excellence in public service provision; the ideological predisposition of governments towards implementing a NPM reform agenda; the general resistance of citizens to paying more tax; and the need to reduce and contain public debt.

The Australian experience is unique in that it is not possible to talk about 'one' PPP initiative. At the macro level this is explained by the federal system: there are potentially many different PPP initiatives at the three levels of government. Policy documentation indicates a process of iterative and evolutionary change in the thinking of governments about the use of PPPs to deliver infrastructure-based services. It is widely acknowledged that the state of Victoria is the leader in both the development of policy documentation and in the implementation of PPPs. English and Guthrie (2003) demonstrate that PPP policy documentation in Australia is very similar, and largely based on, Victorian initiatives, which have been influenced by the UK's PFI. Victoria is also the only government in Australia to have made a commitment to publish PPP contracts. For these reasons this analysis focuses on the Victorian experience of the delivery of human services through the agency of PPPs.

PPPs are defined in government policy documents as '[a] contract for a private party to deliver public infrastructure-based services' (VDTF, 2001:3). However, under this local definition, PPPs explicitly exclude 'outsourcing or other service delivery arrangements where no capital investment [by the government] is required' (ibid., 2001:4). In total some $A87.4 billion in commitments to investment in PPP projects have been made by Australian governments (AusCID, 2004). Victoria accounts for almost $A43.7 billion dollars of investment in a wide range of PPP arrangements.

USING PARTNERSHIPS TO DELIVER HEALTH SERVICES IN VICTORIA

During the period 1997–2004 the Victorian government committed to proceeding with six PPPs to deliver public hospital care. The earliest arrangements, the Latrobe Regional Hospital (VG, 1997) and the Mildura Base Hospital (VG, 1999) can be categorized as Build-Own-Operate (BOO) arrangements. Thereafter, the PPP model changed. In 2002 the Casey (formerly known as Berwick) Hospital (VG, 2002), and in 2004 the Royal Women's Hospital agreements were signed. These are BOOT arrangements. They differ from the Latrobe and Mildura schemes in two important respects: first, the contracts include a clause requiring that the asset be transferred to the state at the end of the term of the contract; and second, that the delivery of core clinical (public hospital services) are excluded. Clinical services are to be delivered by the relevant local health authority. The other two contracts signed in 2004 (St Vincent's Hospital and the Austen and Mercy Hospitals) are once again materially different because they involve the redevelopment, refurbishment and consolidation of existing facilities on existing sites, and novel funding arrangements.

Both the Latrobe and Mildura agreements provide for the private consortium to design, construct, finance and maintain the hospitals, and for the subsequent provision of clinical services to public hospital patients (co-located with private service provision) for 20 (Latrobe) or 15 (Mildura) years. These contracts essentially stipulate that the private partners have total responsibility for every aspect of the provision of public hospital services. Each contract contains an option for an additional term. Payments to operators for the provision of health services are based on the case-mix funding model that is also used to fund public hospitals. In both contracts the contractor paid for a new site, and the construction including fit-out, and agreed to transfer the ownership of the land to the state on the receipt of a 99-year lease. At the end of the term there is no contractual commitment for the asset to revert to state ownership or use. These two hospitals are not recognized in the Department of Human Service's (DHS) financial statements.

As indicated above, the later initiatives are different in a number of ways. Following policy changes in 2000 limiting PPPs to the delivery of non-core services (VDTF, 2000), the 2002 Casey and 2004 Royal Women's hospitals contracts represent a new direction for the state. As previously, the private partners arc required to design, construct, finance and maintain the hospital infrastructure. However, at the end of the term the hospitals revert to state ownership in a condition stipulated in the contract. In relation to the delivery of hospital-based services, the provision of core clinical services is excluded. The private consortium is required to provide only associated 'hotel' services such as cleaning, catering and portering. As for the Latrobe and Mildura schemes, the arrangements governing service provision are renewable every five years.

In this respect these two arrangements are similar to the UK's PFI initiative in that provision of public health services is contracted to a regional health authority. The Casey Hospital, which is 10 be recognized on the state's balance sheet, is to be leased to the state for 25 years, when it will be transferred to the state for zero consideration (VAG, 2003d). Similar arrangements and accounting treatment is proposed for the new Royal Women's Hospital (Minister for Health and the Treasurer of Victoria, 2004).

The St. Vincent's and Austin and Mercy hospitals' arrangements involve significant upgrades and refurbishments, and feature novel financing arrangements, which effectively muddy the waters as far as their accounting treatment is concerned. The St. Vincent's redevelopment is being financed by an issue of indexed annuity bonds and equity finance provided by two banks. Ownership of the redevelopment is initially to reside with the banks, and the building will be leased to hospital management (VAG, 2003b), suggesting that redevelopment costs may initially be 'off balance sheet' for the state. However, the fact that the Department of Human Services (DHS) has guaranteed all repayments to bondholders, suggests that *de facto* ownership may reside in its hands. In the case of the Austin and Mercy hospitals' redevelopment project, the government will pay the actual cost of construction, to an agreed maximum (VAG, 2003a). These hospitals will continue to be recognized in the DHS balance sheet. Thus, it can be seen that the Victorian government is flexible when it comes to structuring partnerships with the private sector to deliver health care to public patients.

As noted earlier, the Latrobe and Mildura head contracts are publicly available. Perusal of these contracts indicates a multiplicity of parties and agreements which is not apparent from first reading. In each contract there are several parties and separate agreements. The state, however, discloses only the one agreement which binds itself and the operator. At first glance, the publication of the hospital service agreements creates an illusion of full disclosure – it is only after careful reading that one realizes the most important and interesting documents are out of the public view. In all cases, the financing documentation remains undisclosed, making it impossible to determine the true substance of the deal. Each contract is divided into two phases, construction and operation. The operating phase of these contracts is of interest here.

THE FAILURE OF THE LATROBE HOSPITAL

Latrobe is of particular interest due to its failure some two years after it commenced operations on 1 September 1998, on time and on budget. Subsequent comment by both public and private bodies (VAG, 2001; 2002; 2003b; IPP, 2003) enable comparison of the *ex post* outcomes with the *ex ante* claims as to the achievement of VFM and risk transfer at the time of contracting. It was not until 2002 that the government had formally to take control of all aspects of the running and ownership of the hospital (VAG, 2003b: paras 2.28–30). The failure of the hospital highlighted weaknesses in the expectations and processes of both the government and the private contractors.

According to lobby group Infrastructure Project Partners (IPP, 2003)[3] there were several reasons for Latrobe's failure, which can be broadly classified as: unreasonable assumptions about government subsidies and costs; misunderstanding of the case-mix funding model and its impact on future levels of funding; and an assumption of the government's willingness to renegotiate the contract. Essentially, the operator was unable to make a profit from the delivery of the services at the performance levels required.

Funding problems relating to the case-mix model also plague public hospitals. Case-mix funding is designed to reward efficient hospitals and to encourage nonperforming hospitals to improve their efficiency. Each Victorian public hospital is expected to make a 1.5 per cent productivity improvement annually, meaning that public funding falls in real terms for a given level of activity each year (VAG, 1998). Auditor-General's reports have highlighted a deterioration of key technical performance indicators[4] in public hospitals due to underfunding, and provide evidence of additional 'one off' funding for many government-run hospitals. For instance, VAG (1999, para. 3.2.37) found that 60 (66 per cent) of public (non-PPP) hospitals run by the DHS incurred a deficit, prior to grants received for capital purposes and transactions of an extraordinary nature; 26 (28 per cent) of hospitals had generated negative cash flows from operating activities, and 35 (38 per cent) had negative working capital positions. Similar comments appear in subsequent reports (VAG, 2001; 2002). By 2003 (VAG, 2003d) there were 15 hospitals, including the Latrobe Regional Hospital, by then back in government hands, showing signs of financial difficulty with unfavourable results in all four Audit Office indicators, and an additional 22 hospitals having unfavourable results in at least two of the indicators.

Thus, the failure to understand the ramifications of the case-mix model of funding, and being ineligible, as a private hospital, for additional top-up funding contributed significantly to the failure of Latrobe, indicating a failure on both the part of the government and the operator to evaluate realistically the cost of providing public health services.

ANALYSIS AND COMMENTARY

Much of the recent debate in the UK has been about the 'nature' of PFI (Broadbent and Laughlin's (1999) second research question). The evidence presented in Table 15.1 and in the previous section suggests that the Victorian government utilizes a variety of different PPP arrangements to deliver public health services to its citizens. These range from full 'in house' delivery, with DHS taking responsibility for all aspects of the provision of public health services, including for the necessary infrastructure and ancillary services, to the use of BOO arrangements, which require the contractor to deliver core clinical and supporting non-core ancillary services. The now more favoured BOOT model lies somewhere between these two extremes, with the private operator being responsible for the design, construction, financing and maintenance of the hospital and the delivery of non-core support services, and DHS responsible for the delivery of core public health services.

Broadbent and Laughlin (1999; 2002) distinguish between the 'macro' and 'micro' drivers of PFI which determine their 'nature', and are also related to their accounting treatment. The 'macro' or policy drivers can be characterized as the macro political and economic policies (such as debt containment/reduction) that drive broad policy decisions. The 'micro' drivers relate to processes of the service procurement aspect of PPPs, and the extent to which individual PPPs have actually achieved value for money (VFM) in reducing costs of service provision. VFM is characterized as being represented by the transfer of risk from the government sector to the private sector. To further complicate matters, the achievement of VFM is also the trigger and justification for the decision to take the PPP option as opposed to the 'in house' (public sector delivery) option.

RISK TRANSFER AND VFM: OPERATIONAL ISSUES

A theoretical benchmark constructed to cost public provision of the infrastructure and related services is used to determine risk transfer and quantify VFM. In Victoria as early as 1994 a financial evaluation, using the Capital Asset Pricing Model (CAPM), was required prior to a decision to take the PPP option (Fitzgerald, 2004). Table 15.1 presents the Government's financial evaluation of the net present value (NPV) of the cost of it providing public health services 'in house' compared to the cost of paying each of the three bidders to deliver public health services at Latrobe. This table does not disclose the estimated savings on the private provision of the hospital and related ancillary services because these estimates have not been made public by the Victorian government.

Table 15.1   Latrobe Hospital provision of public health services: summary of bids and estimated NPV savings (8 per cent discount rate)

| | | Bids | | | NPV savings | |
	Benchmark	AHCL	HCoA	SoC	AHCL	HCoA	SoC
Total costs[a]	482 543	437 982	446 781	482 542	44 561	35 762	1

Note: a. Costs in thousands of dollars.

We can see from Table 15.1 that the AHCL bid appeared to offer the greatest cost savings (VFM), which explains why AHCL was the preferred bidder. In theory, the purpose of this process is to document that VFM is attained, and to prove that risk has successfully been transferred to the private sector. The discount rate of 8 per cent was nominated by the Department of Treasury and Finance. The Auditor-General did not reveal details regarding the construction of the benchmark project. The details in Table 15.1 are taken from IPP (2003).

As noted above, the Victorian Auditor-General's initial *ex ante* analysis of the two BOO arrangements, Latrobe and Mildura, confirmed that substantial risk had been transferred to the contractors, noting only in the case of Latrobe, that the government had guaranteed some of the revenue streams and unrecovered capital costs.

However, in reviewing the failure of LRH, the Auditor-General (VAG, 1997) came to the opposite opinion, *ex post*:

> ACHL's bid was based on the presumption that it could provide hospital services far more economically and efficiently than the public sector and on that basis it had tendered a contract price at a substantial discount (compared with the costs of internally providing the services). The fact that the tender process allowed for what proved to be an unsustainable bid price by AHCL to succeed is one of concern.

The Auditor-General's report suggests that the comparative analysis carried out by DHS was unsatisfactory. It does not make clear whether mandated government processes were in general unsatisfactory, or whether they had been applied unsatisfactorily in this instance. However it appears that no attempt may in fact have been made to determine the benchmark cost of public provision (including the building and maintenance of the hospital) to justify the use of the PPP arrangement (VAG, 2003d, para. 3.22).

The Auditor-General (VAG 2003d, para. 3.23) also recognized that ultimately no government can transfer political risk:

> Although the contractual arrangements ... were successful at transferring financial risk to the private sector, *the social responsibilities of the State meant that any threat to public health and safety or hospital service provision could not be allowed to occur.* In this case, the State stepped in when it appeared that a risk to the provision of on-going hospital services was developing. The final outcome was that ACHL was able to avoid the full financial risk obligations embodied under the contractual arrangements. [Emphasis added]

The use of the CAPM to determine the cost of the benchmark 'in house' cost of provision has been heavily criticized. Debate has raged around the appropriate discount rates to use when applying the CAPM[5] (English and Guthrie, 2003; Officer 1999; 2002; Walker 2002). However, more recently the model itself has also been criticized for its failure to take into account risk of failure and 'over-optimism' bias (Fitzgerald, 2004; Broadbent, Gill and Laughlin 2003b). It is likely that in Victoria, the Public Sector Comparator (PSC) calculation will be overhauled so that it more closely follows revised UK PSC calculations as articulated in *The Green Book* (HM Treasury, 2002).

The Latrobe outcome suggests that despite initial appearances to the contrary, risk was not effectively transferred to the contractor, indicating *ex post* that VFM had not been achieved, that the financial accounting treatment of the arrangement may have been incorrect, and that from a management accounting perspective, the investment strategy adopted by the government failed. In hindsight, Table 15.1 suggests that the highest bid (allowing a NPV saving of only $A1000) may have been the most appropriate.

ACCOUNTING TREATMENT

The accounting treatment of PPPs has raised considerable debate in the literature (Broadbent and Laughlin, 1999; 2002; Broadbent, Gill and Laughlin, 2003a; 2003b; Walker, 2003; Walker and English, 2003, English and Walker, 2004). At issue is whether PPPs involve the purchase of assets (and associated liabilities) which should be recognized on government balance sheets. Broadbent and Laughlin's early work on PFI (1999; 2002) suggests that the achievement of VFM provides evidence that risk has been transferred to the private sector and that, accordingly, an off balance sheet accounting treatment is appropriate for the relevant public sector agency.

In relation to the PPPs discussed in this chapter, the Victorian Auditor-General has been in agreement with the accounting treatments proposed by the Department of Human Services (DHS). However, aside from suggesting concurrence is based on of risk transfer, no reasoning has been made public about the processes undertaken to determine appropriate accounting treatments. It seems that the Auditor-General accepted that risk transfer is demonstrated in the BOO contracts, in part because of the contractor's obligations to provide a range of public health services, with or without income guarantees from the state, and, more specifically, because of the explicit omission in those contracts of the transfer of the asset to the state on termination of the contract. This explains the difference in accounting treatment of the BOO ('off balance sheet') and the BOOT ('on balance sheet') arrangements. In the case of Casey the Auditor-General argued that '[b]ased on out assessment of the risk profile of the contractual arrangements ... we conclude that the key risks associated with the project remain with the State' (VAG, 2003c).

However, in relation to the BOO contracts, Walker and English (2003) question these assumptions, arguing that there is sufficient information contained in published contracts to indicate that the stream of payments in the BOO schemes also give rise to assets and liabilities which should be recognized and disclosed in government balance sheets. They argue that these PPP contracts in fact represent two separate agreements: one arising during the construction phase, the second during the operating phase, and that the obligations arising during the operating phase give rise to liabilities that should be recognized.

Table 15.2   Summary of payments made by the government for the delivery of health services in Victoria

Latrobe Regional Hospital (1997) BOO[a]
Twenty-year term. Service component renegotiated every five years. Contract 294 pages.

Maximum service charge (case-mix based, activity linked)	Some amounts disclosed. Case-mix target set and reviewed on annual basis, based on formula that includes regional and local benchmarks; capital costs borne by contractor. Can be reduced if material default occurs. Payment based on services delivered and increases in payroll tax. Includes the provision of a range of health services: accident and emergency ($A2 840 000 p.a.); outpatients ($A2 106 300 p.a.); community rehabilitation ($A201 300 p.a.); and community mental health services ($A6 559 619 p.a.).
Guarantee of revenue streams	Reimbursement for some services under budget; and payments to state for receipts in excess of budget.
Allocated facilities component	Total amount undisclosed, includes equipment and technology ($A2 575 000), furniture and fittings ($A2 532 000), trustee fees ($A500 000) and water, council rates and land tax ($A7 200 000). Undisclosed amounts include insurance premiums, utility payments, annual rent and senior debt service.

Note: a. Most of the fees payable were monthly in arrears but for simplicity have been reported as sums payable per annum.

Table 15.2 details the basis of payment streams from the state to the operator under the Latrobe arrangement. It is clear that the service payments include what might be loosely be termed 'fixed' and 'variable' components with the fixed components relating to the provision of physical infrastructure and the variable components based on occupancy and levels of delivery of various designated health services. Once the facility was operational, the government was contracted to pay:

1. a client service charge based on levels of activity and the case-mix funding model, which included provision for penalty charges;
2. an allocated facilities charge for accommodation-related services; and
3. guaranteed revenue streams.

Based on their analysis of the concepts of 'substance' and 'form', and the provisions in the Australian Conceptual Framework relating to the definition and recognition of assets and liabilities, Walker and English (2003), and English and Walker (2004) argue that the client services' charge represents ongoing obligations that are quantifiable and should be recognized as liabilities (and not as contingent liabilities as they are currently treated). This analysis appears to be supported by FRS 5 (ASB, 1998; 1994), the relevant UK standard, which provides that if fee components can be separated, they should be accounted for separately.

The question of whether the state had acquired an asset on the date of commissioning is also worthy of consideration (Walker and English, 2003; English and Walker, 2004). In the case of Latrobe, the hospital was built on land bought by the contractor from the government, and then assigned back to the government and leased by the operator on a 99-year lease. Although there was no provision for the government to acquire the asset at the end of the term of the operating agreement it is difficult to envisage circumstances in which the hospital asset would not revert to government ownership, given its ownership of the land. Accordingly, it could be argued that, at the date of commissioning, the government had acquired an asset, and that the facilities services charge actually represents a stream of payments to purchase it. As the Audit Review (2000:8) noted in its review of one Victorian similarly structured BOO project for the construction of a prison and provision of related detention services, it could be 'better classified as a Build Own Operate Transfer (BOOT) project'.

SUMMARY AND CONCLUSION

The stated aim of this chapter was to examine one aspect of the growing partnership in Australia between government and the private sector to deliver infrastructure-based public services. The focus has been an examination of the Victorian government's use of PPPs to deliver health and related services since 1998, with particular emphasis on the failed Latrobe arrangement. The analysis has largely been framed around (the first part of) the second, and the third of Broadbent and Laughlin's (1999) research questions: What is the nature of PFI? How are definitions of PFI in terms of value for money and risk transfer derived and operationalized?

Evidence indicates that the government's policy towards using partnerships with the private sector for the delivery of public health services has evolved from an almost exclusive reliance on the BOO structure to deliver core health and related services, to a more strategic use of PPPs to achieve VFM for the state through risk transfer to the private partner. These developments mirror a shift from the use of PPPs primarily as financing arrangements, a major purpose of which was to provide essential infrastructure without having to recognize debt on government balance sheets, to an acceptance that VFM and risk transfer can be achieved even though PPPs are recognized on balance sheets. Thus the locus between VFM and risk transfer on the one hand, and accounting treatment on the other that is posited by Broadbent and Laughlin in their 1999 and 2002 papers appears to have been broken. As a result, the Victorian government has become more inclined to consider different kinds of strategic partnerships with the private sector to facilitate delivery of crucial infrastructure, and related ancillary services.

As characterized by Broadbent, Gill and Laughlin (2003b), the focus is now more on the strategic management of assets, rather than on the financial accounting treatment. This shift is reflected in the recommendations of the Fitzgerald Report (Fitzgerald, 2004) which are likely to see revision of the calculation of the PSC (to make it similar to its counterpart in the UK), including consideration of political risk and 'optimism bias'.

The failure of the Latrobe Hospital provides an example of the consequences of governments' neglect to factor the cost of these risks into their decision-making processes. It also provides a wake-up call to parliaments about the need to have in place processes to determine the merit and worth of PPPs relating to Broadbent and Laughlin's (1999) fifth research question about the merit and worth of PFI.

Only Auditors-General have mandated statutory access to documents to undertake a thorough evaluation of PPP arrangements. Despite having a full disclosure policy, examination of PPP contracts available to public scrutiny in Victoria reveals that crucial documentation – notably about the calculation of the PSC and financial arrangements underpinning PPPs – is omitted, and is also not provided through the Freedom of Information process.

Thus, as it currently stands in Australia, citizens, including parliamentarians, can only rely on auditors-general to scrutinize and report on whether or not PPPs represent a 'good deal' for the public. The Victorian Auditor-General regularly reviews and reports (briefly) on all PPP projects. However, evidence presented here suggests that in the case of Latrobe at least, the Victorian Auditor-General incorrectly assumed that risk had been transferred to the private contractor. This failure indicates just how difficult it is in practice to recognize risk, to determine with which party it resides and to quantify it. Even if this process could be accurately undertaken at the pre-signing stage that provides no assurance that the identified risks do not change throughout the life of PPPs contracts.

ACKNOWLEDGEMENTS

This work is part of my ongoing interest in 'New Public Management' in the Australian context and builds on previously published works (English and Guthrie 2001; English 2003; English and Walker 2004; Walker and English 2003; English et al., 2005 (forthcoming)). I am indebted to Katie Broadbent, Timothy Haldenby, Adam Weir and Matt Skellern for valuable research assistance.

NOTES

1. The phrase 'joined-up government' was first used by Geoff Mulgan, Head of the UK's Strategic Unit Office, to refer to ways of overcoming problems relating to harnessing and coordination the efforts of strong and competitive top-down administrative units for the overall benefit of implementing whole-of-government policy that cut across functional boundaries (Barrett 2003).
2. PFI is the UK equivalent of PPPs.
3. IPP provides consulting services to facilitate private sector participation in the provision of public infrastructure and associated services.
4. Indicators used by the Auditor-General are: operating result for the year, excluding extraordinary items; operating result prior to special revenue grants; net cash flows generated from operating activities; working capital position at year-end (VAG 2003d).
5. As noted in the Fitzgerald Report (Fitzgerald 2004), increasing the discount rate to reflect greater levels of risk has the paradoxical effect of lowering a project's NPV.

REFERENCES

Accounting Standards Board (UK) [ASB] (1994), *Financial Reporting Standard FRS 5: Reporting the Substance of Transactions*, London: ASB.
Accounting Standards Board (UK) [ASB] (1998), *Amendment to FRS 5: Reporting the Substance of Transactions: Private Finance Initiative and Similar Transactions*, London: ASB.
Audit Review of Government Contracts [Audit Review] (2000), *Audit Review of Government Contracts Contracting, Privatisation, Probity and Disclosure 1992–1999*, Melbourne: Government Printer for the State of Victoria.
Australian Council for Infrastructure Development [AusCID] (2004), *Australian PPP Database*, available on request from AusCID.

Barrett, P. (2003), 'Outsourcing and Partnerships in the Public Sector – Driving a Generic Brand Approach', CPA Australia National Public Sector Convention 2003, Perth.

Broadbent, J. and R. Laughlin (1999), 'The Private Finance Initiative: clarification of a future research agenda', *Financial Accountability and Management*, **15** (2), 95–114.

Broadbent, J. and R. Laughlin (2002), 'Accounting choices: technical and political trade-offs and the UK's Private Finance Initiative', *Accounting, Auditing and Accountability Journal*, **15** (5), 622–54.

Broadbent J, J. Gill and R. Laughlin (2003a), 'Evaluating the Private Finance Initiative in the National Health Service in the UK', *Accounting, Auditing and Accountability Journal*, **16** (3), 422–66.

Broadbent J., J. Gill and R. Laughlin (2003b), *The Private Finance Initiative in the National Health Service: Nature, Emergence and the Role of Management Accounting in Decision Making and Post-Project Evaluation*, unpublished research monograph, available from Professor Richard Laughlin at King's College, University of London, UK.

English, L. (2003), 'Emasculating public accountability in the name of competition: transformation of state audit in Victoria', *Critical Perspectives on Accounting*, **14**, 51–76.

English, L. and J. Guthrie (2003), 'Driving privately financed projects in Australia: what makes them tick?', *Accounting, Auditing and Accountability Journal*, **16** (3), 493–511.

English, L. and J. Guthrie (2001), 'Public sector management in the state of Victoria 1992–1999: genesis of the transformation', in L. Jones, J. Guthrie and P. Steane (eds) (2001), *Learning From International Public Management Reform*, New York: Elsevier Science, pp. 45–60.

English L. and R. Walker (2004), 'Risk weighting and accounting choices in public private partnerships: case study of a failed prison contract', *Australian Accounting Review*, **14** (2).

English, L., J. Guthrie and L. Parker (forthcoming), 'Financial management change in Australia: market experiences', from J. Guthrie, C. Humphrey, O. Olson and L. Jones (eds), *Debating Public Sector Management and Financial Management reforms: an international study*, Greenwich: CT: Information Age Press.

Fitzgerald, P. (2004), *Review of Partnerships Victoria Provided Infrastructure*, January, www.partnerships.vic.gov.au, 12 May.

HM Treasury (2002), *'The Green Book' Appraisal and Evaluation in Central Government*, London: HMSO.

Infrastructure Project Partners [IPP] (2003), 'Latrobe Regional Hospital: case study', www.infraproj.com/latrobe.pdf, 8 August.

Officer, R.R. (1999), *Privatisation of Public Assets*, Melbourne: CEDA.

Officer, R.R. (2002), 'Public value, private good', presentation to Public Sector Finance and Treasury Management conference, Canberra, 15–17 April.

Victoria, Department of Treasury and Finance [VDTF] (2000), *Partnerships Victoria*, Melbourne: Victoria Department of Treasury and Finance.

Victoria, Department of Treasury and Finance [VDTF] (2001), *Partnerships Victoria: Practitioners Guide*, March, Melbourne: Victoria Department of Treasury and Finance.

Victoria Auditor-General [VAG] (1997), *Report of the Auditor-General on the Government's Annual Financial Statement, 1996–97*, October, Melbourne: Government Printer for the State of Victoria.

Victoria Auditor-General [VAG] (1998), *Acute Health Services Under Casemix: A Case of Mixed Priorities: Special Report No. 56: May 1998*, Melbourne: Government Printer for the State of Victoria.

Victoria Auditor-General [VAG] (1999), *Report on Ministerial Portfolios: May 1999*, Melbourne: Government Printer for the State of Victoria.

Victoria Auditor-General [VAG] (2001), *Report on Ministerial Portfolios: June 2001*, Melbourne: Government Printer for the State of Victoria.

Victoria Auditor-General [VAG] (2002), *Report on Public Sector Agencies: Results of Special Reviews and 31 December 2001 Financial Statement Audits: June 2002*, Melbourne: Government Printer for the State of Victoria.

Victoria Auditor-General [VAG] (2003a), *Report on Public Sector Agencies: Results of special reviews and 30 June 2002 financial statement audits: February 2003*, Melbourne: Government Printer for the State of Victoria.

Victoria Auditor-General [VAG] (2003b), *Report on Public Sector Agencies: Results of special reviews and financial statement audits for agencies with balance dates other than 30 June 2002: June 2003*, Melbourne: Government Printer for the State of Victoria.

Victoria Auditor-General [VAG] (2003c), *Report of the Auditor-General on the Finances of the State of Victoria, 2002–3: November 2003*, Melbourne: Government Printer for the State of Victoria.

Victoria Auditor-General [VAG] (2003d), *Report on Public Sector Agencies: Results of Special Reviews and 30 June Financial Statement Audits: November 2003*, Melbourne: Government Printer for the State of Victoria.

Victoria Government [VG] (2002), 'Project agreement in relation to Berwick [Casey] Community Hospital', obtained from the Central Register of Major Government Contracts, accessed at www.contracts.vic.gov.au, 8 August 2003.

Walker, R.G. (2002), 'Public private partnerships: different perspectives', paper presented at The Australian Equities Investment Conference 2002, Sydney.

Walker, R.G. (2003), 'Public–private partnerships: form over substance?', *Australian Accounting Review*, **13** (2), 54–9.

Walker, R.G. and L. English, (2003), 'Do PPP contracts for the construction of infrastructure evolve into liabilities?', presented to the University of Sydney PPP Forum, Sydney, 8 December.

Working With Government Task Force [WWG] (2001), *Working with Government: Emerging PFP Opportunities*, Sydney: New South Wales Government Printer.

16. Public–private partnerships: the Australasian experience with physical infrastructure

Graeme Hodge

Long term government relationships with private business and not-for-profit partners are increasingly popular. Today's public–private partnerships operate with sophisticated and far-reaching contracts and promise better efficiency, improved services and strengthened monitoring and accountability, along with stronger business and investor confidence. Whilst there is some international evidence that these promises are being met, debate in this area remains fierce. As well as the potential for these benefits, there may also be tradeoffs, with revenue guarantees, compensation for future policy changes by governments and reduced flexibility under longer term contracts for the crown to make decisions in the public interest.

This chapter looks at the Australasian experience of public–private partnerships. First, it discusses the historical basis of recent moves towards such partnerships, and notes that the desire for government to marry up its own capacities productively with the private sector through a variety of public–private mix arrangements is not new. Second, it documents the range of modern-day PPPs undertaken to date and comments on the increasing policy support currently being enjoyed by this technique. Finally, the paper reviews the performance outcomes published to date for recent Australasian PPP projects, and compares these achievements against the promises made.

INTRODUCTION AND HISTORICAL CONTEXT

Australasia comprises Australia, New Zealand and the neighbouring islands of the South Pacific Ocean. In this chapter, a picture is painted of the experience with PPPs across this region and we comment on their relative success to date. The chapter focuses mainly on the recent experience of Australia and particularly notes both the leadership position and empirical experience of the state of Victoria. Three case studies are also presented.

Australia has a population of around 20 million people, and a national political system based on the values of the United Kingdom's Westminster tradition. It has a federal system of government, with the federal government sharing power with several state and territory governments. Different Australian governments have adopted quite different stances on PPPs. Whilst states such as Victoria have led the charge with enthusiasm, the federal government has remained entirely sceptical, despite its recent pro-market and pro-privatisation orientation.

The populations of other large Australasian countries such as Papua New Guinea (5.19 million) and New Zealand (4.05 million), and Pacific islands such as Fiji (0.86 million) and the Solomon Islands (0.43 million) are far smaller, but there is a common heritage shared between most Australasian countries in terms of Westminster parliamentary values as well as global geography. Political systems within each of these countries, however, are uniquely dependent on history and culture.

Australia's past has seen a wide range of ownership and regulatory structures. Like New Zealand and other South Pacific nations, Australia has enjoyed a large state owned enterprise (SOE) sector, not through any particular ideological bent for state socialism, but as a pragmatic response to the failure of early market attempts at essential service provision, and the need to meet high community expectations for the provision of comprehensive and effective infrastructure for energy, transport, finance and insurance, and telecommunications. The evolution of widespread public enterprise sector was overseen largely by conservative political parties in the main (Wettenhall, 1983) under the general ethos of stimulating economic development. In essence, it was an early method of combining together the capacity and long term vision of the public sector with the commercial service and efficient production orientation of the private sector in pursuing the community's developmental goals. It was, as Wettenhall (2003) suggests, an early way of the public and private sectors working together in 'public–private mix'.

This method of partnering public and private energies was to become surprisingly well accepted and successful. Often supported by charismatic managerial leaders such as Sir John Monash,[1] Australian SOEs were frequently innovative and creative,[2] and were assisted by the adoption of the independent statutory corporation model in preference to more public service oriented models of State Department, Board or Trust.[3] Not surprisingly, Australia, like its neighbours, saw its public enterprise become a large and well oiled machine. Over the century, Australian public enterprises have also demonstrated progressively more independence and commercial viability and delivered significant improvements in productivity and financial performance at the same time as being highly regarded by citizens.

Australia's history is replete with debates throughout the twentieth century on the benefits and costs of using private contractors for public works in comparison to a public labour force. Today's sensitivity to the public–private divide is therefore not a new phenomenon,[4] and modern-day debates in many ways simply see us further down the path of this 'well rehearsed argument' around the effectiveness, efficiency and probity of these two types of service production systems (McIntosh et al., 1997).

By the mid-1980s to-1990s, though, Australia was increasingly turning to market solutions and private ownership ideas. Likewise, New Zealand was also turning to ideas of fundamental economic reform through privatization and the greater use of markets for traditional government activities.

Other Australasian countries were preoccupied throughout this time with more fundamental concerns for economic development, infrastructure development and economic growth issues along with the pursuit of economic stability and improved governance. Papua New Guinea, for instance, experienced several episodes of intense political and social instability through this time as did other nations including Fiji. In summary then, these parts of Australasia were more concerned with issues of economic growth and improved governance in the context of developing economies.

FOUNDATIONS OF THE AUSTRALASIAN PPP MOVEMENT

The accepted public monopoly paradigm for the past century of Australasian government enterprise was overturned through the past two decades with the consequence that by the 1990s, Australia and New Zealand became two of the OECD's most prolific privatizing countries.[5] Central also to this new philosophy of using private energies for the delivery of government services was the introduction at the national level of competition. These two thrusts – privatization and competition – joined neatly both with the philosophy of outsourcing government services and the idea of purchasing defined services as part of the increased managerialization of government. This new public management ethos was most attractive to its proponents as a way of focusing attention on defined requirements and ensuring that priorities for service provision were being met through the gradual contractualisation of government. Each of these four foundations deserves some discussion.

Privatization

Australia and New Zealand were both willing privatizers through the past two decades. Ranked third in the OECD judging on the size of proceeds from Australia's sell-offs during the 1990s compared to its gross national product,[6] Australia received revenues amounting to some $A96.6 billion from these sales. Revenues were roughly equally spread between federal and state level governments,[7] and covered traditional utility services such as electricity and gas, as well as transport, communications and financial services. Telstra, ($A30.33bn) and the Commonwealth Bank (at $A8.16bn) were the two most important sales along with the sale of Victoria's assets in the electricity ($A22.55bn) and gas ($A6.28bn) sectors. A huge range of business types were divested, mostly through trade sales, with various political justifications and proceeds were mostly used to reduce public sector debt levels.[8] Of the Australian states, Victoria was by far the most prolific privatizer.

Competition

These divestitures occurred in the context of broader moves towards stronger competition and regulatory reforms. The deregulation of banking and financial services in the mid 1980s announced a new era and was a warning to SOEs that protected environments with little real competition were to become a relic of the past. The quantum change in attitudes towards competition was heralded through the arrival of national competition policy, with all Australian governments signing a National Competition Policy Agreement in 1995. This agreement[9] aimed to increase the competitiveness of government businesses by removing unnecessary restrictions to competition, and placed SOEs on the same financial footing as private sector businesses. Broadly, it aimed for 'competitive neutrality' between all providers within a market for services – whether public or private – and was a significant federal Labor government initiative.[10] The Australian Competition and Consumer Commission (ACCC) now comprehensively enforces legislation guarding against anti-competitive and unfair market practices, product safety/liability and third party access to facilities of national significance. National markets in essential services such as electricity and gas have since been established.

Outsourcing

A parallel part of this competition reform was the opening up of government services to external competition and policies encouraging outsourcing of government services. In Victoria, for instance, the Kennett Government adopted a compulsory competitive tendering policy for all local government services with a requirement that 50 per cent of turnover must be competitively tendered.[11] At the federal and state levels, there were also some aggressive policies requiring the outsourcing of public sector services. Prominent outsourcing cases at the federal level included the government's Whole of Government IT Outsourcing Initiative (promising to reduce expenditures by one billion dollars over the contract life) and the Commercial Support Program initiative of the Department of Defence.

The Service Purchasing Ethos

The increasing managerialization of government has been accompanied by a preference to purchase defined services. This trend has occurred across both traditional government services such as cleaning and maintenance through to the provision of infrastructure for travel, and has been part of a broader performance measurement movement underway over the past century. Frederick Taylor's influential observations on the nature of production work efficiency were followed by numerous advances in our thinking about measuring performance such as zero based budgeting, programme budgeting, programme priority and planning, performance indicators and performance budgeting. Today's contractualized 'performance payments based systems' for contracted staff and contracts for the provision of infrastructure to provide particular ('output') service levels are simply the latest in this long line. Each subsequent reform has sought to promote greater specification, greater measurement and greater control over the production agent. The common underlying ethos amongst these advances has been that careful specifications through contracts promotes better performance than more cooperative, flexible traditional staff and work arrangements.

Overall, then, the Australian PPP movement has been built on these four foundations; privatization, competition, outsourcing, and the service purchasing ethos. Given also that the role of the private sector in providing public infrastructure is well acknowledged through the traditional practices of the competitive tendering of public works construction to private companies, the advent of the PPP movement in Australia might also be seen as simply an extension of this practice. Today's PPP era, in this view, has simply been a logical policy stepping stone for governments.

PUBLIC–PRIVATE PARTNERSHIP EXPERIENCE

The more recent predecessors of the PPP movement came out of early moves by the state to get around public finance restrictions on borrowing funds for important capital projects. In Victoria, for instance, the late 1980s and early 1990s saw governments seeking to establish new lines of financing for much needed infrastructure whilst not impacting on the state's borrowing requirements which were restricted under Loan Council agreements. The concern was thus essentially to achieve off-balance sheet financing. Not surprisingly, some of these artificial arrangements were deemed inefficient and were later unwound at high cost to the taxpayer. This was also the case in other states such as New South Wales.

The transition towards our formal adoption of the PFI movement as our own PPP policy seems to have come from an admiration of the British Blair project and a desire by our own New Labour governments to copy their strategies. Saturation advice from increasingly powerful market advisors, such as management consulting companies and merchant banks, to the ruling political heart may also have helped, along with support for the PFI policy as a priority from Treasury bureaucrats who essentially rose to power under previous political regimes whose priority it had been to privatize the state. The PPP movement has, as Wettenhall (2003) remarks, become a 'dominant slogan in turn-of-the-century discourse about government and governance' with little precision as to how the term is used, and a strong belief in its inherent policy worth.

Looking back, it was also fortuitously built on the reactions against the fanatical worship of competition as the salacious solvent for bureaucracy and inefficiency and in the midst of a heightened awareness of the transaction costs and social downsides of over-using such a competitive ethos. The suggestion of a new, warmer partnership ethos[12] came almost as a welcome relief to the abrasive and cut-throat era of competition. And since its ascension, keeping markets happy has become the new mantra for 'Third Way' governments, effectively monopolizing most other social and economic reform ideas. The high priests of market confidence appear to have become the elite consultant advisors, but this seemingly new policy direction has to date exhibited a surreal ignorance in failing to acknowledge the long history of Australia's public–private mix, whether in the form of its mixed enterprise, its progressively stronger willingness for private participation in major infrastructure over the past three decades, its contracting-out and outsourcing history or its willingness to enter partnerships through many varieties as was achieved for the successful staging of the Sydney Olympic Games in 2000 (Wettenhall, 2003).

Our modern day characterization of PPPs might take a number of courses, but across Australasia, the common ground amongst recent definitions appears to be that government has a business relationship within the private sector, it is long term, with risks and returns being shared, and that private business becomes involved in financing, designing, constructing, owning or operating public facilities or services. Thus, compared to traditional contract arrangements for public works or services, the long time frames for the PPP contract, the sharing of risks and rewards and the greater involvement of the private sector particularly in finance arrangements, all describe the new definitional ground. In addition, PPPs might involve joint decision making rather than having a principal–agent relationship. Such partnership arrangements thus have longer term implications, with private potential in decision making possible, bigger financial flows and greater capacity for risks to be shifted to either side of the partnership.

In any event, if one reviews the recent experience of using private finance for the provision of public infrastructure in Australasia there are a wide variety of candidate projects that could be noted over a range of sectors. AusCID (2001) noted that some 177 projects to the value of $A32 billion existed at that time after excluding privatization divestitures.[13] It reported that Victoria was 'clearly the dominant jurisdiction ... accounting for nearly one-third of the total number of projects and almost double that of the next biggest contributor in New South Wales'. It also noted the biggest sector as being power, even when privatizations were excluded, followed by health, airports, water, rail, road and ports with one-third of projects valued at less than $A50 million.

Our more recent request to Treasury Departments for PPP information throughout Australasia linked with other publicly available information revealed a list of 59 candidate projects, ranging from massive road projects in Melbourne such as EastLink ($A3.8 billion) and CityLink ($A2.1 billion), and the $A1.3 billion Alice Springs to Darwin railway line, down to the $A31 million regional police stations and courts project in South Australia and the $A5.5 million Joondalup Hospitality Campus in Western Australia.[14] If we focus solely on current or completed projects above say $A10 million, this yields a list of around 48 projects as shown in Table 16.1. This list is not comprehensive, however, and constitutes simply a set of examples characterizing the modern Australasian PPP territory.

On the basis of this Australasian PPP territory, several preliminary observations can be made. First, the publicly available data for PPPs is poor in quality. This is not only the case in terms of project definitions and financial amounts involved, but as well, there is an absence of good quality monitoring and evaluation information for PPPs. A serious effort is now needed to address this policy evaluation shortfall. Second, to the extent that this table gives projects that are representative of the recent PPP fabric, it is dominated by transport (particularly road projects), buildings and water projects. Third, whilst project roles in areas such as roads/tunnels and buildings are not necessarily controversial, some projects such as hospitals, water treatment plants and prisons have included highly controversial operational and service roles. Fourth, the geographic spread of

Table 16.1 Examples of Australasian public–private partnerships in infrastructure (1990 onwards)

Project	Length of contract	Type of contract	Project size	Year	Comments/portfolio
New South Wales[1]					
M4 motorway[2]	Concession ends 2010	BOOT	$A700 million	The M4 toll road opened in May 1992	• Sydney's oldest privately tolled road. • The motorway is 42 km in length with tolls applying to 12.5km of the link.
M5 South West motorway	30 years (concession ends 2023)	BOOT	N/A	Partially opened in August 1992	• The M5 is a 22km private tollroad owned and operated by Interlink Roads Pty Ltd. Land has been leased to Interlink until 2023.
M2 Hills motorway	45 years (concession ends in 2042)	BOOT	$A650 million	Contract awarded 1994; opened in May 1997	• Operated by Hills Motorway Pty Ltd. 21 km road, with 2 lanes operating in each direction.
Eastern Distributor M1	Concession ends in 2048	BOOT	$A700 million	Construction commenced 1997, with tolling at May 2001	• Links the Sydney CBD and Harbour crossings with the southern suburbs and Sydney Airport. • 6 km in length, with a 1.7 km tunnel.
Sydney SuperDome	N/A	BOOT	$A280 million	Contract awarded 1997 and opened in 1999	• Three projects including the SuperDome, car park and a plaza and external works, operated by Sydney SuperDome Group Pty Ltd.
Sydney Harbour Tunnel	30 year maintenance period	BOOT	$A750 million (total)	1998	
Stadium Australia (Olympic Stadium)	32 years, with expiry 2031	BOOT	$A615 million	Stadium completed in March 1999	• Billed as innovative techniques for financing, etc.

Project	Term	Structure	Cost	Status	Description
New Schools Project	30 years	DC&F	$A80 million (total)	Awarded in 2002	• Nine schools within Sydney, Wollongong, Shell Harbour and on the Central Coast including ancillary services.
Eastern Creek Alternative Waste Technology Facility	25-year contract	F,D,C&O	$A70 million	Completed 2004	• Alternative waste technology
Newcastle Ports Corporation	N/A	N/A	$A100–$A250 million	To begin in 2004	• Redesign and redevelop port into a Multi Purpose Terminal
Cross City Tunnel	N/A	BOOT (FCOM)	$A640 (in total), to be fully funded by the private sector[3]	Completed 2005	• 2 km tunnel under the Sydney CBD.
Westlink M7 (Western Sydney Orbital)	34 years, with end of concession in 2037	BOOT (D,C,F,O&M)	$A1.5 billion	Construction will be complete 2006	• 40km dual carriageway that will link the 'M5/Hume Highway at Prestons and the M2 Motorway at West Baulkhams Hills'.
Lane Cove Tunnel	33 year contract/ concession	BOOT (D,C,F,O&M)	$A815 million	The tunnel will be completed in the first half of 2007	• 3.4 km tunnel.
Northern Territory[4]					
Alice Springs Convention Centre	N/A	DC&M	$A24 million	Opened in 2002	• Construction of 1200 seat Convention Centre and 5-star hotel.

Project	Length of contract	Type of contract	Project size	Year	Comments/portfolio
Alice Springs to Darwin Railway	50 years operating lease	N/A	$A1.3 billion (total), with $A480m from government.	Completed in 2003	• Involves the laying of 1420km of track for railway line between the regional capitals, Adelaide and Darwin.
Darwin Business Park[5]	N/A	N/A	$A600 million (in total)	Construction completion by 2006	• Redevelopment of 25 hectares of waterfront land in Darwin including constructing Darwin Convention and Exhibition Centre.
Darwin City Waterfront Redevelopment Queensland[6]	N/A	N/A	$A1.1 billion	Construction commenced mid-2005	• Development of a 1500-seat convention centre, community and commercial facilities.
Brisbane Airport Rail Link	35 years	Lease, then transfer to state	$A220 million	Project has been operational since 2001	• 8.5 km elevated spur line and new stations to link the Airport to Brisbane and the Gold Coast.
Tweed River Sand Bypass Project	25 years	DFCOM	Approx $A25 million	Commissioned 2001	• Private sector initiated project. • Joint Queensland/New South Wales project providing for the artificial bypass of sand around the entrance of the Tweed River.
Gold Coast Convention and Exhibition Centre	N/A	N/A	Government commitment is $A102 million	Completed 2004	• State will own the Centre, with the private sector (Jupiters Ltd) responsible for the operation of the venue.

South Bank Education and Training Precinct	N/A	DCFM	$A200 million (total)	Estimated completion late 2008	• Redevelopment of South Bank Institute, Southbank Institute of TAFE and Brisbane State High School with private sector meeting state service requirements and State continuing teaching services.
South Australia[7]					
Youth Detention Centre	N/A	N/A	$A46 million	Commencing in 2006–7	
Adelaide Women's Prison	N/A	N/A	$A32 million	Commencing in 2006–7	
Tasmania[8]					
Mersey Community Hospital (MCH)	15 year lease	N/A	N/A	1995	• 130 bed general hospital operated by Australia's largest private health care provider and services both private and public patients.
Victoria					
Melbourne Magistrates' Court	20 years	BOO	N/A	1992 (completion date)	
Loy Yang B	33 years	N/A	$A1016 million	1992	• Provision of power generator.
St. Vincent's Hospital Redevelopment	25 years	DBOL	$A145 million	1996	
Intergraph / BEST/ CAD	8 years	DBOL	N/A	1996	• Emergency communications system.
Latrobe Hospital	20 years	BOO	$A17 million	1997	
New Prisons Project	20 years	BOOT	N/A	1997 (completion date)	• Provision of infrastructure and management of three new prisons.

Project	Length of contract	Type of contract	Project size	Year	Comments/portfolio
Public Transport Franchise Agreements	10–15 years	OF	Approx $A2 billion	1999	• Franchise to provide public transport services.
CityLink	27–54 years	BOOT	$A2.1 billion	2000 (completion date)	• See case study description.
Victorian County Court	20 years	BOO	$A140 million	2000 (completion date)	• First PPP delivered under the recent PV policy. • Owner and Manager is the Liberty Group, a subsidiary of Challenger International.
Coliban, Castlemaine Wastewater Project	25 years	BOOT	$A84 million	Commissioned 2000	
Central Highlands Water Treatment Project	25 years	BOOT	$A50 million	2000	
Mildura Hospital	15 years	BOO	N/A	2000	
Automated Ticketing	9 years	DBOO	$A332 million	2001	• Provision of public transport ticketing systems.
Wodonga Wastewater Treatment Plant	25 years	Design, Build & Operate	$A16 million	2003	• 'Project doubles the capacity of the current plant.'
Echuca/Rochester Wastewater Treatment Plant	25 years	BOOT (BOOT)	N/A	Construction commenced 2003	
Docklands Film & TV Studio Complex	20 years	N/A	$A70 million	2004	• Film studio business development.

Project	Duration	Type	Value	Timeline	Description
Mobile Data Network	5 years	DBFO	State government contribution of $A80 million	Commissioned 2003	• Development of a mobile communication and information system.
Correctional Facilities Project	25 years	DCF&M	$A150 million	Completion 2004	• Project includes a 300-bed correctional centre and a 600-bed remand centre, in conjunction with ancillary services. • Correction services will continue to be provided by the state.
Casey Hospital project (Berwick Community Hospital)	25 years	BOOT	$A80 million	Completed 2004	• Construction and operation of a 229 bed hospital.
Spencer Street Station Redevelopment	30 years	BOOT	$A400 million	Estimated completion end of 2005	• Commercial redevelopment project that will include a new transport interchange, and a retail plaza, offices and apartments.
Ballarat and Creswick Reclaimed Water Project	N/A	DBFO	30 years	Project brief issued 2005	
Enviro Altona	N/A	BOO (DBO)	State government contribution of $A15 million	Construction commencing 2005	
EastLink	39 years	FDCO	$A3.8 billion	Estimated completion 2008	• 45km fully electronic highway across Melbourne's southeast corridor

Project	Length of contract	Type of contract	Project size	Year	Comments/portfolio
Western Australia					
Geraldton Southern Transport Corridor	N/A	D & C	$A88 million	2005 (Stage one)	• Construction of a rail line, a new east-west link road and associated interchanges and connections and improved port precinct.
Tonkin Highway Extension	N/A	D & C	$A105 million	Expected completion 2006	• Dual carriageway highway to be undertaken by Transfield Macmahon Joint Venture.
CBD Courts Project	N/A	N/A	$A127.9 million (total)	To be completed by 2007–8	• First recent PPP project in WA. • Project provides new courtroom facilities to the Perth Courts.

Notes:

BOO = Build–Own–Operate
BOOT = Build–Own–Operate–Transfer
D&C = Design and Construct
DBOL = Design–Build–Own–Lease
DBFO = Design–Build–Finance–Operate
OF = Operations Franchise
N/A = Information not available during search

1. Pierce, J. (2004).
2. Macquarie Infrastructure Group, www.macquarie.com.au/au/mig/assets/aust/m4.htm, 23 February 2004.
3. Huge variations were noted in collecting this information. For example, the costs documented for the Cross City Tunnel in Sydney were recorded at A$640 million on one web site, A$400 million on another and A$1.03 billion on yet another.
4. MacKenzie, L. (2004).
5. Martin, C. (2003).
6. Phipps, R. (2004).
7. Wright, J. (2004).
8. Challen, D. (2004).

PPPs is interesting. Whilst some states such as Victoria have had extensive adoption, none was found at the Australian federal government level, despite its enthusiasm for divestitures and outsourcing, nor in countries such as New Zealand and Fiji.

And what can be learned from these projects? We now focus on three case studies as instances of recent Australasian infrastructure PPPs.

THREE AUSTRALIAN INFRASTRUCTURE CASE STUDIES

The construction of the CityLink transport project and County Court facility in Victoria, along with the provision of the M2 motorway facility in New South Wales, provide relevant recent examples of major public–private partnerships. Each of these is now presented. The major emphasis is on the CityLink case, where there has been the most extensive analysis.

Melbourne CityLink

Melbourne's CityLink road infrastructure project was a massive BOOT[15] undertaking. One of Australia's largest recent public infrastructure projects, it was a symbol of the former Kennett government's approach to public infrastructure. The CityLink project links up three major freeways in Melbourne, the South Eastern, West Gate and Tullamarine freeways, through the construction of 22 kilometres of road, tunnel and bridge works.[16] The project involves the construction, operation and maintenance of several sections of roadway including new and upgraded roads, some elevated, and six kilometres of tunnels through difficult silt conditions, as well as other works.

Following an Environmental Effects Statement in 1994 and the subsequent public inquiry, a brief was issued calling for parties to register their interest in completing the project. Two consortia were chosen for further development of ideas for the links and following a second project brief specifying requirements in 1995, the Transurban CityLink Ltd consortia was nominated as the preferred bidder.[17] The estimated cost of the whole CityLink project was approximately $A2.1 billion, including $A1.8 billion financed by the consortium and $A346 million of associated works and other costs financed by the state. Opened over the period 2000/2001, the consortium has leased land from the state to operate a public tollway for 34 years,[18] with ownership reverting to the state at no cost and in a fully maintained condition.[19] The predicted benefit–cost ratio for these works was 2.0, with a net present value of $A1.3 billion according to economic studies.[20] The Melbourne CityLink also indicated that initial investors should expect to receive a real rate of return of 17.5 per cent after tax for the life of the project according to Walker and Walker (2000:208). To govern the project, specific enabling legislation (the Melbourne City Link Act 1995), was established along with a statutory authority (the Melbourne City Link Authority or MCLA) as the state's contract manager (Russell et al., 2000).[21]

Political and Policy Observations

Both sides of politics agreed to the need for the project, but several factors made this project a divisive political hotbed. Forecasts of net project benefits varied wildly, and were initially inaccessible to the public. The Victorian Freedom of Information Act did not apply to this 'special project',[22] and accusations were made that favourable treatment was given to the consortia[23] and that misleading environmental impact emission information on tunnel air quality was provided by the consortium to the MCLA.[24] Moreover, Melbourne's drinking water was for some time pumped into the tunnel surrounds to ameliorate a lowered ground watertable and structural problems with the tunnel.[25]

After cracks began appearing in the tunnel walls (not acknowledged by CityLink until 17 months later: Davidson, 2001a), the tunnel needed to be redesigned in 1998. Further engineering problems also delayed the tunnel opening (Das, 2001; Davidson, 2001a). State of the art electronic technology was tested, almost on the run.[26] Additionally, direct tolling (rather than a shadow toll paid by government based on traffic volumes) probably diverted between 15–37 per cent of traffic off the link and into adjacent side streets (Russell et al., 2000). A constant stream of legal controversies in the CityLink project between members of the consortium alleged various contract breaches for cost over-runs, construction delays and faulty design.[27] Even the government itself was accused of delays and breaches of contract and, in return it alleged negligence by the builders and designers. These issues, along with the Kennett government's use of a 'crash through' culture legitimized through the legal powers of the project,[28] provided a colourful cocktail of politics and power to deliver this PPP.

Evaluating the CityLink PPP

Substantial risks were indeed transferred to the private sector in this project. Private contractors for instance bore almost all of the construction risks, along with most of the design, construction, operating, financing and market risks based on the contract.[29] In addition, the majority of the legal conflicts were between private parties, with few involving the government directly – despite the good newspaper copy.[30] Overall then, we might conclude that most of these commercial risks were indeed borne by the private sector investors and that they deserved to earn a margin.[31]

The larger concern regarding project risks seem not to be from the commercial side, which was largely well managed, but from the perspective of political governance. Several major shortcomings were evident in governance. No publicly available economic or financial evaluation had been undertaken prior to this project being commenced and no comparison occurred between undertaking this task in the public or private sectors (Victorian Auditor General, 1996). This partnership deal was essentially a two-way affair rather than also including citizens interests directly. The state's enabling legislation even provided scope to override any potential delays from the normal 'complications of due process' (Russell et al., 2000). There was no separate provision for the protection of consumers, and little apparent concern that the concession period may in the end be as high as 54 years in an effort to achieve profitability for the consortia. Magnifying long term governance policy concerns, the former State Treasurer, an ardent supporter of public–private partnerships, took on a top job with Macquarie Bank in its Infrastructure Investment Group, to lead future PPP efforts.

There has been disappointingly little debate on whether the CityLink achievement was worth the price paid. Dufty (1999), for one, argues that investors' interests were protected over citizens' interests, with high returns to private investors being achieved by minimizing risks through concession deed arrangements. The financial arrangement for the annual concession fee payable to the state for this monopoly facility was also far from clear, despite assurances to the contrary. A review by a team of lawyers of metres of legal documents found that payment by the contractor to the state for this monopoly facility could, at the contractor's choice, vary by a factor of four depending on timing options, and only if both a reasonable rate of return had been earned by the private investors and if sufficient cash flow was available. In other words, it was not at all clear, even when the contract documentation had been analysed, what the 'deal' was to which state had committed itself.[32] Citizens of Victoria paid a price in terms of lack of clarity here as well as a financial price. Considerable uncertainty still exists. Some now argue that the state should in future avoid contractual obligations that impact on its discretion for up to 54 years, and that regulatory powers should be established for such projects through the state's Office of the Regulator General.[33] They also stress that future projects should be subject to stronger parliamentary and public scrutiny prior to implementation.

VICTORIAN COUNTY COURT FACILITY

The Victorian County court has been hailed as the most effective example of the new PPP model and of the potential of the state government's 'Partnerships Victoria' policy. The project was certainly completed in under two years following the finalization of the contract, and both the quality of the building and the high level of services provided into the facility have been, in Fitzgerald's words 'commended by the judiciary, the legal profession and by the public'.

This project meets the demand for 46 courts under the contract, with the consortium providing a maintained court building, building management services, security and IT systems. Also impressive was the provision of building related services in terms of a high security holding facility for people in custody, four separate circulation zones for the judiciary, persons in custody, jury members and the public in addition to access for disabled users. Court technology included real time reporting for transcripts, video conferencing and remote witness facilities. Over the 20-year contract life, the state pays an estimated \$A519 million. One interesting additional feature of this PPP was the provision by the consortium of an extra two floors 'at their own risk' (Maguire, 2002).

Fitzgerald (2004) in his final review report noted that the Auditor General provided an opinion that the consortium did in fact bear substantial risks associated with the construction, financing and operation of the court facility. As well as this observation, however, this review also noted the absence of any real life benchmarks as the foundation for cost comparisons (compared to the more nebulous and potentially manipulatable public sector comparator framework) in his analysis. This was implicitly viewed as disappointing, given the recent construction of another Court facility nearby. As well, Fitzgerald also questioned the degree to which any demand risks existed in reality, given that government had signed up, and was highly unlikely to be unable to pay its agreed contractual obligations.

SYDNEY'S M2 ROAD

The M2 Motorway comprises 21 km of roadway, with two lanes operating in each direction and was constructed by the Abigroup–Obayashi Joint Venture on behalf of Hills Motorway Limited. A concession arrangement for a 45-year period until 2042, the roadway is a BOOT scheme at a cost of \$A650 million. Opened some six months ahead of schedule in May 1997 and underpinned by finance from the Macquarie Infrastructure Group, the road services an expanding middle-class residential area in north western Sydney.

Like CityLink, this deal has also been the subject of political interest and sensationalism. For instance, the returns available from this deal have been criticized by those opposing PPPs. Walker and Walker (2000:208), for instance, quote early projections for investor returns of over 24 per cent even after large transaction costs.[34] Interestingly, the Macquarie Bank web site is explicit in its judgement of the performance of its project – following a purchase price for an economic interest in 15 million stapled securities at $A1.04 per security in 1999, the sale prices of these securities as at December 2003 was $A6.61. In this light, perhaps, concerns that governments are prone to making bad business deals for the sake of delivering conspicuous infrastructure projects to voters are understandable.

Like CityLink, the M2 motorway was also dogged by concerns on matters of governance. A wide range of figures and claims surfaced as to who was paying for what and who was bearing which risks. As well, Walker and Walker (2000) report that the Transport Minister failed to table legal documents underpinning the deal, as requested by the parliament. Consequently, a motion of no-confidence in the Transport Minister was then moved. Despite this, 'the NSW Parliament was denied access to the contract deed between the public sector roads authority and the private sector counterpart' (Barrett, 2003:40).

PERFORMANCE OF PUBLIC–PRIVATE PARTNERSHIPS POLICY

Like our national $A97 billion privatization programme, there has been no comprehensive evaluation of Australia's PPPs thus far. There have nevertheless been some assessments attempted on the general issue of PPPs which provide clues on relative performance and likely public benefits to date. In this section we briefly review the PPP evidence available and interpret these findings.

The foundation of Australasian assessments on the effectiveness of PPPs has mostly rested on the international evidence rather than any local empirical data. Praise for the policy on the one hand and criticism on the other have been ubiquitous, in much the same way as polarized debates characterized the privatization debate in previous years. Examples of this rhetorical battle include commentators such as Davidson (2001b), who coined state transport franchise contracts in Victoria a 'failed experiment' and Crosweller (2002), who quoted a newly elected Minister nominating prisons partnership contracts[35] and hospital contract arrangements as 'time bombs'. At the international level, similar rhetoric has been seen, with Hodge (2002) noting that some that UK observers view PPPs as 'yet again screwing the taxpayer' and with private project sponsors appearing to be 'evil bandits running away with all the loot', whilst in Canada, PPPs have been labelled as 'Problem, Problem, Problem'.[36] Alternatively, the other side of this war of words has seen PPPs characterized as a marriage made in heaven and an arrangement which successfully draws on the skills of the private sector to deliver superior infrastructure at reduced cost (Shepherd, 2000). Both rhetorical extremes continue today.

The solid PPP research is less colourful, and more informative. By far the most often quoted study of the benefit of PFI projects has been the initial work of Arthur Anderson and LSE Enterprise (2000) and the National Audit Office (2000).[37] Arthur Anderson and LSE Enterprise investigated 29 business cases from UK departments at the request of the UK Treasury Task Force for public–private partnerships and estimated average cost savings of 17 per cent compared with the projected costs under public provision.[38] These findings were also supported by the assessments of the UK National Audit Office which reviewed seven specific Private Finance Initiative projects. For these seven projects, cost savings of 10–20 per cent were estimated. Later work by Pollitt (2002) also saw PPPs as effective. He observed firstly that in the late 1990s even the UK Treasury did not appear to know what its PFI commitments were, that unions were critical of the PFI initiative and that the IPPR (2001) had judged PFIs as being 'successful for prisons and roads but of limited value to date in hospitals and school projects'. Importantly, though, he also summarized the findings of National Audit Office work in 1999 (NAO, 2000) showing that in a sample of ten major PFI case evaluations undertaken by the NAO, the best deal was probably obtained in every case, and good value for money was probably achieved in eight of the ten cases.

On the other hand, Monbiot's regular criticism of PPPs in the UK press have presented a stinging attack and have accused the UK Treasury in failing to represent the public interest in their haste to sign-up for these deals. Across the Atlantic, a US case study from Bloomfield et al. (1998) reviewed a $US73 million Massachusetts correctional facility constructed as a PPP and argued that the lease purchasing financing arrangement used was, far from being less expensive, 7.4 per cent more costly than conventional general obligation financing. Not surprisingly, this arrangement was labelled as 'wasteful and risky'. Similarly, the analysis of Walker and Walker (2000) likened off-balance sheet infrastructure financing deals being undertaken through early Australian PPPs as misleading accounting trickery and an erosion of accountability to Parliament and to the public. In support, they cited the pre-tax return estimate of 24.4 per cent for Sydney's M2 Motorway.[39]

Of course the context in terms of the empirical experience of public sector provision is also important here in the UK. On this score, the Department of Transport (2002) remarks that the London Underground under public ownership 'has had a history of completing investment projects over budget and late'. Experiences cited included the recent line upgrade for the Jubilee Line which was six years late and 30 per cent over budget, and an analysis of some 250 projects by LU between 1997 to 2000 that revealed cost over-runs averaging 20 per cent.[40]

Remaining empirical research studies, particularly of Australasian PPPs have been few and far between, despite many colourful commentaries. One exception to this has been the recent 'independent' analysis undertaken for the Victorian Department of Treasury and Finance by Peter Fitzgerald (2004). This encompassed eight case studies. The analysis documented the arrangements entered into by the state for each of these cases and made some initial qualitative assessments on methods of delivering PPPs more cost-effectively. Importantly, he argued that 'the discount rate and risk adjustments were integral to the issue of whether the commercial arrangements proposed in a tender offered value for money over the public procurement alternative'. Overall, this review found benefits in the provision of PPPs in terms of innovation, timely delivery and cost certainty, but also a need to base risk assessments on better evidence of the frequency and quantum of risk experience – i.e., be more evidence based. It also suggested a revision be made to the use of the current 8.65 per cent discount rate in public sector comparator evaluations and instead, adopt a figure of 5.7 per cent. Critically, the consequence of using this smaller discount rate on a 'hypothetical' example presented in the report (2004:23) was that, whereas the higher discount rate led to the conclusion that a 9 per cent cost saving was being achieved against the public sector comparator, the use of the smaller discount rate suggested the opposite. At a discount rate of 5.7 per cent, the PPP arrangement indeed led to an estimated 6 per cent greater cost.[41]

In addition to this analysis, there have been several recent parliamentary inquiries across governments into the public–private partnership and contracting-out phenomenon. Notable throughout these assessments, including the most recent Fitzgerald review, has been the paucity of quantitative information relating to risk experience and weak financial evaluations of the comparative performance of work being done through traditional mechanisms compared to the policy preference for PPP deals. Better quality empirical assessments as a basis for future policy are therefore a high priority for both publicly funded and privately funded projects.

Likewise, a broad and still unresolved issue common to many of these developments remains the question of how government can best fulfil the multiple conflicting roles bestowed on them in the PPP process. Whilst PPPs are only around 7 per cent of overall Australian public infrastructure provision at present, this is likely to increase. Government may act in the roles of policy advocate, economic developer, steward for public funds, elected representative for decision making, regulator over the contract life, competitive builder of infrastructure, infrastructure funder using public taxes, commercial signatory to the contract and planner. The optimum ways in which long term public interests can best be protected and nurtured need more debate and consideration in the light of experience. This is particularly so in view of citizen transparency concerns and the high complexity of such deals.

This set of challenges covers much governance ground and should be detailed at another time. Until then, it remains a critical research priority in view of the financial sums being devoted to PPPs. It is also timely in view of candid admissions by even those within the industry itself, that empirical experience to date has too often not been favourable from the perspective of taxpayers. As one anonymous industry analyst put it recently, 'clear accountability mechanisms will distinguish [future] PPPs from the first round of private infrastructure projects in which the State did not always get a good deal'.

CONCLUSIONS

This chapter has presented a range of PPP experiences from Australasia. With a largely pragmatic approach to government and business relations in the past, Australasia has had a strong history of building a productive marriage between its own government capacities with those of the private sector through a variety of public–private mix arrangements. It is concluded that the desire for such business–government relations is not new, but that it has generally been unacknowledged during the more recent evolution towards a narrower perspective of public–private partnerships. This chapter concludes that there is a wide range of modern-day PPPs completed or currently underway and that the policy support being enjoyed by this technique is increasing. The cause of this appears to be the need for governments to be seen as reliable economic and fiscal managers, and builds on the fact that PPPs essentially offer governments the capability to purchase new high quality infrastructure quickly on a credit card and out of immediate sight of traditional public sector debt monitoring. Our attempt at reviewing the performance outcomes for Australasian PPPs to date found that we effectively relied on the international assessments, mostly from the UK.

The absence of any rigorous and transparent evaluations of Australasian PPPs represents a significant accountability shortfall, and we are left relying on only a few pieces of empirical evidence when attempting to make up the accountability jigsaw. These incomplete jigsaw pieces suggest that much of the political promise has not yet been delivered, and whilst there is always some potential to meet these promises in time, the jury is still out at present given the huge time lengths of PPP contracts. Overall, then, the recent performance of Australasia's PPPs has been mixed. Governments clearly need to approach future PPP deals in terms of the old adage 'caveat emptor'. And as the complexity and sophistication of these financial and contractual schemes increases in future, and citizens demand progressively more accountability of governments, it may well be that PPP decisions become more sensitive. To the degree that this occurs, governments who are unable better to balance their PPP policy advocacy role against their stewardship role for public funds, will do so at their own political peril.

NOTES

1. Sir John Monash oversaw the creation of a vertically integrated coal mining and electricity generation and distribution system across Victoria.
2. Russell (1990).
3. See Wettenhall (1965), Russell (1990).
4. The Royal Commission of 1896 into competitive contracting and tendering is an early example of such tensions.
5. Australia's divestiture activities through the 1990s ranked either second or third in the OECD depending on the measure used (Hodge, 2003). Likewise, New Zealand also consistently ranked in the first three.
6. Using the same economic yardstick (enterprise sales proceeds as a proportion of gross regional economic product), Victoria ranked number one as the world's most ardent privatizer through the 1990s.
7. For details of these transactions, see Hodge (2003).
8. Having said this, we ought note that large slices of SOE sectors still nonetheless remain in public hands in most Australian states. For instance, whilst electricity provision in Victoria is now effectively entirely privately based, New South Wales continues to provide electricity through a wholly government-owned electricity sector. Likewise, whilst public transport in Victoria now operates largely under a series of private franchises, most public transport across other States has remained essentially in public hands.
9. This followed the recommendations of the Hilmer report (Hilmer et al., 1993).
10. A notable sweetener encouraging states to review legislation for anti-competitive clauses was the fact that in return for such progressive reviews and the opening up areas of government service provision to competition, a series of 'competition payments' were made by the federal government.
11. Under this policy, targets were set at 20 per cent, 30 per cent and 50 per cent of local government services to be subject to competitive tender by mid-1995, 1996 and 1997 respectively. Over one half of all Victorian local government operating expenditure is spent on services now provided by external contractors.
12. Note that the British label of Private Finance Initiative, including the dirty words 'private' and 'finance', was rejected in favour of the more attractive and warmer partnership label.
13. The published details of these projects were limited to title, however.

14. Not included in this listing are planned projects such as the $US3 billion PNG-Queensland gas pipeline project (with 18 per cent PNG Government ownership).
15. This project outline is based on Hodge (2002). Further description of the project is provided in Grumsey and Lewis (2004), and early analysis of risk was also reported in Arndt (1998).
16. This description draws on the previous work of Hepburn et al. (1997).
17. Transurban CityLink Ltd is a joint venture between Transfield Pty Ltd and Obayashi Corporation.
18. This project life had stretched out to 37.75 years by the time of the review by Russell et al. in 2000.
19. Victorian Auditor General (1996).
20. See Allen Consulting Group et al. (1996).
21. In addition, an Office of Independent Reviewer was also established to approve the technical adequacy of the project throughout the design and construction phases.
22. See Walker and Walker (2000:216).
23. For example, land valued at $A80m was rented for the concession period for a paltry $A100 p.a. according to Costa (1997).
24. See Holmes (2000).
25. See Das (2001).
26. The experience of Melbourne's abysmal 'Met Ticket' Automated Ticketing System debacle in the background did not help here, with public transport ticketing being regarded widely as a mess after a decade of ticket machine problems and constant criticism.
27. See Hodge and Bowman (2004) for details of these controversies.
28. The often cited example here was the use of the State's infringement notice system of debt collection.
29. From a technical point of view the CityLink project was indeed a very challenging one, requiring a large technical advance in the tolling technology, real construction risks in tunnelling through soft Yarra River River silt and considerable risks in environmental issues concerning air quality and the height of the water table around the river. The private sector took on these risks fully and in accordance with the signed contracts. This conclusion is strengthened by the comments of an anonymous reviewer of this book who argued that 'most of the problems were due to political meddling. Basically, a decision was made at an early stage for the tunnel to be a wet one, that is, it would require continuous pumping of water. At the very last stage the politicians took fright and decided that it had to be a dry tunnel. Almost all of the problems can be attributed to this late change of heart'.
30. In reality, notwithstanding the colourful political symbolism of legal actions against government, the one-off A$10 million settlement in relation to alleged project delays and the ongoing $A37 million claim against government for constructing a new public road nearby were small relative to the size of project achievements. Government litigation nevertheless does raise serious questions of accountability and good governance in terms of publicly funding both PPP projects and legal defences in contractual suits. In this regard, the $A10 million 'taxpayer saving' settlement to the project consortium and the ongoing A$37 million compensation claim for reduced earnings, both appear to have tarnished the project's political success (Hodge and Bowman, 2004).
31. A more conservative conclusion might also be that in recognition of the early stage in the life of the project, the jury is essentially still out at present.
32. As documented in Hodge (2002), this information was 'not readily ascertainable from the Concession Deed in the Schedule to the Melbourne City Link Act 1995, but Russell et al. (2000) report that 'the stipulation that the fee can be paid in Concession Notes appears in a separate agreement, the Master Security Deed' ... and ... 'in Exhibit W inserted by the First Amending Deed cl 3.1 (b)'.
33. See Russell et al. (2000) and Hodge (2004). The first claim is opposed by policy proponents who see PPPs as providing governments with 'strategic flexibility'.
34. Walker and Walker (2000) note transaction costs of some $A28 million, an extraordinary amount considered against a private sector investment level of only $A156 million.

35. One outcome of the Kennett regime was the construction of three new private prisons. Consequently, Victoria had the highest proportion of privately housed prisoners in the world prior to one of these private prisons having their contract cancelled for poor performance and the state now managing the facility.
36. See Bowman (2000).
37. Hall's earlier judgement regarding PFI value-for-money was also important, noting that despite its sparcity and qualifications, the evidence on performance nevertheless provided 'some grounds for optimism' (Hall, 1998).
38. The majority of these cost savings were attributable to the assumed transfer of risks from the public to the private sectors in these business cases. (Arthur Anderson and LSE Enterprise, 2000).
39. Walker and Walker nonetheless noted that 'there can be situations where BOOT schemes are good deals for both government and private sector'.
40. Likewise, National Audit Office (2001) in the UK indicates that for their survey of PFI projects let prior to 2000, some 81 per cent of authorities viewed the value-for-money from PPPs as either excellent (6 per cent), good (46 per cent) or satisfactory (29 per cent), whilst 19 per cent saw PPPs as being of marginal (15 per cent) or poor (4 per cent) value.
41. Symbolically, whilst no detailed quantitative analysis figures were presented by Fitzgerald in his report to the Treasurer, the overall cost savings found by Fitzgerald for the eight case studies against the public sector comparator (using the higher discount rate) was 9 per cent (the same figure as presented in his 'hypothetical' case.) As well, in financial terms, the $A2700 million presently being repaid by the government for the eight PPPs reviewed in Victoria by Fitzgerald was seen to be excessive by around $A350 million.

REFERENCES

Allen Consulting Group, John Cox and Centre for Policy Studies (1996), 'The economic impact of Melbourne City Link Transurban Project', consultancy report to the Melbourne CityLink Authority, April, Melbourne.

Arndt, R. H. (1998), 'Risk allocation in the Melbourne CityLink project', *Journal of Project Finance*, **34** (3), 11–24.

Arthur Anderson and LSE Enterprise (2000), 'Value for money drivers in the Private Finance Initiative', report commissioned by the UK Treasury Task Force on public–private partnerships, London.

AusCID (2001), 'Delivering for Australia: a review of public–private partnerships and privatisation', a report by the Australian Council for Infrastructure Development, September.

Barrett, P. (2003) 'Public private partnerships – are there gaps in public sector accountability?', presentation to the 2002 Australasian Council of Public Accounts Committees, 7th Biennial Conference, Melbourne, 3 February.

Bowman, L. (2000), 'P3 – problem, problem, problem', *Project Finance*, **206**, 25.

Challen, D. (2004), 'Research project: major Australian infrastructure projects since 1990', personal communication, Hobart: Secretary, Department of Treasury and Finance.

Costa, G. (1997), 'A case study on competition and private infrastructure: the Melbourne CityLink project', *AQ*, **69** (2), 39–49.

Crosweller, A. (2002), 'Premier left to hold Kennett's "time bombs"', *The Australian*, 4 January, 4.

Das, S. (2001), 'Tunnel expert urged delay: the man who oversaw CityLink was worried about the water tables', *The Age*, 7 February, 1.

Davidson, K. (2001a), 'The tunnel of error: the warnings were ignored, whatever investors may lose is dwarfed by the public loss of liveability', *The Age*, 22 February, 17.

Davidson, K. (2001b), 'A Failed Experiment', *The Age*, 13 December.

Department of Transport (2002), *London Underground PPPs: Value for Money Review*, London: Department of Transport.

Dufty, G. (1999), 'CityLink 2000 to 2030: a hard road for Victorians', report into the impacts of the CityLink tollway on low-income Victorians, Melbourne, Victorian Council of Social Services.

Fitzgerald, P. (2004), *Review of Partnerships Victoria Provided Infrastructure, final report to the Treasurer*, January, Melbourne: Growth Solutions Group.

Grumsey, D. and M.K. Lewis (2004), *Public–Private Partnerships: The Worldwide Revolution in Infrastructure Provision and Project Finance*, Cheltenham UK and Northampton, MA, USA: Edward Elgar.

Hall, J. (1998), 'Private opportunity, public benefit?', *Fiscal Studies*, **19** (2), 121–40.

Hepburn, G., M. Pucar, C. Sayers and D. Sheilds (1997), *Private Investment in Urban Roads*, staff research paper, Canberra: Industry Commission (Australia).

Hilmer, F., M. Rayner and G. Taperell (1993), (Hilmer Report) *National Competition Policy, Report to the Independent Committee of Inquiry into Competition Policy In Australia*, Canberra: AGPS.

Hodge, G.A. (2002), 'Who steers the state when governments sign public–private partnerships?', *The Journal of Contemporary Issues in Business and Government*, **8** (1), 5–18.

Hodge, G.A. (2003), 'Privatisation: the Australian experience' in David Parker and David Saal (eds) *International Handbook on Privatisation*, Cheltenham, UK and Northampton, MA, USA: Edward Elgar.

Hodge, G.A. (2004), 'The risky business of public–private partnerships', *Australian Journal of Public Administration*, **63** (4), 37–49.

Hodge, G.A. and D.M. Bowman (2004), 'PPP contractual issues – big promises and unfinished business' in A. Ghobadian, N. O'Regan, D. Gallear and H. Viney (eds), *Public–Private Partnerships: Policy and Experience*, London: Palgrave.

Holmes, D. (2000), 'The electronic superhighway: Melbourne's CityLink project', *Urban Policy and Research*, **18** (1), 65–76.

IPPR (2001), 'Significant reforms of PPPs necessary for Labour to deliver on public services', *Current Topics*, www.ippr.org.uk, 25 June 2001.

Maguire, G., Assistant Director Commercial Division, Department of Treasury and Finance (2002), personal communication, Melbourne.

Mackenzie, L., Assistant Under Treasurer, Northern Territory, (2004), 'Public–private partnerships in Northern Territory', personal communication, Darwin.

Macquarie Infrastructure Group (2004), www.macquarie.com.au/mig/assets/aust/m4.htm, 23 February.

Martin, C. (2000), 'Government to spend $100 million on convention centre as part of Darwin City waterfront project', media release, Chief Minister of Northern Territory, www.nttc.com.au/MediaCentre.mediarelease.asp?version=59, 11 August.

McIntosh, K., J. Shauness and R. Weltenhall (1997), *Contracting Out in Australia: An Indicative History*, Canberra: Centre for Research in Public Sector Management, University of Canberra.

Monbiot G. (2002), 'Very British corruption: the Private Finance Initiative is rigged and now we have a chance to stop it', *The Guardian*, 22 January, p. 15.

National Audit Office (2000), *Examining the Value for Money of Deals under the Private Finance Initiative*, London: Stationery Office.

National Audit Office (2001), *Managing the Relations to Secure a Successful Partnership in PFI projects, a Report by the Comptroller and Auditor General*, HC 375, 29 November, London: Stationery Office.

Phipps, R., Principal Treasury Analyst, Queensland Treasury, (2004), 'Public–private partnerships in Queensland', personal communication, Brisbane.

Pierce, J., Secretary, New South Wales Treasury, (2004), 'Public–private partnerships in New South Wales', personal communication, Sydney.

Pollitt, M. (2002), 'The declining role of the state in infrastructure investments in the UK', in Sanford V. Berg, Michael G. Pollitt and Masatsuga Tsuji (eds) *Private Initiatives in Infrastructure: Priorities, Incentives and Performance*, Cheltenham, UK and Northampton, MA, USA: Edward Elgar.

Russell, E.W., E. Waterman and N. Seddon (2000), *Audit Review of Government Contracts: Contracting, Privatisation, Probity and Disclosure in Victoria 1992–1999, An Independent Report to Government*, vol 3, May, Melbourne: State Government of Victoria.

Shepherd, T. (2000), 'A practitioner's perspective', presentation to the Productivity Commission Workshop on Private Sector Involvement in Provision of Public Infrastructure, 12–13 October, Melbourne.

Victorian Auditor General (1996), *Report on Ministerial Portfolios, May 1996*, Melbourne.

Walker, B. and B.C. Walker (2000), *Privatization: Sell Off or Sell Out?*, Sydney: ABC Books.

Wettenhall, R. (1965), 'Public ownership in Australia', *Political Quarterly*, **36** (4), 426–40, also in R. Wettenhall (1987), *Public Enterprises and National Development: Selected Essays*, RAIPA (ACT Division) monograph.

Wettenhall, R. (1983), 'Privatisation: a shifting frontier between private and public sectors', *Current Affairs Bulletin*, **69** (6), 114–22.

Wettenhall, R. (2003), 'The rhetoric and reality of public–private partnerships', *Public Organisation Review: A Global Journal*, **3**, 77–107.

Wright, J. Under Treasurer, Department of Treasury and Finance (2004), 'Public–private partnerships in South Australia', personal communication, Adelaide.

17. Public–private partnerships: a policy for all seasons?

Graeme Hodge and Carsten Greve

INTRODUCTION

We began this book by making some policy observations of PPPs, noting that despite their increasing popularity around the globe, and despite the fact that government has contracted with the private sector for centuries, few people agree today on what a modern PPP is. In this context, it was argued that there were three good reasons for publishing a book such as this one. First, we wanted to re-examine the huge range of meanings given to the concept and assess whether the notion of PPP was itself worthwhile keeping. Second, we aimed to review the empirical experience of PPPs globally and learn from the outcomes achieved across a range of different experiments to date. Third, we noted that huge financial commitments were currently being made by governments and as a consequence, careful and balanced assessments of PPPs are now needed rather than louder shouting from one side or other in the debate.

The PPP phenomenon has certainly grown. From a recurring historical theme but very much a background public policy matter, it has evolved to become a central and for some governments, almost obsessive, policy tenet which commits citizens for decades to come through increasingly complex and technical legal arrangements. In this closing chapter, we will firstly reconsider the central policy questions posed at the outset, before we then draw together the bigger themes that have evolved throughout the book. Last, we will close by contemplating issues for the future.

CRITICAL POLICY QUESTIONS

In the initial chapter of this book we asked a series of specific questions concerning PPPs:

1. From an historical perspective, which aspects of PPPs are new today, how have PPPs evolved over time and how should a better understanding of PPP history inform our actions now?
2. From the perspective of finance and risk transfer, what are the financial drivers of PPPs, how are these financial deals constructed, and how successful in financial and economic terms have PPPs been for citizens and other parties to date?
3. On what criteria ought PPP success be evaluated and which criteria are currently adopted?
4. To what degree do PPPs adhere to traditional stewardship requirements in accounting and to what extent do risk transfer promises match risk transfer experience?
5. In terms of legal issues and getting the contract right, do different models of PPPs exist and what have we learned to date from a legal perspective about PPP contracts?
6. In the field of politics, what are the important political interests at stake in typical PPPs and what are the implications for making future governance decisions in the public interest?
7. When managing and governing PPPs, how is management and governance practised if decision-making is shared between public actors and private actors and what challenges arise?
8. Lastly, in terms of accountability issues, how is accountability practised in PPPs and what are the resulting accountability challenges for the future?

This book sought not only to answer some of these questions, but also to extend the PPP agenda further. Throughout our deliberations, the emphasis was to be on learning from the empirical evidence of international experience in order to better meet tomorrow's PPP challenges. The emphasis throughout investigations was also on outcomes for citizens as well as policy successes for governments and bottom line results for commercial businesses. These characteristics set this book apart from other recent additions to the PPP literature including Ghobadian et al. (2004) and Grimsey and Lewis (2004) who view PPPs more through the eyes of businesses, economists and policy proponents.

In searching for answers, the editors of this book have not sought to enforce a comprehensive rational unitary analytical approach along any single lens, but have encouraged a diversity of views from a range of commentators each of whom applied a different lens in their analysis. Each commentator has contributed a different piece of the jigsaw. Now, whilst acknowledging we are still missing pieces of the picture, we need to begin drawing our own themes together and making tentative conclusions.

So, after the dust has settled, how might we reconceptualize PPPs? And how have PPPs performed?

RECONCEPTUALIZING PPPs: A POLICY FOR ALL SEASONS?

There are many insights in reconceptualizing PPPs and the canvas is broad.

First, from an historical standpoint, PPPs ought to be viewed as a label covering a huge range of different potential approaches to the cooperative delivery of public sector services going back centuries. At the broadest level, and using Wettenhall's words, 'there is nothing new about the mixing of public–private endeavours ... whatever the new enthusiasts may think'. PPPs inevitably cover a broad family of approaches, and despite the rhetorical advertising of reformist governments around the globe, there is no one single approach to PPPs. To some governments, partnership is defined through the existence of a shared equity company and arrangements incorporating shared decisions, shared costs and shared profits. To others, partnership refers to a two way government–business deal, whilst others insist on a three way deal with citizens explicitly represented. Yet other governments see the availability of private finance as a precondition for the label of partnership. Whilst some governments believe partnership is intimately connected to privatization, others reject this. Some governments regard partnerships as being all about trust in an uncertain environment, whilst others operate their partnerships through watertight and complex contracts more like a traditional commercial relationship. Governments around the world will no doubt continue to try and differentiate their own policies from the PPP experiments of other jurisdictions as well as past PPP failures. But the fact remains that PPPs are a family of techniques rather than the one best way.

Second, from the contributions in this volume it would seem fair to say that governments around the world have been generally thinking of partnerships in two ways: social (or organizational) partnerships and economic partnerships.

Social (or organizational partnerships) refer to new forms of organizing collaboration between actors from the public sector and the private sector. These arrangements can take the form of a joint organization, but they may also be looser cooperative efforts built on previous contractual relationships. The north European way of extending corporatist-like arrangements as PPPs (such as in Germany or in Sweden) are examples here. The purpose of social or organizational partnerships is to go beyond the present way of organizing in order to learn new ways of producing and delivering service and to share risks, as well as reaping rewards, in doing so.

Economic partnerships are what many refer to as PFI-style arrangements, modelled after the British initiative in the 1990s. In an economic partnership, public sector bodies depend on the private sector to provide finance and capital for infrastructure projects. Most of these infrastructure projects have been fairly large such as the construction of a new road system or building a new prison facility, although there are examples of smaller projects as well. Economic partnerships bring with them the 'alphabet soup' of BOO, BOT, DBO and vocabularies found in the construction and finance sectors.

In this volume, we have learned from experiences with both social (or organizational) partnerships and economic partnerships, although many of the recent headlines worldwide seem to have been taken up by economic partnerships. The research agenda from now on must concentrate a part of its efforts on communicating the message that partnerships involve more than just economics.

A third point in reconceptualizing the PPP phenomenon results from its breadth, which in many ways has become one of its enduring strengths. Like 'progress' or 'improvement', the warm glow of the partnership ethos cannot easily be dismissed. The nuance of cooperative production of public services inevitably appeals to a diverse range of applications, with the consequence that the notion of partnership itself, central to PPPs, has a huge rhetorical and hence political, appeal. In the context of the language games played in the public policy domain (Edelman, 1985; Parsons, 1995), it is unsurprising that PPP language games have fitted like a glove. It has certainly acquired higher political legitimacy than the alternative aggressive culture of competition through competitive tendering, for instance, or any romantic thought of yesteryear's concept of cooperative service provision through bureaucratic arrangements. It has also provided important symbolic differences for New Labour in the UK (Correy, 2004). These two characteristics have combined to ensure the rise of PPPs as a politically attractive policy, particularly when added to the triad of promises in the case of PFI including cheaper infrastructure, quicker project delivery and the availability of private finance, all amidst a fear of public sector debt.

These attractions have in many countries provided a convenient solution to a myriad of pressing political concerns. Little wonder that we view PPPs as 'a policy for all seasons',[1] with positive appeal across many interest groups, numerous jurisdictions around the world and over some time as well. Having said this, we might also observe that the reasons behind PPPs have changed over time, and are (like the rationale behind outsourcing policy decisions) somewhat slippery. As Jean Shaoul suggests in Chapter 10, the rationale seems to have begun with broader macoeconomic concerns in terms of public sector debt levels, and then moved to more direct value-for-money concerns. More recently, the rationale has again been reshaped firstly towards quicker service provision and then towards 'innovation'. Watching the evolving political profile and its policy rationale, the interesting question is whether or not PPPs represent anything other than a temporary policy window in time where political pressures are for a period married to financial availability and business opportunity in difficult times. The answer to this question is yet to be found.

Fourth, in thinking further about the history of partnerships between governments and the private sector, there are inevitably some lessons that stand out with current relevance to PPPs. Whether we look at the history of the public–private mix in terms of privateer shipping or the history of privately held Treasury functions, the lessons appear consistent. Privateer shipping, for instance, 'was vital to England's rise as a major sea power' and the establishment of overseas empires for both England and Spain, as Roger Wettenhall notes (Chapter 2). Having said this, though, privateer shipping was also a 'feeble and corrupt system' in which political interference and leading officials promoted partnership ventures intent on plunder. Again, in the case of early state treasury functions, interestingly undertaken by a body of businessmen 'functioning as private accountants', whilst the system was 'dynamic and flexible', it also 'depended on corruption to sustain it'. The paradox here, as Wettenhall reminds us, is that whilst both of these theatres of public–private mix helped shape expansionist state policies with strong end social benefits, they also demanded clearer lines of distinction between the state and private interests. So, in the midst of today's policy marketing and spin, there are clear and relevant lessons to be learned from history. And governments currently intent on marketing PPP policies and slogans in preference to learning from history and empirical experience need to understand that, as Wettenhall put it, 'continued shouting from the rooftops that seeks to eulogize these slogan-processes is scarcely helpful'.[2]

Fifth, the institutional history of the Falck company in Denmark presented by Greve and Ejersbo is informative, as well as fascinating. Looking at the impressive expansion of the Falck company over the past century, they question the degree to which competition can successfully coexist with partnering over time. Partnership to them, is not necessarily a stable relationship – and certainly not inevitable. Greve and Ejersbo point out the growth of the Falck company from an initial inability of local government in Denmark to provide its own fire fighting (with ambulance driving and security interests added later) to a stage now where it covers 108 countries amidst global competition. The move observed, in their words, was from 'a semi-public company' which was able to combine the 'advantages of a public organisation with the value of a private initiative' to nowadays being regarded more as a 'private company – with special privileges' and increasingly subject to scrutiny from competition regulators and suffering criticism from citizens. The lesson here has been the observation that partnerships are to an extent dependent on market structure and take some years to build. Partnerships depend to a degree on secure and stable conditions to thrive and the introduction of competition puts them under pressure. And in the words of Greve and Ejersbo, public–private partnerships are certainly different in the local and national context from the global context. This understanding again contrasts the most frequent public–private partnership literature in the contemporary uni-dimensional business context.

Lesson six was from the political perspective. It is interesting to observe that in political terms PPPs have failed to become a major issue in many places according to Coghill and Woodward (Chapter 5). To their mind, PPPs are even in danger of being presented as a technical solution to inherently political questions. They observe as well that their popularity is likely to continue in the absence of any alternative ideology but suggest that paradoxically, the time has come for PPPs to take a more prominent place on the political agenda. The need now, to their mind, is to subject PPPs to greater scrutiny as part of the democratic process. Of course, one underlying question here is the issue of political differences between jurisdictions. Trade union opposition to PPPs in the United Kingdom, for instance, appears to have been much stronger and more consistent than the opposition shown under Thatcher's initial enterprise divestiture policy.[3] Other countries may see differing experiences.

Seventh, and this time adopting a legal lens, getting the contract right is fundamental to the success of a project if we intend pursuing the PFI version of partnership. Several elements are central to an appropriately structured contract arrangement. In any case, with legal disputes now almost an expected part of the partnership approach, it is clear that from a legal perspective, the jury is still out on PPP success because we are only a few years into contract arrangements usually lasting several decades. Cautious implementation and evaluation ought guide us here, according to Evans and Bowman (Chapter 4). In a broader sense, getting the contract right is also only one aspect of a far more complex need to understand better the behaviours of contracting parties – whether public or private. The issue is getting the project outcomes right – not just the black and white contract. When 83 per cent of long term European outsourcing contracts in information technology are renegotiated within one year, perhaps questions of renegotiating project outcomes and renegotiating contracts loom larger than the theory of the perfect initial contract. A better understanding of the commercial behaviour of governments under PPP arrangements may require us to better understand the real behaviour of successful commercial contract partners in the business world. Similarly, we ought also investigate and better understand the practical tensions between commercial goals and political ends as well as the theoretical synergies. It appears our legal research efforts in PPPs have only just begun.

Eighth, there is little doubt that 'public–private partnership has everything going for it' and that it is 'one of the most important new horizontal forms of governance in the modern network society', in Klijn and Teisman's words (Chapter 6). But when partnership is seen not as a contract but in a more pure sense as co-production through organisational cooperation, it is likely to be a 'difficult marriage'. Indeed, in line with Wettenhall's earlier judgement, Klijn and Teisman argue that it is highly debateable whether the contract form of public–private partnership, as it is found in the English PFI, should be considered as PPP at all. To them, this service delivery form is in fact no different to classic forms of contracting out and tendering. It is a well known way of collaborating with relatively little risk, but limits co-production, joint decision making and the search for solutions. To these authors, then, real partnership between public and private spheres requires a lot of work and often has to conquer many institutional obstacles in its pursuit of meeting partnership objectives in a truly cooperative and productive manner.

Lastly, David Corner's reminder (in Chapter 3) of the importance of getting financial matters right related to both social partnerships based on trust as well as economic partnerships characterized by contracts. With some 563 PFI contracts signed by 2003 in the UK and noting the critical independent work of the UK National Audit Office, he remarked, quite rightly, that 'public service delivery is a risky business'. This identification of risk in public activities and the easy availability of private finance for public purposes both represent new dimensions for governance in the twenty-first century. We ought now seek 'optimum not maximum risk transfer' in his words, be better aware of the types of partnership risks as well as risk allocation principles and seek incentives that encourage risk bearing, so that private financiers step in if need be when a private operator fails. He also reminds us that some £123 billion may well be committed over the next 25 years to the UK's PFI version of PPPs, and that, as always, considerable care will continue to be needed to assess value for money estimates with any degree of independence and veracity.

Ongoing careful analysis will no doubt unpack the degree to which promises of better defined and measured delivery of public services are being met, the degree to which the use of private finance is done at a cost or at a saving, and the degree to which the partnership language game camouflages commercial games from 'the consultocracy' of business players whose objective is only to chase commissions.[4] Perhaps it is as simple as the pursuit of more refined processes for providing infrastructure and services and giving communities better value for money. But we doubt it. The PPP phenomenon is all of these characteristics, and we need to understand each phenomenon better.

So, looking at the international empirical experience presented in this book, how then have PPPs performed? How have PPP outcomes for citizens compared with alternative approaches available around the world, and who have been the biggest winners and losers in these changes?

PERFORMANCE INSIGHTS: LEARNINGS ON PARTNERSHIPS AS CONTRACTING-OUT SERVICES

Both Johnston and Romzek (Chapter 7), looking at accountability, and Martin (Chapter 8), looking at contractor performance, use the typical United States perspective and view partnerships simply in terms of competitive, even short term, service contracts with government. Johnston and Romzek suggest that accountability effectiveness varies across contracts and that 'effective contract structures and management of contract accountability are elusive goals'. Further, the tendency to under-invest in contract management led to difficulties in holding contractors accountable to their mind. They observe several factors influencing the effectiveness of accountability in contracting, and noted that even in fairly straight forward contracting environments, contract management becomes very complicated. Their work is sobering.[5] And they are right that many accountability matters are indeed complex and unresolved.

Martin notes that in the case of the USA, the recent arrival of performance based contract (PBC) practices have replaced the two competing historical modes in the field of human services. Thus, the market model and the traditional partnership model have been superseded by a new notion of public–private partnership focused on performance. The result, in Martin's words is that 'PBC may be the mechanism that will lead to more public–private partnerships in human service contracting'. He reports that initial experiments have demonstrated significant increases in contractor performance, and notes reduced client service waiting times, increased numbers of job placements and a higher number of adoptions in his case studies. These improvements in service delivery saw governments, contractors and service recipients all winning. Clearly, insofar as the broader PPP movement is based on the philosophy that performance based incentives are a key reason for improved performance delivery, these positive results suggest that governments should continue their efforts along this path.

Almqvist and Hogberg on the other hand presented evidence in Chapter 12 suggesting PPPs in Stockholm's social sector are changing in nature. Three strategies for opening up municipal activities to competition were reviewed, and costs and quality gains through competition observed. They also, however, highlighted both the change in the structure of markets, and the ironic dimensions of measurement and trust. On the first score, ten years of competition strategies in the City of Stockholm appear to have resulted in the market behaving as an oligopoly, with the threat of insufficient competition and cartel formation. The current need was therefore seen to be the redevelopment of competitive contracting markets or even the cessation of external service procurement as an option. On the second score, detailed measurement and monitoring systems seem to reduce the degree to which partes involved in economic and social transactions trust each other. Whilst this is not surprising in abstract, we might reflect that in global terms, as well as their observations in Stockholm, the vast majority of today's partnerships seem dependent on formal and explicit legal contracts rather than any softer notions of trust.

In Chapter 14, Oppen, Sack and Wegener look at Germany's experience in PPPs in the context of the German corporatist social sector. They note that the PPP construct has been burdened by a monetary bias around the world. Their perspective, though, is one of organizational innovation, and they argue that in the area of social services, the focus is on collaborating and on sharing responsibility, visions and criteria of relevance rather than on cofinancing. The motive then is joint problem solving. Interestingly, they argue that experimentation has widened the scope for bottom-up initiatives and has seen the long overdue development and spread of performance standards, pointing to 'a potential social dynamization of such partnerships that goes beyond the service provision itself'.[6] They note that a growing number of partnerships are taking their place amongst familiar traditional corporatist arrangements and comment that the trend is towards gradually more competitive subsidy arrangements, dissolving monopolies and more service and quality measurement standards. And new forms of self organization, planning and debating quality and service standards have occurred. But whilst acknowledging this innovation, it is also not yet clear what the results and lessons from such experiments have contributed or the degree to which these have spread.

PERFORMANCE INSIGHTS: LEARNINGS ON PARTNERSHIPS AS INFRASTRUCTURE CONTRACTS

It would be fair to observe that citizens have been somewhat apprehensive of the political promises made for major PPPs. This is hardly surprising. History provides us with plenty of examples of citizens being subjected to governments ideologically bent on applying the latest fashionable policy prescription when neither was the patient ill, nor was the policy effective. Moreover, a range of examples from supplying electricity in Manila[7] through to the London Underground rail transport debacle[8] show that government reforms undertaken in the name of 'partnership' can easily go wrong for a host of reasons.

Our global experience with PPPs reviewed here has been as fascinating as it has been mixed. Five chapters viewed the empirical experience of partnerships in terms of the PFI phenomenon. Boardman, Poschmann and Vining reviewed experience in North America (Chapter 9), Shaoul and Pollitt (Chapters 10 and 11) each reviewed experience in the United Kingdom, and English and Hodge (Chapters 15 and 16) reviewed experience from Australasia. Their findings present some interesting contrasts. Pollitt, at one end, showed not only the popularity of PFI with the UK government typically raising some 15–20 per cent of its capital budget each year through this mechanism,[9] but also its empirical success. Indeed, his conclusion after looking at five case studies was that despite the lengthy and costly bidding process amongst a small number of bidders, and despite observing government's extreme positive stance in the face of high-profile problems with individual PFI projects, compared to the previous government procurement system 'it seems difficult to avoid a positive overall assessment'. Thus, relative to the counterfactual of what might have happened under conventional public procurement, Pollitt argues that projects under PFI 'are [now] delivered on time and to budget a significantly higher percentage of the time' ... with construction risks 'generally transferred successfully' and with 'considerable design innovation'. Importantly, whilst he acknowledges that it is possible many of the assumed benefits of PFI projects are hypothetically available through conventional procurement, the reality is that these would not be achieved without the learning and leverage provided through the PFI initiative.

At the other end is the contrast provided by Shaoul's evidence. In the midst of the government's rationale, itself described as an 'ideological morass', she presents a litany of failed PFI project examples, a VFM appraisal methodology biased in favour of policy expansion, pitiful availability of information needed for project evaluation and scrutiny, and projects in which the VFM case rested almost entirely on risk transfer but for which, strangely, the amount of risk transferred was almost exactly what was needed to tip the balance in favour of undertaking the PFI mechanism. Added to this apparent manipulation of the PSC process were the observations that in hospitals and schools 'the PFI tail wags the planning dog' with projects changed to make them 'more PFI-able', highly profitable investments being engineered for private companies with 'a post tax return on shareholders' funds of 86 per cent', several refinancing scandals, and conspicuously unsuccessful IT projects and risk transfer arrangements that in reality meant that risks had not been transferred to the private sector at all but transferred over to the public. Not surprisingly, Shaoul concludes that at best, PFI has turned out to be very expensive with, moreover, a lack of accountability leading to difficulty in learning from past experiences. Partnerships, in her view then, were 'policies that enrich the few at the expense of the majority and for which no democratic mandate can be secured'.

Other evidence from the United States and Australasia lay in between these extremes. Boardman, Poschmann and Vining, for instance, note the difficulty of capturing transaction costs in any comparison between partnership and traditional project delivery and catalogue major North American 'P3' projects. They note that less than half of these P3s include a significant private financing role. Five transport, water provision and waste projects are then presented show-casing a series of 'imperfect' partnership projects with high complexity, high asset specificity, a lack of public sector contract management skills and a tendency for governments to be unwilling to 'pull the pin' on projects once underway, all conspiring against the simple notion that partnerships guarantee either political or commercial success. They particularly point to private entities being 'adept at making sure, one way or another, that they are fully compensated for risk-taking' and even to strategic behaviour such as declaring bankruptcy (or threatening to go bankrupt) in order to avoid large losses. The tensions here with governments needing to hold their nerve and watch commercial failures materialize as risks are borne by commercial entities on the one hand, and yearning to be viewed as governing a growing and vibrant market economy on the other, is clear.

The Australasian empirical evidence on PPP performance likewise appears patchy. Linda English notes the failure of the Latrobe Regional Hospital case in the state of Victoria and provides a reminder of both the importance and the difficulty of VFM estimates. A 20-year BOO project, this arrangement failed only two years into the contract due to a commercial failure to understand the government's case-mix funding model as well as ineligibility for additional top-up funding. Importantly too, she notes that amidst the appearance of full disclosure by the state government, crucial documentation in terms of PSC calculation and financial arrangements underpinning the PPPs were still withheld from citizens and were also not provided through Freedom of Information requests. Imperfect PPP arrangements indeed. The Auditor General's line in reviewing this situation was also interesting – apparently seeing this case not only as a financial failure of the private hospital, but as a governance failure by government as well. Interpreting English's observations here, it had not behaved as an intelligent and informed buyer. The government had accepted an unsustainable price bid in the first place, had not undertaken any comparative analysis to benchmark public provision in the second place and had thirdly not recognized that government was unable, in reality, to transfer the social responsibility of hospital provision at all.[10]

Hodge's observations of Australasian experience noted the logical policy stepping stones in terms of privatization, competition, outsourcing and the service purchasing ethos as well as Australia's desire to copy Blair's New Labour policies. He looked at three cases and observed that whilst commercial risks may well have been largely well managed, the same success could not be claimed for the governance dimension. Governance risks appear to have increased with PPPs. For these cases, the unavailability of project economic evaluations, the fact that most deals were two-way affairs between government and business without explicitly including citizens, the length into which past governments can tie up future governments, the apparent willingness to protect investors' returns above citizens' interests, the lack of clarity of commercial arrangements and the desire of governments to proceed with hasty project construction for political purposes all appear to have contributed to this conclusion.

Importantly as well, evidence from an evaluation of eight PPP case studies in Victoria was presented. Two important observations were made here. First, the superiority of the economic partnership mode over traditional delivery mechanisms was dependent on the discount rate adopted in the analysis. Indeed, opposite conclusions were reached when using 8.65 per cent at one extreme (leading to the conclusion that the PPP mechanism was 9 per cent cheaper than traditional delivery) compared to evaluation adopting 5.7 per cent (where the PPP mechanism was apparently 6 per cent more expensive). Second, the point was also made that government has clearly moved from its traditional stewardship role to a louder policy advocacy role, and that government now finds itself in the middle of multiple conflicts of interest acting in the roles of policy advocate, economic developer, steward for public funds, elected representative for decision making, regulator over the contract life, commercial signatory to the contract and planner. Far more debate is now needed to discuss the optimum ways in which long term public interests can best be protected and nurtured in the light of experience, particularly noting citizen concerns around low PPP transparency and high deal complexity.

Interestingly, the reviews of Boardman et al. and Hodge both concluded independently that 'caveat emptor' is the most appropriate philosophy for governments to take as we move forward with infrastructure PPPs. Such a learning provides a contrast between the empirical reality of global experience on the one hand and the notion that 'all the evidence that I have ever read has been positive', as one Australasian government Minister responsible for billions of dollars of partnership investments recently argued to one of the editors.

So, where does that leave us? And what of the future of PPPs?

THE FUTURE OF PPPs

Some factors here are crystal clear. PPPs are currently enjoying policy popularity on the global political stage, as well as commercial attractiveness in the business sector. It is an attractive policy to third way governments eager to please markets. But transaction costs are high, competition is weak and VFM is debateable, despite being more reliable in terms of on-time delivery of major projects. Other factors in our assessment are less clear. We know for instance that any assessment we make of PPPs must recognize that insufficient research has been undertaken thus far to be fully informed on outcomes to date. As well, the counterfactual of traditional delivery, but with minimal improvements, is rarely defined let alone properly costed or evaluated. It will also remain easier to criticize PPPs compared to perfection rather than against realistic counterfactual alternatives. So, are we better off now having experienced the most recent PPP wave? This is debateable. But we ought to remember firstly that as with other members of the privatization family of reforms, public–private partnerships and contracted government service delivery have all been highly controversial policy arenas. And the theatre of change here attracts advocates and critics with almost religious enthusiasm. More rigorous and independent economic assessments at the policy level are obviously needed for PPPs.

The less visible consequences of PPP reforms also need airing and debate. There are numerous issues needing public debate and political recognition here whether it is the concerns expressed by many over VFM issues; the unavailability of simple performance information such as the expected economic return on taxpayer funds invested in PPPs; contract complexity or secrecy; or concerns over the longer term governance issues that are at stake. Clearly, PPPs are not simply a technical service provision question, but an inherent part of how public governance occurs in our time. One operational prospect from this insight is that PPPs could potentially alter the way that both the public sector and the private sector are organized internally. If cooperation between the two sectors is extended, then the public sector will have to stop thinking about itself as 'purchaser' and the private sector will not only be 'provider', but instead be a 'partner' and share organizational attributes, responsibilities and citizen expectations.

Politically, PPPs have reached a fascinating stage in evolution. Moving forward, there is no doubt that governments will need to keep their governance responsibilities clearly separated from commercial performance concerns. This will present new dilemmas and pressures on government. The question of governance risks was mentioned earlier in reviewing the Australasian experience, but to the extent that governments signing PPPs put their own capacity to govern at risk, this situation is common to all countries around the world. Governments clearly now need to consider more fully the various kinds of risks that PPPs pose to their ability to govern wisely in the future. Ministers will need to strenuously resist business pressures to alter the rules of the PPP game in favour of specific ongoing commercial business interests. There will continue to be huge temptations for Ministers to craft new rules for the PPP game that support the appearance of a positive, growing and thriving state business sector rather than maintain rules of the game initially set to provide optimal competition in the interests of citizens.

Put simply, Ministers will increasingly need to hold the line, and watch the downside of their favoured market-based PPP policies play out. Ministers will increasingly need not only to think of economic risks when entering PPPs, but governance risks. As part of this, we will need far more serious debate in contemplating whether we should trust legal commercial contracts alone to regulate our future public infrastructure services. Citizens in the privatized state are these days most concerned about the appearance of reduced public accountability in politics. So with PPPs, citizens will increasingly ask who will oversee new related legislation and planning? Who should look after the contract deals, and regulate how risks are handled for decades to come? And who will protect users and evaluate these projects on behalf of citizens? Perhaps the transparent work of parliamentary committees, auditors general and regulators all needs strengthening here, but government will no doubt need to begin by understanding far better how to separate and strengthen the intelligent long term governance role from any commercial responsibilities.

Moreover, it will be important to be more aware of who is pushing for PPPs around the world. Greater clarity will be required in articulating the interest groups at play, the extent of their influence and the pay-offs going to stakeholders. Governments have made the partnership ethos a priority in some countries, notably the UK, but how much priority will be given to PPPs in the long run in other countries? What will happen to PPPs when they are not as high on the policy agenda as they have been in the current period around the millennium? It was noted above how central ministries, usually the Treasury or the Ministry of Finance, find themselves occupying several roles, including policy advocate and steward for public funds. Many countries seem to have established single-purpose organizational entities that promote PPPs (Britain and the Netherlands are examples), but other countries have organized themselves in a more decentralized way for PPPs (the Nordic countries). If countries make special organizational units for PPP policy, this would indicate a clear top-down push for PPPs across government. If countries have not established centralized units, a more bottom-up approach to PPPs might be expected, with room for greater local experimentation. Germany, Sweden and Denmark seem to be examples of that trend. Examining who is responsible for PPP policy and who is pushing for PPPs will be a continuing factor to watch carefully in the years ahead.

Looking back at our recent PPP history, there is much that can be observed in the evaluation literature. It is clear that no matter how PPPs are defined, they fall far short of a perfect mechanism for delivering public sector services. But this is hardly surprising, surely. It is not empirical experience compared to perfection that is really at issue here, since an imperfect PPP reality will always fall short. It is an imperfect PPP compared against an imperfect next best alterative that needs more investigation. The huge achievements of PPP projects should not be underplayed as these were impressive in political terms and gains have often gone to citizens with such government initiatives. But this is also a side issue in the sense that it is the mode of infrastructure or service delivery that is really at issue here not the delivery of a 'Taj Mahal' project per se.[11] And in any event we are only a few years into lengthy contracts spanning decades. So, despite the political chest beating on this issue, the jury is still out on the overall benefit of PPP mode of delivery.

Another interesting development is the fact that governments have begun buying back into enterprises only recently privatized. Whether it is New Zealand buying back into Tranzrail (Boyle, 2003) or the British government buying back into the London Underground (Dow Jones, 2003), the point is clear. Governments will, if pushed, consider major interventions into privatized markets and even the option of re-nationalising parts of a production system. But the swing of the pendulum back away from maximizing the use of private markets will not be done lightly, and certainly not on an ideological basis. Of course we all want better service outcomes for citizens. And new organizational forms, new financial techniques and new project delivery and contract options for governments present new political opportunities. But learning from the past is not always easy in politics, and governments who say there are no risks and only good news with PPPs need to go back to history classes.

CONCLUSIONS

The PPP movement has had a long historical pedigree. And today, it continues to see a huge diversity of approaches around the globe. A distinction between social (or organizational) partnerships and economic partnerships seems to be appropriate in order to grasp the division between the various uses of the term 'PPP' around the world. Certainly, the contemporary phenomenon of private finance dominated partnership arrangements now represents an important element of the partnership family, although often viewed only through a narrow commercial lens. A range of PPP experiences in terms of successes and failures has been presented in this book. There is little doubt that some of the glowing policy promises of partnerships have been delivered. Equally, though, PPPs have, in reality, also led to ideological blind spots for treasuries more intent on policy advocacy than on their stewardship role. Whilst PPPs continue to promise much, careful continuing evaluation away from the loud noise of cheer squads is needed in order to ensure that governments maintain their intelligence as to policy effectiveness as well as the desire always to be seen as building infrastructure and reforming in order to be noticed by voters and the business sector. Good government, after all, is effective government.

NOTES

1. This paraphrases the observation of New Public Management made by Hood (1991).
2. We might also add to these lessons the observations of Bovaird (2004) who recounts the history of PPPs in the United States of America from around 1938. He notes that by the late 1970s, city officials had become PPP 'deal-makers'. Also relevant are his observations on the public infrastructure concession arrangements common in France since the seventeenth century, albeit we need to acknowledge that the French system is very different to the PFI experience of the UK.
3. Personal communication with David Parker (2004), October, London.
4. See Saint-Martin, D. (1998).
5. It might on reflection be noted that the control case, or the counterfactual alternative, was not put forward in this analysis. This begs the question – effective compared to what alternative – perfection, or the reality of less than perfect in-house provision?
6. By involving private as well as not-for-profit companies, they also argue that firms gain through enhancing their reputations and competitive positions.
7. See for example Hodge (2004:241) who notes that following independent power producers being contracted to build greater capacity, an increase of over 200 per cent occurred to the

'purchased power adjustment' – an additional charge remitted to private power producers for unused power. Moreover, whilst overall electricity power bills have almost doubled, power prices have also been double those in neighbouring countries such as Thailand and Malaysia. This situation has understandably outraged citizens in the Philippines.

8. See for instance *The Economist*, (2002), or more recently, Redwood (2004).
9. Pollitt also notes that this proportion is as high as 50 per cent in sectors such as Transport.
10. Note that we also ought ideally keep the business or policy idea of government separate to the policy delivery mechanism in our assessment here. In other words, the terms on which this hospital was transferred back to government after the 'political failure' would presumably need to be known before we assessed the relative overall success of the subsequent commercial transaction to the taxpayer.
11. It is important to recall that in any evaluation of PPP effectiveness, the question of evaluating the policy decision itself (such as the infrastructure project endorsed, the building constructed or public service provided) ought to be separated from the question of the chosen delivery mechanism – the PPP. Success or failure is possible at either level here. Thus, a high public benefit project such as say, infrastructure, could hypothetically be provided through an inefficient mechanism because too much was paid for the availability of private finance. Alternatively, a low public benefit project may have been endorsed, but delivered through an efficient PPP mechanism which was highly competitive and lowest cost compared to traditional means.

REFERENCES

Bovaird, T. (2004), 'Public–private partnerships in Western Europe and the US: new growths from old roots' in Abby Ghobadian, David Gallear, Nicholas O'Regan and Howard Viney (eds), *Public–Private Partnerships: Policy and Experience*, Basingstoke: Palgrave Macmillan, 221–50.

Boyle, J. (2003), 'Tranzrail out of loop in toll takeover', *The Australian Financial Review*, 8 July, 14.

Correy, D. (2004), 'New Labour and PPPs', in Abby Ghobadian, David Gallear, Nicholas O'Regan and Howard Viney (eds), *Public–Private Partnerships: Policy and Experience*, Basingstoke: Palgrave Macmillan, 24–36.

Dow Jones (2003), 'London takes over the tube, delays still expected', *The Australian Financial Review*, 16 July, 10.

Economist (2002), 'Enron-on-Thames: Railtrack and British public finance', 30 March.

Edelman, M. (1985), 'Political language and political reality', *Political Science*, **18** (1), 1–19.

Grimsey, D. and M.K. Lewis (2004), *Public–Private Partnerships: The Worldwide Revolution in Infrastructure Provision and Project Finance*, Cheltenham, UK and Northampton, MA, USA: Edward Elgar.

Ghobadian, A., D. Gallear, N. O'Regan and H. Viney (eds) (2004), *Public–Private Partnerships: Policy and Experience*, Basingstoke: Palgrave Macmillan.

Hodge, G.A. (2004), 'Conclusion', G. Hodge, V. Sands, D. Hayward and D. Scott (eds) in *Power Progress: An Audit of Australia's Electricity Reform Experiment*, Melbourne: Australian Scholarly Publishing, 233–41.

Hood, C. (1991), 'A public management for all seasons?', *Public Administration*, **69** (Spring), 3–19.

Parsons, W. (1995), *Public Policy: An Introduction to the Theory and Practice of Policy Analysis*, Cheltenham, UK and Northampton, MA, USA: Edward Elgar.

Redwood (2004), 'Public–private partnerships and private finance', in Abby Ghobadian, David Gallear, Nicholas O'Regan and Howard Viney (eds), *Public–Private Partnerships: Policy and Experience*, Basingstoke: Palgrave Macmillan, 15–23.

Saint-Martin, D. (1998), 'The new managerialism and policy influence of consultants in government: an historical–institutional analysis of Britain, Canada and France', *Governance*, **11** (3), 319–56.

Index